The
FIVE GEORGE MASONS
Patriots and Planters
of
Virginia and Maryland

PAMELA C. COPELAND *and* RICHARD K. MACMASTER

Published for the Board of Regents of Gunston Hall
by the University Press of Virginia
Charlottesville

THE UNIVERSITY PRESS OF VIRGINIA
Copyright © 1975 by the Rector and Visitors
of the University of Virginia

First published 1975

Frontispiece: The opening of a letter from George Mason
of Gunston Hall to
William Cabell, 6 May 1783.
(Courtesy the Emmet Collection, Manuscript and Archives Division,
the New York Public Library,
Astor, Lenox and Tilden Foundations.)

Library of Congress Cataloging in Publication Data

Copeland, Pamela C   1906–
  The five George Masons.

  Bibliography: p.
  Includes index.
    1. Mason, George, 1725–1792. 2. Mason family.
I. MacMaster, Richard Keith, 1935– joint author.
II. Board of Regents of Gunston Hall. III. Title.
E302.6.M45C58   973.3'092'4 [B]   75–8565   ISBN 0–8139–0550–8

Printed in the United States of America

The Five George Masons
Patriots and Planters of
Virginia and Maryland

Dear Sir, Fairfax County Gunston-Hall May 6: 1783.

              You

I congratulate you most sincerly, upon the Establish=
=ment of American Liberty & Independence. Happiness
& Prosperity are now within our Reach; but to attain
& preserve them must depend upon our own Wisdom & Virtue.
I hope the Assembly will revise several of our Laws, and
abolish all such of them as are contrary to the fundamental
Principles of Justice. This, & a strict adherence to the
Distinctions between Right & Wrong for the future,
is absolutely necessary, to restore that Confidence &
Reverence in the People for the Legislature; which
a contrary Conduct has so greatly impair'd; and with=
=out which, their Laws must ever remain little better
than a dead Letter. Frequent Interferance with private
property & Contracts, retrospective Laws destructive
of all public Faith, as well as Confidence between man
& man, and flagrant Violations of the Constitution
must disgust the best & wisest part of the Community;
occasion a general Depravity of Manners, bring the
Legislature into Contempt, and finally produce Anar=
=chy & & public Convulsion. I write to You with
                      the

Preface

THIS BOOK is the outgrowth of research efforts to help the Board of Regents of Gunston Hall appropriately furnish the home of George Mason and better interpret its history through a greater knowledge of Mason's personal life, business enterprises, and political activities.

The undertaking soon proved to require more research than I had the time to do. Francis Henninger, who was then a doctoral candidate at the University of Pennsylvania, was engaged by the Board of Regents to assist me in this work. Mr. Henninger collated the papers in the files at Gunston Hall and then interviewed many members of the Mason family in Virginia and Kentucky concerning their early ancestry. When Francis Henninger accepted a teaching position at the University of Dayton, he was succeeded by Richard K. MacMaster, Ph.D. in history from Georgetown University. He continued the research under my direction, traveling to California to interview Mason descendants and to England to check many court and parish records. But just as Mr. Henninger entered the academic world, so did Mr. MacMaster, at Western Carolina University in North Carolina. It then became necessary to ask Mr. Dale Fields and Mrs. Gladys M. Coghlan, executive director and library director, respectively, of the Historical Society of Delaware to give editorial advice and assistance to pull the manuscript together.

The material resulting from the research required for this book is deposited in the Library at Gunston Hall as the Pamela C. Copeland Mason Family Research File. Part of it consists of correspondence with many members of the Mason family, some of whom I have had the pleasure of meeting. All of them have been gracious in replying to my letters and most cooperative in answering my questions. Nevertheless, some members are so deficient in genealogical data that an accurate pedigree of their branch seems impossible. In some instances the repetition of the same name without benefit of dates makes it impossible to be sure of accuracy. I hope that this study will stimulate further research to fill the many omissions of dates and biographical material. Indeed, there must be rich stores about such an interesting family.

Given the uncertainty of the times and the lack of roots that have led to a weakening of family ties, the Mason family is fortunate to have the house of their ancestor preserved as a symbol of their fine heritage.

After a hundred years, or after about four generations, curiosity arises as to the place of origin of the immigrant settler. For help on this search, I enlisted the services of Sir Anthony Wagner, Garter Principal, King of Arms, the College of Arms, London, as little was known (except by tradition) of the English background of George Mason I. This now seems proved and documented. Although some descendants may regret that the immigrant was of yeoman stock, this is probably nearer the truth than the tradition that he was a member of Parliament and a courtier of Charles I. George Mason I literally had to hew down trees in the endless wilderness in order to erect a crude dwelling against the elements, plant corn in order to eat, and grow tobacco for support. This, then, was the sort of labor that went into the very first plantation. It required men accustomed to work and fearless women in order to survive. Four generations later George Mason IV was able to enjoy and embellish the cleared lands left him by his forebears. George and his brother, Thomson, also benefited by better educations, as tutors were also looking for opportunities in the new world. Thomson took advantage of the increased trans-Atlantic travel to study in London at the Inns of Court. The political and the legal mind appear in every generation; but although there are Masons who have been eminent in medicine, education, the ministry, and the military, apparently only one became a notable merchant. In the present generation one of the leading hotel corporations of the world is operated by a descendant of Thomas, youngest son of George Mason IV.

Mr. Lucius Randolph Mason, who until his recent retirement had a distinguished legal career, is descended from George Mason's son Thomson Mason. Through his generosity the Board of Regents in 1954 was able to purchase the portrait of Ann (Mason) Selden, the sister of George and Thomson Mason. Since that time Mr. Mason has continued to take a personal interest in Gunston Hall and in the reassembling of the eighteenth-century Mason-Mercer Library, which is being collected by the First Regent of the Board of Regents of Gunston Hall, Mrs. Frederick Frelinghuysen.

The Reverend Melvin Lee Steadman, Jr., has been of the greatest help in genealogical matters. He is a descendant of Thomson Mason of Raspberry Plain and, in my opinion, knows more about the Mason family as a whole than any other member. He has contributed family papers and a portrait of George Thomson Mason to the Board of Regents.

Members of the Mason family in and about Alexandria, Virginia, and Washington, D.C., have lent precious family heirlooms for special exhibitions and given of their time and talents to aid in some of the special events at Gunston Hall to honor George Mason IV. I should like to express my appreciative thanks to the members of the Mason family already mentioned as well as to all the others who are equally deserving of my thanks if space permitted naming them all. I hope that their personal interest will continue, and in order to encourage the Masons to know one another, a file of living members and their addresses is being maintained at Gunston Hall.

I hope that every Mason will be able to find his line of descent from the genealogical tables, which were drawn with meticulous care by John Thayer of Wilmington, Delaware. The tables have been broken down into family branches, which then may be found on the master table in less detail. Any mistakes are my responsibility. All dates and the spelling of names were carefully checked through wills, deeds, tax lists, church records, and Chancery suits, as well as with members of the Mason family. For the spelling of Virginia place names, I have followed, whenever possible, *Approved Place Names in Virginia*, Mary Topping et al., comps. (Charlottesville, Va., 1971).

I must thank my husband and family for their patience and good humor in letting me "live" with George Mason IV. Without their understanding this work would never have been accomplished. To Marion Graham Bailey I wish to express my deep appreciation for the hours she spent in typing and retyping and for her forbearance with my frustration when I could not solve a problem. But the thrill of solving a problem and finding a missing link by piecing together clues and bits of seemingly irrelevant information has been a facinating task that was impossible to put aside. I also wish to thank Mr. Richard Stinely, assistant director of the Publications Department, Colonial Williamsburg, Inc., for preparing the map of the region of the upper Potomac as it appeared in George Mason's time.

I have been given every courtesy and consideration by Mr. John Melville Jennings, director of the Virginia Historical Society; Mr. Howson W. Cole, curator of manuscripts, Virginia Historical Society; Mr. John W. Dudley, assistant state archivist, Virginia State Library; Mrs. Mary K. Meyer, genealogical librarian, Maryland Historical Society; Mrs. Bryce Jacobsen, archivist, Hall of Records, Annapolis, Maryland; Miss Charlotte R. Lutyens, librarian, the Honourable Society of the Middle Temple, London; Mr. A. E. J. Hollaender, keeper of manuscripts, Guildhall Library, London; Mr. E. K. Timings, head of Search Department, Public Records Office, London; Mr.

Daniel Hay, librarian and curator, Public Library and Museum, White-haven, Cumberland, England; John B. Rigg, curator of manuscripts, Eleutherian Mills Historical Library, Wilmington, Delaware; Miss Margaret C. Cook, curator of manuscripts, Earl Gregg Swem Library, the College of William and Mary, Williamsburg, Virginia; and the Reverend Albert N. Jones, Pohick Church, Truro Parish, Lorton, Virginia.

And, finally, I must name three men who gave me valuable critical advice during the past year when I needed it most. They are J. A. Lloyd Hyde, Edward P. Alexander, and Walter Muir Whitehall. Each in his way has been my guide, philosopher and friend.

PAMELA C. COPELAND

Mt. Cuba
Greenville, Delaware
March 18, 1975

Contents

Chapter I

Colonel George Mason I

ENGLISHMEN BEGAN TO SETTLE on the Virginia shore of the Potomac River about 1648, seeking lands beyond the settled areas of the York and James rivers. These Potomac pioneers transplanted the institutions of rural England to the Virginia borderland and adopted the tobacco economy of their Chesapeake neighbors. Land grants and local offices obtained by these settlers launched many Virginia families into wealth, which they held for generations, as well as into long traditions of public service. The first George Mason was one of these Potomac pioneers. His descendants became one of the great Virginia families whose history is that of the settlement of a region and the building of a nation.

George Mason I was born in 1629 to Thomas and Ann (French) Mason in Pershore, in the rich farming country of the Vale of Evesham in Worcestershire, England.[1] The complex web of tradition made subtle distinctions between Pershore and its neighboring hamlets as the traditions and events accumulated over the centuries. Pershore, a market town on the banks of the Avon, was a more important place than its immediate neighbors, and tradesmen and innkeepers were led to settle within its bounds, drawn by the number of people who came there for the market.

English villages in the seventeenth century were composed of a clearly stratified society, each landholder sharing with his neighbors certain rights and obligations inherited with the land itself from a distant past. The lord of the manor, the publican, the craftsman, the miller, the yeoman, and the yeoman farmer were alike absorbed into the life of the community, each taking his appropriate part in the meeting of the parish vestry, which inherited its function from the court baron.[2] The very stratification of village society led to easy intercourse between classes; everyone knew his place and rank and could converse and mingle with his betters or his inferiors on a stable basis. Moreover, the very nature of village life, isolated as it was from that of other towns and villages, led to an intermingling of high and low on a social as well as a business plane. This isolation resulted in a stable,

nonmobile population and led to marriages made within the confines
of the village or with neighboring farmers.

The persistence of names is always a striking feature of village society. There are still George Masons in the Vale of Evesham. In an
examination of the records of the sixteenth and seventeenth centuries
for the village of Pershore, we find Masons and Frenches described as
yeomen, farmers, craftsmen, millers, smiths, innkeepers, gentlemen,
and esquires. Their exact relation to one another has for the most part
been obscured by time, but some names appear in enough legal and
church records to enable us to trace their descendants to this day.

Thomas and Ann (French) Mason were married in the Abbey
Church of the Holy Cross, Pershore, on 2 February 1624/25. That the
ceremony was held there attests to the prominence of the families, as
only the more important people kept their holy observances at the abbey rather than at the parish church.[3] Seven of their children were baptized in the Abbey Church, one of whom was their third child and
eldest son, George Mason I, who was baptized on 10 June 1629. Not
much is known of Thomas Mason. He was a yeoman farmer and presumably not of a quarrelsome nature. His name does not appear in any
legal cases of the time except one, when he journeyed to Worcester in
1642 to post bond for his friend William Southerne of Walcott, a village near Pershore, to appear at quarter sessions to answer certain
charges.[4] Southerne was appointed by Mason as an executor in the settlement of his estate in his last will, made orally in February 1655,
which was admitted to probate in July of that year. The closeness of
this branch of the Mason family to the Frenches is attested to by
Thomas Mason's calling on Grace (Baugh) French and Chrisagone
(French) Hungerford to be witnesses to his will. In 1657/58 Ann
(French) Mason witnessed the will of Grace (Baugh) French.[5]

The French and Baugh families were two of the most important
families in the village at this time. Their ownership of lands and houses
placed them on the commissions of peace, on the vestry of the parish,
and, in the case of George French, Gentleman, at the head of the court
baron of the manors of Old and New Pershore. This last position was
one that was included in the ancient rights and privileges belonging to
the manors of Old and New Pershore, which he had purchased from
John Richardson in 1598.[6] As lord of the manor, he was the most prominent man in Pershore in George Mason's boyhood. He lived until
1647, a staunch supporter of the old order in church and state. It is
indicative of the respect he commanded in the countryside that his
children contracted marriages with other notable families of the area
even though his wife, Cecily (Grey) French, and their daughter,

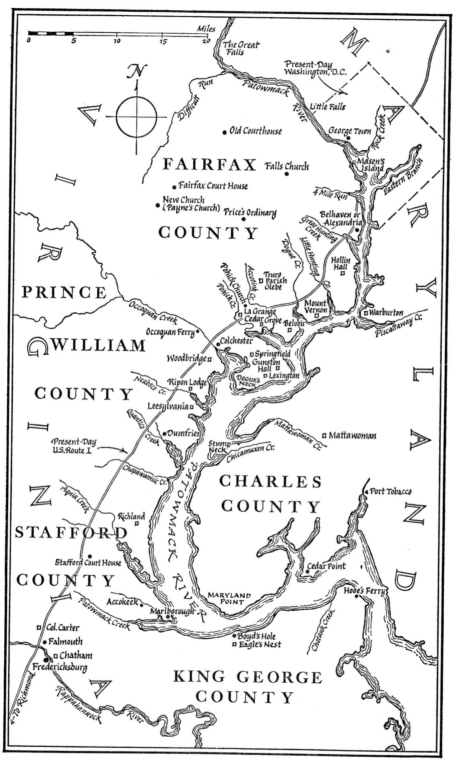

The region of the upper Potomac as George Mason knew it. Locations of plantations (□) and townsites, ferries, and public buildings (•) are approximate. *Prepared by Richard Stinely.*

Chrisagone (French) Hungerford, were named among the Catholic recusants of 1642.[7] In 1643 George French conveyed the manors of Old and New Pershore to Edward Baugh, whose daughter, Grace, was married to George French's son, George.[8] This conveyance was possibly a means of safeguarding the inheritance of George French's children from confiscation in such troubled times. It is also of record that a "French, Gentleman of Pershore" was among those who defended the city of Worcester for Charles I in 1646 and marched out with the garrison to surrender to the Parliamentarians.[9]

The kinship of the members of Thomas Mason's family with the Baughs and Frenches would have made them more than ordinarily aware of the workings of village and county justice as well as decisions concerning parish affairs. Acts of Parliament clearly defined the method by which parish business was to be carried out by the vestry and the justices of the peace. All the freeholders of the parish met once a year at Eastertime to elect the churchwardens. The acts of Parliament of 1598 and 1601 had greatly expanded the churchwardens' duties.[10] Originally they had served primarily as parochial officers, keeping the church in repair and seeing to the maintenance of all that was needful for divine worship. The new legislation extended their authority to the whole area of public welfare. The churchwardens acted as overseers of the poor, levying and administering the poor rate, with the approval of both the vestry and the justices. They were obliged to submit careful accounts of all their collections and expenditures for the needy and for the upkeep of the church itself. In September the vestry met again to compile a list from which the justices would appoint men as waywardens to maintain the public roads. As the representative inhabitants of the parish, the vestry had the power to administer common property and make bylaws on matters of public concern. It had absolute control over the assessment, levy, and expenditures of the poor rate and the church rate, as well as the election of at least one of the churchwardens. In actual practice the vestry often had a good deal to do with the election of overseers and constables as well as waywardens.[11]

Local officials, such as constables, fieldmen, chimney searchers, flesh searchers, ale tasters, and bread and butter weighers, were normally chosen by the court baron. At different times in different places the vestry took the place of the manorial court, giving itself a rather wide authority in local affairs. In other parishes there was a tendency for the vestry to shrink from an assembly of all the freeholders into a select vestry or committee of the more substantial inhabitants.[12] The Virginia vestry system developed from the English vestry system and incorporated parts from both of these contemporary trends. It became in practice the preserve of the more substantial inhabitants and extended its concerns into several areas of economic and social life.

The court baron of the manors of Old and New Pershore, over which George French presided, was a penal court and a court of record, not a meeting of villagers to discuss new approaches to social issues. It was a court held principally for the benefit of the lord of the manor and normally met once a year in the Easter season. Every tenant of the manor was expected to attend, and the court levied fines on those who did not. The major business of the court was the recording of land transfers; the judicial proceeding relied on the fact that every man in the village knew the traditional bounds of every man's fields. The court assessed fees for recording transfers and fines for misdemeanors on the lands of the lord of the manor. It also performed some of the functions of local government in appointing petty officials where this function had not passed to the vestry.[13]

Country gentlemen usually held the office of justice of the peace as a matter of course. These gentlemen justices presided at the sessions of the county court, which met generally every twenty-eight days in any town in the county at the pleasure of the sheriff. The holding of the county court was one of the oldest of his duties. Its jurisdiction extended to personal actions of debt, replevin, detinue, and trespass theoretically amounting to less than forty shillings but by privilege extended to much larger sums. The justices of the peace assembled four times a year for the quarter sessions to deal with such crimes as petty larceny, assaults, forcible entries upon land, sheepstealing, housebreaking, trespass, and the like. They left the more serious offenses to the more experienced judges of the assizes.[14]

The sheriff notified the county of the place and date of the next quarter session and notified all justices of the peace, stewards, constables, and bailiffs to be present. The county court of assizes was assembled by proclamation, the sheriff notifying all officials and others with business at the court to appear before the King's judges at such and such a date. Besides organizing the courts, the sheriff executed their orders, judgments, and sentences. In social distinction the sheriff ranked above the justices of the peace. He was normally the great man of his county and presumably the wealthiest and largest landowner. These property qualifications were necessary because of the heavy expenses incurred upon the assumption of office and in the entertainment of the judges and country gentry at the assizes. The high sheriff headed the hierarchy of county civil officials, just as the lord lieutenant was head of the military organization of the county. Below the high sheriff ranged undersheriffs, bailiffs, bailiffs of the hundreds, high constables of the hundreds, petty constables, and the justices of the peace. Below the lord lieutenant were the deputy lieutenants and the officers of the trained bands.[15]

The functions of all these officials were familiar to every English settler on the frontier of the New World. The Englishmen who settled in Virginia in the seventeenth century nurtured the familiar institutions of local government in a new setting. The transplanting of these traditional forms was not the work of a day but a slow process of evolution and the blending of elements more familiar in one part of England with those common in another.

The vestry system had taken firm root in Virginia by 1644, when the Virginia Assembly provided for the election of vestrymen by a majority of the inhabitants of the parish. Despite this legislation, the Virginia vestry developed steadily in the direction of a self-perpetuating select vestry in the exclusive control of the principal inhabitants. Reformers decried this abuse and sought remedial legislation in 1676. Not only was the vestry itself evolving in the middle years of the seventeenth century, but its functions were no more uniform in Virginia than in England. Levying the parish tithe was clearly the inherent right of the vestry. In some places it served a judicial function; in others, the presentment of offenders to the county court belonged to the churchwardens alone. The relationship between the vestry and the wardens was still somewhat hazy. In one area the care of the poor belonged exclusively to the churchwardens; in another, they shared this function with the vestry or the gentlemen justices of the county court. In some places in Virginia the justices appointed the churchwardens, while in others they were chosen by the vestrymen. By the end of the century the vestry and the county court were composed of the same propertied gentlemen, so that this distinction became a purely nominal one, and for all the efforts to reverse the trend, the development into a select vestry was complete.[16]

The earliest judicial system in Virginia consisted of the governor and his Council sitting as the General Court of the colony. In 1619 the authorities began to create monthly courts in each precinct to settle petty civil and criminal cases. In its scope, if not in its frequency, the precinct court bore a certain resemblance to the manorial court. It was only in 1634 that Virginia's first counties began to be governed like the English shires and to have sheriffs with the same powers as in England. Not until 1642 did the governor authorize the monthly meeting of a county court in some convenient location and appoint the first gentlemen justices for each of the new counties. The membership of the county court came, in practice, to be restricted to the principal inhabitants, extensive landowners or an occasional prominent merchant. The governor had the ultimate authority to appoint the justices of the peace for each county. He shared his power in the 1650s with the members of the House of Burgesses. The right of the county bench to nominate its own members with a recommendation to the governor that was tantamount to appointment gave that body a greater measure of autonomy as time passed. Generally speaking, the gentlemen justices took to themselves the rights and privileges of the justices of the peace of their English counties. In this way they gradually built up a squirearchy of their own in Virginia. The close connection between the sheriff and the county court was regularized by an act of 1661 restricting appointment to men already on the county bench. The county lieutenant had long existed under another name as the commander of the county militia with authority to name his subordinate officers.[17]

The local institutions of the land watered by the Avon loomed large in the shaping of the local institutions of the Potomac settlements, for a number of George Mason's friends and neighbors in the Vale of Evesham had already settled in Virginia. Thomas Baugh, one of Ann (French) Mason's Bredon Hill cousins, went to Virginia in 1629 in the ship *Supply,* according to the muster of the inhabitants of the College-land in Virginia (Henrico) taken 23 January 1624. Thomas was unmarried on his arrival and credited with a house, a canoe, a gun, and a complete armor.[18]

Another family with Bredon Hill connections was that of the Brents. Giles Brent, Esquire, arrived on the Potomac in 1637. His brother, Fulk Brent, Esquire, and their sisters, Mistress Margaret Brent and Mistress Mary Brent, landed in Maryland in November 1638. They were the children of Richard Brent, of a notable and wealthy Catholic family, lord of the manors of Stoke and Admington in Gloucestershire. His lands were located about twelve miles east of Evesham and some twenty miles east of Pershore. Richard Brent had married Elizabeth, daughter of Giles Reed, lord of Tusburie and Witten. For some unexplained reason, Elizabeth was buried with her parents rather than with her husband. Giles Reed had ordered a great tomb erected in his memory as befitted one of his station in the church at Bredon just south of Pershore. This great canopied monument of 1611 in the thirteenth-century chapel of the church is astonishing for its rich detail. The fine figures of the lord of Tusburie and Witten and his wife are shown lying with hands at prayer, he in armor, she in elaborate dress, surrounded by their children, including Elizabeth Brent, who are kneeling at each side of their parents.

That the Brent family into which Elizabeth married was highly regarded is shown by the fact that though they were all Catholic recusants, Richard served as high sheriff of Gloucestershire, England, in 1614. Children of this Richard Brent held lands at Defford, Worcestershire, in the parish adjacent to Pershore. One of his sons, George Brent, lived at Defford and married Marianna Peyton, daughter of Sir John Peyton of Doddington; one of their younger sons, Robert, married in 1686 Anne, daughter of Edmund Baugh of Pensham and a niece of Grace (Baugh) French, mentioned earlier. In the year of their marriage he took his bride with him to Stafford County, Virginia, to settle near his Brent kinfolk.[19]

Capt. Giles Brent rose to considerable prominence within a short time of his arrival in Maryland. He was swiftly appointed deputy governor, treasurer, and chief justice of the province of Maryland as well as granted large tracts of land in the Chesapeake wilderness. He married the daughter of the emperor of the Piscataway Indians, after she had been converted by Jesuit missionaries and baptized with the name Maria. She was educated as became her new station by her redoubtable sister-in-law Margaret Brent, whom Governor Leonard Calvert considered the most able person to administer his estate. In 1647 Margaret Brent succeeded Calvert as attorney for his brother Cecil, the lord proprietor. Captain Giles Brent, following his marriage, laid claim before the proprietor in his wife's right to the greater part of Maryland. When Lord Baltimore failed to accept his argument, Brent withdrew across the Potomac to the peninsula in Virginia formed by Aquia and Accokeek runs. Captain Brent lost his Piscataway wife early in their married life, but she had borne him one son, who was also to be known as Capt. Giles Brent. This half-Indian son, born in 1651, the year of Mason's arrival in Virginia, was to be closely associated with him in later years in the defense of the Potomac borderlands.[20]

Brent's choice of the mouth of the Aquia Creek as the site of his new home in Virginia determined the pattern of some of the earliest settlement on the Potomac River. Newcomers like George Mason, who had connections with the Brent family in England, sought land near Giles Brent's cleared acres and clustered their plantations along that particular stretch of the river. James Clifton, Gentleman, who married Ann Brent of Defford, Worcestershire, came to Virginia in the 1650s to take up land adjoining that of his wife's uncle. Two of Giles Brent's nephews later left the same parish and took up lands on the Potomac. Others, who were members of the Peyton family, may well have come to Virginia under Brent's influence. For instance, in 1654 Valentine Peyton patented 1,000 acres on Aquia Creek near Giles Brent's land. Peyton was a native of London, but his father had come to the city from the same corner of Gloucestershire as the Brents and was of the same family as Giles Brent's sister-in-law, Marianna (Peyton) Brent.[21]

The final defeat of the Royalists at the second battle of Worcester in 1651 caused many young men to leave England and seek their fortune in other lands. Some went to the continent; others, like George Mason I, came to the Virginia plantations. There is a strong tradition in the Mason family that he was a colonel in the royalist cause at this decisive battle, although his name cannot be found on the military rolls. Usually there is some truth to these traditions, and the fact that he left Pershore in 1651, the year when the policy of confiscating the lands of supporters of the Crown was introduced, lends credence to the fact that it was considered best for him to leave the country. That he was able to take up a certain number of headrights * indicates that he was not without monetary backing.[22]

George Mason left his home in Pershore when he was about twenty-two years old and settled on the Potomac River in 1651 or 1652, first appearing as a juryman in Northumberland County in 1652.[23] When he acquired his first land grants in 1656, Mason's acres were mostly bounded by the unbroken wilds of the main woods, but he was not without neighbors. Earlier pioneers already had cleared lands on the banks of one of the creeks that emptied into the Potomac, but they had only to wander a short distance from their cabins to be lost in a trackless wilderness. However, before this generation passed away, the patches of corn and tobacco at the edge of the forest became broad acres of cultivated land, and the rough shelters at the head of the creek were replaced by more comfortable dwellings. Within approximately twenty years the line of Virginia settlements extended as far as the Great Falls.† As the settlers pushed on, they carried their English heritage of local government and common law with them—petitioning for new counties and new parishes, electing justices, churchwardens, and representatives to the lower house at Jamestown.

When George Mason came to the colony, the Virginia settlements scarcely extended north of the York River. The Northern Neck, lying between the Potomac and the Rappahannock, was still considered Indian land. Some few settlers, discontented with the Maryland govern-

---

* "Headrights were issued in the names of persons of all social classes. The persons named as headrights in a patent did not necessarily arrive in the colony the year the patent was issued. Before a patent was issued the claimant was required to show receipt as proof that passage money was duly paid" (Annie L. Jester, comp. and ed., in collaboration with Martha W. Hiden, *Adventurers of Purse and Person, Virginia, 1607–1625* [Princeton, N.J., 1965], p. xxiv).

† Great Falls "derives its name from the falls of the Potomac River near Georgetown, Md." (John T. Scharf, *History of Western Maryland* [Philadelphia, 1882], 1:788).

ment, had crossed the Potomac and taken up lands along one or other of the creeks and runs of the Northern Neck. In the 1640s a number of these Maryland settlers and some others from Virginia clustered at Coan, near the mouth of the Potomac, opposite Point Lookout in Maryland. In 1648 they were officially organized as Northumberland County, Virginia. However, by the end of the decade few settlers had gone up the Potomac beyond the cluster of Maryland settlements on the opposite bank of Saint Marys. When Mason began to cast about for land, the whole stretch of the Potomac lay vacant, or nearly so.[24]

George Mason obtained a patent for land in the same way most of the Potomac landowners did, by presenting a certificate for the importation of eighteen persons into Virginia. The original certificate is no longer extant, and no copy of it was ever made, so that the identity of these individuals is not known. He may have brought all of them with him when he first arrived, and some, or all of them, may have been members of his family. He may have paid their passage at intervals over several years, bringing some of them as indentured servants. He may even have purchased a list of passengers from a merchant or ship's captain on a ship coming into Virginia. Whatever method he used to transport them, Mason required money to do so. The passage of a single person would cost perhaps as much as £5, and the passage money for eighteen persons, including himself, would amount to a respectable sum.

Very soon after landing in Virginia, he began to appear in county records as Capt. George Mason. On 20 February 1653/54 Capt. George Mason of Westmoreland County registered his mark for identifying his hogs and cattle by a crop on their ears.[25] He had not then been more than two years in Virginia and had not yet obtained any land, but the title indicates that he had been appointed to command a company in the county militia. The militia officers were generally drawn from the members of the wealthier and more influential men of the county. In the 1640s under the Commonwealth, authority over the militia and the power to appoint militia officers was placed in the hands of four militia commissioners appointed from the membership of the county court. In 1653 the commissioners of militia from Westmoreland County were Col. Thomas Speke, Lt. Colonel Nathaniel Pope, Maj. John Hallows, Capt. Thomas Blagg, and Capt. Alexander Burnham.[26] It may be that in a frontier county like Westmoreland the commissioners judged a man's natural ability more than his acreage or his family connections; at any rate, young George Mason was accepted as an equal by the gentlemen justices of Westmoreland County.

From his first arrival in Virginia, Mason was associated with a number of other young men of similar backgrounds in England. One of these early friends was Thomas Fowke, Gentleman. On 10 June 1654 Thomas Fowke obtained a patent for 3,350 acres in Westmoreland County on the south bank of the Potomac River at the head of Potomac Creek in what would be modern Stafford County. He obtained this land by including himself in the list of headrights.[27] Gerard Fowke, whose mother was Mary Bayley, and John Bayley, her nephew, head the list of names. The others are less easy to identify, but Gerard Fowke, John Bayley, and Thomas Fowke obviously had come to Virginia together from their homes near Wolverhampton in Staffordshire, England. A family tradition that links these men with George Mason in England is that in spite of their separate headrights they traveled together to Virginia.

"During the period of settlement," as Louis B. Wright has pointed out, "the fundamental fact determining social status was capital. That some families were founded by the sons of gentlemen was of far less importance at the moment than whether they had money enough to bring over servants and take up large tracts of land. The tradesman, the merchant, and the gentlemen who were adequately financed at the start gained a similar foothold in the economic structure of the colony, and, if they prospered sufficiently, they all became members of the ruling class, and, in the course of time, developed similar ideas about family, position, and social obligations."[28] Once they became landed proprietors, they sought to become English country gentlemen, and whatever their background, that is what they became.

Many of these early Virginia gentlemen were drawn from the ranks of the merchants and traders of London and Bristol as these men had sufficient capital to take up land grants, import servants under the headright provision, and develop their landholdings. Others, such as the Fowkes, were genuine country squires from the Midlands but came to Virginia as merchants and obtained their first land grants by headrights for imported servants. Gerard Fowke, Esquire, was fairly typical of the country gentleman who came to Virginia. His uncles and aunts were people of substance in Staffordshire. One of his uncles had been a vicar, the others small landowners.[29] He belonged to the Fowke family who had owned the manor of Gunston, in Brewood Parish, from the fourteenth century, although neither he nor his father actually possessed Gunston Hall. His descendants, both in the Fowke and in the Mason families, cherished the memory of Gunston Hall and built new Gunston Halls in the Chesapeake area.[30]

George Mason settled near the Brents, Fowkes, and Peytons on lands drained by Potomac Creek and Accokeek Run, as evidenced by Robert

Hubbard's patent of 12 December 1654 for 1,600 acres on the Potomac at the branch of Aquia Creek, which is described as bordered on the west by lands owned by Capt. George Mason. Actually he did not obtain patent rights to his land until 17 March 1655/56. The original grant, as preserved in the Mercer Land Book and in the records of Westmoreland County, described the land as in Northumberland County; this would indicate that Mason applied for his patent before the county lines were redrawn in 1653 with the creation of Westmoreland County.[31] By this document Governor Edward Digges granted Capt. George Mason 900 acres of land abutting northeast upon Aquia Creek, southeast upon the land of Richard Godsford, northwest upon the small creek that issues out of Aquia Creek, and southwest upon the main woods. This land would appear to be south and west of Aquia Creek and not far distant from the Fowke lands. On 26 February 1658/59 Mason and his wife, Mary, sold 500 acres of this land "in Oquion River in Potomack adjoining to my now dwelling house" to John Lear, who paid five cows with calves and 2,500 pounds of tobacco for the property. Thus before 1659, and probably as early as 1654, Mason made his home near the mouth of Aquia Creek. He may possibly have been engaged in trading of some sort as the will of Thomas Boys in 1657 mentioned that Captain Mason was indebted to Boys for eight pounds of beaver.[32]

In 1664 James Clifton complained in Stafford court that Captain Mason "doth unjustly detain a Servant maide" who belonged to Clifton. The court ruled that the girl belonged to Mason and that Clifton had no claim on her services. Thus it would appear that he had indentured English servants working for him at this time.[33] Mason was prospering in his new home. In 1664 he purchased land on Accokeek Creek in Stafford County from Col. Valentine Peyton. After the purchase of this property, he petitioned for a new grant in his own name in 1669. He then described the property as bounded on the northwest by land of Col. Giles Brent. This Accokeek property was Mason's home plantation and later passed to his eldest son.[34]

George Mason was fast becoming a man of considerable importance in Stafford County. In 1664 he was added to the court as one of the justices of the county. The county court at this date was holding its sessions at "the house of Colo. Fooke at Parsbitansy." In October 1664 Mason first presided in court as Maj. George Mason, the new rank indicating a recent promotion in the militia. In April 1665 he was sworn high sheriff of Stafford County. As sheriff his duties encompassed the defense of the frontier as well as many more routine duties. In 1665 the Stafford justices ordered two ferries to be established in the county, one at Potomac Creek and the other at Aquia, and ordered that "Major Mason see to have it effected." In 1667 the Stafford County Court was concerned to secure a place for divine services and ordered the churchwardens to prepare a house for divine worship. The house of Robert Townsend was selected. George Mason was among those listed as members of the vestry on 12 June 1665.[35] The extant records break off abruptly in December 1667, but Maj. Mason was still sheriff of Stafford County in 1670. He was also continuing to increase his landholdings with the patent of an additional 300 acres in the same year.[36]

The number of land patents granted in the 1650s shows that this was a period of tremendous expansion in the Virginia settlements. The Northern Neck shared this growth of population with the other frontier districts. The settlers spreading out along the Potomac had gradually engulfed the villages of the Potomac Indians. Pressure on the Indians increased as these new families took up lands and scattered the game on which the natives depended. Brushes between Indian hunting parties and English settlers were frequent—sometimes ending in tragedy, sometimes only confirming the frontier belief that Indians were responsible for every petty theft. In 1654 the militias of Northumberland and Westmoreland were called out against the depredations of the Rappahannocks.[37] In 1656 the Virginia Assembly realized that the Indians faced extermination and needed some direct assistance to enable them to live side by side with their new neighbors in peace and to preserve their identity. Some of the planters had bought out the Indian titles to complement their Virginia patents, as did the London merchant Henry Meese, who became the first representative of the House of Burgesses from Stafford County in 1666.[38] Others resorted to fraud and violence.

In 1662 the House of Burgesses disciplined Capt. Giles Brent, Col. Gerard Fowke, John Lord, and Capt. George Mason for trouble with some of the Indians. This had developed from some brushes between the settlers and Wahangonche, the king of the Potomacs. Capt. Brent had brought charges of murder and treason against the king, but the Indian was acquitted by the authorities at Jamestown. The House of Burgesses appointed a committee to inquire into the situation on Potomac Creek, and after due investigation the committee censured Brent, Fowke, Lord, and Mason for "several injuries and affronts done to Wahangonche, King of the Potomack Indians."[39] Brent was obviously the most compromised. He was obliged to pay the king 200 arm's lengths of roanoke (wampum), while Mason, Fowke, and Lord paid only 100 apiece. Brent and Fowke were to be barred from holding office. Mason and Lord were simply suspended. Colonel Fowke was also fined for permitting the murderer of an Indian to escape unpunished. Faced with the removal from public life of the four most prominent men in the county, the burgesses considered either reuniting Westmoreland to Northumberland County or asking the governor to send some able men to Westmoreland County to take their places.[40]

This was at most a temporary setback for Fowke and Mason, for within two years Fowke patented a tract of land known as "Machapungo formerly enjoyed by the King of Pottomack," which he deeded to his cousin Richard Hope; a different tract of land formerly in the possession of the king of Potomack was described in 1679 as in the tenure and possession of the orphans of Col. Gerard Fowke.[41]

Relations between the Virginians and their Indian neighbors steadily grew worse. In May 1664 the justices of Stafford County Court authorized Capt. John Alexander to press six men and horses in the king's name "to see if he can discover which Indians they were that had lately committed that Murther above at Potomack." In November 1664 Maj. George Mason and the Stafford justices decreed that "whereas many sad Accidents have happen'd by the Indians hunting in the Woods, by firing the same, and the P'ticular P'sons soe harbor them; Then the Court doth Order that noe Indian by any P'sons whatsoever shall be suffer'd to hunt in any P'ts of the English habitations."[42]

As the commanding officer of the Stafford County militia, Mason soon found himself involved in more serious Indian problems. The Conestoga Indians of Pennsylvania, who were known to the English settlers as the Susquehannocks, traditionally hunted in the country above the falls of the different Virginia rivers. These Susquehannocks also had developed a trade in furs along the same route, bartering for pelts with the tribes in the Carolina Piedmont and carrying their furs to the Dutch at New Amsterdam. They were much more independent and warlike than the Potomacs or the Doegs and were often blamed for frontier depredations. In 1675 the whole frontier was stirred by the Iroquois conquest of the Susquehannocks, who took refuge in Maryland on the Potomac with the Piscataway tribe after being driven from their homes along the Susquehanna River, near the head of the Chesapeake Bay.[43] Numerous incidents of strife between the Indians and the settlers continued. Thus, when an Indian murder took place on the edge of Stafford settlement in 1675, George Mason and his cousin, the half-Indian Capt. Giles Brent, took the field in hot pursuit.[44] During one of these clashes, the English captured the eight-year-old son of the king of the Doegs and brought the boy to Colonel

Mason's. The boy lay as one dead for some time. It was decided that he was bewitched and that, to break the trance, he should be baptized in the Church of England liturgy. Both Colonel and Mrs. Mason stood as godparents. Following the ceremony the men returned to drinking punch while Mrs. Mason (Mary French) stayed with the child, who regained consciousness when Mrs. Mason gave him a cordial by spoon to aid in his recovery. Not long after the curious incident, he returned to his tribe, who were well known for their practice of witchcraft.

On 26 September 1675 the Virginia forces commanded by Col. John Washington and the Maryland troops led by Maj. Thomas Truman beseiged the Susquehannock fort and committed an atrocity that left the frontier in flames for many months. When the militiamen approached the fort, the Indians sent four of their great men to parley. Truman and Washington ignored their peaceful overtures and ordered the four sachems shot down in cold blood. This brutal murder roused the Indians to make a desperate defense of the fort that cost the lives of many of the attacking party. The Piscataway fort stood a six weeks' seige. Then, on a moonlit night, some seventy-five warriors with their women and children passed safely through the English lines. They moved up the Potomac to the Little Falls and then crossed over from Maryland into Virginia. Keeping beyond the English settlements as much as they could, they made their way south crossing the Rappahannock and the York rivers. As they retreated across Virginia, they committed brutal acts of vengeance. Altogether they slew thirty-six settlers on the upper reaches of the Potomac and the Rappahannock. When the war party reached the falls on the James River, they killed Nathaniel Bacon's overseer and one of his servants.[45]

Early in 1676 Nathaniel Bacon, Jr., emerged as the leader of a group of volunteers intent on protecting the Virginia frontiers if the governor would not do so. Bacon's men warred on the Pamunkeys and other friendly or neutral tribes close at hand. In the heated passions of 1676 frontier settlers made little distinction between friendly and hostile Indians, nor, for that matter, did the Susquehannocks make any distinction between one Englishman and another in avenging their fallen leaders. Bacon and his friends sought an official appointment from the Virginia authorities to place the defense of the frontiers in his hands. Thomas Mathew was approached by the Bacon faction and went immediately to Col. George Mason for his advice. As Mathew recalled:

That evening I made known what had past with Mr. Bacon to my colleague Coll. Mason (whose bottle attendance doubled my task) the matter he liked well, but questioned the govern'rs approbacon of it.

I confess'd the case required sedate thoughts, reasoning, that he and such like gentlemen must either command or be commanded, and if on their denials Mr. Bacon should take distaste, and he constrained to appoint comanders out of the rabble, the govern'r himself with the persons and estates of all in the land would be at their dispose, whereby their own ruine might be owing to themselves; in this he agreed and said If the govern'r would give his own commission he would be content to serve under generall Bacon (as now he began to be intitutled) but first would consult other gentlemen in the same circumstances; who all concur'd twas the most safe barier in view against pernicious designes, if such shoud be put in practice; with this I acquainted Mr. Lawrence who went (rejoicing) to Mr. Bacon with the good tidings, that the militia commanders were inclined to serve under him, as their generall, in case the governor would please to give them his own commission.[46]

Col. George Mason took no further part in Bacon's Rebellion. Capt. Giles Brent, on the other hand, led a contingent of volunteers from the Potomac frontier to fight with Bacon against the Indians, but then turned his standards against Bacon when he rebelled against constituted authority. The rumored advance of Brent's men from the Potomac freshes led Bacon to put Jamestown to the torch, according to the contemporary *History of Bacon's and Ingram's Rebellion.*[47]

On the exposed and thinly settled Potomac frontier there were few men of the ability, social standing, or wealth of George Mason, Gerard Fowke, or Giles Brent. They were the natural leaders of their county, and their leadership was not disputed. By the time Col. William Fitzhugh of Bedfordshire, England, arrived on the Potomac in 1670 with the qualities and status to challenge the older leadership group, the Masons and the others were too deeply entrenched to be shaken from their positions.

Thomas Mathew of Stafford County, who was George Mason's colleague in the Virginia Assembly in 1675/76, wrote this interesting testimony to Mason's standing among his neighbors:

In March 1675–6 writts came up to Stafford to choose their two members for an assembly to meet in May; when Colo. Mason, Capt. Brent and other gentlemen of that county, invited me to stand a candidate; a matter I little dreampt of, having never had inclinacons to tamper in the precarious intrigues of govern't, and my hands being full of my own business; they press't several cogent argum'ts, and I having considerable debts in that county, besides my plantation concerns, where (in one and th' other) I had much more severly suffered, than any of themselves by th' Indian disturbances in the sumer and winter foregoing. I held it not discreet to disoblige the rulers of it, so Colo. Mason and myself were elected without objection.[48]

Stafford County seethed with disaffection during these troubled years and the property of certain influential gentlemen was destroyed in the Potomac region. Some twenty "rebels" craved the pardon of Stafford County Court at its session in March 1677. Mason and Brent were considered favorable to the complaints of their neighbors, but no record exists of their need to ask pardon for treasonable acts.[49] Col. George Mason brought the complaints of Stafford County to the House of Burgesses after Bacon's Rebellion. In 1680 Stafford County had two committees, military and civil, and Colonel Mason served on both; but he was particularly concerned with the committees on public claims and local grievances. However, he often conferred with the governor and the Council regarding the Indian affairs of the province.[50]

He was again returned a member for the 1684 session. This was the first session held under Francis, Lord Howard of Effingham, who had arrived in February with pomp and politics. Only nine acts were passed during this session; among them were the royal order that no persons should "use a printing press in Virginia on any occasion whatsoever" and the act, the first of its kind in Virginia, which laid a duty on all liquors imported from other English colonies, exempting, however, those imported by wealthy planters in their own vessels for their own use. These unfortunate laws remained in effect, a constant irritant to the people. Virginia was not to enjoy the advantages of the printing press until 1730, and George Mason's grandson was to dispute taxation without representation.

Regarding his personal and family life, George Mason was married twice. His first wife was named Mary, as shown on a deed of 1658. Family tradition has called her Mary French; this would account for the name *French* being used as a baptismal name in the family and further attests to family ties with the Frenches of Pershore. As the records indicate, Mason arrived in the colony a single man. It appears that the marriage took place in Virginia after 1652, when he arrived there, and before 1658, the date his wife Mary joined with him in signing the deed.[51] They had one son, George, who reached maturity. There may have been other children, but positive proof is lacking. At any rate, Capt. George Mason was recognized in Stafford County Court as the son and heir of the now Col. George Mason.

A legal dispute in the Stafford County Court records has preserved some details of Colonel Mason's second marriage. At a court held at the home of Thomas Ellsey 10 June 1691, Capt. George Mason, son and executor of George Mason, deceased, and Dr. Edward Maddocks were ordered to bring in an inventory of the goods and chattels of Dr. Maddocks's late wife, Frances Maddocks. Dr. Maddocks had married Frances, widow of Colonel Mason. At the time of her marriage to Mason, she was the widow of Capt. John Norgrave. A daughter of this marriage had wed Sampson Darrell, Gentleman, who in 1690 claimed 600 acres on Potomac Creek on behalf of his children as heirs of Capt. John Norgrave and of Frances (Norgrave) Mason Maddocks. Captain Norgrave died in 1664, but the exact date of his widow's marriage with Colonel Mason is unknown. Although George and Frances (Norgrave) Mason had no children, the families were later joined by the marriage of William Darrell, a grandson of Frances and John Norgrave, to Ann (Fowke) Mason, the granddaughter of George Mason I, sometime around the year 1711.

George Mason I was buried at his home plantation on Accokeek Creek in Stafford County, Virginia.[52] The date of his death is believed with good cause to be 1686 because on 27 October 1686, Capt. David Fox and Henry Jenkins were appointed by the House of Burgesses to inquire of George Mason II, who was then lying sick in Jamestown, whether his late father had provided a boat for the use of the garrison, in keeping with orders of the burgesses, for the protection of the settlers in the Occoquan area from Indian raids.[53] This entry in the records of the House of Burgesses is the earliest extant reference to George Mason II.

George Mason I had come to a wilderness area and helped to make it into a settled one with laws and regulations governing its future growth. Obviously, he was a man of stature among the other settlers, as is borne out by the number of appointed and elected offices he held during his lifetime. He left to his heir a position of importance in the new society developing along the shores of the Potomac, and a heritage of lands and goods much in excess of what he had in hand when he came to Virginia after the Battle of Worcester.

Chapter II

Colonel George Mason II

FAMILY TRADITION PLACES the birth of George Mason II at Accokeek plantation in 1660. In the absence of both church and county records for Stafford County in this period, most details of births and deaths must rest on traditional accounts preserved by later generations. He succeeded to his father's political offices as well as to his Potomac estates. He built wisely on the foundations laid by his father, increasing and developing his inherited lands and securing his hold on political leadership in Stafford County. The defense of Virginia's exposed frontiers and the problems arising from a too rapidly expanding tobacco economy occupied much of his time in public life. As commander of the Stafford County militia, Mason often took the field against marauding Indians and advised the governor on Indian policy. Otherwise reluctant to leave his Potomac borderland, he had little to do with the political factions of the Virginia capital. A power in his own county, the second George Mason furthered the transition of the Northern Neck from a frontier to a plantation economy.

In his lifetime the pattern of the economic and social development of Tidewater Virginia took definite shape. Tobacco emerged as the staple of the Virginia economy, and as it became dominant, the vast landholders began to displace the small subsistence farmers on many of the Virginia rivers. With the importation of African slaves, the large planters became more or less self-sufficient. They opposed the settling of towns and the establishment of ports that, by their nature, would regulate trade.

Chesapeake society reflected some of the stresses within British society in this period of rapid change. The continued hostility with France was accompanied by threats of attack along the frontier by Indians allied with the French. Even more disturbing than foreign wars was the deposition of James II in 1688. It reverberated across the ocean with repercussions in the American colonies, from Massachusetts Bay to the Chesapeake. Conflicts between the Roman Catholic proprietary in Maryland and Protestant planters blazed in open revolt. Fears of Jacobite invasion ushered in a period of renewed Indian warfare on the Potomac.

The two sister colonies on the Chesapeake had a number of common problems, among them their economy and the defense of their frontiers. At a time when most transportation was by water, the Potomac River and Chesapeake Bay served to unite, rather than separate, Maryland and Virginia. The frontier problems of Maryland were echoed in the Northern Neck of Virginia, and the two colonies pooled their resources in joint efforts to restrain the Indians on the upper Potomac. George Mason helped to shape plans for defensive operations in Maryland and Virginia, and the light-armed cavalrymen of his Potomac rangers patrolled the frontiers alongside their Maryland neighbors.

His interest and association with Maryland was strengthened by his marriage in 1680 to Mary Fowke, the daughter of Col. Gerard and Ann (Thoroughgood) Chandler Fowke of Charles County, Maryland.[1] The association of the families in the New World was an old one. George Mason I had been a neighbor of Colonel Fowke in their early plantation days in Virginia. Colonel Fowke's property was extensive, as he owned plantations in both Virginia and Maryland. In Virginia he was a burgess from James City in 1658–59, and later he served Westmoreland County in the same capacity. In Maryland his holdings included Cedar Hill, Gunston Hall, Hilltop, and other properties near Nanjemoy and Port Tobacco in Charles County, where he held the office of justice in 1667.[2]

Ann (Thoroughgood) Chandler Fowke's marriage to Gerard Fowke on 12 February 1661 was her second marriage. Her family was a distinguished and wealthy one. Her father, Adam Thoroughgood, who had come to Virginia as an apprentice, became wealthy; at one time he owned as many as 49 sheep and 117 cattle.[3] He built the first mansion in the Virginia settlements, which was located in the Norfolk area, and was a powerful man in his community. Her mother, Sarah Offley, was descended from a lord mayor of London who in 1556 was granted arms "peculiar to his branch."[4] Ann Thoroughgood's first husband was Job Chandler, receiver general of Maryland and a member of the Maryland Council, 1651–54 and 1656–59. He died in 1659. His will, dated at "Portoback in the Province of Maryland," 24 August 1659, made his wife, Ann, his executrix and bequeathed his home plantation of 1500 acres as well as 500 acres on Goose Creek and other lands recently surveyed on Nanjemoy to her during the minority of their children.[5]

In the first years of her marriage to Gerard Fowke, they lived in Westmoreland County, Virginia. Before they removed to Charles County, the signature of Ann Fowke was recorded in the Westmoreland County deeds as confirming a sale made by her husband on 11 November 1663 to Raleigh Travers, whose descendants intermarried with later generations of Masons.[6]

Four children were born to Ann and Gerard Fowke: Adam (named for his grandfather Adam Thoroughgood) who died young; Elizabeth, who married William Dent; Gerard, whose wives were Mary Lomax and Sarah Burdett; and Mary, who became the wife of George Mason II.* One of the few extant contemporary references to this marriage was in a letter from William Dent to Sir Edmund Andros, governor of Maryland, written 30 November 1697 from Nanjemoy, saying that he expects his "Brother Mason every day" and that he has had information concerning the Indian situation from his "Brother Gerard Fowke." [7]

William Dent represented Charles County in many capacities for many years. The considerable scope of his abilities is shown by the various kinds of duties he filled as a lawyer, legislator, council member and defender of the province. He was elected a member of the vestry of Nanjemoy Parish (now Durham Parish), as was his brother-in-law, Gerard Fowke. His will of 2 October 1702, probated 17 February 1704, shows that he was a man of substantial means who provided considerable estates for all of his five children. Two of his sons were to take possession of their estates at the age of seventeen, the other two at nineteen; but none of them were to have their money in England until they became twenty-one.[8]

The marriage of George Mason to Mary Fowke joined him in kinship with a number of illustrious families in Maryland. Of this marriage seven children were born: George, probably born at Accokeek; French, presumably named in memory of his Pershore ancestors; Nicholson, undoubtedly for Governor Nicholson, who was a good friend of the Mason family; Ann Fowke, for her Fowke grandmother; Mary, for her mother; Elizabeth, in all likelihood for her aunt, Elizabeth Dent; and Simpha Rosa Ann Field, for whose name we can hazard no guess.

The date of Mary (Fowke) Mason's death is unknown, but by 1706 George Mason had married Elizabeth Waugh, the daughter of Elizabeth and the Reverend John Waugh, with whom Mason was closely associated in politics in Stafford County. Elizabeth (Waugh) Mason died in giving birth to their only child, Catherine.[9] His third wife was Sarah Taliaferro, the daughter of Francis and Elizabeth (Catlett) Taliaferro of Essex County, Virginia, by whom he had three sons, all

---

* Mary (Fowke) Mason probably died in the summer of 1701, although there are no positive church or county records to support the inference.

of whom died in infancy, and a daughter, Sarah, who grew to maturity.*

Family ties drew him into the circle of discontented Protestant Marylanders chafing under the proprietary government of Lord Baltimore and the Roman Catholic establishment. Charles County was always the seedbed of Protestant disaffection, while neighboring Saint Marys County was the Roman Catholic stronghold in colonial Maryland. The Protestant Fowkes had close ties with Col. Josias Fendall, who had twice stirred up resistance to the lord proprietor. In 1681 Colonel Fendall and Capt. John Coode played on the lingering animosities of their Charles County neighbors toward the Catholics across the county line in Saint Marys County and on their fear of Indian uprisings. Moreover, they promised to obtain greater political power for the Protestant majority. When Fendall was arrested, his rescue by the Charles County militia was plotted in several of their meetings held at Chandler's Hope, the house of the widow Ann (Thoroughgood) Chandler Fowke in Nanjemoy.[10] Thus George Mason's marriage in 1680 made him conversant with the aims and intentions of the Protestant party in Maryland, particularly as they related to Indian problems and to conflicts with the lord proprietor.

The settlements in the upper reaches of Stafford County were under constant alarm in the 1680s by the passage of Iroquois war parties along the path that crossed the Potomac near the mouth of the Monocacy River and ran along the Catoctin Hills and the Bull Run Mountains to ford the rivers above the fall line. From time to time the remnants of the Piscataway Indians ranged from their settlement along Mattawoman Creek in Charles County to hunt in the backcountry of Stafford County, circling around the limits of English settlement by crossing the Potomac above the Little Falls, in the region of modern Washington.

Threats to the stability of the frontier country had come also from another source. The grants of all the lands between the Potomac and the Rappahannock, which had been made by Charles II as his way of rewarding faithful followers, were surrendered in May 1671. New letters patent were issued in their stead in 1673. These still included the right of the proprietors to collect quitrents from settlers on any lands that the proprietors made available to them.[11] Between 1680 and 1682 Thomas, Lord Culpeper bought out the rights of the other proprietors. He took advantage of "the Confusion that happen'd in the End of

---

* Francis Taliaferro was the son of Robert Taliaferro, who settled in Virginia before 1647. For his ancestry see Anthony Wagner and F. S. Andrus, "The Origin of the Family of Taliaferro," *Virginia Magazine of History and Biography* 77 (1969):22–25.

King James the Second's reign, viz. in October 1688 he got an Assign-
ment from the other Patentees, and gain'd a favorable Report from the
King's Council, upon his Patent for the Northern Neck." With the
grant confirmed by William and Mary, Culpeper appointed Nicholas
Spencer his agent. Spencer "did but little in his Lordship's Service"
and was succeeded by Col. Philip Ludwell, who "went over with this
Grant in the Year 1690 and set up an office in the Neck, claiming some
Escheats; but likewise could make nothing of it." [12]

The proprietor had made his subjects uneasy by abolishing the headright system as a means of obtaining land in the Northern Neck. Moreover, on both sides of the Potomac planters were held fast in the grip
of a depression in agricultural prices through the 1680s. Efforts to
regulate the tobacco trade in 1688 by prohibiting the exportation of
low-grade bulk tobacco had further alarmed planter and merchant
alike. [13] All of these fears and resentments coalesced in the name of religion and loyalty to William and Mary, the Protestant king and
queen.

In March 1689 the Piscataways made their usual hunting trip across
the Potomac. Burr Harrison of Chopawamsic was fishing in the river
off Potomac Creek as the Indians left their winter camp in Maryland.
He brought back news that connected the migration of the Indians
with events in England and closer to home. He spread abroad accounts
that the Marylanders planned to rise in favor of King James and that
Col. Edward Pye had threatened at Saint Marys City "before Easter
day to wash his hands in the Protestant blood" of his neighbors in
Virginia. Capt. George Brent of Woodstock, he further asserted, had
conspired with the Piscataways to attack the Virginia outposts. The
Piscataways had drawn in the Senecas by telling them "that they must
make haste and Kill the protestants before the shipping did come in
for after the shipping came they will then Kill the papists and then
they would Kill all the Indians." [14]

This was the kind of wild talk that inspired the followers of Jacob
Leisler, who became governor of New York in 1690, to seize the reins
of government in New York before traitors turned the city over to
French and Indian marauders. [15] Noised abroad by John Coode in
Maryland, it overturned the proprietorship of Lord Baltimore by open
rebellion. The planters in Charles County armed and "gathered themselves together in great parties to defend themselves" against the
threatened attack by Roman Catholic conspirators and their Indian
allies, of which they had received reports from Stafford County. In a
short time Coode's Protestant Association had seized the power of the
area from the representatives of the proprietor. [16] In the frontier settle-

ments of Stafford County the alarm ran like wildfire. The people armed and prepared to defend themselves. Garbled accounts of the Glorious Revolution in England and fears of Roman Catholic plots in support of the deposed James II only added fuel to the local fears of new Indian troubles and for the security of present land titles under a renewed proprietorship of the Northern Neck.

Burr Harrison gave the signal, but Capt. Mason and the Reverend John Waugh seized the torch from his hands and inflamed the back-country. Waugh, as the minister of Potomac Parish of the Church of England in Virginia, and Mason, as one of the Stafford County repre-sentatives of the House of Burgesses, gave a certain respectability to the tumultuous proceedings. Mason was sent to the Assembly by Staf-ford County in 1688 and took the oath of office as a member of the House of Burgesses on 25 April 1688. His only major contribution in his first term in the House was to serve on the committee that pre-sented a bill on the legal status of Negroes to the Governor's Council for approval. On 26 April 1689 Mason was suspended by the Gover-nor's Council from his duties as a justice of the peace and commanding officer of the Stafford County militia, charged with spreading danger-ous rumors and encouraging lawlessness.[17]

Mason joined wholeheartedly with Parson Waugh in stirring the embers of revolt in Stafford County. Some considered him the moving spirit in what came to be called "Parson Waugh's Tumult." [18] The un-settled state in England between the flight of James II to France and the arrival of King William to take his place had repercussions in America. Local factional fights reflected the enmity between Protestant and Catholic such as the one that arrayed Mason and Parson Waugh against Captain Brent and the Stafford County Catholics. George Brent and Col. William Fitzhugh, both of whom arrived in Stafford County circa 1670, drew around them the faction opposed to that led by Mason and Waugh. Fitzhugh had sat as a justice of the peace for Staf-ford since 1684 and served frequently as its representative in the House of Burgesses. Captain Brent, who was Fitzhugh's law partner and his close associate in land speculation efforts, was more vulnerable to at-tack because of his Catholicism. The evidence presented by Burr Har-rison of a plot between George Brent and the Indians made Brent the natural target of any ill-feeling stirred up by Waugh. A Maryland shipmaster testified that Brent was in peril of his life and that a large body of Stafford County freeholders were prepared to plunder him of all his goods. To allay the clamor against him, Nicholas Spencer, who was both the secretary of state for Virginia and the agent of the North-ern Neck proprietors, ordered Brent's house to be searched for arms and ammunition and directed Brent to retire to Fitzhugh's home.[19]

Mason and Waugh put themselves at the head of the Protestant freemen, who pledged unquestioned loyalty to King William and Queen Mary and armed themselves against an invasion of Catholic Jacobites from Maryland. John Coode was raising a Protestant militia across the Potomac for use against Lord Baltimore, the Jesuit priests of southern Maryland, and Catholic settlers in general. These movements occurred in districts where the rights of a proprietor threatened the rights of individual landowners.[20] As the Maryland storm blew to gale force, Waugh continued to preach dangerous doctrines. In the interim between the flight of King James and the accession of King William, Waugh asserted that "as there was no King in England, there was no lawful government in Virginia" and urged the people to remain armed for their own defense. The alarm spread from Stafford to the upper settlements on the Rappahannock. Three members of the Governor's Council took immediate steps to arrest Waugh, Burr Harrison, and another of his followers and to suspend Mason from all his offices and emoluments. Waugh "made a publick and humble acknowledgement" before the officials at Jamestown and was restored to his parish, "with a hearty penitence for his former faults and a promised obedience for the future." [21]

George Mason was also restored to his former position. It is a tacit indication of his power in his native county that he was merely suspended from his post as commanding officer of the militia when he was suspected of being the prime mover in an insurrection. He continued to be the staunch defender of Protestant Virginia. Presiding over the session of the Stafford County Court on 12 December 1689, he granted the petition of William Barton of Stafford County, who protested that Francis Hammersley, the Roman Catholic executor of his father's estate, kept Barton's two brothers and sister from him and might well bring up the children as Catholics. The suit is of interest because Hammersley's wife was Mary Brent, a Roman Catholic of Woodstock, Stafford County, Virginia, and the daughter of George and Marianna (Peyton) Brent from whom was descended Sarah Brent, who married George Mason IV, whose grandfather granted Barton's petition.

Col. William Fitzhugh was less than pleased to see Mason restored to his duties as a magistrate. Writing to his brother-in-law in 1690, Fitzhugh rehearsed the grave troubles that the Waugh Tumult had presented for Stafford County and for himself. Fitzhugh insisted that he himself "stood in the gap and kept off an approaching Rebellion, to my no small charge and trouble." He had been in daily expectation of being plundered by the rabble and once of being murdered. All this he counted as nothing. "But to be disregarded nay & slighted too, & to see those mischievous active Instruments as you well enough know Waugh & Mason &c, the only men in favour, & the only men taken notice thereof, grates harder than the non payment for powder shot & other disbursements." Fitzhugh relied on his kinsmen to bring the whole matter to the attention of the new governor, Lord Howard of Effingham, "and fully set forth to him the wickedness of Waugh & Mason & Co. the at present grand favourites."

The pardons issued to Mason and Waugh aggravated the bitterness between the two factions, which was carried over into the 1691 election for burgess. Martin Scarlet defeated Fitzhugh and deeply injured his feelings as well by publicly asserting "that neither Law nor Justice has been adm'r'd in this Country since [Fitzhugh] sat upon the Bench for nothing was law or Justice but what [he] said was soe." [22] When Stafford County voters again returned Mason, the triumph of Waugh's faction and the discomfit of Fitzhugh's followers were complete. Mason took the oath of office and was admitted again to the House of Burgesses on 18 April 1691. Two months later at the court held at the house of Thomas Ellsey on 10 June 1691, Mason and Scarlet took the oaths appointed and were sworn as justices of the peace of the county of Stafford. On the same day Mason was sworn in as high sheriff of Stafford County for the ensuing year and as county lieutenant. [23]

Colonel Fitzhugh rose in the same court to enter his protest against Martin Scarlet's aspersions. He pointed out that he had served on the bench since 1683, when he had been the colleague of the late Col. George Mason I. Perhaps with an eye on Capt. George Mason, Fitzhugh recalled that Colonel Mason had seldom or never presided and, on the rare occasions when he did, had left tedious legal matters to Fitzhugh. Since Mason's death in 1689 Fitzhugh had presided in his own name and in that of the freeholders of Stafford County. To declare that there had been no justice done in those years was a slur on the jurymen, the attorneys, and the whole body of freemen. [24]

The factional squabbles brought to a head in Parson Waugh's Tumult continued. Neither side had yet exhausted its weapons. Richard Gibson registered his first protest against "Mr. George Brent, Robert Brent, and all other Popish recusants" in Stafford County at the October 1691 session of Stafford County Court. On the same day Gibson sued a tenant for arrearages of rent for land at the head of Quantico Creek, with Mason as his surety. Gibson again lodged information in 1692 and in 1693 against the Brents, who appealed to the governor against these continued aspersions against their loyalty. [25] In November 1691 Fitzhugh sent the Stafford justices a long criticism of John

Waugh and the loose accusations he had made against Fitzhugh. In 1692 Colonel Fitzhugh's brother-in-law, George Luke, entered an action of trespass against the Reverend John Waugh "of overwarton plantation on Potomack Creek" on behalf of Mary, widow and executrix of the late Henry Meese, merchant of London. Mason stepped forward as Waugh's surety and posted bond for him.[26]

In November 1693, when Fitzhugh took his seat in the House of Burgesses as a representative from Stafford County, his colleagues made a special point of imposing the Test Act on him as suspicions of disloyalty or Catholicism still hung around his name. Fitzhugh and George Brent were then proprietary agents for the proprietors of the Northern Neck. Mason and Fitzhugh made their peace the following year, when George Mason renewed his land patents as a new grant from the proprietors of the Northern Neck.[27]

The Mason and Fitzhugh factions composed their differences after a political quarrel that had brought their Stafford County neighbors to the verge of armed insurrection and anarchy. But there was little likelihood that the settlers on the Virginia frontier and the nearby Indian tribes could live together on a basis of mutual forebearance and understanding. While the fluctuating price of tobacco occupied much of the thought of the local magnates who came to the capital city for the sessions of the Assembly in the 1680s, men like George Mason, who represented frontier districts, were much more concerned with the peril of Indian raids. The House of Burgesses vacillated between the desire to protect the frontier and the wish to avoid expense. In 1680 they determined that the forts at the headwaters of the four great rivers of Virginia, including the garrison house at the Occoquan for the protection of the Potomac, should be kept up and maintained. In 1682 they determined that the danger was for the present removed by peace treaties with the Indians and that the forts could be dismantled.[28]

It was at this time that the light-armed volunteer cavalry units known as rangers were called into being to give the backcountry some means of defense against hostile Indians. No warfare between the Indians and settlers troubled Virginia, but the incursions of war parties of Iroquois against vassal tribes like the Rappahannocks had an unsettling effect on the frontiers of the colony. Under a treaty negotiated with the Iroquois at Albany in July 1684, they agreed to keep away from the settlements and to use a new path east of the Blue Ridge for their thoroughfare to the south.[29]

Captain Mason and his neighbors on the upper reaches of the Potomac were naturally concerned about the defense of their frontier plantations. This concern led them to give credence to widespread rumors of impending Indian attacks when Waugh appealed to the freemen of Stafford County to defend themselves. They needed little urging to take alarm at the passage of hunting parties of Indians through the forests that began just beyond their fields, but the real danger came from the violence of the frontier reaction to even minor provocation.

In October 1691 a party of Seneca Indians who had been trapping beaver on the Rappahannock crossed the Potomac near Hunting Creek, just north of Mason's lands at Pohick, and visited the emperor of the Piscataways at his fortified town in Maryland. The emperor, who knew from experience how small incidents could lead to angry confrontations between the settler and the Indian, urged the Senecas to keep their hunting dogs in check, lest they kill the sheep or cow of some English settler and cause trouble for the Indians. The Seneca band returned to Virginia and went hunting toward the Sugarlands above the Great Falls of the Potomac, far beyond any Virginia settlement. Before they left the neighborhood, they told a planter near Hunting Creek of the advice they had been given and of their future plans.

A short time later Robert Brent reported that a mare had been stolen from his brother's plantation near Little Hunting Creek and a cow killed by some dogs belonging to the Indians. Lt. David Strahan and his rangers followed the tracks of an Indian hunting party until they surprised and captured six Indians in a cabin, with the tail and part of the skin of Brent's mare in their possession. The rangers delivered the prisoners to Mason, sheriff of Stafford County. Mason immediately sent a report to Governor Francis Nicholson, who authorized Mason to continue his patrols of rangers if the Indian danger made such patrols necessary.[30]

The Indian prisoners continued in Mason's custody. He and his deputy, Capt. Malachy Peake, took them before the justices of Stafford County on 22 December 1691. They examined the chief prisoner, whom they found to be none other than the king of the Doegs. He explained that the mare had been killed by a young Mohawk, who had been a member of their party. It was ironic not only that the king of the Doeg Indians had fallen into the hands of George Mason as sheriff of Stafford County but that the sheriff was the son of the man who had captured the Indian in 1675 when he was eight years old and had arranged for his baptism. He explained to the justices that he had been taken prisoner by the Senecas in 1677 and had remained with them until the previous year, when he came to live in Virginia with his kinsmen, the Nanticoke Indians on the Rappahannock, as he was one of the last of his tribe. Whether they believed that the young Indian was the king of the Doegs or not, the justices kept him and his companions under the watchful eye of Captain Mason through the winter of 1691/92. Mason and David Wheatly, the official interpreter for the Northern Neck, brought the six prisoners back to Stafford County Court on 9 March 1691/92 along with Tahooka and Tahnquan, "two of the great men of the Nanticokes." The emissaries from the Nanticokes paid for the cow, and the Indian prisoners were given their freedom.[31]

It is interesting to note some of the expenses incurred by those engaged in defending the Virginia frontier. Mason entered his claim for the support of the Indians he had kept in custody for 106 days and was allowed 20,000 pounds of tobacco. Robert Cropper entered his claim for expenses incurred when Mason sent him to the governor in the dead of the winter. Lt. David Strahan was allowed 2,000 pounds of tobacco for his troubles and expenses in ferrying men and horses over the Occoquan between April and October 1691, as well as those for the previous three years.[32]

Indian affairs continued to trouble the settlers. On 17 March 1692 Captain Mason addressed the Governor's Council regarding the Piscataway Indians of Maryland. In April of that year he served on a committee of the House of Burgesses concerned with munitions needed for the defense of Virginia and was reappointed sheriff of Stafford County. In June 1692 Lieutenant Strahan and his rangers came to Pohick and learned that Mason's manservant was missing. They followed his tracks about half a mile to a deserted house, where they found the tracks of a great many Indians whose trail they followed for ten miles without finding the missing servant.[33]

Captain Mason and Lt. Sampson Darrell carried reports of incursions of strange Indians to the Stafford County Court. On 8 June 1692 the magistrate authorized the raising of an additional troop of ten men under the command of Capt. Thomas Owsley, Mason's neighbor on Pohick Creek, "to Range and Scout from above Occoquan to the head of this River." They sent Capt. Martin Scarlet and Capt. John Withers to present a petition from the "Frontier Plantations" to the governor and the Council.

Mason was "ranging" with Strahan and his men during most of June 1692. They requested the emperor of the Piscataways to come across the Potomac on parlay, but he refused. Mason, Owsley, and Strahan then went over to the Piscataways' palisaded town in Maryland, where they held a council with the Piscataway chiefs. The Piscataways sent twenty of their braves to go after the Indians who had carried off Mason's servant. This accomplished, Mason returned to his home at

Pohick, and the two companies of rangers returned to their patrol of the frontiers, with Mason's house as their headquarters.[34] Disturbances continued on the frontier, for in July 1694 Mason sent information to the Governor's Council concerning the murder of a Negro and more Indian problems.

Mason returned to the House of Burgesses in April 1695 as a newly elected member from Stafford. His first action after taking his seat in the House was to petition on 23 April for payment of the arrears due to the Potomac rangers for their services and expenses. Two days later he requested the appointment of additional rangers on the frontier. Mason was appointed to a committee to prepare a bill for the defense of the colony and to a committee drafting a bill authorizing the appointment of additional rangers for the better defense of the frontiers.[35] He also presented a bill to regulate the size of hogsheads for tobacco.

Again returned to the House of Burgesses in 1696, Mason continually pressed for frontier defense measures. He complained to the Council about the state of the Indian problem on the upper Potomac. In the autumn session he introduced a bill to pay a bounty to Indians who killed wolves on the Virginia borderlands and presented a series of propositions from Stafford County relating to the Indian problem, the Potomac rangers, and problems of trade and horsestealing. Captain Mason had long been active in enlarging the patrols of rangers on the Potomac frontier as commander in chief of the Stafford militia. When additional rangers were authorized in 1695 in response to legislation he had introduced, Mason took command of them himself. In October 1696 he presented his accounts for two months active duty as captain of rangers.

The Indian problem, as Mason and his neighbors saw it, could be rendered more manageable if the Piscataways and the other Maryland Indians could be restrained from crossing the Potomac into Virginia on their periodic hunting expeditions. Mason prepared a bill to close the Virginia boundaries to the Indians of Maryland to prevent them from using their former hunting grounds.[36] While the Virginia burgesses discussed means of closing their frontiers to the Piscataways, the council fires burned late in the fortified town of the Piscataways by the marshes of Zachia Swamp. As the Maryland and Virginia settlements pushed relentlessly up the Potomac, the Indians found themselves surrounded by white settlers and increasingly hemmed in by the snares and meshes of the white man's law. The emperor and his older councillors had long ago accepted the policy of acting as a buffer state between Maryland and the powerful Indian confederacies of the north and west, all of them more or less tributary to the Iroquois. In return, the Marylanders and Virginians had tolerated the Piscataways and given them a measure of autonomy in their old homeland. The Iroquois, however, continued to harass the Piscataways, and the younger and more militant men taunted their leaders with the failure of Maryland to come to their assistance at Zachia in 1681.[37] They must have prevailed upon the chiefs to join the Iroquois because suddenly, in the early spring of 1697, the whole tribe moved out of the protective swamp and crossed the Potomac into Virginia below Occoquan Creek, leaving behind them a trail of slaughter and cruelty. As they passed Aquia Creek on their way to the mountains, the Indians, led by one named Squire Tom, murdered a woman and three children in an isolated farmhouse.

Mason went after the murderers and informed Col. John Addison, who had taken the field with the Maryland rangers, that the woman and children stabbed by the Indians were likely to recover.

I did light of 8 Indians that was accused for the Murther & Ordering my men to seize them all to a Popol'r immediately to Execute them all; & telling them I knew them to be Murder'rs one Esqr. Thom & Choptico Robin desired that they might discourse me at which I did; they told me if I would not hang them they would discover the Murder'rs; Soe I admitted them their Pardon; so immediately they told me it was three of them; & two of them was there and the other was Gon to the New fort, soe immediately seizes the Two and sent to Prison; & I have sent to Emperor for the other Indian, whom I know. Our Country is so Dam'd full of lyes; that I know not how allmost to Act but God direct for the Best that I may Act both for the Good of King and Country.[38]

Squire Tom insisted that he was innocent and that the emperor of the Piscataways and his men had committed the murder. The emperor crossed over to Virginia and gave himself up to the Stafford County authorities as proof that his tribe had not broken the peace by such a cowardly murder. Eventually one of Squire Tom's companions confessed that Squire Tom had killed the family as an act of revenge for the wrongs done to Pamunkeys by the English and had contrived to throw the blame on the Piscataways as the allies of the settlers. Tom escaped but the seven other Pamunkeys were hanged. Mason wrote long accounts of the affair to the Governor's Council. Later that summer the Piscataway Indians abandoned their fort in Zachia Swamp and crossed the Potomac into Virginia. Governor Andros sent immediate orders to George Mason and the other local authorities to prevail with them to return to Maryland, but still the Piscataways remained "back in the Woods beyond the little mountains." [39]

They built a new fort and planted corn that summer at the new home they had chosen beyond the Bull Run Mountains in Fauquier County. The Council of Maryland sent two commissioners, Thomas Tench and John Addison, to try to persuade the Piscataways to return. Tench and Addison began their journey with a visit to Mason at his home at Pohick to obtain his advice. For as commander in chief of the militia he was responsible for the defense of the backwoods and took the field as the commanding officer of the Stafford rangers during the Indian troubles.[40]

Indian affairs continued to occupy Mason's attention in the 1698 and 1699 sessions of the House of Burgesses, when he was spokesman for Stafford County's grievances. At the same time the Piscataways, who had spent all of their lives by the shores of the Potomac, where fish were always in plentiful supply, now found life intolerable far from their staple food. As they were ill equipped for hunting, they soon found themselves close to starvation. Therefore they moved to Point of Rocks far up the Potomac, and once again were blamed for several more murders that had been committed on the lower Potomac. Mason demanded that the Virginia authorities destroy the Piscataway fort and punish the marauders.[41] It was soon discovered that the murders were not committed by the Piscataways but by roving Senecas on their way to the hunting grounds of the upper Rappahannock.

In June 1699 Captain Mason was reappointed commanding officer of the Stafford County militia raised in rank to lieutenant colonel and sheriff. In October he received instructions from the Governor's Council to investigate the condition and number of the Piscataway Indians. Colonel Mason sent David Strahan and Giles Tillett to treat with the Piscataways in April 1700.[42] That June the Piscataways agreed to come back within the Maryland jurisdiction and live in peace as before their migration. But they did not return.

On hearing a rumor that the emperor and his people had come back from their camp beyond the mountains, Mason sent Robert Colson over the Potomac to the Indian town at Pamunkey, directly opposite Mason's Neck on the Maryland shore, where he found the wandering emperor and a few of his braves. The emperor told Colson of the movements of the Senecas and of a party of Indians sent by the French to the upper Potomac and assured him that he would gladly return to the Maryland jurisdiction if his people were willing to do so. Mason observed to the governor that the Christian King Peter and his Pamunkey Indians, allies of the English settlers, "doe continue at Parmunkey Town in Maryl'd and doe make corn there, there's about 100 men women and children of all sorts and *they* say the Emperor is a great

Rogue" and was in league with the Senecas.[43] Mason suspected trouble, and when it came it was closer to home than he had perhaps anticipated.

On Sunday 16 June 1700 about three o'clock in the afternoon, twenty or thirty Indians came to the house of Thomas Barton, "about 20 miles above my house," Mason reported to Governor Nicholson. The man and his wife and brother were away and had

left his three children and an orphan boy at home and had gotten a man and his wife and three children from a plantation of mine about 2 miles from home to stay to look after the house until they came home; the Indians fell on them and killed Barton's three children, the man and his wife and his three children. The orphan boy ran away, he being out to play, blessed be God, got to a Neighbor's House and is safe.

On the news I went immediately with a small parcel of men and buried the poor people. This murther was the most horrible that ever was in Stafford, and I thank God, we have not had the least harm on this side of Occoquan since. I have been in the Freshes * and have kept the people bravely on their plantations, but God knows what I shall do now, for this has almost frighted our people out of their lives and Interests, and besides the Emperor and his Indians being still about, which did as surely do the murther as God's in heaven.

The man himself [Thomas Barton] coming home called at the Mill and took a bagg of meal with him, and about 400 yards from his house about 20 Indians as he guesses, started up and immediately had him in a half moon; he well mounted, put on, endeavoring for his house, but he being loaded, they had like to have gotten him, but with great difficulty [he] got his bagg off, and broke through the Woods, and got safe to a neighbor's house. . . .

Sir I have raised 12 men and have sent every way to search the frontiers and back-forest-plantations, and I intend, God willing, to keep constantly moving myself with them, until [I] have your Excellency's Commands, but trust in God, shall be able to give our people better satisfaction than at present can, for I am afraid that we shall have a bad summer; but if please God, can but keep them upon their plantations, it will be some discouragement to the Enemy but those too are deserted for this Year. I do not doubt your Excellency's Christian care for the good of his Majesty's subjects, for without immediate Care,[44] [we] shall have but few plantations in Stafford.

Governor Nicholson and Colonel Mason crossed the Potomac to consult with Governor Blakiston of Maryland about joint action

---

* "Freshes: The water is salty at the Capes and in the lower parts of the Bay, and fresh at the head of the Bay and in the upper courses of the rivers. The creeks and those portions of the rivers that are fresh are known in the Chesapeake region as 'freshes' " (Arthur P. Middleton, *Tobacco Coast: A Maritime History of Chesapeake Bay in the Colonial Era*, p. 35) .

against the Indians. They met at the house of Col. John Addison on the south side of the Anacostia River. On his way back to Jamestown, Nicholson wrote to Mason: "I hope in God that we shall have no more mischief done by the Indians and that the people are all returned to their plantations. I'm also in hopes that all the militia officers and justices will meet you this Week attending to appointment, and I pray God Direct you for the best." [45]

The safety of the Potomac frontier rested on Col. George Mason and his rangers. He ordered six men under Ens. Giles Vandegasteel to patrol the outlying settlements. "I have raised them from Guiles Vandecastiall's house up to the uppermost plantation, the Neighbors having fitted out their Sons and other young men well equipped; so their ranging is as low as my plantation at Pohick so round all the works up to the uppermost Inhabitants, so down upon ye back plantations, and Cornet Burr Harrison from Acaquan down to the Potomack Creek. . . . The Inhabitants still continue from their houses, but abundance [are] better satisfied since part of the Rangers is constantly ranging among them." [46] Mason and his hastily raised levies scoured the woods for signs of hostile Indians through the dismal summer of 1700.

Frightened refugees left their outlying farms and fled to friends and neighbors below Pohick, perhaps below the Occoquan, spreading stories of danger in the backcountry. Mason found "every one under great dread and fear, but few gone home as yet, some going quite out of these parts," when he wrote to the governor in August.[47] Mason's own tenants could hardly be expected to stay on his lands above Little Hunting Creek, where one family had been so cruelly butchered. Gentlemen might talk of the price of tobacco and slaves over a leisurely glass of Madeira in the security of York or Gloucester County but in the frontier world of Col. George Mason the struggle to survive was still uppermost in men's minds.

Mason heard of a man on board a Potomac river sloop who had spent a long time with the Indians and immediately sent men up river to bring him to Pohick for examination. The young white man, twenty-two-year-old Thomas Monck, confessed to Mason that he had been with the Piscataways at their mountain camp in the summer of 1699 and had seen Squire Tom bring in a scalp. This renegade tried hard to ingratiate himself with his captors, while freely offering details about most of the murders committed on the frontier since 1698.* He

---

* In answer to a question Monck admitted that there was a Frenchman living with the Piscataways on the upper Potomac; probably this was Martin Charetier, a French trapper with an Indian wife, who had long been in the area.

had helped Squire Tom plot the murders of the families of Thomas Pearson and Humphrey Peake, but at the last minute they decided to kill the Barton children. After the murders Squire Tom and his band had crossed into Maryland and fled to the upper reaches of the Potomac. While Monck passed himself off as an innocent observer, Mason thought he knew too much about too many of the murders to be innocent and sent him to Jamestown in chains.[48]

The Virginia council authorized Colonel Mason to raise a new troop of volunteer rangers to patrol the lower part of Stafford County against the Indians. The problem still seemed threatening to Mason in October 1700, and he asked permission to continue his rangers on the frontier. In December 1700 the governor and the Council decided that the situation no longer required such extraordinary precautions and ordered Mason to disband his rangers. Their common efforts to bring the Indian menace on the Potomac frontier under control brought Governor Francis Nicholson and Col. George Mason into frequent and amicable association. From the tone of their surviving correspondence and the evidences of close collaboration on the political issues that disrupted Stafford County, it is reasonable to conclude that Colonel Mason was on friendly terms with the governor. At least one letter indicates that Nicholson expedited legal business for Mason. The friendship between the two men was probably of long standing. Col. Francis Nicholson arrived as lieutenant governor of Virginia in 1690, serving under Francis, Lord Howard of Effingham, the actual governor, who was away from Virginia at the time. In February 1692 Nicholson was transferred to Maryland as governor and was succeeded in Virginia by Sir Edmund Andros. In November 1698 Nicholson returned as governor of the Old Dominion, which office he held until 1705.[49]

In 1702 as commander in chief and president of the county, Col. George Mason sent an address to King William III from the civil and military officers of Stafford County, promising their allegiance and expressing their disgust on learning that "the French King Imediately upon the Death of the Late King James did Cause the Pretended Prince of Wales to be solemnly proclaimed King of England Scotland and Ireland."[50] Among the militia officers who attested that Jacobites would find no support in northern Virginia was a Lt. George Mason, who was almost certainly the son of Edward Mason and possibly Col. George Mason's nephew, but documentary proof has not been found.[51]

In 1704 Colonel Mason reported to the council about new Indian menaces on the Stafford frontier. Depredations by some of the Nansiattico Indians on the upper Rappahannock were alarming the frontier settlements. Mason was granted a commission of oyer and terminer to try Indian prisoners believed to be guilty of the murders. In November 1704 he expressed to the Council his fears of the possibility of an Indian war because of the dangerous situation still existing on the frontier. Though problems concerning the defense of the frontier continued to be of grave concern to Mason, his wish to absent himself from his political obligations and devote his time to his plantation and family became increasingly noticeable after 1701. He asked to return home during the 1701 session of the House of Burgesses because his wife was then seriously ill. After 1705 he was reprimanded by the House of Burgesses for his failure to attend sessions. Even so, in 1706 he again asked to be excused from the session of the House.[52] His attendance improved over the succeeding years as there is no record that he asked permission to leave the assembly until 3 December 1711. Over the long period that he served as burgess he was appointed to many committees concerned with the making of laws although there is no indication that he had more than a very simple education. The first settlers were involved with the hard work of building the homes they desired, but the next generation realized that it was only by law they could safeguard these lands hewn from the wilderness for their successors. This respect for law fairly administered as a means to live comfortably in one's community was to be a dominant characteristic of George Mason's grandson.

George Mason II, by careful husbandry and shrewd land investments, had solidified the inheritance received from his father into a considerable estate. His marriage, and connections by marriage, added to his prestige. These factors combined to raise him to a position of considerable importance in his county, as his offices and continued services to the House of Burgesses testify. Vast acres set out in tobacco did not necessarily lead to wealth and social prestige. Worn-out lands or the depressing effect of overproduction on the price of tobacco could drive a man from prosperity to ruin. But men of property and influence could survive the waves of prosperity and depression that passed over Virginia much better than men who possessed only marginal lands or lacked the credit of important family connections. The depression of the 1680s thinned the rows of future leaders of the colony, eliminating some "new men" and insuring the greater prominence of others. Mason was not a man of great wealth in the 1680s, but he was a man whose strategically placed landholdings and inherited position enabled him to survive in a changing economic and social pattern.[53] For the man of means and good family connections, land was still available. From various records it is certain that in 1692 George Mason had moved up the Potomac River to the peninsula

known today as Mason's Neck. This neck of land between the Occoquan River and Gunston Cove is one of the most attractive headlands
on the Potomac. In Mason's day it was still untenanted, and the Indian
clearings, fast being overtaken by honeysuckle and scrub pine, were
the only tangible relics of the Doeg Indians, who had once made it
their home. Doegs' (or Dogues') Neck, as it was known in Mason's
time, offered a rich field for the expansion of his farm and tobacco
fields.

The land on and around this peninsula had had claimants some
forty years earlier. In 1651 Richard Turney sailed up the Potomac
until he saw the fields of the Doegs, separated from the mainland by
swamp, on the most outstanding neck of land in the Potomac freshes.
Turney claimed the land and registered a patent for 2,109 acres "commonly called or known by the name of Doeg's Island." Two years
later Thomas Speke of Nomini, presiding justice of Westmoreland
County, claimed 1,000 acres "on Potomack River opposite against the
Meompses Island," which was the Indian name for Doegs' Island.
Later land grants made Col. Thomas Speke's patent rights somewhat
clearer. His lands lay "above the Doeg's Island." Reference is made
to "Colo. Speake's poynt" on a "great creek" called "Doeg's Island
Creek" (now known as Gunston Cove) into which emptied two
branches, one called the "West or North West" and the other called
the "Main Branch" (now known as Accotink Creek). Colonel Speke's
property passed in 1657 to Thomas Brereton, clerk of the council, and
to Richard Bushrod of Gloucester County in 1660 and 1662. None of
these early owners of the tract did anything to improve it, so far as
can be discovered, and did not reside on this remote frontier. Several
other patents of land adjoining Doegs' Island on the west, that is, on
the north bank of the Occoquan, were also granted in 1653. They
were immediately consolidated by John Drayton and later passed to
Thomas Baxter.[54]

Mason's name first appears as a landholder in Stafford County in a
case at law presented before the magistrates of that county on 8 October
1691. John Tillett represented to the magistrates that "coming a
Stranger into this County" he had bought two "parcels of Land upon
Ocoquan River within the Jurisdiction of this Court, which land lyes
bounded between the Land of Captain George Mason, Mr. Thomas
Bushrod, and Land formerly of Thomas Baxter and Mr. Wilks." Tillett petitioned the Court "to put an end of lawsuits between the
aforementioned neighbors" by ordering Capt. George Brent, as the
attorney for William Sherwood, to survey Sherwood's "Doge's Island'
tract." The Stafford County magistrates granted his request and or-

dered Brent "to lay out the land of the said Sherwood lying upon Doegs Island."

In the absence of more complete land records for Stafford County, the petition of John Tillett is a clear indication that sometime before 1691 Mason had acquired a tract of land on what was later to be known as Mason's Neck. It can be identified a little more definitely from the patent of land taken out in 1694 by Thomas Owsley, which refers to the upper part of the tract granted to Colonel Speke as "now in tenor and occupation of Captain George Mason." Thus by 1694 George Mason II was definitely living with his family on the former Speke tract, bounded in part by Pohick Creek and present day Gunston Cove and extending toward the tract owned by Tillett on the banks of Occoquan Creek, which completed the bounds of his own property. In 1696 Mason purchased the Doegs' Island tract that had previously belonged to William Sherwood and repatented it under a grant from the proprietors of the Northern Neck, thus rounding out his title to Mason's Neck.[55]

Mason had not taken up his residence above the Occoquan before 1691, for the ferry rights over that river, which were granted to his father in 1684, were still not exercised by Capt. George Mason as late as March 1691. Mason's friend, David Strahan, appeared in Stafford County Court on 11 March 1690/91 to assume the "keeping of a ferry for man and horse over the River of Occoquan," and was authorized to agree with each person for whatever ferriage seemed convenient. The magistrates determined at the court session of 9 October 1691 that as a ferry over the Occoquan was "found absolute necessary for the inhabitants of the upper parish of the County," David Strahan should be paid 25,000 pounds of tobacco to maintain a boat for that purpose.[56]

By 1692 there are several references showing that George Mason II had taken up residence at Pohick. This is further borne out by records of a meeting of the Stafford County magistrates on 10 February 1692/93 in which they appointed Richard Fossaker to take Mason's place as surveyor of the highways for the "whole Precincts of Aquia and Aquakek with the County." That he was already regarded as an important citizen by his new neighbors above the Occoquan is indicated by his appointment to receive the census report listing tithable inhabitants and their slaves in the area from the Occoquan up to the head of the river which had been authorized by the Stafford County Court in May 1693.[57]

However, Mason was still a landholder in the Aquia area. In October 1694 he patented, under a new grant from the proprietors, the

1,150 acres of land he had inherited from his father. In that year he
sold to Richard Wright, a merchant of Stafford County, 150 acres of
his property on Accokeek, including "the late mansion house of Col.
George Mason deceased," together with all "houses, outhouses, barns,
stables, tobacco houses and all other edifices," but reserving "the Tomb
of the said Colonel George Mason and the Burying Place in which it
stands." In 1701 he conveyed an additional 200 acres of the tract as a
gift to Thomas and Mary Barbee. He sold the remaining 800 acres in
1705 to Edward Mountjoy.[58]

While he gradually disposed of the lands he had inherited on Accokeek Run, Mason increased and consolidated his holdings on the
upper Potomac at Doegs' Neck until by 1704 he had established himself as a major landholder on the Potomac. For in that year on 8 February he compounded with the proprietors of the Northern Neck for the
payment of the rents and arrearages of rents due from the lands that
he then owned. He described his property at that time as including
"divers tracts of Land in Stafford amounting to about 8,000 Acres in
Stafford County, my home Seat of Doegs Island being part thereof."
Mason spent considerable time and thought on the development and
improvement of his lands—erecting mills, acquiring acreage for his
tobacco crops, and adding to his lands for speculative and investment
purposes. The transition of his Potomac homeland from rough frontier
to a settled plantation economy had been completed. The Indian raids
that had retarded settlement little more than a decade earlier faded
into a dim memory of heroic deeds and violent reaction. Col. George
Mason left to his children a secure place in Chesapeake society, threatened only by the vagaries of the uncertain tobacco economy.

Land was more than an idle speculative venture. It was a hedge on
the uncertain tobacco economy. As early as 1648 planters south of the
York River had complained that their "lands had become barren from
cultivation" and petitioned for new grants of untilled acreage. The
scientific parson, the Reverend John Clayton, found the same practices
of soil exhaustion and abandonment in full swing in the Jamestown
neighborhood in the 1680s, where planters assured him that their
lands were so worn out "that they had not ground altogether that
would bring forth tobacco." The breaking in of new ground and the
abandonment of the old fields was already becoming the pattern as
tobacco marched into the forest at the head of the succession of crops
leaving behind fields that would bear no more.[59]

This depletion of the soil was deplored, but tobacco brought such
abundant returns for the planter that the problem of overproduction
was a more serious one than wasteful methods of agriculture. There

was still an abundance of land, but, unfortunately for the tobacco grower, there was a superabundance of tobacco. The duty of two shillings for every hogshead of tobacco exported to England was the primary source of revenue from the colony. The amount collected by customs officials in 1677 amounted to nearly £100,000 and is a fair indication of the agricultural productivity of Virginia. The number of tobacco plants set out in 1680 was till then the greatest in the annals of Virginia. A vast quantity of tobacco already lay in warehouses as a surplus of the preceding season. The total amount of tobacco available to be shipped would glut British markets for at least two years, even if not a single plant was set out in 1681.

The tobacco planters were in desperate straits, and they sought in vain to obtain some alteration in the Navigation Acts to open foreign trade to their produce. As a remedy for the dangerously low price of tobacco, brought about by the competitive efforts of the Virginia growers to make more abundant crops, the burgesses recommended a voluntary abandonment of their one cash crop and concentration on grain, pork, and other produce that could be shipped to the West Indies. The Virginia authorities also petitioned the home government for a farm holiday, but officials in London, fearing the loss of an entire year's revenue from Virginia, listened more readily to the complaints of English merchants and shipmasters than to the petitions of the planters.

Voluntary methods of crop limitation did nothing to ease the depression that clung tenaciously to Virginia through the 1680s. In the Tobacco Riot of 1682 some desperate planters leveled the crops of their neighbors on the lower reaches of the York and Rappahannock. Militiamen called out to quell the disturbance restricted the planters' war to night raids and tobacco barn burnings. The crop destruction of 1682 permitted prices to begin a slow recovery, despite even more abundant crops in 1683. When tobacco rose on the British market, Virginians were stimulated to set out more and more plants. The salutary lessons of the last depression were quickly forgotten. By 1685 despite the alternation of high and low prices for tobacco, authorities in England and in Virginia abandoned their efforts to diversify the economy of the colony. If tobacco was not a sure path to wealth, it remained the only path in seventeenth-century Virginia.

The tobacco economy, in which the settlers on the Potomac were engaged, did not encourage the growth of towns and villages. The river itself was the broad highway of commerce, and the planter brought his crops by water to some central place where the British merchants gathered. The hogsheads of tobacco were then taken out in flatboats to a ship riding at anchor in the mouth of an inlet or in a sheltered cove of the Potomac itself. The need of a safe anchorage for the ships led to a consolidation of individual tobacco shipments. Some of the planters acted as consignment merchants and lined up the tobacco of friends and neighbors to be shipped to a particular British merchant. Col. William Fitzhugh of Stafford County was active in recruiting customers for British merchants. In 1689 he wrote to John Cooper of London that he had advised and persuaded Samuel Hayward and Sampson Darrell to make their tobacco consignments to him and should be able to persuade others to deal with him if the terms were worthwhile.[60] That Fitzhugh was not idle is shown by the cargo carried by the *Mountjoy*, James Scott, master, which cleared the Potomac for Bristol in 1689 with 100 hogsheads of tobacco and an additional 70,000 pounds of tobacco in bulk, consigned to John Cooper.* Colonel Fitzhugh secured a number of additional customers for Cooper, among them George Mason. Fitzhugh told Cooper that "Capt. Mason may consign again but pay no more money then he has effects for in your hands." In 1690 Colonel Fitzhugh sent another London merchant a bill of exchange drawn by Captain Mason on Thomas Storke, a London merchant with considerable interest in Stafford County.[61] The tobacco trade was a speculative business, and the merchants were wary of prior commitments that would bind them to take a certain quantity of tobacco at disastrously low prices or to receive the consignment of the Stafford County planters when the crop on the Rappahannock or the James might promise better profits.

Through his brother-in-law, William Dent, George Mason II had close associations with Jonathan Mathews and Company of London, one of the leading firms in the Chesapeake trade. William Peel, a factor and partner in this firm, took a cargo of manufactured goods and indentured English servants into some part of Stafford County above the Occoquan and established a temporary store there. Quite possibly he located at Colonel Mason's property at Pohick or at Shop Point, possibly nearer the Chapel land near Dogue Creek. On 15 December 1702 William Dent gave Mason a power of attorney "in behalf of himself and Jonathan Mathews and Company of London, Merchants," explaining that

in carrying on our Trade from London to this place and making returns again in Tobacco it was judged necessary to send a Cargo of Goods and Servants to Stafford County in Virginia under the Care and management of William Peel Merchant as factor and Part Owner thereof who accordingly

* The *Mountjoy* was owned by George Mason, a Bristol merchant.

in the year 1701 sat down with a Cargo of Goods and servants at the upper parts of Stafford County in Virginia and sold or disposed the same or the Greatest part thereof among the Inhabitants and rec'ed divers Quantitys of Tobo, but divers other Quantitys and sums of Tobo. and Money remains yet due and owing from several persons in the County aforesaid for Goods delivered as aforesaid of the said Cargo and Servants and the said William Peel being since dead.[62]

The difficulties of debt collections were aggravated by the wide dispersement of the population with no general centers of assembly. This lack of towns in the area was considered by some Virginians a deplorable situation. One of the results of this lack was the excessively high price of labor and the scarcity of skilled draftsmen. The Potomac settlers tended to import many kinds of goods that easily could have been produced at home. Builders, masons, free laborers of every kind, as well as more specialized artisans and craftsmen could not survive very well in a completely rural society. The rare craftsman to be found on the Potomac or the Rappahannock demanded a high price for his labor in an unsettled country. Col. William Fitzhugh found this almost reason enough to leave Virginia, for it was next to impossible to find a blacksmith to forge a nail or a carpenter to raise a roof beam in Stafford County in the 1690s.

In 1680 Lord Culpeper made a determined effort to create towns in Virginia, especially in the Northern Neck. There his grant as lord proprietor would give him added emoluments from the developing towns and cities to be planted there. Culpeper's efforts came to nothing, but the idea that towns would prove advantageous to the colony survived this setback.[63]

In 1691 the House of Burgesses officially determined that towns should be fostered in Virginia. In the April session the legislators designated a public port in each county and decreed that no tobacco should be exported or any goods landed except at the designated port of entry, under pain of forfeiture of the offending vessel. The act designated a site on Potomac Creek as the town land in Stafford to be called Marlborough and to be the port of entry for Stafford County. On 10 June 1691 at a session of the Stafford County magistrates, determinations were made for the "Towne to be surveyed and the port established." In November the magistrates authorized Capt. John Withers to keep the ferry over Potomac Creek to the town point. Since the remote settlements above Occoquan Creek would be obliged to use Marlborough-town, a ferry over that river was considered necessary "for the conveniency of the town or port." [64]

Marlborough-town was surveyed in October 1691 by Burr Harrison and laid out on land owned by Giles Brent on the neck of land formed by Potomac and Aquia creeks. Trustees were then appointed in February 1691/92, with Captain Mason among their number. On 11 February 1691/92 Mason purchased several lots in Marlborough-town from Mathew Thompson and John Withers. He certainly built in the new town, for in 1691 he petitioned for a license to "keep an ordinary at the Town or Port for this County." His petition was granted on condition that he "find a good and Sufficient Maintenance and reception both for man and horse." Mason sought to turn a profit as the owner of the only tavern in Marlborough-town. He was still a feofee or trustee, in 1708 when he sold a lot to William Robinson.[65] Marlborough failed to develop into a port, for the same House of Burgesses that created it and sought to make it grow by ordering all the trade of the upper Potomac to pass through it soon strangled it by suspending the 1691 act and allowing trade to be carried on as it had been in the past by the tobacco planter-merchants.[66]

The failure of the legislature to develop towns in Virginia, thus making available a pool of free labor for the planter and merchant to draw on, made the Potomac economy dependent upon forced labor. Whether it was that of Negro slaves or white servants, competition with this unfree labor tended to make free labor scarcer and more costly. Thus the failure of the towns accelerated the development of a plantation economy—which was precisely what the British merchants and the British government wanted for Virginia. When the House of Burgesses in 1704 made a second attempt to encourage the growth of towns with an act for ports and towns, it was set aside by the Crown in 1709 as not being subject to the best interests of the mother country. As such an "Act is designed to Encourage by great Privileges the settling in of Townships, and such settlements will encourage their going on with the Wollen and other Manufactures there . . . and take them off from the Planting of Tobacco, which would be of very ill consequence, not only in respect to the Exports of our Wollen and other Goods and Consequently to the Dependance that Colony ought to have on this Kingdom, but likewise in respect to the Importation of Tobacco hither for the home and Foreign Consumption, Besides a further Prejudice in relation to our shipping and navigation." [67]

The suspension by the burgesses of the act of 1691 chartering towns and ports acted as a stimulus, and one might say a charter, for the development of plantations on the upper Potomac. Even though George Mason II had been a trustee of the incipient town, he and a number of others did not take up large grants of land on Pohick Creek until the fate of Marlborough-town was sealed. Sweet-scented tobacco thrived best in the lands between the York and the James, while the lands along the Potomac were better suited to the stronger Oronoco tobacco, developed from strains brought originally from the Orinoco River in South America. It was grown extensively in the back settlements by small planters who relied on the labor of an indentured servant or two brought from England and sold at the smaller ports. Many of these remote farms were worked entirely by indentured servants while the owner continued to make his home in one of the older settlements. Sampson Darrell, who lived near the mouth of Aquia Creek, owned farms near the Little Falls of the Potomac that were farmed by indentured servants. He protested the calling of these servants in a case of Stafford County Court in 1692 because their presence in court would leave his plantation defenseless.

Overproduction, underproduction caused by drought, and intercolonial competition all affected the tobacco planter. In his need for more and more land to replace that worn out by his tobacco crops, the large-scale planter bought increasing acreage. His plantations pushed the frontier farther and farther up the Potomac toward the falls and at the same time pushed the small farmer out of business.

By the beginning of the eighteenth century the increase in number of large plantations produced far-reaching social changes that were to affect the social and economic life of Virginia. It became increasingly difficult for small landholders to take up more lands or to enlarge their income by working for one of the large landholders. They were being driven out by the compounding of the great plantations, which were worked by tenant farmers, white indentured servants, and black slaves. One observer wrote in 1700, "There was no encouragement for persons of small means to come and settle in the plantations as the greatest parts of the lands that lye any thing convenient being taken up, some persons having tracts of land of twenty-thirty or forty thousand Acres." Not only was land difficult to acquire when the great landed families amassed so much of it, but life was hard for the poor man in Virginia, "for a man had really better be hanged than come a Servant into the Plantations, most of his food being homony and Water, which is good for Negroes but very disagreeable to English Constitutions. I have been told by some of them that they have not tasted flesh meate once in three months." [68]

The development of such large-scale tobacco growing led to changes in the labor system. Virginia had depended for its laboring force on an annual influx of some fifteen hundred white indentured servants from England, a flow that continued unimpeded until the end of the seventeenth century. However, during the second half of that century the number of Negroes grew by leaps and bounds. In 1650 there were some three hundred Negroes; in 1671 there were two thousand, and by 1681 three thousand.[69] The larger planter found Negro labor most useful and encouraged the flow of African slaves to Virginia. Col. William Fitzhugh, for instance, was one of the most extensive tobacco growers in Stafford County. He introduced the slave-run plantation into that part of Virginia and proved that the use of slaves was not only profitable but necessary to make a profit. Fitzhugh was more typical of the planters in Westmoreland County and in the older sections of Virginia than of his neighbors in Stafford County, a frontier that still depended primarily on indentured servants for working its farm lands rather than the slave gangs of the plantation. He was, however, the forerunner of the plantation economy that was to sweep over this frontier area. Governor Nicholson reported in 1705 that over eighteen hundred Negroes were brought into the country in that year to serve as slaves and were sold for the high price of £54 for man or woman. Cargoes of African slaves were still rare on the Potomac in the early years of the eighteenth century. Only an occasional ship, like the *John of Lyme* in 1702, brought Negro slaves from Barbados to the upper Potomac. Most slaves of this period came from other parts of the colonies to the still backward Potomac frontier.[70]

Never a large slave owner himself, George Mason always remained fearful of Negro uprisings. In the 1710 session Indian problems were still a concern of the Assembly, and Mason was appointed to a committee on frontier defense. Mason's chief concern, however, appeared to be his fear of a possible uprising by Negro slaves. He urged the need to take stern measures to prevent such an outbreak and asked for instructions to be given to the militia in the event it should come about.[71] At this date the proportion of whites to Negroes in Virginia was about four to one; but only five years later this ratio had narrowed to almost three to one.[72]

Within his lifetime George Mason II had seen the frontier pushed back and a plantation economy developed in what had been a wilderness in his younger days. In spite of the contacts he made during the sessions of the Assembly and his visits to Williamsburg, he always remained a rough-and-ready frontiersman. In his famous diary William Byrd records an incident that involved Mason during the 1710 session. Byrd had written an anonymous lampoon that put the House of Burgesses "in a ferment." A day or two later, while Byrd and some friends were dining in a Williamsburg coffee house, "in came George Mason very drunk and told me before all the company that it was I that wrote the lampoon and that Will Robinson dropped it. I put it off as well as I could but it was all in vain for he swore it." [73]

Although the primary concerns of Col. George Mason II were the protection of his lands from the incursions of the Indians and the acquisition of more land to produce more tobacco, his affiliation with the church must not be overlooked. He accepted the established church as the root of the society of which he was a part and acknowledged his responsibility to it by serving as churchwarden of Stafford Parish in 1699.[74] The first settlers had built a church at Aquia and a chapel near Quantico Creek, both by 1667. As the Masons, the Owsleys, the Wests, and others pushed back the forests and built homes beyond the Occoquan, the need arose for a house of worship. Reverend John Waugh obliged his far-flung parishioners by establishing a chapel on land owned by Mason on the south side of Dogue Run, just below the mouth of Piney Branch. This "land of the said Col. George Mason called the Chappel land" is described in a deed of 1715, when the chapel was evidently still in use.[75]

Five years later, on 21 October 1704, George Mason as churchwarden of Overwharton wrote to Governor Nicholson that glebe lands to support the incumbent of the parish would "be Laid out as soone as it shall please God to Supply us with a Minister." Mason added that the parish had not received "any of the great Bibles given by Sir Jeffery Jefferys" to the Virginia churches, but humbly begged two of them. The vestry would have met earlier in the year, Mason averred, "but the dread of the Indians hindered us meeting." * Even when the Reverend John Frazier, who was more likely a lay reader, read the service from the prayer book at the little chapel on Mason's land, "the dread of the Indians" was never far away.[76]

The second George Mason drew up his will on 29 January 1715/16, providing for his children, as his father had done for him, a fundamental legacy of land that would enable them to maintain the position of prominence the family had attained. He bequeathed to French Mason "all the Land which I bought of Martin Scarlet and Thomas James," that is, the land along the northeast side of Pohick Creek, including Shop Point, that he had purchased from James in 1690 and from Scarlet at about the same time. He confirmed French in his possession of six Negro slaves, whom he had already given him, and gave him the right to the labor of a mulatto boy named Charles, who was to be freed at his majority. His son Nicholson Mason, born 1696/97, inherited "all the Land which I bought of Edward Smith, James Joyner and William Betty" as well as "all the Land which I bought of

* John West, who lived near the Masons on what was later called "Belvoir," just across Gunston Cove, wrote on 8 Nov. 1704 to Mason, "I thought to come to Court but my son Pearson seeing great signs of Indians and the Inhabitants in great fear of them that I cannot come. If I come I leave but one man at home . . ." (Stafford D.B., W-Z, fol. 248).

Edward Rockwood in Maryland" and seven Negro slaves. But Nicholson died before the will was probated. The Maryland property was part of a tract known as "Christian Temple Manor" in Charles County. The other lands were in Stafford County. Mason left his son Francis Mason "all the Land that I bought of Madam [Margaret] Brent, Rawleigh Travers and William Lambeth" and "all the Land which I bought of John Harper, John Simpson and Bryant Foley" and three Negro slaves. These lands were all located in Virginia in the vicinity of Great Hunting Creek. Thomas Mason received the lands that his father had purchased in Charles County from William Moss and those lands he bought in Stafford County from Michael Vandlandingham and two Negro slaves. All of the land that Mason had purchased in partnership with James Hereford, consisting of 909 acres on Mason's Neck, he left to two of his daughters, Elizabeth and "Simpher Ross" [*sic*]. Each of the girls also received a Negro slave. Catherine Mason inherited "all the Land where Thomas Brooks doth now live and the rest of the Land at the head of Potomack Creek which my brother-in-law, Joseph Waugh, did grant and convey until me" as well as a mulatto girl called Sarah.

George Mason, the third of the name, received only two candlesticks, a snuffer, and a snuff dish of silver because at his coming of age he had already received the greater part of his father's lands lying on the neck of land between Occoquan and Pohick creeks by a deed of gift. On 18 May 1731 he leased some land to his sister, Simpha Rosa Ann Field (Mason) Bronaugh, and her husband, Jeremiah Bronaugh, Jr., which he described as "on the lower side of Pohick Creek where the said George Mason lately dwelt" and "commonly called and known by the name of Newtown." This was Mason's father's house on Pohick Creek, to which he had moved his family in 1691 or 1692. When he repatented his lands in 1703, George Mason II described Doegs' Island as his "home seat." This was the place adjoining "Douges Island old field" that George Mason IV designated in 1754 as "the place where my Grandfather formerly lived," located on the Occoquan Creek side of Mason's Neck at a spot now just offshore in Occoquan Bay near High Point.

The will lists the names of twenty-two Negro slaves and two mulatto slaves, but would not include those of any already given to George Mason III when he had received the major portion of his lands. Similarly, the household goods, including "furniture, potts, pewter, either iron or wooden ware," divided among his widow, Sarah (Taliaferro) Mason, and his sons Nicholson, Francis, and Thomas could only include such things as were at Doegs' Island. Nicholson Mason received his father's riding horse, half of his sheep, and all of his hogs and cattle in Maryland. His widow, Sarah (Taliaferro) Mason, was to inherit all the rest of his horses and sheep and all his hogs and cattle in Virginia. Mason's will also included bequests of 500 pounds of tobacco to each of his sons-in-law, William Darrell and George Fitzhugh.[77]

His children contracted marriages with other prominent families of the area to carry on the traditions and duties of landed proprietors. Ann Fowke Mason, probably the eldest daughter of George and Mary (Fowke) Mason, married William, the son of their neighbor Sampson Darrell and his wife Margaret (Norgrave) Darrell. William and Ann (Mason) Darrell had at least one child, Sampson Darrell, born 1712, who served as sheriff of Fairfax County. William Darrell died in 1716, perhaps of the same epidemic that killed his father-in-law, in whose will he is named as a son-in-law. His young widow married Thomas Fitzhugh, who had inherited 4,334 acres in Stafford County and seven slaves from his father, Col. William Fitzhugh of Bedford. Thomas Fitzhugh died in 1719, leaving his estate to his wife, Ann (Mason) Darrell Fitzhugh, and their daughter, Mary Fitzhugh. A posthumous son, Henry Fitzhugh, was alive in 1723 but evidently died in childhood. Ann, widow of Thomas Fitzhugh, was also living in 1723. She later married Thomas Smith. George Fitzhugh, a burgess from Stafford County in 1718 who wed Mary Mason, was also a son of Col. William Fitzhugh. He too inherited 5,975 acres of land in Stafford County and seven negroes from his father. George Fitzhugh died in 1722, leaving his widow and two sons, George died in childhood; and the other son, William Fitzhugh, was the owner of Rousby Hall in Calvert County, Maryland. Later the widow, Mary (Mason) Fitzhugh, married Benjamin Strother.[78]

Mason's other three daughters married equally well. Simpha Rosa Ann Field Mason married John Dinwiddie, a member of the distinguished mercantile family of Glasgow, Scotland, and brother of Robert Dinwiddie, lieutenant governor of Virginia 1751–58. After his death in 1726 she married Jeremiah Bronaugh, Jr. Elizabeth Mason married William Roy of Essex County. Her death took place about 1734. Catherine Mason, born 21 June 1707, married John Mercer of Marlborough 10 June 1725. The wedding took place at the home of her half sister Ann, Mrs. Thomas Fitzhugh, with the Reverend Alexander Scott officiating. John Mercer had come from Ireland to Virginia in 1720 at sixteen years of age, bringing with him a tremendous ambition and little else, but he soon left an indelible mark on Potomac society.[79]

In the first months of the year 1715/16 an exceptionally virulent epidemic struck the family of George Mason II, causing his death, the death of his third wife, Sarah (Taliaferro) Mason, and of his son Nicholson. The wills of George Mason and his wife were admitted to probate on the same day, 14 November 1716, at Stafford County Court-house. Her will was dated 13 February 1715/16. Her husband had undoubtedly predeceased her, as according to provisions in her will she divided the property left her by her deceased husband among her children and appointed George Mason III and Nicholson Mason, Gentlemen, her executors and guardians of her minor children. Nichol-son was unable to serve as he died shortly after her death.[80] By the terms of her will she left two Negro men, Stafford and Nicholas, to her daughter, Sarah Mason, and bequeathed all the silver plate left her by her husband to her sons, Francis and Thomas. All the movables left her by her deceased husband were to be equally divided among their three children. Her sons, Francis and Thomas, died very young, and her daughter, Sarah, was contracted in marriage to Thomas Brooke of Saint Marys County, Maryland, on 3 December 1734.[81]

At their father's death in 1716 the eldest sons were living at their own plantations on Gunston Cove (Pohick Creek) : French Mason on the northern side and George Mason III on the southern side at Newtown. George inherited the largest share of his father's estate and the prop-erty left to his stepmother and brothers as well. Their inheritance of property and position gave these two brothers a standing in Virginia that marked the achievement of stability and prominence by the first and second generations of their family in America.

Chapter III

Colonel George Mason III

G EORGE MASON III was about twenty-seven years old at the time of his father's death and was already a man of standing and property in the Potomac area. Family tradition has assigned 1690 as the year of his birth. This date is supported by a transcript of an entry from the no longer extant family Bible, which stated that he was forty-five years old when he drowned in the Potomac in 1735. As a planter-merchant on the Potomac River with interests in both Maryland and Virginia, he survived a period of disastrously low prices by taking advantage of the divergent laws of the two colonies regarding the control of tobacco production and by leasing the greater portion of his lands to tenant farmers. He played a significant part in assisting Glasgow merchants to gain a foothold in the Chesapeake tobacco trade as buyers of the Oronoco leaf that was grown in large areas of both Virginia and Maryland and was considered unmarketable by the English traders. Furthermore, he carefully increased his landholdings in both Maryland and Virginia despite the agricultural depression and left a substantial estate in real property to his eldest son.

The earliest extant reference to the third George Mason is in a Stafford deed book and has reference to a decision reached by the vestry of Overwharton Parish. On 18 March 1707 Capt. Edward Mountjoy, one of the churchwardens, bound over an apprentice to "Mr. George Mason, Junr. son of Coll. George Mason of the said County."[1] According to the family records George Mason III would have been seventeen years of age, old enough to receive his estates and to accept apprentices. The 1702 will of William Dent, mentioned before, shows that this was the age at which sons often received their estates and were legally of age.

Before 1716, by deed of gift from his father, George Mason III had acquired large tracts of land on Doegs' Neck and on both sides of Chopawamsic Creek. After his father's death he inherited other lands between Pohick Creek and Accotink Run, lands along Little Hunting Creek, and lands in Charles County, Maryland. Like his father before him, he began to expand and consolidate his holdings.

As mentioned in the preceding chapter, George Mason II had tired of public office and had withdrawn completely from public life by 1710. George Mason III succeeded to many of the offices he had held; on 25 April 1713, at the suggestion of his father, he was appointed to the lucrative and much sought-after office of sheriff of Stafford County, to which he was reappointed in 1714. On 8 December 1715 Governor Alexander Spotswood appointed him county lieutenant and commander in chief of the militia of Stafford County. He was thereafter Col. George Mason.[2]

The freeholders of Stafford County sent Mason as their representative to the House of Burgesses, and he duly made his appearance in Williamsburg on 3 August 1715. He was appointed to the Committee for Propositions and Grievances and was one of a body who presented an address to the governor at the close of the session. Otherwise, his career as a new member of that august body was without event.[3]

Williamsburg was no longer the wilderness capital of Governor Francis Nicholson's dream, "where fancy sees squares in Morasses, obelisks in trees." Since his arrival in 1710 as governor of Virginia, Alexander Spotswood had made every effort to transfer Nicholson's visions into brick and mortar. He had prevailed on the House of Burgesses to provide money to construct the official residence, soon derisively labeled the Governor's Palace, which he had himself designed. In 1711 Commissary Blair had submitted to the vestry of Bruton Parish a "platt or draught of a Church," also designed by Governor Spotswood. The House of Burgesses again appropriated money, if somewhat begrudgingly. By the time Mason came to Williamsburg as a member of the Lower House in 1715, Bruton Parish Church was nearing completion, the Governor's Palace and the new Magazine were well underway, rapidly outstripping appropriations from a reluctant House of Burgesses.[4] In short, Williamsburg had become the proud capital of Virginia that Nicholson had intended. In the crowded hours when the Assembly was in session, merchants and lawyers came to town to settle accounts with the county grandees and peddlers, while horse traders and strolling players vied with the local tavernkeepers in turning an honest or dishonest penny.

Mason's official duties brought him into frequent contact with Governor Alexander Spotswood. The dreams of this brilliant and ambitious Scotsman were not limited to embellishing the capital of Virginia. He saw the possibilities of an empire beyond the fringe of settlements clinging to the waterways and strove manfully to open the frontiers to settlers. New settlers meant new tenants or potential purchasers of undeveloped land grants, and Spotswood's passion for expansion was colored by his own land interests. Alexander Spotswood was the prince of land speculators, obtaining grants in his own name that exceeded by tenfold the nibbling efforts made by the Masons and McCartys on unclaimed woodlands and western lands. Colonel Mason shared with Spotswood a combination of practical sagacity and a desire for high adventure. He was a member of the expedition led by Governor Spotswood in the summer of 1716 across the Blue Ridge down into the valley of the Shenandoah. The vast panorama of streams, forest, and meadows that spread before them gave intimations of the richness of the great stretches of land held by France—land the English colonists hoped to wrest from the French.

The expedition consisted of Governor Spotswood, several Virginia gentlemen, twelve rangers, and four Indian guides. They rendezvoused at Germanna, in the backcountry of the upper Rapidan, where Mason joined them, and then headed for the distant mountains. They cut their way through trackless underbrush and forest up the Rapidan to Swift Run Gap and followed the meanders of Elk Run to the Shenandoah. The Governor buried a bottle with a paper inside it "on which he writ that he took possession of the place in the name of and for King George the First of England." They struggled to the summit of the highest mountain in sight, and there, after a good dinner, "drank the King's health in Champagne, and fired a volley." The explorers turned back early in September. When again they drew near Germanna, George Mason left them to cut across the back settlements to his home on the Potomac.[5]

Alexander Spotswood realized as few men did that the new French settlements on the Gulf of Mexico connecting with the older bases in Canada would form the extremes of a great arc along which French power would steadily expand until the British colonies were limited to a narrow stretch on the Atlantic seaboard. His ride over Swift Run Gap into the Shenandoah Valley was a gesture of defiance and a promise that Virginians would push westward and turn the flank of the French advance.

Spotswood's plans matured in 1720 with the creation of two frontier counties—Spotsylvania, on the Rapidan and the Rappahannock Rivers, and Brunswick, on the southern frontier of the colony. He promised the settlers courthouses, churches, arms and ammunition at public expense, and he begged the Crown to relieve them of quitrents for ten years, as Virginia had freed them of taxes for ten years.* This benev-

---

* The quitrent, adopted in 1618, required all persons whose tenure of their lands was based upon the ordinary headright to pay an annual rent of twelve pence for every fifty acres conveyed to them. This charge was payable after seven years of possession (Philip A. Bruce, *Economic History of Virginia in the Seventeenth Century* [New York, 1896], 1:556).

olence offered more to speculators than to actual settlers, and the governor and his associates were swift to take advantage of their own liberality.[6]

In 1722 he secured a treaty with the Iroquois that pledged them to keep to the east of the Blue Ridge. The hunting parties of Senecas who had so terrified Stafford County two decades earlier would thus come no closer to the Virginia frontier than the distant Shenandoah Valley. The final removal of the Indian threat made possible the development of the backcountry. By the same treaty Governor Spotswood bound the Iroquois and their vassals to return runaway slaves: "if any such Negro or slave shall hereafter fall into your hands, you shall straightway conduct 'em to Colo. George Mason's House on Potowmack River."[7]

Like his father before him, George Mason III was a somewhat reluctant burgess. He was reelected a member of the House of Burgesses in 1718, and during this session served on a committee concerned with the building of the Governor's Palace. For absenting himself from the sittings of the House of Burgesses he earned a public reprimand by giving only frivolous reasons for his absence. Apart from some purely formal duties, he appeared principally on the records of the House as requesting permission to go into the country during periods when the House was in session. Returned again in 1720, Colonel Mason served on the Committee on Public Claims. He performed the same duty in the 1722 and 1723 sessions.[8]

During the 1723 session Mason petitioned the House for permission to bring in a bill to sell the land of the former townsite of Marlborough, as it was neither built upon nor inhabited. Mason still owned lots there that he had inherited from his father. He and Rice Hooe were trustees of the town. After due consideration, on 21 May the House gave Mason leave to withdraw his petition. The members of the House of Burgesses evidently saw no need to erase Marlborough-town from the statute books, where alone it had any existence. Towns no more populous sent elected representatives to the British Parliament, so George Mason and Rice Hooe might just as well continue to conduct the affairs of an imaginery town on the Potomac.[9]

During Mason's 1726 term in the House of Burgesses, he was much concerned with a proposal to divide Stafford County. This one large county that covered the whole of northern Virginia was no longer a workable unit of local government. The gradual spread of settlements into the Potomac backcountry and upriver above the Little Falls made it difficult to administer justice and settle legal disputes. Civil and criminal cases had to be adjudicated at the Stafford County Courthouse on the south side of Potomac Creek. When the Courthouse at Marlborough-town burned, the freeholders of Stafford County urged in 1720 that a new site be found as it was then in a "Situation very inconvenient for the greater part of the Inhabitants" of Stafford County. The problem that surfaced was one that would recur again and again in the eighteenth century as the machinery of county and parish government failed to keep pace with the expansion of the frontier in Virginia and the southern colonies as a whole—but with a difference. It was proposed that Stafford County be divided to accommodate a proposed convict settlement. All convicts thereafter imported into Virginia would be confined to "a county by themselves under the care of proper overseers" who would "keep them to their labour by such methods as are used in Bridewell." Their labors would be concentrated on raising hemp and flax, and the new county was to be designated Hempshire. Such a plan was not to the advantage of those already settled in the area and certainly was not in the mind of those who petitioned for a new site for a courthouse. As representatives of Stafford County, Colonel Mason and his brother-in-law, George Fitzhugh, were not pleased with such a proposition, nor were their constituents. The problem of law and order in the frontier settlements was difficult enough without adding a large concentration of convicts to the population. The motion was rejected.[10]

In his career as a member of the House of Burgesses from Stafford County, Mason never departed far from the norms of his fellow members. He did not introduce any startling legislation but dutifully sat on the committees of which he was a member and begged leave to return home at the earliest opportunity. Like his grandfather and father before him, he felt no strong attachment to Williamsburg. After 1726 he never came again as an elected representative and, as often as not, employed agents to conduct his business in the capital.

However, when it was necessary for him to go to Williamsburg during the "public times," his visits were not without their lighter moments. As the son of a former burgess he would be accepted in the official society of Williamsburg, and as an eligible bachelor he would be invited to receptions by Governor Spotswood and to the parties given by members of the House of Burgesses. As it was the clearly defined duty of a mother of unattached daughters to see that they were presented to all eligible males, he would in the ordinary course of events have met Mrs. Stevens Thomson, the widow of the former attorney general, and his family. No record remains of how or when Ann Thomson and Colonel Mason met, but meet they did, and in 1721 they were married.[11]

Stevens Thomson, Esquire, had come to Williamsburg in 1703 to be attorney general. Governor Francis Nicholson was pleased with his new colleague and wrote to the Board of Trade and Plantations, "I'm very glad yt yr. Lordships have been pleased to send so good a man and able a lawyer as Stephen Thomson, Esqr. to be her Majtys. Attorney genll." Governor Nicholson had appealed to the board for the appointment of a qualified attorney general for Virginia and particularly requested that the new attorney general be obliged to reside in Williamsburg. The Commissioners forwarded Nicholson's request to Attorney General Sir Edward Northey and asked him to nominate a suitable candidate. Northey suggested "Stephen Thomson, Esq., who was the eldest son of Sir William Thomson, one of his late Majesties Serjeants at Law, and was educated first at the University (Cambridge), and after in the Study of the Law in the Middle Temple (where he is fifteen years standing) as a fit person to serve her Majesty as Attorney General in Virginia." A group of distinguished members of the legal profession gave Thomson an equally strong recommendation, noting that he had "been educated at ye University about three years, After for neare four years in ye science of special pleading, And acting about two years more as Prothonotary to ye Sheriffs court in London, [he had] since applyed himself to ye study of ye law being above fifteen years standing in ye Middle Temple." [12]

Stevens Thomson was born in London in 1674, the eldest son of Sir William Thomson, of Yorkshire, and his first wife, Mary (Stephens) Thomson.[13] In his will, probated in 1696, Sir William left to his son Stevens Thomson lands in the parish of Ripon in the West Riding of Yorkshire, which, he said, had belonged to the Thomsons from time immemorial.[14] These lands had passed from Sir William's father, Henry Thomson of Hobbinghose in the parish of Ripon, into the family of his second wife through the legal complications of their marriage settlement. Stevens Thomson never inherited his ancestral home and may never have visited it.

In the 1674 records of the Middle Temple is the petition of William Thomson to consolidate his chamber in Vine Court with that of Mr. J. Stephens. At some later date William must have taken chambers in the New Court, for on 15 June 1688 the Benchers of the Middle Temple, being informed that his sons were being enrolled, decided that "Mr. S. Thomson shall be admitted to his father's chamber in New Court for a life and two assignments on his father's surrender, who is now called to the degree of Serjeant." On 28 March 1690 Stevens Thomson, aged about sixteen years, a native of London, was admitted to Trinity College, Cambridge, wishing to broaden his education by university training. However, he was sent down in 1693 without taking his degree and returned to the study of law. His father died not long afterwards. The records of the Temple Church disclose that Sir William Thomson, Serjeant at Law, was buried there on 25 January 1695 on the side of the Middle Temple.[15] The following month, on 4 February 1695, Stevens married Dorothea Tanton, or Taunton, of Saint-Giles-in-the-Fields Parish, London, at the Church of Saint James, Duke Place, Aldgate, London.[16]

The new attorney general of Virginia was twenty-nine years old when he received his appointment and living in London with his wife, Dorothea, and their five small children: Mary, Elizabeth, William, Ann, and Stevens. Queen Anne gave Thomson his official appointment on 30 July 1703.[17] He and his young family were unable to sail with the regular summer convoy to the Chesapeake and were obliged to wait for the October fleet. This was always a difficult passage, made longer and more tedious by the need for caution in a wartime winter season. He took the oath of office as attorney general in March 1704.[18] Thomson's arrival at Williamsburg gave Governor Nicholson some much needed assistance and encouragement, and the Thomsons were quickly drawn into his circle of friends for the short time that Nicholson was to remain in Williamsburg.

Stevens Thomson did a thorough job as attorney general of Virginia, but his promising career was cut short by his early death in February 1714 at the age of forty. His salary was paid over to his executrix, Dorothea Thomson, on 1 May 1714.[19] Dorothea Thomson and her fatherless children did not return to England but continued to make their home in Williamsburg. Taunton (or Tanton) Thomson, the youngest of the family, born after their arrival in Virginia, died in childhood, as did his sister Elizabeth and their brothers, William and Stevens. Mary and Ann Thomson alone reached maturity. Mary "married one Booth and after Captain Graves Pack. She had but one child by Pack who died at six months old." Ann Thomson "married Colonel George Mason of Stafford County in 1721." [20]

George and Ann Mason had three children. George Mason IV, their eldest, was born 11 December 1725 at Doegs' Neck at the house known as Newtown overlooking what is now called Gunston Cove. Colonel Mason later moved with his family to Charles County, Maryland, to Christian Temple Manor, on Chickamuxon Creek, where Mary Thomson was born in 1731. Mason still used the house at Chopawamsic Creek in Stafford County as an occasional residence, and Thomson Mason, youngest of the family, was born there 14 August 1733.[21] It would be interesting to know if the change of residence was prompted by Governor Sir William Gooch's legislation against trash tobacco, which stirred up resentment and even rebellion among the small planters and tenants of Prince William County. Quite possibly the mob violence of the Northern Neck impelled him to seek a safer place for his wife and children.

At the time of his marriage in 1721 Colonel Mason was already a wealthy and successful tobacco planter. He had increased the considerable estate left him by his father through careful investments in the expanding Chesapeake economy. The clearings at the edge of the forest where tenants or indentured servants once tended a few acres of tobacco had broadened into tilled fields of corn and tobacco edging the wanderings of every creek and run of the Potomac River. The tenant cabin, once deserted at the first rumor of an Indian raid, had been replaced by farmhouses and overseers' houses, tobacco barns, and other outbuildings. A patent for 200 acres of marsh and woodland on one of the Potomac tributaries could be developed into a profitable farm while the landowner ran new survey lines into the wilderness to protect his investment with further grants of land beyond the frontier.

The lands in the Northern Neck presented a special case. They were available as grants from the proprietary of the Northern Neck through a resident agent and were thus a fairly safe investment as they could not be thrown open by such devices as the suspension of quitrents. Virginians were never slow to claim wilderness land as tobacco depleted the soil of their Tidewater plantations, and Governor Spotswood's policies gave impetus to the drive to acquire new lands beyond the pale of settlement. Colonel Mason shared that drive with most of his neighbors in northern Virginia.

He bought extensive holdings in compacted areas in Charles County and in what would be Stafford, Prince William, and Fairfax counties in northern Virginia. In 1721 he bought 150 acres on the north branch of Little Hunting Creek from James and Priscilla (Vandegasteel) Hay; later he purchased another 253 acres from them. John and Catherine (Sandiford) Lewis sold Mason an additional 105 acres also on the north branch of Little Hunting Creek in 1723. All these tracts were adjacent and were repatented in 1771 by George Mason who deeded them to his son Thomson Mason of Hollin Hall in 1786.[22]

In 1717 George Mason had purchased the island of Barbadoes in the Potomac River, opposite the mouth of Rock Creek, from the heirs of the original patentee. This island (now officially named Theodore Roosevelt Island) was variously known in the seventeenth century as My Lord's Island, Anacostian Island, Barbadoes Island, and Analostan Island. After the Hammersleys sold the seventy-five acre island to

George Mason it became known as Mason's Island.[23] Later, when John Mason inherited the island, he restored the name Analostan; hence his sobriquet General John Mason of Analostan.

In 1717 Mason also acquired large grants of land south of the Occoquan. This property in later years formed the estate known as Woodbridge, which George Mason bequeathed his youngest son, Thomas. In the lifetime of George Mason all of the property he owned on the south shore of the Occoquan was leased to tenants. At the same time he was engaged in developing his property in Charles County almost directly across the Potomac from Doegs' Island, he was buying additional land on the north side of Mattawoman Creek. One tract of 450 acres at the mouth of Chickamuxon Creek was called Doegs' Neck. This Mason renamed Stump Neck to avoid confusion with the similar name on his Virginia properties. Another, which lay farther upstream, was part of Christian Temple Manor. The acreage in between was simply designated as "Adjoining Doegs' Neck." These purchases were made by William Woodford, a London merchant who handled the business interests of George Mason in England. Woodford wrote to Mason in November 1723: "I have yrs. of 18th & 23 Septr. with Copys of Deeds of Land to Buy of Mr. Blayden whose Lodgings I have been twice at but could not meet with him. Intend in a few days to go againe, his Living at the other End of ye Town makes it ye more difficult to light of him however hope to see him to give you an Acct pr this Opportunity what can be gone in ye affair." In December of the same year Woodford wrote that he had seen "Mr. Blayden who [would] have taken £150 and not under for ye land mentioned in ye deeds but I haveing no money of yrs. in my hands and it not suiting me to advance that sum so could not Confirm and Bargain; he has promis'd to take that sum for ye lands and to stay a reasonable time for you to make a Remittance which I told him I Expected very Soon." [24] Thomas Bladen, later governor of Maryland but then living in London, inherited these lands from his father, William, in 1718.

Mason apparently made no great haste in remitting the purchase price, for the deed to him was not executed until 23 February 1725 and was not recorded until 29 March 1727. By that time title to these lands was vested in Thomas Cowper, of the Parish of Saint Paul, Covent Garden, in the county of Middlesex, by a deed from Thomas Bladen; the transfer of the property was from him.[25]

Mason continued to buy land, but he rarely sold any. His practice was to lease out small farms to lesser planters, most of whom held their land on leases for three lives. Mason leased his lands because he did not consider the large-scale plantation feasible or profitable. But apparently he, too, was a lessee of land, for in a letter of 3 July 1720 Robert Carter wrote to Capt. Thomas Hooper that "Colonel Mason and I have fully settled. He paid me his arrears in money and give me his obligation for tobacco for his last year's rent and told me he had lodged tobacco in Mr. [James] Carter's hands for the payment of it." [26]

But to turn a profit by renting farm lands, a planter required a steady flow of potential tenants since idle farmsteads brought no profit. One of the waves of Irish emigration was reaching its peak in the 1720s when some sturdy Ulstermen made their way to Virginia. Many of these immigrants came as indentured servants and survived the four or five years of their indentures to begin their lives as freemen with a long-term lease on a small tobacco farm. Between 1723 and 1725 the proprietors of the Northern Neck made more than seventy grants to small planters with recognizably Irish names; the proportion of Irish redemptioners who took up lands from individuals would obviously be much greater. With the fluctuations in the market for Potomac tobacco, Mason found indentured servants a better source of labor than slaves because the former formed a ready source of tenants when their indentures were served.

A deed from Colonel Mason to William Murfey of Stafford County, dated 5 November 1722, gives an illustration of this practice. In exchange for an annual rental of tobacco, Mason leased 100 acres of land on Chopawamsic Creek to William Murfey and permitted him to select the tract of 100 acres that he desired, including "the said William's present dwelling house." A series of similar leases made between 1722 and 1728 shows that Mason gradually settled tenants on his Chopwamsic property while busily leasing other lands farther up the Potomac.[27] An annual rental of 600 pounds of marketable tobacco was his standard agreement with his tenants for the use of 150 acres of land. This is borne out by a number of leases inscribed in the deed books of Prince William County.* Small tracts, such as 100 acres on "one of the falling branches of Accotink" leased in 1734, brought in a smaller rental, in this case 500 pounds of tobacco a year.[28]

No account books or ledgers have been found relating to the business dealings of George Mason; so we can only conjecture whether his leases were profitable. The accounts kept by his close friend Ed-

* A similar deed (bk. B, fols. 191–92) leasing 100 acres on the Potomac to William More (Moore) enables us to see one of Mason's tenants in some depth. Moore had patented a 500-acre freehold on Accotink Creek in 1727 and perhaps needed better land in 1733. When he died in 1769, he left an estate amounting to 459 pounds and included five slaves. More was an Irishman who came to Virginia in the 1720s. His daughter married William Buckland, carpenter and joiner of Gunston Hall (Rosamond R. Beirne and John H. Scarff, *William Buckland,* pp. 29–31).

mund Bagge of Essex County are illustrative of some contemporary
business practices. In 1727 Bagge agreed to allow his overseer eleven
shillings in money for every hundred pounds of tobacco he raised, not
to exceed thirty or forty shillings. He further allowed him fourteen
shillings per hundred pounds in credit for store goods. The overseer
made a crop of 3,984 pounds of tobacco and something more than 900
pounds of corn as well. The overseer's share of the crop would have
worked out to some £27 8s., mainly in credit. The cost of providing
clothing, salt, and medicine for seven adult slaves and two boys at
twenty-two shillings for each adult and ten shillings for each boy
totalled £9 16s. for the year 1727. Two adult male slaves bought from
an African slaver in the same year cost £46, or an average of £23 each.
During the year 1727 Bagge sold all together twenty-one hogsheads of
tobacco averaging about 900 pounds to the hogshead for prices that
netted, after shipping costs, a high of £11 4s. per hogshead and a low
of £3 6s. depending on the quality. In this year his total sales from all
of his plantations amounted to £167 13s.[29]

As Mason's income was derived from leases rather than worked plantations, different factors would enter into his scale of profits. Though it
is dangerous to generalize from one example, such as the Bagge account book, still one might not go too far afield in suggesting that the
annual rent of one of Mason's tenant farms of 150 acres might give him
a net yield, after paying shipping and commission costs, of from £3 to
£9, perhaps averaging closer to the lower figure. Tenants were no-
toriously careless in the preparation of tobacco to be used for paying
their rent. In an average year Mason probably would earn no more
than £5 on each of his 150-acre leased properties. His costs, on the
other hand, were limited to the negligible quitrent due for every acre.
Edmund Bagge's costs included such items as clothing and medicine
for each adult slave, amounting to £1 2s. per annum. His overseer took
as his part, roughly, half a hogshead of tobacco, about £2 in money,
and £25 in goods for making little more than four hogsheads of tobacco. Assuming that the tobacco made in this plantation was of better than average quality, Bagge might have netted from £36 to £40,
perhaps less, which in terms of profit would not put him much ahead
of what Mason received from his leases. Mason's only disadvantage was
that he could not control the quality of his tenant's crop and became,
perforce, a dealer in trash tobacco.

Colonel Mason was not the only Virginia landowner whose tenants
obliged him to ship inferior grades of tobacco. The quality of Virginia
tobacco fell to a low level in the first quarter of the eighteenth century.
Careless overseers and unwilling slaves and redemptioners made poor

crops without giving the matter much consideration; tenant farmers deliberately paid off their fixed annual rent in the poorest quality tobacco and kept the better grades for market. The universality of the practice gave it a kind of sanction. If Mason's tenants had been the only farmers who paid their debts in trash tobacco, he soon would have faced financial ruin. Since the practice was commonplace, Mason and his neighbors found a way of making it profitable. Great landowners followed the example of their poorest tenants, when they themselves did not lead, and paid their taxes, parish levies, and quitrents in the worst tobacco they had on hand. If the London merchants protested the inferior quality of the tobacco remitted them for their debts, they were not the only tobacco buyers on the river.

The sharp division in demand and prices between Oronoco and sweet-scented tobacco tended to disappear because the continental market favored the peculiar quality of Virginia and Maryland Oronoco. The Reverend Hugh Jones differentiated between "Oroonoke . . . with a sharper leaf like a fox's ear, and the other rounder and with finer fibres," but added that "each of these are varied into several sorts, much as apples and pears are." [30] Differences in soil and cross-hybridization developed new strains of tobacco, generally classified as Oronoco, and the old sweet-scented variety that had charmed the Jamestown pioneers gradually disappeared after 1735. When the merchants of London discovered that some varieties of Oronoco were as mild as the sweet-scented and cost far less on the open market, the demand for the latter declined and tobacco prices were depressed. The merchants of the smaller ports, who had always dealt in the cheaper varieties of Oronoco, were now in a more advantageous position to secure shipments than were their rivals in the metropolis.

Whether he dealt in sweet-scented tobacco or in Oronoco leaf, the British consignment merchant necessarily dealt in quantity. If he could possibly avoid it, the odd hogshead at a distant planter's landing was not worth the trouble securing it. Indeed, the London merchants strove continually, if not always successfully, for limited number of ports of entry and for the regulation of the staple. Even without the advantages of official regulation, the merchants made it a matter of practical necessity for the larger planters to combine for the sale of their produce or to become merchants themselves—buying a hogshead from a neighbor or purchasing the parish levy for resale. In 1700 the London merchants enjoyed a comfortable monopoly in the commerce of the Chesapeake. If they suffered the competition of the shipmasters of Cornwall and Devon or even parceled out part of their overseas market to the Bristol merchants, the lion's share of the Virginia trade in quantity and value found its way to the Thames. When Micajah Perry frowned in a London coffeehouse, the credit of a James River baron withered away. These London merchants were nearly all consignment merchants, taking a man's crop to be sold at a commission, then filling his orders with other merchants for everything from hoes to Flemish lace for another commission. A poor grade of tobacco meant lower prices and a lower commission. The merchants eagerly solicited the business of those planters who were known to raise crops of a generally higher grade and were reluctant to handle the tobacco grown by men with a reputation for raising crops of poor quality.[31]

After the 1707 Act of Union the merchants and shipmasters of Kirkcudbright, Dumfrieshire, Scotland, made a bid to enter the Virginia market that had so enriched their English neighbors. How could Glasgow compete with London? Quite simply by taking tobacco that London would not accept, thereby squeezing London firms out of the Virginia market. For if the London market sniffed at trash tobacco, there were those who would buy it. The era of trash tobacco and tenantry had some long-range effects on the Mason family fortunes and those of many another family as well. Mason was a man with considerable influence in mercantile circles, although he dealt primarily in trash tobacco of the lowest grade. Mason and the outport merchants were thus natural allies, and the Burgess Records of Glasgow preserve their treaty of alliance.[32] On 2 March 1720 John Bowman, the lord provost of the city of Glasgow extended the privileges of a burgess and guild brother of Glasgow to "the Honble. George Mason, Esqr., Collonel of the County of Stafford, in Potowmach River, Virginia." As a symbol of his new status Provost Bowman sent Colonel Mason a handsomely mounted Burgess Ticket, illuminated with the coat of arms of Glasgow. In an accompanying letter the lord provost explained that:

having received certain information of the many Extraordinary Favours you have done to our merchants or their agents in Virginia we thought ourselves obliged in the name of our City to ackknowledge your Goodness, and in Testimony hereof we do send you the Compliment of the City a Burgess Ticket by which you are entitled to all the Rights and privileges and Immunities of a Burgess or Citizen of Glasgow. Hitherto your favours to our people have flowed from the wider motives of Hospitality, in time coming you will if possible multiply your goodness towards them when you can consider them not only as strangers but as Fellow Citizens with yourself.[33]

A Burgess Ticket was a tangible proof of citizenship and gave the owner the right to vote in municipal elections and to hold public office. It meant that a man was a citizen of no mean city and a man of substance in his community. It was not the sort of thing to be idly handed to every likely business prospect or associate. New York and a few other American cities saw fit to make honorary citizens of a naval hero and a peer or two, but Glasgow paid the honor of honorary citizenship to Col. George Mason.

The entrance of the enterprising Scots and Irish into the tobacco market resulted in an increased demand for Oronoco, which could be sold on various European markets. This further depressed prices on the colonial and London markets. At this point the interests of the London merchants and the colonial governor coalesced; the result was an attempt to regulate the tobacco trade. Regulation of the staple would they hoped, raise the market price of tobacco and generally improve the Virginia economy.

In one of his efforts for the betterment of Virginia, Governor Alexander Spotswood proposed an act to provide for the official inspection and grading of tobacco at fixed locations in each county. The bill passed the House of Burgesses on 12 December 1713. The avowed aim of Spotswood's legislation was to drive trash tobacco from the market and prevent the clandestine shipments of the small packets of bulk tobacco that could so easily be disposed of in England. The merchants in the British port towns and the Virginia planters, who had learned to make a profit of necessity, protested vigorously. In June 1717 Spotswood's attempt to regulate the trade came to an end.[34] No amount of legislation seemed capable of lifting the tobacco trade out of the doldrums of depressed prices. The English merchant William Woodford commented on this condition while on a business trip to Virginia in 1729, when he wrote, "Our stable Commoddity being of late of little Vallue has made severall Gentn. here go on different projects & not trust wholly to makeing Tobacco."[35]

The author of *Sotweed Redivivus: Or the Planters Looking-Glass,* published at Annapolis in 1730, touched on the problem of overproduction and condemned those planters who,

> To glut the Market with a poisonous Drug,
> Destroy sound Timber, and lay waste their lands
> To head a Troop of Aethiopian Hands,
> Worse Villians are, than Forward's Newgate Bands.

Even the comic poet could not avoid alluding to the depression on the Chesapeake. In his flowery dedication of *Muscipula: The Mouse Trap,* printed at Annapolis in 1728, Richard Lewis looked to a time when

> The Markets for our Staple would advance
> Nor shall we live, as now we do, by Chance,
> Nor more, the lab'ring Planter shall complain
> How vast his Trouble! but how small his Gain.[36]

The protracted depression in the 1720s led Governor Gooch to turn once again to Spotswood's rejected legislation. He was able to persuade the Board of Trade and Plantations that the traffic in trash tobacco had been carried on primarily by smugglers who paid little duty and that reestablishment of an inspection law was absolutely necessary to safeguard Virginia's staple commodity. While the new measures differed only slightly from the old proposals and the Board of Trade objected that the bill was no more than a reenactment of one already rejected, Sir William had a more secure political position and secured the passage of the inspection act through the House of Burgesses in 1730. It revolutionized the tobacco industry by establishing public warehouses, providing for the appointment of official inspectors, and requiring planters to transport every hogshead to an official warehouse for inspection. The inspectors were salaried officials who were expressly forbidden to be in any way concerned in the tobacco trade, had authority to open every hogshead, to weigh and grade the tobacco, and to burn any trash tobacco they found. In this way the merchants would be sure the tobacco they bought or received on consignment would be of a standard quality. In a land where taxes, rents, and debts were payable in tobacco, regulation of the staple seemed the only way to avoid economic chaos.[37]

The smaller planters did not agree. The necessity of transporting their saleable tobacco to a central warehouse seemed burdensome. They were concerned, moreover, that the merchants would discontinue trading in the Potomac, where trash tobacco played such an important role; and they were afraid that their rents would be consumed in the inspectors' fees. Rumors of every sort ran through the upper Potomac, as in Parson Waugh's day. Mobs assembled to burn the accursed warehouses and pitch the inspectors into the river. James Bland, Thomas Furr, and Henry Filkins, all respectable planters on the Occoquan, marched across Prince William County in March 1732 at the head of a band of fifty armed men. Warehouses along the Rappahannock were burned to the ground. Riots and rick burnings become so epidemic by early 1732 that the militia had to take the field to restore order. The realization that trade would continue quieted the respectable elements. But the Northern Neck had a large population swept from British jails and brought to the Rappahannock under a lucrative contract made by Jonathan Forward with the British Government in 1722. Some honest debtors made new lives for themselves, but there was a dangerous rabble who scarcely needed a crossroads Catiline to lead them on a career of rape and plunder. From 1729 on, the Northern Neck seethed with insurrection, crime, and violence. An unpopular justice might be burned out; a Glasgow factor plundered of his stock; even the Lees and the Carters ran out into the night as bands of arsonists put the torch to their houses and outbuildings. When grievances against Gooch's inspection act linked honest yeomen farmers with Newgate cutthroats, no man was safe in his own home.[38] Such incidents as these, coupled with the fact Maryland did not have a regulatory act governing the shipment of tobacco probably influenced Mason to take up his residence in Maryland and rent his Virginia properties to tenants.

The passage of the inspection act no doubt brought to a head the problems George Mason III was having with his London agent in regard to the quality of his tobacco. Mason and the Reverend John Bagge put together cargoes of tobacco from the Potomac and Rappahannock for William Woodford, a London tobacco merchant, but their shipments were not of the best quality. "The hogsheads and Stript per Colo. Mason in ye John and Robert I never saw a worse," Woodford wrote to Bagge in 1723. In 1725 he told his agent Captain Reuben Welch, "Mr. Bagge advises me of his buying me 14 hogsheads. I wish they may prove good." If the cargoes Mason and Bagge sent him disappointed their London correspondent, the British market left much to be desired from Mason's viewpoint. In May 1723 Woodford wrote to Colonel Mason:

By the John & Robert I answered yours & wrote the Needful. Am glad to hear Shes safe Arrived with you & I hope my Charter is Complyd with. You have Inclosed George Grants bill of £30 returned protested. I have writ several times to my friend at Kendall abt Sturdys Affair but have not recd any Satisfactory Answer.

The Tobacco Business is still depending, a Regulation in that Trade is soon Expectd per an Act of Parlmnt wch I fear will not Answer ye design of our Petition, in a few Days we shall know how it will be & I hope in time to advise you per this Opportunity. Tobo, is a dull Comodity & Much fallen in price & am afraid ye Crop Yt is comeing Home to a poor Markett.

The London merchants placed great faith in the act regulating the tobacco trade that passed in Parliament on 10 May 1723. Writing to the Reverend John Bagge, William Woodford rejoiced that London and "the outports are now upon a Levell in Respect to Damages, all manner of Stript Tobo. is prohibited from 1st of June 1724."

Like most Virginia tobacco growers, Colonel Mason constantly faced the problem of debts owed to British merchants. In 1725 Woodford pressed for payment of a debt of £32 5s. 6d. that had been outstanding since 1723. Later in the same year Woodford sent to his factor on the Rappahannock "four Accts, proved with ye City Seale Annex'd to them,

Viz. Robert Taliaferro, ye Son of John Taliaferro dec'd, Colo. John Robinson, Colo. George Mason and John Roy." [39] Mason and Woodford each had their grievances. The London merchant justly complained that poor quality tobacco injured his own reputation, but Mason was at his mercy in the actual sale of the tobacco. Woodford could arbitrarily strike a third of the shipment off the account. The precise weight of a hogshead varied, but one might safely wager that each was in the range of 900 pounds. [40] Poor grade or not, four hogsheads represented at least 3,600 pounds of tobacco, the rental of seven good farms. Mason could not stand beside each of his tenants at every stage in the process of making their tobacco crop nor supervise every detail of pressing down the tobacco into casks with a prise, where crop tobacco was often spoiled.

Colonel Mason found it even more difficult to supervise the prising and shipping of his tobacco when the session of the Assembly at Williamsburg ran into the last weeks of August or early September, the usual season for the return of the fleet. Woodford not only complained that his ship lay idle while Mason was detained at Williamsburg through September 1723 but that Mason himself had been imposed upon by the inferior tobacco sold him, "the worst parcell I ever saw," and went on to advise: "for ye future youl take better Care in re Tobacco you Ship, for such Tobo as yrs was is not only a loss to you but a discredit to those that dispose of yrs. If I may Advise you Ship none to this Port of any Sort but what you are well assur'd is good & well managed, & then you may expect the Market price" [41] as only the finest York River tobacco obtained the list price.

Had Mason limited his capital to intensive cultivation of high-grade tobacco or confined it to the production of trash tobacco, he would never have left his children the tremendous landed heritage that he did. His policy of diversification of capital and the leasing of his lands to tenant farmers assured him a measure of prosperity while other landholders were going hopelessly in debt.

Besides his investments in tobacco and land leased out to tenant farmers, George Mason III found other profitable uses for his domain on Doegs' Neck and his other property in Maryland and Virginia. For further diversification he purchased the exclusive right to fish for shad, herring, and all other kinds of fish in the body of water known as Simpson's Bay (or Baxter's Bay) at the mouth of Occoquan Creek. He also obtained the right to erect any necessary buildings for salting and packing or otherwise conducting a fishery. This monopoly was given in the form of a lease from Thomas Simpson, dated 31 January 1727, which was to be valid for three lives and would expire after the death of Colonel Mason, his wife, Ann (Thomson) Mason, and their son, George Mason, then a baby little more than a year old.[42] In 1756 George Mason of Gunston Hall, the third party to the original lease, granted the reversion of these rights to Catesby Cocke in return for an undisputed title to the fisheries during his own lifetime.

Fisheries were an important investment in the eighteenth century. Barrels of dried and salted herring and other fish were packed away to feed family and dependents alike in the winter months and frequently entered into the intercolonial trade. A bit of verse published in the *Maryland Gazette* declared that in March and April the Potomac and Patuxent

> were stained from shore to shore,
> And ran purple to the Main,
> With the Blood of H—rr—gs slain.

Mason's fishing rights on the present Belmont Bay were part and parcel of his development of Mason's Neck into an independent and profitable domain. The shad and herring of the Potomac figure in the miscellaneous trade that Mason and his partner John Mercer of Marlborough were developing and doubtless helped provender Mason's household as well. A little notebook containing some household accounts of the Mason family of the 1791–93 period discloses that herring still played an important part in the domestic economy at Gunston Hall, while a letter of General John Mason written in 1821 alluded to "an Excursion to my Fishery in Virginia."[43]

Another source of income was the money he received from the ferry monopoly that had long been the preserve of his family. In 1703 the unwieldy parish of Overwharton was finally divided. A new church "above Occoquan ferry" replaced the earlier chapel on the land of George Mason II, near Dogue Run. Occoquan Church stood north of the ferry, where the Potomac path began to curve down to the ferry landing after it crossed Pohick Creek. After creating a new parish in 1730, to include all the territory from Chopawamsic Creek to the farthest reaches of settlement on the upper Potomac, the Virginia Assembly created a new county with the same boundaries in 1731 and named it Prince William in honor of King George II's son, the duke of Cumberland. The site selected for the Prince William County Courthouse was on the south side of Occoquan Creek, at the ferry landing, on property owned by Colonel Mason. Everyone above the Occoquan who had business with the County Court of Prince William County used Mason's ferry and paid the stipulated tolls, as did everyone below the Occoquan who came to Sunday services at the Occoquan Church.

Among the earliest Glasgow firms to venture into the Virginia trade was that composed of the brothers Matthew, John, and Lawrence Dinwiddie. John Dinwiddie represented the family interest in Virginia and established himself as a merchant on the Rappahannock River. In 1716 he married Simpha Rosa Ann Field Mason, daughter of George and Mary (Fowke) Mason.[44]

Maj. John Dinwiddie may have had difficulty in getting his business built up, because a letter written to Captain Thomas Hooper by Robert Carter, 3 July 1720, suggests that the major might be slow in payments.[45] The 1725–26 accounts kept by John Mercer of Marlborough, who was Major Dinwiddie's brother-in-law, produce another side of his business dealings. The Mercer account books indicate that they were partners in the sale of earthenware. Mercer's accounts yield one more clue to Dinwiddie's business associates. Mercer had run up some debts with Thomas Monteith, a merchant of King George County, Virginia, which he credited to John Dinwiddie's account in his own ledger. The simplest explanation of this is that Dinwiddie and Monteith were connected with the same firm, so that Mercer's debt to Monteith canceled Dinwiddie's debt to Mercer. On 10 February 1734 French Mason, Gentleman, a brother of Simpha Rosa (Mason) Dinwiddie, leased a tract of land on the upper side of Pohick Creek known as Shop Point to Thomas Monteith of King George County, merchant.[46] A landing on the Potomac would be of value to a Scottish merchant on the Rappahannock as a place to establish a branch of his business, and French Mason may have wanted to help his brother-in-law in a new venture.

King George County was not formed from Richmond County until 1721, when Governor Spotswood, who was always on good terms with the Masons, appointed Maj. John Dinwiddie its first Sheriff. The choice was not a popular one, as the early settlers considered Major Dinwiddie a newcomer, and they had hoped to have the distinction and financial benefits that went with the office go to one of their own people. Major Dinwiddie's tenure was stormy and short. He was replaced in this office in 1724, and he left for Glasgow in September of the same year, perhaps frustrated by his failures.[47] Well aware of the hazards of a sea voyage, he left a will dated 21 August 1724. This will was proved at King George County Court on 2 September 1726, as it was probably not known that Dinwiddie had written a subsequent will in Glasgow on 21 February 1726.[48] He was taken ill with little hope of recovery and presumably forgot that he had left a will in Virginia. The second will named as executors his brothers, Robert and Lawrence Dinwiddie, merchants in Glasgow; his brother-in-law, John Baird, also a Glasgow merchant; and John Stark, another Glasgow merchant. Since they also submitted a list of sums due to him at his death, they were very likely his partners in business. He left his lands, stock, Negroes, and servants in Virginia in equal shares to his wife, Rosa (Mason) Dinwiddie, and their two daughters. He also insisted that his widow bring his children back to Scotland and sell the Virginia estates for their support. If she herself should be unwilling to leave her native land, she was to send the children to his relatives in Scotland. It was not until December 1726 that news of the second will reached Virginia, and this presented some legal complications. Simpha Rosa Dinwiddie declared that she was unwilling to leave her native land, nor would she send her daughters to Scotland. Instead she married Jeremiah Bronaugh, Jr., of King George County, and kept her children with her.[49]

At this same time another family wedding took place, that of Catherine Mason to the aggressive John Mercer, who was busily engaged in trade on the Potomac and the other rivers and inlets of Chesapeake Bay. It is not known when Mercer and his brother-in-law, Col. George Mason III, made their first joint business venture, but by 1725 they were in partnership in a trading sloop operating in those waters. Their earlier ventures had clearly been successful, for John Mercer owned more than £322 worth of tobacco at the falls of the Rappahannock in 1725 and sold his tobacco to the firm of Whiting and Montague of Gloucester. Mercer dealt not only in tobacco but in other goods as well. He sold 710 pounds of raw deerskins to the Yorktown merchant Richard Ambler and bought a very considerable amount of dry goods from him. In the same year he purchased £12 3s. 6d. worth of earthenware from William Rogers of Yorktown, along with fourteen dozen small books, eleven dozen pamphlets, and eighty-three full-sized books, paying for them partly in sterling and partly two-and-half bushels of wheat. Mercer's account with Colonel Mason recorded a joint investment in oyster shells, probably to be made into mortar, with a share given to the skipper of the sloop as his payment for hire of his vessel.

The Mercer accounts include such items as "to my half of the Hire of the Sloop to Capt. John King," "to my half of the Hire of the sloop to Capt. Browne." Mercer's account with Mason from October 1725 to August 1726 consisted of a long list of drygoods purchased by Mason from Mercer's stock. After 1726 the balance of the ledger shifted from small purchases by Mason from Mercer to small purchases by Mercer from Mason. Mercer's side of the ledger began to include fees for legal cases in Mason's behalf; these items increased with the years.

Following John Mercer's marriage on 10 June 1725 to Catherine Mason, they settled on Marlborough Neck, site of the long-deserted town of Marlborough, and occupied the last surviving structure in the abandoned port town. In January 1729 John Mercer paid Anthony Linton and Henry Suddath 2,000 pounds of tobacco or £10 for "building a house at Marlborough" and an additional £3 for "covering my house and building a chimney." In October of 1730 James Jones received £3 for "9 days work of your man plaistering my house and making 2 brick Backs."

Mercer had dealings with a number of British merchants, factors, and shipmasters. In March 1725 his account with John Wilson recorded on the debit side two hogsheads of tobacco "order'd you at Colo. Mason's" and one hogshead each from George Rust, Michael Judd, and Henry McDonnel. The credit side of the ledger showed that John Wilson paid Mercer with one hogshead of rum containing 113.5 gallons and one barrel of sugar, together valued at 3,005 pounds of tobacco. John Wilson and Company, merchants of Kilmarnock, Scotland, were involved in the settlement of John Dinwiddie's estate. Doubtless Mercer made his connections in Glasgow through his brother-in-law and business partner.[50]

The Whitehaven merchants were at this time looking for bright tobacco, a strain of Oronoco found on the Potomac that had proved itself in the Dutch market. Maryland tobacco was considered less desirable than that grown in Virginia. This did not dampen the ardor of the factors who settled along the Potomac and Patuxent. After 1725 Whitehaven and Scottish factors began to establish stores there, although after 1730 the merchants were at something of a disadvantage on the Maryland side of the river. There was no official inspection in Maryland until 1747, and the factors had to keep a weather eye on the grade and weight of the hogsheads they bought. In 1725 Aderton and How of Whitehaven dispatched William Eilbeck to Virginia as their agent. When Eilbeck sailed from Whitehaven on the *George,* he was instructed to take on 200 gallons of brandy at the Isle of Man or else 50 gallons of brandy in Dublin on credit. If they were to be had without delay at Dublin, he was to take on four or six male servants, as indentured servants not only commanded ready tobacco but were engaged to substantial planters for their entire crops. Eilbeck and his companion factor were to divide their stock of goods and set up two stores at a suitable distance from one another. Once the *George* had taken on her cargo of tobacco, Eilbeck was to take all the store goods that remained unsold and set up a new store for the next season. If need be, he was to reduce his prices until all the goods had been sold for tobacco, as they were of little value when reshipped to England. Both factors were instructed to give encouragement to those who prised their own tobacco but to be careful of the quality and weight of the tobacco they accepted from the Virginians.[51] They were to be careful to protect their own interests, even at the expense of truth. "Alarm the planters if possible and tell them Tobacco is fallen in England, and that there will be few Ships in this Year. And let none deliver any letters, unless you see them and that they may not be prejudicial to you, which sometimes does great harm." [52] Customs records show that the *George* cleared Port South Potomac for White-haven on 11 July 1726 with a cargo of 171 hogsheads of tobacco and 2,500 staves.[53]

William Eilbeck remained as a storekeeper on the Potomac and built up two extensive properties in Charles County, one located in Pomonkey Quarter and the other on Mattawoman Creek at a place known in his day as Mount Eilbeck and currently as "Araby." [54] The factor from Whitehaven became a country magnate in due course and a neighbor of Colonel Mason when Mason moved to his Maryland estates. The nearness of the two families was one element in the marriage in 1750 of William Eilbeck's daughter with Mason's son George Mason IV.

Excerpts from the Mercer and Bagge account books indicate that George Mason was a genial fellow who enjoyed playing games of chance. John Mercer, for instance, lost heavily at a game of cribbage at Mason's house in Maryland, while Philip Key had a run of good luck. Colonel Mason lent some books to Daniel Dulany the elder, the distingiushed Maryland jurist, and purchased some law books for him in Williamsburg. Robert Spotswood, John Mercer, Edmund Bagge, nephew of the Reverend John Bagge, and George Mason made up a party at loo during the long Christmas holiday in 1725, when Bagge and Spotswood were guests at Newtown. On another occasion the merchant John Wilson won a little money in a card game at Mason's.[55]

One of his house guests in 1727 was a gentleman named Ebenezer Cook, no doubt the reputed poet laureate of Maryland. In 1728 John Mercer sent eighteen shillings and eightpence to George Mason to give to the poet laureate, the author of *The Sot-Weed Factor,* a satire on Maryland customs and manners printed in 1708. In 1730 William Parks, the Annapolis printer, ran off a little tract in verse called *Sotweed Redivivus: Or the Planters Looking-Glass.* This slight volume presented arguments for the regulation of the tobacco trade by an inspection act in the guise of a sequel to *The Sot-Weed Factor.* It, too, purported to come from the pen of Ebenezer Cook. A serious poem, "An elegy on the Death of the Hon. Nicholas Lowe, Esq.," appeared in the *Maryland Gazette* in 1728 over the same signature. Colonel Mason's interest in poetry and satirical verse was shown by his subscription to *Muscipula: The Mouse Trap, or the Battle of the Cambrians and the Mice* in a new translation by Richard Lewis published in Annapolis in 1728. Edward Holdsworth's original poem was a popular Latin satire on the Welsh. Colonel Mason was the only advance subscriber in Virginia for Lewis's translation of the original Latin verse into rhyming couplets; he subscribed for three copies.[56]

Mason's friends were surprisingly bookish for their rather remote frontier residence. The Mercer accounts show that Edmund Bagge purchased a copy of *Expeditio Ultramontana* "Eng & Lat" from John Mercer on 21 February 1726. Like the Lewis translation, this was an original satire in Latin rendered into English verse by another hand. It was written by Arthur Blackmore and translated by the Reverend George Seagood. It recounted the adventures of the Spotswood expedition over the crest of the Blue Ridge in 1716. Because of his participation in that journey, as well as from the fact that two of his closest associates owned copies, one might suppose that Colonel Mason read this work as well. John Mercer was already building up his notable library while engaging as a bookseller himself.

Mercer was the son of a Dublin merchant who left him not a farthing beyond his education. The belief that he attended Trinity College in Dublin seems to be without foundation, as there is no record of his ever having been a pupil, let alone a graduate.[57] But his interests in the classics and in literature indicate that he was a man of culture. He read law by himself, qualified as an attorney, and practiced law at intervals. Steeped in the classics, with a partiality for satire and the comic muse, John Mercer formed the center of a literary circle on the Potomac and exchanged quips and capped verses with his friends. He purchased a large selection from Governor Spotswood's library from John Graeme in 1726 and forty law books from Robert Beverley in 1730. In the course of a single month in 1730 John Mercer lent a *History of the Netherlands* to John Savage, three works on mathematics to Edmund Bagge, a narrative of a tour through Italy to Captain Peter Hedgman, a *History of the Royal Society* to Col. Henry Fitzhugh, a law book to the Reverend Robert Rose, a book on gardening to Ralph Falkneer, and some poetry to Andrew Forbes. John Graham, one of the early Dumfries factors on the river, sold an interesting collection of ancient and modern classics in translation to Mercer.

In the last years of his life Colonel Mason entered into an agreement with the vestry of Durham of Nanjemoy Parish in Charles County for building a new church in Nanjemoy Parish.[58] His sudden death prevented him from carrying out his intention, and Ann (Thomson) Mason contracted with John Hobson to complete the structure. Since Old Durham Church, located near modern Welcome, was begun in 1732, it is highly probable that Colonel Mason had a good deal to do with the design and the construction of the handsome old brick church before his tragic death made it necessary for Hobson to complete it.

On 5 March 1735 Colonel Mason attempted to cross the Potomac in his sloop. The vessel was overturned and he was drowned. He was buried at Newtown. His busy life came to a sudden end, and he left a young widow to manage his estates and raise three small children. On 18 August 1735 an inventory of Mason's property at his Charles County homestead was taken by William Eilbeck and W. Williams, both designated as creditors of the estate, and by John Mercer of Marlborough and Jeremiah Bronaugh, Jr., both designated as kin of the deceased.[59] A similar inventory was made of his Virginia property.

According to the inventory Colonel Mason had at the time of his death twenty-three slaves on his estate at Chickamuxon Creek. Eleven of them were adults and the rest were children. Among them were three skilled workers—Rush and Dublin, ship carpenters, and Dick, a shoemaker. He also had six indentured English servants in his employ on the Maryland property. One of them was a carpenter, the rest laborers. The movable property in Maryland was appraised at £721 18s. 11d. The detailed accounting of every article owned by Colonel Mason gives a picture of his home on Chickamuxon Creek in Maryland. One room contained a corner cupboard, table, an end table, several old prints, an escritoire where Mason kept sixteen quires of paper, a penknife, and a pocket case. He owned thirty-three earthenware plates and forty-three miscellaneous pieces of earthenware. Beds and furniture, quilts, blankets, old curtains, and glasses appear over and over again on the inventory, as do six chairs, four cushions, and window curtains in one room and twelve chairs in another. The household goods included a pair of steelyards for weighting "kasts" of tobacco and a pair of sheepshears. Mason owned a periagua (a small sloop-rigged vessel), a spyglass that he probably used on board it, a speaking trumpet, and various other nautical implements. The house in Virginia was sparsely furnished. The inventory made there included one old looking glass, two old leather chairs, two flag, or rush-bottomed, elbow chairs; an old cane chair; one old chest of drawers; one old slab table; and the usual feather bed, rug, and blanket, as well as another bed and another table. This is in accord with the fact that his Virginia estate was appraised at only £304 7s. The inventory showed that Mason employed a Negro man, a mulatto woman, and three Negro children on one plantation, and two Negro men and a Negro boy on another. He also had two white indentured servants on his Virginia estate; an indentured servant man and a boy were on a third property.[60]

Ann Mason was appointed the administrator of her husband's estate. She presented an account of the charges against the estate and the debts due to Colonel Mason's heirs at a session of Prince William County Court in 1737. The charges for the funeral expenses amounted to 270 pounds of tobacco, or £3. She had paid several of Mason's creditors, including John Graham, Thomas West, Richard Blackburn, and the vestry of Overwharton Parish. Mr. Aderton of Whitehaven had paid £42 to the estate, probably for tobacco sold in England. An additional £23 came by way of Captain Gale, a Whitehaven shipmaster in the tobacco trade.[61]

With her husband's sudden death in 1735, Ann Mason was left on her own to provide for her three small children: George Mason IV, then nine, Mary four, and Thomson, barely two years. She had to manage the affairs of the tobacco plantations and tenant farms in Maryland and Virginia; get her crops to market at the most advantageous price; look to the needs of the indentured servants and slaves; and supervise the education of her children. Continuing in her husband's path, she became a successful planter-merchant as well as an astute land speculator. She looked beyond the pale of settlements and saw the promise of the future in the unspoiled lands on the frontiers of Virginia.

Although she took the property on Chopawamsic Creek as her dower, she did not move there until late in September 1735. Her nephew, John Fenton Mercer, was born at her home in Charles County on 31 August 1735, while his parents were visiting their recently widowed sister-in-law. He was baptized there on 7 September by the Reverend William Michinchie.[62]

George Mason IV inherited the rest of his father's property, his mother to administer the estate in his name. All the ordinary expenses incurred in educating and providing necessities for her children had to be presented for approval to the officers of the Prince William County Court before being charged to the estate, such as those for five-year-old Mary Mason, who began to attend classes at the family home in Chopawamsic in 1736. For that year, the expenses came to 1,000 pounds of tobacco for her board and 200 pounds for her tutor. In 1738 the charges for her dancing lessons at home are recorded. Charges for young Thomson in 1739 included payments for his early tutors, who taught him his first lessons, as well as 1,000 pounds of tobacco for his board.[63]

George Mason's school days began while he was living with his mother on the Chopawamsic plantation. In 1736 Ann Mason paid a certain Master Williams 1,000 pounds of tobacco for tutoring her son and charged the estate 1,200 pounds of tobacco for her son's board. Williams kept a school on the Mason plantation, teaching his pupils in a separate schoolhouse on the property, and boarding with the family or with a neighboring family. The sons of other Stafford County families came up to Chopawamsic to attend classes with George Mason. One of them was Richard Hewitt, who eventually became a clergyman of the Church of England and rector of Hungars Parish on the Eastern Shore of Virginia. Richard Hewitt was the son of an Anglican minister who came to Virginia in 1725 and who died when his son was quite small. His mother then married Thomas Heath of Stafford County. The two fatherless boys doubtless had a good deal in common, and George Mason remained close to his "old schoolfellow" and his family for the rest of his life.[64]

When Williams migrated across the Potomac to Maryland, his boys followed him. In 1737 twelve-year-old George Mason left Chopawamsic to board with a Mrs. Simpson in Maryland, where Williams continued to supervise his lessons through this year. In 1738 and 1739 Williams continued to draw his annual stipend of 1,000 pounds of tobacco as George Mason's tutor. There is no charge for board in the accounts for these years as all of the school expenses were drawn against the Maryland estate. George Mason memorized the rules of grammar, parsed Latin sentences, and penetrated the mysteries of mathematics under the guidance of Williams for at least four years. A Master Wylie received 545 pounds of tobacco for additional lessons during 1738–39. He may have initiated George Mason's study of Greek and Latin authors. In 1740, however, young George was definitely back with his family at Chopawamsic. Williams had been dismissed, and a Dr. Bridges received £12. 10s. 1d. for teaching the boy.[65]

The name Bridges as one of George Mason's tutors raises some tantalizing speculation. It is quite possible that he was the Charles Bridges who had a great deal to do with the development of the charity schools established by the Society for the Promotion of Christian Knowledge in London and in his native Northamptonshire. As a nonjuring Anglican who refused to acknowledge George I as the legitimate heir to the throne, Bridges found all avenues of preferment closed to him after 1715. He eked out a living in various ways before coming to Virginia with his family in 1731. Charles Bridges tried to interest the authorities in England and Virginia in providing free schools for black children. Old Commissary Blair favored the plan, but nothing came of it. Bridges lived mainly in Williamsburg and in Hanover County in the 1730s, apparently painting portraits of some of the first gentlemen of Virginia and their ladies. He visited the Potomac in 1740 or 1741 and was a guest of William Fairfax at Belvoir, his newly built house on the lower side of Pohick Creek.[66] Thus he could be the Dr. Bridges who directed some of George Mason's more advanced studies.

Ann Mason was not entirely alone in meeting the responsibilities of her children's upbringing as the children's uncle, John Mercer of Marlborough, had been appointed guardian along with her on 21 May 1735, and both were required to post bond.[67] John Mercer offered a helpful presence to his sister-in-law, who was affectionately regarded by her husband's family. Between the two of them, the children grew into capable adults.

As an uncle and legal guardian, John Mercer of Marlborough had some say in George Mason's education. His opinions were not to be lightly regarded, though they did not suit everyone's palate. An opinionated man with a sharp wit and a mordant sarcasm, he sometimes ruffled the feathers of his neighbors, but he never bored them. In 1734 the gentlemen justices of Prince William had reason to complain to the governor and Council of John Mercer's insolence in court.[68] He was suspended from his legal practices and reinstated in 1738, still unrepentent; he was again disbarred in 1739. Ten years later he was made a justice of the peace in Stafford County, though there is no indication that he had mended his ways.[69] But John Mercer won the final round of his skirmishes with the legal profession: he compiled the standard compendium of Virginia laws for the use of the gentlemen who had turned him out of their profession.

John Mercer had one of the best collections of books in Virginia at his Marlborough plantation in Stafford County. His splendid library of fifteen hundred volumes doubtless lay open to his nephews. George and Thomson Mason probably listened intently when their brilliant and witty uncle discoursed on the politics and personalities of Williamsburg. John Mercer's library was a gathering place for many Northern Neck planters who had taste for literature. He purchased books from his friends, lent or sold his own books to them, and took their orders for British publications.

John Mercer kept a careful record of every book that passed through his hands, but his ledgers for Mason's formative years are missing. In his library catalogue he recorded the initials JM and GM for all those volumes ordered for his sons, James and George. George Mercer's books are the usual schoolbooks of the day: a Greek grammar and a Greek New Testament; Cornelis Schrevel's Greek-Latin lexicon; editions of Sallust, Virgil, Terence, Horace, and Lucian; a translation of Plutarch's lives; three books on Roman history and antiquities; and a geography of the ancient world. Young George Mercer also owned a copy of Pope's translation of the *Iliad,* sets of the *Spectator,* the *Tatler,* the *Guardian,* and Addison's *Works. The Seasons* by the Scottish poet James Thomson was the only representative of strictly contemporary writers among young Mercer's books.

If John Mercer selected these works for his own sons in their school-days, he might well have recommended the same texts to his nephew. He visualized a solid grounding in Latin and some familiarity with Greek as essential to a young man's education. He preferred that the student cut his teeth on Sallust, rather than Caesar, and move rapidly to the riches of Latin poetry, not bothering with the soaring periods of Cicero's orations that lurk behind so many English prose styles. The student's Greek could be quite rudimentary, with an exposure to the Koine of the New Testament, and he could use the interlinear Latin translation and ample English notes such as he would find in Edwin Murphy's edition of the *Dialogues* of Lucian, which George Mercer used.

In 1750 George Mason purchased one book from John Mercer that was among those the latter recommended to his sons. This is the only book that Mason is definitely known to have bought or borrowed from his uncle's library. *The Method of Teaching and Studying the Belles Letters, or, An Introduction to Language, Poetry, Rhetoric, History, Moral Philosophy, Physics, &c.* was a translation of an immensely popular work by Charles Rollin, rector of the University of Paris from 1720 to 1741.[70] He also compiled *An Ancient History,* an equally popular textbook, that was among the volumes Mercer supplied his sons. George Mason owned another set of books of a similar character that he bought from his friend the Reverend James Scott in 1747. This was *An Universal History, from the Earliest Account of Time,* in twenty volumes. Mason's set is still on the shelves in the Little Sitting Room at Gunston Hall. Books of this sort served the busy planter as a guide to self-education and provided the common reader with a vade mecum to the ancient and modern classics. They equally served the eighteenth-century gentlemen as a treasury of anecdote and illustration from ancient history and literature.

John Mercer had strong opinions about the proper character of a schoolmaster, as he had about every other subject: "My opinion of a Tutor," he wrote in 1768, "is, that besides instructing his pupil in such branches of learning as he is designed for, he should also be particularly careful of his Religion, morals, & behavior, in short he should be a gentleman." A thorough classicist himself, Mercer could afford to sniff at the impracticality of the classics. He considered a sound understanding of mathematics preferable to "Greek, Hebrew, or any other learned languages, which would be of little use here, whereas the other is of the greatest use not only here but everywhere else & may enable a man of ingenuity to make his fortune in any part of the world."

Many of the schoolmasters on the Potomac were Scotsmen, and John Mercer, being Irish, acknowledged that he was prejudiced against Scottish schoolmasters:

I have known several of them who understood & were capable of teaching the latin Authors, some of them Greek (whose language was so uncouth that Catesby Coke used to swear they translated one strange language into a Stranger), & have known some of them who understood the mathematicks, but I never knew one of them who upon his first arrival did not surprize the company he was introduced to by his awkward & unpolished behaviour. They are almost to a man bred Presbyterians & tho none of them scruple to become Episcopalians for a parish, their religion is to be much questioned, I mean whether they have any or no, for I have known some without either religion or morals, & I attribute it to George Mason's tutor that I have long doubted with a good deal of concern that he had very little improved in either.[71]

The account books kept by Ann Mason indicate that the Reverend Alexander Scott, the rector of Overwharton Parish, selected books for young Mason's use and ordered them from England. Scott lived at Dipple, a short distance from the Masons at Chopawamsic, and served as the minister of their parish from 1711 until his death in 1738. He had received the Master of Arts degree from the University of Glasgow before coming to America and was as well qualified as any man on the Potomac to direct young George Mason's reading. Scott was also an active and successful land speculator; therefore, he could be considered among those who shaped George Mason's mind and sharpened his business acumen. Scott, whose wife was Sarah (Gibbons) Brent, the widow of William Brent, had no children of his own and invited his younger brother, James, to join him in Virginia. At the death of his brother, James Scott inherited Dipple, on Quantico Creek (now a part of the United States Marine base), and extensive lands on the upper reaches of the Potomac and the Rappahannock. He went home to Scotland to be ordained and returned as the rector of neighboring Dettingen Parish in Prince William County.[72]

Ann Mason's accounts indicate that the family physician was Dr. Gustavus Brown, a Scottish gentleman. He was the son of a small landowner in Lanarkshire and came to the colonies to make his fortune.

Brown, "Laird of Wainside and House Byres and of the Stone Middleton in Scotland, and of Rose and Rich Hills, Maryland," settled in Charles County in 1708. He married Frances Fowke, daughter of Gerard and Sarah (Burdett) Fowke and granddaughter of Gerard and Ann (Thoroughgood) Fowke. Mrs. Brown was thus a first cousin of George Mason III, the grandson of Gerard and Ann (Thoroughgood) Fowke.[73]

Frances (Fowke) Brown died at Dipple in Stafford County and was buried there. Her tombstone, now in Aquia churchyard, carries a proud inscription:

Here lyeth the body of Frances, the wife of Dr. Gustavus Brown, of Charles County, Maryland. By her he had twelve children, of whom one son and seven daughters survived her. She was a daughter of Mr. Gerard Fowke, late of Maryland, and descended from the Fowkes, of Guston Hall, in Staffordshire, England. She was born February the 2d, 1691, and died, much lamented, on the 8th of November, 1744, in the fifty-fourth year of her age.

Brown took his family to Scotland for a time but returned to Charles County in 1734. His daughters won the hearts of a number of promising young men, who, like their father, had come to the Potomac from Scotland. Sarah married the Reverend James Scott, rector of Dettingen Parish. They made their home on the glebe lands on the banks of Quantico Creek in Prince William County until James came into his inheritance, when they moved to Dipple. Dettingen Parish was created by an act of the Virginia Assembly in 1744 and took as its parish church the small and somewhat neglected chapel near Dumfries that had been erected many years before by the vestry of Overwharton Parish.[74] Frances Brown married the Reverend John Moncure, another young Scottish minister, who succeeded the Reverend Alexander Scott in the cure of souls at Overwharton, and they lived on its glebe land. When George Mason wrote his will, he referred to the esteem he held for these ministers and noted that James Scott was an "old and long-tryed" friend. Jean Brown married the Reverend Isaac Campbell, and Margaret became the wife of Thomas Stone of Charles County. Christian married John Graham, a factor for a Dumfries firm doing business on Quantico Creek, and died a month after her wedding. Mary wed the Reverend Matthew Hopkins of Maryland, and after his early death the young widow married Henry Threlkeld, who had also come to Quantico Creek as a factor for a Scottish firm.[75]

Colonists from Scotland began to have a marked influence on the Chesapeake in these years and gave a decided Scots burr to the more intellectual conversations on the Potomac as well as to the business dealings of the tobacco traders. Graduates of the Scottish universities came to Maryland and Virginia in substantial numbers to teach, practice medicine or the law, or to take a parish of the Church of England. Scottish parsons, doctors, and lawyers formed little circles of their own in every one of the colonies. Gustavus Brown relied on his wife's kinsman, Lawrence Dinwiddie of Glasgow, to send him an apprentice to his medical practice.[76]

The resident agents, or factors, sent out by tobacco firms in Glasgow and Dumfries to handle their business on the Potomac came from the same Scottish social grouping as did the professional class. The son of a minister or a landowner counted himself fortunate to be employed as the representative of a family firm in the colonies. The Scottish factor, like the Scottish parson and physician, moved easily in the planter society of the Chesapeake. John Graham married as his second wife Elizabeth Catesby Cocke and, by a family arrangement, succeeded his new father-in-law as county clerk of Fairfax County.[77] His story was repeated again and again as young merchants from Glasgow and Whitehaven married into Virginia families and became important planters in their own right.

The factor, in ordinary usage, was no more than the agent employed to transact business. In the Potomac tobacco trade, however, the factor was the most important man in the business transaction. For a consignment merchant, the ability to deal in volume and knowledge of his home market counted most. He took his percentage of the gross, whether tobacco prices were high or low. The Scots factor had to buy his tobacco at a price high enough to keep the planters from shipping it to England at their own risk but low enough to make a profit in Glasgow six months later. He had to order his stock of goods a year or more in advance and try to forecast accurately what kinds of goods farmers or housewives would need and whether his competitors would glut the market with iron hoes or bolts of calico—perhaps of a quality that would leave his stock unsold because it was shoddy or too expensive.[78] The factor was, consequently, a great deal more than a shop assistant. He was usually working either for a percentage of the firm's business in his own district or was actually a full partner in the firm. Not infrequently he was a son, nephew, or son-in-law of a company director in Scotland.

Whitehaven merchants did not lag behind their Scottish neighbors in exploiting the trade of the Potomac and the Rappahannock. If anything, they showed the way. The shipowners of Whitehaven chartered their vessels to companies of traders in Glasgow or Dumfries. With certain Scottish ports, particularly Kirkcudbright, there was a special relationship.[79]

Ann Mason almost certainly continued to sell her son's Maryland tobacco through William Eilbeck, and it seems likely that some of her tobacco passed through the hands of John Graham because of the family connections. However, the only merchants in the tobacco trade known to have had business dealings with Ann Mason were William Hunt and James Buchanan of London. The accounts of William Hunt record transactions with her husband crediting him on 22 November 1728 with £1,000; credits of smaller sums from 15 August 1735 to 9 August 1742 would be to Ann as administrator of his estate.[80]

Although Ann Mason moved her family back to Virginia in 1735, she continued to improve the property in Charles County acquired by her late husband. In Maryland the quitrents were calculated at one penny the acre. Since she paid four shillings for lands held in Prince Georges County in 1736, apparently she owned 463 acres in Maryland at this time. By 1740, with skillful purchase and patent, Ann Mason had rounded out the Mason family holdings between Chickamuxon Creek and Goose Bay in Charles County and made them into one plantation.[81]

She was equally careful in leasing her son's Virginia lands. In 1737 Ann Mason paid quitrents on 12,574 acres of land in the Northern Neck of Virginia. On 3 September 1737, as guardian to George Mason she leased 150 acres on the south side of Occoquan Creek, lately in the possession of Thomas Dent, to John Mercer. She explicitly enjoined Mercer and his heirs or assigns from keeping the ferry over the Occoquan, "neither shall any Ferryman board there or any house be built or other provisions made for any person who shall have the ferry or row any boat or boats belonging thereunto." [82]

In addition to the lands left by Colonel Mason, Ann Mason owned ten slaves valued at £150. In 1736 no crop of tobacco was made, "but the negroes would have brought the estate considerably in debt if any Account had been made for their maintenance at the island where they all lived except London and Porus. London this year worked in Maryland and made for his share 1,817 pounds of tobacco." In 1737 London and Matt made 2,806 pounds of tobacco in Maryland, while Porus, Windsor, Nan Wilson, Jack, and Stephen made 3,500 pounds of tobacco in Virginia. In 1739 the Maryland plantation produced 3,436 pounds of tobacco, the Virginia plantations 4,547. Crops of corn, wheat, and beans were made on all of the Mason plantations, but the cost of maintaining the slaves and providing them with clothing, bedding, tools, and other necessities more than equaled the value of these crops, according to Ann Mason's reckoning.

A much greater amount of tobacco came to George Mason in rents than was raised on his property by his slaves. In 1735 nineteen tenants on his Virginia property paid him 11,390 pounds of tobacco. In 1736 rents on the Virginia property produced 13,166 pounds of tobacco and £20 in cash. In 1737 the rents amounted to only 10,800 pounds of tobacco, but by 1739 the number had increased to 19,035. The Maryland rents brought in 4,686 pounds in 1736, a figure that varied little in the next few years. In 1739, an unusually good year, Mason's tobacco plantations produced 7,983 pounds, but rents in that same year amounted to 23,188. Obviously the lease of tobacco lands to tenant farmers was by far the most important aspect of Ann Mason's management of her husband's estate.

She also took care that the buildings of the estates were kept in good condition. In 1736 she repaired houses on the Doegs' Neck estate, where she built a fifty-two foot tobacco barn in 1740. When George Mason reached his majority, this Doegs' Neck property became his home. In 1741 she also built new tobacco barns on the Stump Neck property in Maryland.[83] During the period of her guardianship, Ann Mason had improved all of the plantations that were soon to come into her eldest son's management.

Ann Mason's ability to understand the potential of the frontier and to make wise investments is well documented from the records of her contacts with the sturdy Pennsylvania German and Quaker families. As these families moved across the Potomac into Virginia, they gave an immediate value to lands that had been all but worthless before the migration of the 1730s. In 1731 Governor Sir William Gooch reported to London that "the people of this Dominion, as well as many Strangers from Pennsylvania, have discovered a strong Inclination to extend our settlements on the western side of the great mountains and on the River Cohongarooton [the upper Potomac], under grants from this Government to hold their lands of the Crown." [84] Quakers from Pennsylvania and New Jersey settled along the Monocacy in the 1720s, and in 1732 a group of Friends secured a grant in the Shenandoah Valley. Ten years later the Friends in modern Loudoun County gathered for the Fairfax monthly meeting. The first German families were building and planting in the future Loudoun County in 1731. From this beginning, the movement spread southward, frequently increased by large migrations from Pennsylvania and Europe.[85]

Even before the migrations increased the value of these lands, farsighted speculators began to buy up large holdings in these remote areas. Col. Robert Carter, the agent for the proprietary of the Northern Neck, began to carve out vast holdings for himself. John Mercer and Catesby Cocke were also active in land speculation, particularly in the region along Catoctin Creek. Though Capt. Francis Awbrey did not operate on the scale of "King" Carter, he managed to turn a nice profit on the speculations he ventured. In 1728 Awbrey obtained a warrant for survey of 5,316 acres from the proprietor of the Northern Neck and a deed for a tract of 962 acres. In 1730 he obtained a grant for an additional 454 acres.

Captain Awbrey is of especial interest with regard to the Mason estates because Ann Mason purchased a number of tracts of land from him. On 21 August 1738 Francis Awbrey of Prince William County, Gentleman, leased 4,054 acres above Goose Creek and an additional 962 acres five miles above the mouth of Goose Creek to Ann Mason of Stafford County, widow. The next day, upon receipt of £350 from Mrs. Mason, Awbrey gave her a deed to the land. On 23 August 1738 Awbrey agreed to obtain a deed to the 5,316-acre tract, and Ann Mason agreed to purchase 4,000 acres of this tract for £450.[86] On 8 July 1740 Ann Mason purchased another 2,998 acres from Francis Awbrey for £74.10. The plat of this tract is preserved in the Mercer land book. It ran along Wood's Branch, below Pimmitt's Run, somewhat north of modern Falls Church.[87]

Ann Mason developed her lands by leasing out over 600 acres in small farms to individual planters of Cameron Parish. She continued this practice through 1756 when, on 15 June, Christopher Perfect of Cameron Parish, planter, obtained a lease for 150 acres of the same tract from her.[88]

On 23 December 1756 Ann Mason deeded to Thomson, her youngest son, 4,650 acres of land purchased from Francis Awbrey and located in Cameron Parish, Fairfax County, which was cut off from Truro Parish in 1749. She made a similar gift on the same day to her daughter, Mary Thomson (Mason) Selden and her husband, Samuel Selden, whom she had married on 11 April 1751, when she was twenty years old. Mary Selden died 5 January 1758, leaving three little children: Mary Mason Selden, Miles Cary Selden, and Samuel Selden, Jr.[89]

In the midst of her land development, Ann Mason learned that her uncle, Sir William Thomson, puisne baron of the Exchequer, had died in 1739 in England. Her first intimation of that fact came from John Ambler of Yorktown, to whom John Thomson of the Exchequer Office had written inquiring about the heirs of Stevens Thomson. This was apparently in 1743. Ann Mason wrote to her British kinsman:

I lately received a Letter from Mr. Ambler acquainting me that you had desired him to enquire after the Heirs of my Uncle the late Baron Thomson, there being a Suit in Chancery for the Sale of his Estate. . . . Whether your own Interest may be concerned in the Enquiry or whether you are induced to it by a Desire of Serving the Baron's Relations I thought it would not be improper to let you know that I am his Heir which you will be fully convinced of when I inform you that my Father Stevens Thomson who was Attorney General of this Colony came hither from London about forty years ago bringing my Mother Dorothea & five children Mary Elizabeth William myself and Stevens & after his Arrival here had another Son born named Taunton. Elizabeth William Stevens & Taunton died under age and without Issue. Mary married one Booth & after Capt. Graves Pack. She had but one Child by Pack who died at Six months old, so that I am the only Child now living of my father. I married Colo. George Mason of Stafford County in 1721, by whom I had several Children, of which only three are living: George about 18, Mary about 12 & Thomson about ten. This will no doubt convince you as I said that I am my Uncle's Heir tho' if it is necessary I can have the most authentick proof possible of it. If it lies in your way to be of Service to me with regard to my Uncle's Estate you may depend not only on my reimbursing any Expence you may be at about it but of acknowledging your good offices in the most greatful manner & if you will favour me with a Letter please direct for me in Stafford County Potomack River.[90]

At the same time Ann Mason wrote to the London firm of Haswell and Hunt, repeating the facts she had learned from John Ambler:

That Letter being delivered to Mr. John Mercer a Relation of mine who was then at Williamsburg as he was informed of the Contents of it he was so kind to take the opportunity (as he informed me) of writing to you by Capt. Dansie who sailed the next morning, being induced thereto by the Information he had received some time before from Messrs. Thos. & Wm. Nelson that you had requested them to enquire after me or my family tho' they could not tell upon what Occasion, & as they were so kind to promise him to write by the same opportunity to desire you to give me Credit for what Cash you might think proper to advance for employing one or more Lawyers to take Care of my Interest I take this opportunity to let you know how kindly I approve of those measures and to request you to be so good as to acquaint me what you have thought proper to do in the Affair & to send me a full State of the Case or Copies of such Papers as may be necessary to give me a sight into it & Particularly to let me know whether my Uncle made any Will a copy of which (if he did) I should be glad to receive. As I could not tell how much trouble this matter might be attended with or how agreeable it might be to you to act in it I have wrote to Mr. James Buchanan to apply to you & hope if it will be too great trouble to you that you will undertake it. . . .[91]

Sir William Thomson had drawn up a very complicated will, but without any provision for his niece in America, and apparently she gained nothing from his estate.[92]

The careful accounts that Ann Mason kept show her son George passing from boyhood into manhood. In 1742 charges were recorded for a new beaver hat, a wig, and razors, as well as schoolbooks. He attained his majority at his twenty-first birthday in 1746, but he continued to live at Chopawamsic with his mother, brother, and sister.

Ann Mason died on 13 November 1762 at her house in Stafford County. She made the Reverend John Moncure, her husband's cousin, the executor of her will together with her sons, George and Thomson. To her son George she left her largest silver salver; to her son Thomson "my ring and castors, two salts, my soup spoons and all the rest of my silver spoons, large and small." She made a bequest of land in Loudoun County "to John Bronaugh, son of my sister Bronaugh of Fairfax County." A codicil left the portrait of Mary (Mason) Selden "now in my hall to my cousin Frances, the wife of John Moncure, Clerk," in trust for her grandson, Samuel Selden.[93]

The *Maryland Gazette* published a brief obituary:

To give her true Character at length would, to those who had the Pleasure of her Acquaintance, be unnecessary; and by Strangers would be thought Flattery. Let it suffice therefore to observe, that she discharged her Duty, in her several Characters of a Wife, Parent, a Mistress, a Friend, a Neighbour, and a Christian with that distinguished Lustre, which everyone would wish to imitate, but few have ever equalled. Providence was accordingly pleased to reward her Virtues in this way, by gratifying her in the Accomplishment of the first and dearest Wish of her Heart (the Happiness of her Children) and after preparing her by a long and painful Illness, which she bore with exemplary Resignation; permitted her in the 63rd year of her age, to exchange the transitory Pleasure of the World for those never failing Joys which Goodness like hers may reasonably be assured of meeting with in the next.[94]

Inventories of Ann Mason's estate were filed in both Fairfax and Stafford counties. The Fairfax appraisal would indicate that the property was farmed by the Negro couple who lived there. The man was appraised at £70, and the woman at £55. The other items listed were livestock and farm implements. The only odd item was "one old ferry boat at Occoquan." On the other hand, the inventory filed in Stafford County gives a very good idea of how Ann lived at Chopawamsic. Her Negro woman, Lotty, was worth £75, but her "old bay chair horse" was only worth £50. Ann had seven cows and a yoke of oxen at the homeplace; six beds and furniture with curtains, but only one set of curtains and "vallins" and one pair of window curtains. She had a number of tablecloths and napkins both damask and diaper cloth, and "two Linon table cloaths." Also one pair of "old fine shoos" was valued at 15 shillings. The silver was all carefully described, some of which was not mentioned in her will, as "Appraisal of old plate, viz: 2 tankards, 1 beaker, 2 porringers, 1 nutmeg grater, 1 pepper box, 1 mustard box, and 1 siphon." A marrow spoon was also listed. Among the furniture were one large oval table, one tea table, four small pine tables, two smoking chairs of gold leather; one large looking glass (these items were listed in Ann's husband's inventory), two small dressing glasses, two Dutch glasses, two old gilt trunks, one large chest, and one large case of bottles. There is no description of the china, except that all of it was cracked or broken. But "2 Delf" chamber pots were carefully noted and two more in "pewter," two pairs of money scales are recorded, but only a "parcel of old books" for 25 shillings, and two "old" spinning wheels and six sides of tanned leather. Ann's "worn saddle" was listed, but the girth was new, since "the old chaise and harness" were "worn out," she was not driven out in an elegant equipage.[95]

Ann Mason's home no longer exists. Only a hole full of rubble overgrown with weeds indicates its location on a slight rise overlooking Chopawamsic Creek, which too is becoming choked with silt and weeds. She was a woman of strong character and considerable native ability. Widowed at thirty-six, she never remarried. Her capable management secured the landed estate amassed by her husband and left their eldest son with a richer inheritance than his father had provided. She made wise investments in land for their younger son that provided him with a substantial income. Their two sons' education was received primarily under her direction, and she formed their own strong characters under her roof. If we know nothing of Ann Mason, the mere fact that George of Gunston Hall and Thomson of Raspberry Plain were her sons would tell us a good deal about her.

Chapter IV

George Mason IV: Country Gentleman

GEORGE MASON IV CAME OF AGE on 11 December 1746 and took possession of his estates and tobacco plantations in Maryland and Virginia. He now assumed the duties and responsibilities of a landed gentleman and those required of him as the head of his family. He was a good-looking young man with dark hair and skin, well built, a little inclined to stoutness, and generally of good health. His strong even features were enhanced by thoughtful and piercing eyes. A manner of polite reserve in company may have covered a certain shyness, but he could converse well on topics of interest to him. Men found themselves drawn into conversation with him on subjects of weight and matter. Even as a young man his friends deferred to his intellect. They were, in the main, serious young men, several of them of the clergy, and nearly all somewhat older than he. Horse racing was one of his pleasures, and he enjoyed the purse racing and the racing for cups that were a regular event at every county town during the holding of court. Appreciation of good horses was almost universal in the Chesapeake colonies. Both George and Thomson Mason managed race-meets at one time or another and visited the racecourse at Boggess's, near Pohick Church. George Mason was something of an outdoorsman —proud of his hunting guns, his horses, his hounds; enjoying riding out with his friends after deer or fox; shooting on the Great Marsh; or visiting his fishing stage on the Occoquan.[1]

His main interest, however, lay with his lands. His extensive property holdings in Maryland were centered in Charles County along Chickamuxon and Mattawoman creeks. In Virginia his lands lay along Occoquan and Neabsco creeks and at Cockpit Point in Prince William County; in Fairfax County along Pohick and Accotink creeks, on Hunting Creek, Analostan Island, and on the Virginia shore opposite Rock Creek.[2] He had also acquired the right to the ferry over the Occoquan and, after 1748, to the ferry over the Potomac at Analostan Island. The family property on Chopawamsic Creek in Prince William and Stafford counties remained as his mother's share of the estate of George Mason III, with the understanding that it would pass at her death to her son Thomson.[3] He selected lands on Doegs' Neck in Virginia as his home plantation and moved there in 1749, where he chose for his first home a site on a high bluff overlooking the Potomac near Sycamore Point. He began at this time his long association with Truro Parish and Fairfax County.

As head of the family, Mason assumed another responsibility in 1748. French Mason, his uncle, died leaving five small children, and the Fairfax County Court appointed Mason their guardian. French Mason had inherited 1,455 acres of land, mainly on the north side of Pohick Creek, most of which he leased to tenant farmers. He owned the official warehouses for the inspection of tobacco near the mouth of Pohick Creek and a mill on the south side. French Mason, Jr., stood to inherit the greater part of his father's property. His younger brother, George Mason, known as George Mason, Jr., or George Mason of Pohick, inherited the mill and certain other lands in Fairfax County.[4] From family records we know that Leannah Mason, who married William Talbott, had already received some lands on Pohick Creek as a gift from her father in 1741; Lucretia Mason married Robert Speake (or Speke) in 1759; and Rosanna Mason married Gilbert Simpson. The husbands of Leannah and Rosanna took up western lands and removed to Kentucky.

George Mason brought his cousins to his own house on Doegs' Neck for their school years. He wrote of young French Mason in 1758, "He has lived a good while with me. . . . He never was a flashy fellow. He has been but little in company, and has not that address which is requisite to set a man in advantageous light at first, but he is a very modest lad, and does not want parts."[5] Since French Mason had been a member of his household for ten years, George Mason makes it clear that flashiness and forwardness were not valued at Doegs' Neck. He himself was by nature a private man, and his closest friends were often members of his own family.

Capt. Jeremiah Bronaugh and his wife, Simpha Rosa Field (Mason) Dinwiddie Bronaugh lived at Newtown plantation. It was here that Jeremiah, with whom George Mason had always been close, died 11 November 1749 and was buried. His widow and children continued to live at Newtown. Elizabeth Dinwiddie, the older of Simpha's daughters by her first marriage had married, on 26 November 1745, her first cousin, Gerard Fowke III and had gone down the Potomac to live at his plantation, Gunston Hall in Stafford County. There they raised ten children. The second daughter, Jane, married William Waite of Fairfax County, a builder by trade. He was highly regarded by the Mason family, and he and George Mason worked closely together in

planning Pohick Church. He removed his family to Fauquier County
and apparently lived upon a plantation inherited from her father.
There were no children from this marriage.[6] The Bronaugh cousins,
Ann and Elizabeth, although younger than George, were particular
favorites of his. Ann, who was born 25 August 1735, married Martin
Cockburn, a Scot.* Elizabeth, born three years later, married the
Reverend Lee Massey, becoming his third wife.[7] When George Mason
drew his will in 1773, he made bequests to both his cousins Ann and
Elizabeth and referred to their husbands as his "worthy friends." He
named Martin Cockburn one of the executors of his estate and guardian to his children and called upon Massey to assist his executors in
the direction and management of his estate. The Reverend James Scott,
who married Sarah Brown, and the Reverend John Moncure, who
married Frances Brown, are also referred to in George Mason's will
as being "old and long-tryed friends." [8]

The Moncures, and very likely the Scotts as well, lived a quiet and
remarkably happy life. One of the Moncure children recalled that their
father read aloud every evening, while his wife worked with her needle.
"They were rarely seen asunder. . . . Whenever she could do so, she
accompanied him in his pastoral visits. They walked hand-in-hand and
often rode hand-in-hand, were both uncommonly fond of the cultivation of flowers, fruits, and rare plants. . . . While he wrote or read,
she worked near his table, which always occupied the pleasantest place
in their chamber, where he chose to study, often laying down his pen
to read and comment on an impressive passage." Mason's friendship
with these cousins is a key to his own character, and the picture of the
Overwharton rectory could have been sketched at Gunston Hall a few
years later. George Mason was a frequent guest of the Moncures and
stood as godfather to all of their children. John Mercer stayed with the
Masons on 3 March 1747 at Chopawamsic and went with them to the
christening of John Moncure, Jr., which was performed by the Reverend John Phipps, the tutor of the Mercer children.[9]

John Mercer's old friend Catesby Cocke, clerk of Fairfax County,
lived nearby on the Occoquan; and the Reverend Charles Green of
Truro Parish, that genial Irish physician turned parson who was the
first minister of Pohick Church, made his home nearby. John Barry,
Charles Green's parish clerk, lived at Belmont on the Occoquan.[10]
From his journal we know that Mercer frequently came up the Potomac to see these old friends more often than he visited his nephew,

* Martin Cockburn was the son of Dr. Thomas and Rachel (Moore) Cockburn of
Kingston, Jamaica (Sir Robert Cockburn, *The Records of the Cockburn Family* [London,
1913]).

but there is no doubt that he would have introduced George Mason to them.

Early in June 1748 John Mercer stopped at Ann Mason's house at Chopawamsic and then went on to the Greens by way of the Neabsco Ordinary. On 13 June 1748 he attended the Fairfax elections to support Mason's candidacy for the House of Burgesses. Virginia freeholders were a conservative lot, and they did not rally to the cause of a young man of whom they knew little and who was not yet a resident of the county, though he was one of the larger landowners. They chose instead to send Lawrence Washington and Richard Osborne to Williamsburg as their representatives.[11] Mercer records in his journal that he rode from the polls to Hamilton's Ordinary and then to Charles Green's. Two days after the election he rode from Neabsco Ordinary to Mrs. Mason's and stayed there for two more days. He did not stop at Doegs' Neck even though he rode across it twice, a fair indication that George Mason was not yet in residence at Sycamore Point.

One of the most important events in George Mason's life was his marriage on 4 April 1750 to Ann Eilbeck, the only child of William and Sarah (Edgar) Eilbeck. They were married at the home of her parents in Charles County. Mason's old friend, the Reverend John Moncure, performed the ceremony. George Mason was then twenty-five, and Ann was just sixteen. The *Maryland Gazette* of 2 May 1750, in reporting the marriage, said Ann was "a young lady of distinguishing merits and beauty and a handsome fortune."

The close ties between the Mason and the Eilbeck families dated back to Mason's birth. Their plantations on Mattawoman Creek made them neighbors, and they had been associated in a number of land and tobacco dealings in Charles County. Young George had spent his boyhood and part of his school days on his Maryland plantations and had many close friendships with his Brown and Fowke cousins, whose lands lay near his. One, Richard Brown, son of Gustavus and Frances (Fowke) Brown, had been (according to family tradition) betrothed to Ann Eilbeck before he went to Edinburgh to study for the ministry. While there he met Helen Bailey, fell in love with her, and married her privately in 1750. Upon his ordination they returned to Maryland, where he became known as a heavy preacher and a "strange man." Helen appears not to have been happily married because she returned to her native Scotland, where her second son was born and where it is supposed she died, as the Reverend Richard Brown married twice again.[12]

Ann Eilbeck's father was born in Gardends (now known as Guard End Farm), near Gosforth, Cumberland, England. He was a son of

William and Margaret (Dixon) Eilbeck and was baptized at Gosforth on 4 October 1696.[13] The Eilbecks were an old family of Gosforth and neighboring Irton. William was the third son and sought a career for himself away from the land as a factor with Peter Howe and Joseph Aderton on the Chesapeake. About 1730 he married Sarah, the daughter of John and Johanna Edgar, of Prince Georges County, Maryland. The will of Johanna Edgar probated in 1731 made bequests to her daughter, Sarah Eilbeck, and her son-in-law, William Eilbeck. One bequest excused him for paying charges for "storage" at her plantation, that is, for rental of his store.[14]

William Eilbeck was a member of the county militia with the rank of colonel; by 1745 he was one of the gentlemen justices of Charles County. He was still a justice on 5 May 1755, as he sat with Gustavus Brown and Thomas Stone on the murder case of Jeremiah Chase, who had been poisoned by one William Stratton. He was also a vestryman of Durham Church, where Gerard Fowke had acted in the same capacity.[15] His brother-in-law, John Edgar, Jr., was a vestryman of King Georges Parish.[16] In his will, dated 1736, among other bequests he left "for the use of the Lower Chapel of King George Parish for the use hereafter mentioned £5 Sterling to purchase a communion plate with the inscription, 'the gift of John Edgar for the Lower Chapel of King George Parish' on the outside and on the inside 'Holyness to the Lord.' " He made a further bequest of £5 to purchase a Bible, a Book of Common Prayer, and what other books the Rev. John Fraser should think proper. He made his brother-in-law, William Eilbeck, executor and bequeathed him certain personal property as well as 1,500 pounds of tobacco in Eilbeck's store. His sister, Sarah Eilbeck, received 200 acres of his home plantation, known as Wheeler's Purchase; 100 acres of Long Acre; 100 acres of Dent's Levells; and The Horse Pen, all located in a corner of Prince Georges County that was later restored to Charles County.[17]

By the time of his death in 1764, William Eilbeck had become one of the wealthiest men in Charles County. The inventory made of his estate in 1765 appraised his wealth of slaves and personal property at £2,213. After the charges on the estate and payment of certain debts, his tobacco, tobacco notes, Maryland currency notes, pounds sterling, and debts owed to him came to £2,369.[18] This figure does not include the value of his lands. According to the studies done by Aubrey C. Land, this places him in the upper 2 percent of those planters producing more than 2,000 pounds of tobacco a year, while his personal property places him in the upper 6.5 percent of the wealthy planters.[19] The inventory of the furnishings of his plantation at Mattawoman gives a picture of the comforts a man of means could now enjoy along the shore of the Potomac, which not so long ago had been a wilderness. There were six beds complete with furniture, "viz, bolsters, feather beds, pillows, 2 pr. blankets, 2 pr. sheets, 2 quilts or counterpanes, 4 pillow cases, bedsteads and curtains"; six other beds "with the same furniture, except for curtains"; several clocks and looking glasses; "two large oval tables; four small framed pictures, 'The Seasons'; and four very small Dutch pictures." There were four Kilmarnock carpets for the floors and two small rugs for the bedside, "one old painted floor cloth and two small old linen painted floor cloths." Among the chairs were "one dozen with worsted buttons [they probably were covered in a worsted fabric kept in place by the buttons], ten leather bottomed chairs; 6 chair bottomed chairs, 4 very old leather bottomed ones," as well as a number of flag- and rush-bottomed ones, and two children's chairs. There were glass cannisters with silver tops and a service for twelve of black and white china dishes. There were two tea chests, one of mahogany and one of shagreen with silver cannisters valued at £20; his silver plate was valued at £31 16s.8d. This was as much as many of the lower 40 percent of tobacco planters could hope to obtain for a year's crop. The large number of chairs and beds, dishes and table accouterments listed show that the Eilbecks could, and no doubt did, entertain on a large scale, providing accommodations for guests who came from a distance for parties and visits that sometimes lasted for a number of days. Thus William Eilbeck by his own efforts, though no doubt assisted by an advantageous marriage, had risen from the position of a third son with few or no prospects to that of a man of property and influence in the New World. While his wealth was not on the scale of the Carrolls, Dulanys, or Carters, it was considerable, particularly when it was to be the inheritance of an only child, his daughter, Ann.

Before marriage George Mason had already assumed many of the obligations that were to dominate his life. Upon paying his share, he was admitted to a full partnership in the newly formed Ohio Company on 21 June 1749. At a meeting held on 25 September of that year, Nathaniel Chapman, who was the first treasurer, requested that George Mason succeed him as "Cashier of the Company," a position held by Mason until his death forty-two years later.[20] In August of the same year he was elected to the vestry of Truro Parish along with his uncle, Jeremiah Bronaugh; his neighbor, Daniel McCarty of Cedar Grove, who had just married Sinah Ball; Abraham Barnes; and Robert Boggess.

The scheme of running a lottery at Bellhaven, Fairfax County, to build a church and marketplace was announced on 24 January 1750 and was to be under the direction of George Mason, Nathaniel Chapman, Col. William Fairfax, Col. William Fitzhugh, the Washingtons (Lawrence and Augustine), and John Pagan.[21] Thus when Ann (Eilbeck) Mason assumed the traditional duties of wife, household manager, hostess, and mother, her role was further widened as the wife of a man of public affairs.

As no correspondence describing her life in Virginia has come to light, it is not known to which "dwelling house" in Doegs' Neck she went as a bride, but it was here that she lived for the first eight years of her married life. Nor is it known how she felt about becoming a member of a large family who were closely joined by their interests and responsibilities in their plantations, parishes, and politics. The sixteen-year-old bride must have been a well-balanced, competent young woman to have filled all the duties expected of her in managing a household and conferring with the overseers of the plantation while her husband was absent attending to his civic and public duties as well as his private business affairs. Her sphere of activity was one where individual initiative, executive ability, and other talents were necessary. The food and clothing for her family were prepared under her supervision, and as the hostess of a large plantation the calls on her hospitality for invited and unexpected guests were many. She had to oversee the spinning, weaving, and dyeing of cloth as well as the making of garments for the household, the plantation slaves, and her family. While much of the clothing for the family came from goods purchased abroad, nonetheless many articles of clothing were made from cloth prepared on the estate. Only a few items, such as spices, tea, and coffee, were purchased; all the rest of the food was raised in the gardens, poultry yards, and fields; flour and meals were grown and milled on the plantation; meat came from the herds and flocks; cheeses and butter were prepared from the dairy herds. All these had to be preserved, stored, smoked, or dried for provender against the changing seasons. The actual labor was done by slaves or indentured servants, but the responsibility was hers to see that all was done in a manner that would reflect credit and grace not only in her family's style of living but also in the hospitality offered to guests, invited or unexpected.

Girls from well-to-do families and large plantations were trained by their mothers in the numerous duties of a wife, chatelaine, and hostess. There were a number of books of household advice advertised in the newspaper, such as *The Compleat Housewife, The British Housewife,* and *Mrs. Glasse's Art of Cookery.* However, the standards of service in Virginia were not always as we would like to imagine them, for Chastellux in his *Travels* noted that the service was apt to be crude: "I have frequently seen in Virginia, on visits to gentlemen's houses . . . young negroes from sixteen to twenty years old, with not an article of clothing, but a loose shirt, descending half way down their thighs, waiting at table where were ladies, without any apparent embarrassment on one side, or the slightest attempt at concealment on the other." [22]

The first family gathering at which Ann was present after her marriage was not a happy occasion. It was for the burial of her husband's aunt, Catherine (Mason) Mercer, on 15 June 1750, at Marlborough. The funeral oration was not preached until four weeks later at the parish church. The grieving John Mercer spent much of the following summer at Chopawamsic with his sister-in-law, Ann (Thomson) Mason, but his diary gives no indication that he called upon the newlyweds. John Mercer did not remain a widower long, for on 10 November 1750 he married Ann, the daughter of his great friend Mungo Roy, of Essex County, Virginia.[23] His remarriage did not break his close association with Mrs. Mason, as his diary continues to record visits to her.

Another family marriage took place on 11 April 1751 when Mary Thomson Mason married Samuel Selden of Salvington, near Fredericksburg, Virginia. He was the son of Joseph and Mary (Cary) Selden of Elizabeth City County, Virginia.[24] This event was followed by Thomson Mason's departure for London, where he was to study law at the Middle Temple.

Why the decision was made to send Thomson abroad to study law is not known, but George Mason advanced the money. Thomson's early schooling was similar to that of George; the records of the College of William and Mary do not support the tradition that Thomson attended the college before he studied law in the Middle Temple.[25] He was admitted to the Middle Temple on 14 August 1751, where his grandfather, Stevens Thomson, had studied. His sponsors were Griffith Griffith, milliner of Devereaux Court, and John Richards, merchant, who signed his admission bond on 1 November 1751. There were other young students from the colonies in the Middle Temple while Thomson was there and with whom he must have been acquainted; on their return home they were conspicuous as lawyers before the Revolution. Often their political views were governed by the principles of English law they had studied in the Inns of Court. Two of his compatriots with whom he maintained ties in later life were John Dickinson and John Ambler. In the spring of 1754 Thomson received a letter from his brother asking him to find a well-trained joiner or architect to assist him in the completion of a house that he had already begun. Thomson immediately set about inquiring for such a man among his circle of acquaintances. William Buckland of Oxford was recommended to him. Buckland must have impressed Thomson favorably, for he engaged him on a four-year indenture and immediately advanced him money on his future salary.

Thomson must have supplied his own lodgings for the first three years that he was in London. He was not admitted to chambers until 19 November 1754, upon the death of Zouth Troughton, when Thomson paid £2 for number 6, a ground-floor room with appurtenances. He was called to the bar on 22 November 1754. He surrendered his chambers on 6 August 1755, and his certificate was sent to Virginia on the same day.[26]

Tobacco prices had been on the rise since the 1740s because of the increased trade with France. The war in 1740 between England and France, known as King George's War, had not resulted in any disruption of the trade. Both France and England were unwilling to forego the lucrative revenues that accrued from it.[27] Thus after a decade of prosperity tobacco planters in Maryland and Virginia were in a position in the 1750s to turn their profits toward the improvement and enlargement of their houses. About 1753 George Washington began to transform the comparatively humble Mount Vernon he had inherited into a mansion, while Carter Burwell brought skilled craftsmen from England during the years of 1751–53 to make Carter's Grove one of the handsomest houses on the James River.[28] The tobacco boom of the 1750s placed George Mason in a more financially secure position than he was to achieve at any future time. His standing in the world was growing and so was his family. George Mason V, the first child of Ann and George Mason IV, was born at Dogues' Neck, Monday 30 April 1753. There must have been some concern for his health as he was privately baptized the following week by the Reverend Charles Green of Truro Parish.[29] Aware of the building plans of his neighbor George Washington and other planters, Mason's thoughts turned toward building a house suitable for the needs of his family and his position as a country gentleman. In February 1754 he had all his land on Doegs' Neck surveyed and chose the site for his house.[30]

In April 1754 the French and Indian War broke out, resulting from the conflict between French and English colonists on the North American frontier. It was an extension of the Seven Years War, in which France and England were the major antagonists, and was resolved on the North American continent by the defeat of Montcalm by General James Wolfe at the Heights of Abraham. Governor Dinwiddie, alarmed

by the chain of forts being built by the French from Presque Isle to
the forks of the Ohio, sent George Washington with an advance party
of 150 men to construct a fort at the junction of the Allegheny and
Monongahela rivers to protect the English frontier. He was unsuccessful, for the French had already constructed one there. While the war
interfered with Washington's plans and those who were called to serve,
again the tobacco trade was not disrupted, and business was conducted
"as usual." Life in the Potomac settlements and the rest of Virginia
also went on much as usual. The legislature was concerned with the
first issuance of paper money in Virginia; Mason was appointed a
trustee of Alexandria to succeed Philip Alexander; on 21 June 1754
the vestry of Truro Parish was concerned that William Waite was not
keeping to the letter in the building of the new Pohick Church; and
Mason's plans for building his new house went forward with the signing of the indentures between Thomson Mason and William Buckland.

On 4 August 1755 William Buckland, carpenter and joiner, became
indentured to Thomson Mason, Esquire, of London, to "serve the said
Thomson Mason, his Executors or Assignes in the Plantation of Virginia beyond the Seas, for the Space of Four Years, next ensuing his
arrival in the said Plantation, in the Employment of a Carpenter &
Joiner." Buckland was then not quite twenty-one years of age. He had
been born 14 August 1734 in the city of Oxford; had spent his childhood amid undergraduates and dons; then, at fourteen, had gone to
London as an apprentice to his uncle to learn the craft of a joiner.[31]
His seven-year apprenticeship had run out in April 1755, and the
indenture to Thomson Mason would give him a scope that he could
not hope to achieve in England, where, by the rules of the guild, he
would have to serve many years as a journeyman before he could become his own master.

The year 1755 began with the birth on 13 January of a daughter,
Ann Eilbeck, at the house in Doegs' Neck. Perhaps there were fears for
her survival, for the family Bible records, opposite the entry of her
birth, that she was privately baptized at the age of two weeks by the
Reverend Charles Green.[32] On 14 June 1756 she was formally baptized
in Pohick Church. The weather was somewhat unusual, and 1755 was
known as "the year of the great drought." John Mercer recorded in his
diary on 1 April 1755 that he was windbound at the Masons, but continued to Marlborough the next day "through a very great gust—24
miles." It was probably during this summer that the bricks were laid
for the walls of Mason's new house. Although he was expecting Buckland to come as the architect for the house, the shell of the house was
constructed by a professional builder whose indentured servants, slaves,

and hired skilled craftsman supplied the labor. It was customary to provide for a son's future by apprenticing him to a master builder as well as binding a number of slaves at the same time to learn building trades, who would then be a part of his business when their training was at an end. John Mercer had bound his son, James, in 1753 as an apprentice to William Waite of Alexandria, "a master carpenter and undertaker [builder], who covenanted to instruct him in all the different branches of that business. At the same time I bound four young Negro fellows (which I had given him [James]), to Mr. Waite, who covenanted to instruct each of them in a particular branch. These, I expected, when they were out of their time, would place him in such a situation as might enable him to provide for himself, if I should not be able to do any more for him." [33] At the end of the apprenticeship, young James Mercer and his slave-craftsmen would be able to undertake the building of churches, courthouses, and Tidewater plantation houses.

William Waite may conceivably have been the builder of Gunston Hall. His relationship by marriage and friendship was close; he and Mason had been associated in the building of Pohick Church. There is no surviving record as to who was the master builder, but we do know that George Mason supervised every detail of the construction. "When I built my house," he recalled years later, "I was at some pains to measure all the lime and sand as my mortar was made up and always had two beds, one for out-side work $\frac{2}{3}$ Lime and $\frac{1}{3}$ sand, and the other equal parts of Lime and Sand for inside-work." [34] Not a brick was laid without Mason's knowledge and approval.

In its structure Gunston Hall does not differ essentially from any number of houses in Maryland and Virginia built at the same time. It is a simple one-and-a-half story building of brick laid in Flemish bond with Aquia sandstone trim. Dormer windows provide light and air for the bedrooms under the roof. Two chimneys stand at each gable end, and the corners are strengthened and decorated with quoins of Aquia sandstone. The floor plan is equally simple in its essential design: a central hallway with two large rooms on each side, a stairway leading up to the smaller rooms under the roof, a narrow corridor between the two rooms on the left side of the house leading to the separate kitchen building, a cellar the length of the house, divided for the storage of wines and other comestibles. Its architectural details can be traced to the standard pattern books and could as easily be the work of James Wren and James Parsons, who built Falls Church and Christ Church, Alexandria, in the 1760s as that of Daniel French, Jr., the original "undertaker" of Pohick Church in 1769.[35]

Virginia builders drew their inspiration from pattern books and volumes of architectural plans prepared by English and Continental masters. The builder usually owned a selection of these books and would allow his customer to select overall plans and specific details that he wanted executed. William Buckland and Daniel French, Jr., owned a considerable collection of such works. A planter who commissioned a new house often had such books in his own collection. For instance, in 1748 John Mercer purchased from Sydenham and Hodgson of London a copy of William Salmon's *Palladio Londiniensis, or the London Art of Building* (1734) ; *The City and Country Builder's and Workman's Treasury of Designs* (1741) ; *The Gentlemen's and Builder's Repository or Architecture Displayed,* by Edward Hoppus (1749) ; and an English edition of Andrea Palladio's *Architecture,* all of which he sold to William Brent. The vestry of Truro Parish contracted with William Copein, a mason, to make a baptismal fount for Pohick Church identical with figure 150 in Langley's *City and Country Builder's and Workman's Treasury of Designs.*[36] Mason would have been familiar with these books and could have drawn freely from them in building Gunston Hall.

On 21 August 1755 Mason wrote to George Washington, "I find myself very unwell after my ride from court." [37] Therefore, the arrival of William Buckland to help in the supervision of the building must have been most welcome. If the walls, roof, and main structural and masonry work of Gunston Hall were completed by October 1755, when Buckland arrived, Mason probably paid off the contractors and masons at that time to permit Buckland to assume the work for which he had been engaged, that is, the direction of the carpenters' and joiners' work on the house. At the end of his indenture period in 1759, George Mason unqualifiedly recommended him: "having behaved very faithfully in my Service I can with great Justice recommend him to any Gentleman that may have occasion to employ him, as an honest sober diligent Man, & I think a complete Master of the Carpenter's and Joiner's Business both in Theory & Practice." Only William Buckland is remembered of those who built Gunston Hall. If he had little to do with the external construction, he certainly had a free hand in the carving and design of the interior. If the external lines of the building could be the work of any contemporary builder, the interior betrays the hand of a master. Following the completion of Gunston Hall, there was considerable work remaining to complete the farm buildings. Among Buckland's assistants was a journeyman, James Brent, whom he left behind to complete the outbuildings. Brent was paid for more than a year's work on the Gunston Hall plantation for 1759–60.[38]

It is unfortunate that none of James Brent's outbuildings have survived, because the historian Robert Beverley tells us that the "drudgeries of cooking, washing, dairies, etc." were performed in outside offices in order to keep the mansion "more cool and sweet." [39] It was the number of these outbuildings that made the plantations of persons of importance seem like a village.[40] Virginia gentlemen lived in the center of a farmyard, like good husbandmen everywhere. The cackle of poultry, the lowing of cattle, the shouts of servant boys and stable hands, the steady babble of the kitchen staff—these formed the background noises of Gunston Hall from early morning until late at night. John Mason (1766–1849) recalled in his later years that in his youth

to the west of the main building were first the schoolhouse, and then at a little distance, masked by a row of large English walnut trees, were the stables. To the east was a high paled yard, adjoining the house, into which opened an outer door from the private front, within, or connected with which yard, were the kitchen, well, poultry houses, and other domestic arrangements; and beyond it on the same side, were the corn house and granary, servants houses (in those days called Negro quarters) hay yard and cattle pens, all of which were masked by rows of large cherry and mulberry trees. And adjoining the enclosed grounds on which stood the mansion and all these appendages on the eastern side was an extensive pasture for stock of all kinds running down to the river, through which led the road to the Landing, emphatically so called, where all persons or things water borne, were landed or taken off, and were kept the boats, pettiaugers and canoes of which there were always several for business transportation, fishing and hunting belonging to the establishment. Farther north and on the same side was an extensive orchard of fine fruit trees of a variety of kinds. Beyond this was a small and highly fenced pasture devoted to a single brood horse. The occupant in my early days was named Vulcan, of the best stock in the country and a direct descendant of the celebrated Old Janus. The west side of the lawn or enclosed grounds was skirted by a wood, just far enough within which to be out of sight, was a little village called Log-Town, so called because most of the houses were built of hewn pine logs. Here lived several families of the slaves serving about the mansion house; among them were my father's body-servant James, a mulatto man and his family, and those of several negro carpenters.[41]

Mason's new house was assuredly a Virginia gentleman's residence. He chose for it a name that would reflect its character. Doegs' Neck might do well for a tobacco farm, but the new house should recall his proud ancestry and link his home on the Potomac to the manor houses in old England. He called it Gunston Hall. His Fowke cousins, Gerard and Elizabeth (Dinwiddie) Fowke, had earlier preserved that same link to their English heritage, and Frances (Fowke) Brown had had carved on her tomb that her ancestors were of the family of Gunston Hall in Staffordshire, England.[42] These were closer memories than those of his Thomson ancestors at Hollin Hall, Yorkshire, or the Mason connections with Pershore. Thereafter he would be Col. George Mason of Gunston Hall.

During the four years the house was being built there was happiness and sorrow in the Mason family. A second son, William, was born 16 April 1756. Two months later he and his older brother, George, and his sister, Ann Eilbeck, were baptized publicly at Pohick Church by the Reverend Charles Green. Thomson Mason, having returned from his studies in England, was one of the godfathers and John Moncure, the other. The godmothers were Sarah (Edgar) Eilbeck and Margaret Green, the wife of the rector. Little William died when he was only fifteen months old and was buried in the family burying ground at Newtown. Another son was born on 22 October 1757; he too was named William. He was baptized at home by the Reverend James Scott, who was visiting the Masons at the time. Another death in the family came on 4 January 1757 with that of Mary Thomson (Mason) Selden; George had gone to Chopawamsic on the third to bid her farewell. Thomson was made the guardian of her two children.[43]

The year 1759 opened with an event of considerable interest to the Masons. Their friend and neighbor George Washington was married on 6 January to Martha (Dandridge) Custis, whose first husband, Col. Daniel Parke Custis, had been an intimate friend of John Mercer. Mercer was her attorney.[44] Early in that year Ann and George must have moved into their handsome new house as the birth of their son Thomson is the first recorded in the family Bible as taking place at "Gunston Hall on March 4, 1759." The next entry is of the birth of a daughter, "Sarah Mason born on the 11th of December 1760, abt. 9 o'clock at night at Gunston Hall, and privately baptized by the Revd. Mr. Charles Green." She was named for her maternal grandmother, Sarah Eilbeck, who bequeathed her namesake "my gold watch and my emerald ring, set round with sparks." [45] Mary Thomson Mason's birth followed there on 27 January 1762. Four years later a son, John, was born on 4 April 1766 at Mattawoman, Charles County, while Ann Mason was visiting her widowed mother, Sarah (Edgar) Eilbeck. Two years later Elizabeth was born at Gunston Hall on 19 April 1768 and baptized by the Reverend Lee Massey. Martin Cockburn was "standing Godfather," Mrs. Cockburn and Elizabeth Bronaugh were godmothers. Next in the Bible was recorded another son: "Thomas Mason was born on Tuesday the 1st Day of May 1770 about two o'clock in the After-

noon at Gunston Hall and was baptized by the Revd. Mr. Lee Massey,
Mr. Martin Cockburn & Capt. John Lee standing God Fathers & Mrs.
Mary Massey & Mrs. Ann Cockburn God Mothers." The Capt. John
Lee who stood as godfather was the John Lee of Chopawamsic and the
uncle of Hancock Lee, who was a surveyor for the Ohio Company.[46] As
the sponsors in baptism for George Mason's children were always members of his family, the choice of Captain Lee as a godfather attests to
the high regard that George Mason must have felt for him.

These years were happy ones. The improvement of the grounds of
the plantation, experiments in agriculture, the laying out of orchards
and the husbanding of game, seeing to the education of their children,
the exchange of hospitality with friends and neighbors made a busy
and happy life at Gunston Hall. These were the years that made a close
and happy marriage.

The diaries of George Washington mention a number of examples
of improved nursery stock that George Mason sent to Mount Vernon.
In 1760 Washington received several kinds of cherries and plums, a
dozen Spanish pears, and a dozen butter pears from Gunston Hall. In
1761 Mason sent his neighbor some black pears of Worcester, winter
boon cherries, summer boon cherries, and early (June) pears. In 1762
Washington noted receiving bergamy pears and Newtown pippin apples from Mason, who had originally obtained them from James Blair
of Williamsburg. In 1764 he gave Washington some bullock heart
cherries, early May cherries, large Duke cherries, and some magnum
bonum plums. Similar gifts are recorded in 1765.[47]

The British Government had long advocated the growing of grapes
for wine making in an endeavor to cut down the importation of wine
into British colonies. Many experiments had been made. The most successful was that of some Huguenots settled for that purpose by the British government in South Carolina.[48] Perhaps the success of this group
encouraged Mason to patronize several experiments in viticulture, one
of which was headed by Maurice Pound from the Rhineland, who settled in Colchester in 1756. What led Pound to settle at Colchester is
not certain. The climate was thought to be suitable, and undoubtedly
some of the Scottish and Irish factors along the Potomac were interested in the venture, having numerous contacts with the Rhine through
their agents in Rotterdam. There is correspondence between John
Pagan of Glasgow and Mason about arranging passage for a group of
German Protestants. They were not redemptioners or indentured servants, for they had a fair amount of capital invested in their venture.
They brought with them vine cuttings and vine crowns from the

famous vineyards along the Rhine and the Moselle rivers. Mason gave them considerable support, and in October 1759 he circulated an appeal for funds to help the infant industry weather the bad times:

Maurice Pound a native of Germany having settled at Colchester in the said County about three years since on two lotts which he purchased (one of which he has improved according to law) and planted a vineyard on them; during which time he has lived at his own expense without any profit from his vineyard having been much retarded in his undertaking by these two last dry summers and having one of his lotts yet to save by building the legal improvements; with a wine press & other conveniences, proposes to any gentlemen who are desirous to help him & encourage and promote an undertaking likely to be so useful & beneficial to this colony to oblige himself to improve his other lott, & to mortgage both the said lotts to any gentlemen who will advance him one hundred pounds current money the interest of which he proposes to pay yearly & the principal sum advanced within five years, and the whole time to prosecute with industry all measures possible to bring his vineyard to perfection (a thing not to be done at once) of which he has a most encouraging prospect if seasons will permit.

N.B. the lotts to be mortgaged to any one or more of the subscribers in trust for all. —I have known Maurice Pound ever since he lived in Colchester he has the character of a very honest industrious man. I have been frequently in his vineyard upon which he has expended an infinite deal of labour, & I really believe if our soil & Climate is capable of producing good wine that he will with proper encouragement bring it to perfection tho' I don't think less than £150 will do—as I am sensible that his present circumstances are too low to carry on this undertaking without assistance & from my opinion of the integrity and capacity of the man I will advance him ten pounds upon the above mentioned terms, & I will readily join with other subscribers in making up whatever sum they shall judge necessary for the purpose.[49]

The circular drew support from fellow Virginians, and the sum was fully subscribed. Thomson Mason advanced £20, while Charles Broadwater, Daniel French, Jr., George William Fairfax, Spencer Grayson, Benjamin Grayson, and George Washington brought the full subscription up to £118 Virginia currency. Unfortunately, Pound was unable to produce Virginia wines at a profit, for in 1772 George Washington wrote off as a bad debt the £15 he had advanced.[50]

The failure of the Colchester colony did not deter other Virginians from seeking to emulate its attempt to make native wine from imported vines grafted on native stock. The drift toward home industry and self-sufficiency gave a further stimulus to a project that aimed at independence from a one-crop economy. George William Fairfax helped Frederick Zimmerman, one of this group, to obtain land in the Shenandoah Valley when the experiment along the Potomac proved a failure. Later Pound also settled in the Shenandoah Valley in Augusta County.[51] Andrew Estave had some success with French vine stocks as early as 1770 and succeeded in obtaining official backing from the Assembly for his experiments.[52] A network of enthusiasts soon sprang up across the Old Dominion. As in most of the projects that dealt with improving nursery stock, the Quakers led the way. Robert Pleasants and Edward Stabler were soon passing vine cuttings, grafts, and slips to Robert Bolling, along with some antislavery propaganda. Col. Robert Bolling of Chellowe appealed in 1772 to the members of the House of Burgesses to foster a native wine industry by helping experienced vintners from France and Italy settle in the Old Dominion:

> Think, you hear the run-burnt livers.
> all around the land of rivers,
> Cry, Give wine! Exert your cunning;
> You'll soon set the vats a-running.
> that you're wise and great—we know it
> But to future ages show it.[53]

Bolling was the chief missionary of the winegrowers. In 1773 he filled the *Virginia Gazette* with little essays on the utility and method of vine culture during the session of the Assembly and immediately thereafter.[54] Tobacco had fallen to eighteen shillings Virginia currency on the James River and as low as sixteen shillings eightpence and fourteen shillings in some other parts of Virginia. Serious hearings were given to schemes to obtain vine cuttings from the different European powers through an official request by the British government and to import families of Italian wine makers.

Philip Mazzei, a brilliant Italian physician, took to London a plan for growing wine grapes in America and then migrated to Virginia. He received a good deal of encouragement from George Mason of Gunston Hall. By the summer of 1774 he had received various kinds of nursery stock and seeds from Italy and had begun an experimental farm in Albemarle County. Mason and others took slips from him for their gardens. In the early spring of 1774 Mazzei circulated "proposals for forming a Company or partnership, for the Purpose of raising and making wine, oil agruminous plants and silk." Shares in the enterprise were sold for £50 each. Mason subscribed for one share. Robert Pleasants also took one share "on condition that he may withdraw his subscription in case, that any slaves should be purchased on account of the Company." Thomas Jefferson was also a shareholder and his accounts with "the Wine company" show that it continued to operate through 1778.[55]

Mazzei was able to report considerable success in 1775, and he believed Bolling's vines would be ready for wine making in 1776. Andrew Estave had taken apprentices to the wine making business in 1773, and both Estave and Mazzei were meeting with considerable success in their ventures. A letter from Mazzei to Col. John Page in 1778 was intended to be passed on to Mason, Bland, and others "actuated by the same principles as you are" with regard to the vineyard experiment.[56] Mazzei had put in Spanish and Portuguese vines in 1776. These had all been killed by frost, but his Italian vines survived, full of promise.

Mason took personal interest and pride in the gardens of his estate, and on the land approach to the main house, he planted a long row of cherry trees, arranged so symmetrically that they created the optical illusion of a single tree on either side of the road. Mason was proud of this carefully planned trompe l'oeil and liked to watch the reaction of his visitors when they discovered the clever illusion. On the river side of the mansion he planted a row of boxwood (still a feature of the Gunston Hall gardens), set out beds of flowers, and made a large kitchen garden. The land sloped away from the "garden falls" and gave way to woods and wild lands enclosed as a fenced deer park. Here Mason developed a herd of native deer that he and his friends thinned out with a day's hunting when necessary. But only when necessary. Mason was much concerned with the protection of the wild deer, and in a letter to Alexander Henderson he declared himself to be fully prepared to punish the offenders even though they might be acquaintances, such as Robert Boggess. "There has been such a shameful Havock made of the Deer during this Snow, when the poor creatures cou'd not get out of any Body's way, that I hope the Magistrates & Gentlemen of the County will think it their Duty to make an Example of the Offenders; and as I understand many of them intend to avoid half the Penalty by informing against each other, I now make [an] Information to you against such Offenders as have come to my Knowledge." [57] George Washington records in his diary on 28 November 1771 that he "set off before sunrise with John Custis for Colo. Mason's and went adriving in his neck after breakfast. Two deer killed." Although they went out with Colonel Mason the next day, they killed nothing, but Washington remained at Gunston Hall. On the twenty-ninth the two friends went together to a vestry meeting at Pohick Church. These were the years that Mason creatively developed Gunston Hall and entertained with widespread hospitality.

The depression of the 1760s, that followed the inflated tobacco economy of the fifties caused plantation owners to turn to crops other than tobacco, and wheat began to make its appearance in these years. George Washington first began to experiment with wheat and other grain crops at Mount Vernon in 1760, and thereafter wheat became an important part of his farm income. Advertisements for land in the vicinity of Gunston Hall frequently referred to the possibility of raising wheat. James Mercer, a cousin, offered two tracts of land, one on Pohick Run and another on Four Mile Run, noting that "the soil of both is stiff and well suited to wheat." George Mason acted as Mercer's agent in selling this particular property.[58]

George Mason, too, had become engaged in the wheat trade, as the account books of Hooe and Stone and of Jenifer and Hooe include many references to his sales of wheat to these two firms. In 1775, for instance, the accounts show that Colonel Mason delivered 1,064 bushels of wheat on 30 January for which he received £266. On 13 February he sold 864 bushels for £216; two lots of 260 bushels and 628.5 bushels brought £222 on 4 March 1775. On 26 April 1775 George Mason V of Lexington sold 1,435 bushels of wheat at four shillings the bushel for a total price of £358 12s. 6d. Since George Mason V was then farming some one thousand acres on Doegs' Neck, it is clear that the greater part of the future Lexington plantation must have been in wheat in 1774 and very likely the home plantation at Gunston Hall as well. A further account of Jenifer and Hooe with George Mason V included the purchase of 3,312 bushels of wheat in May 1775 for five shillings the bushel and 584 barrels of corn in September 1775 at eleven shillings the barrel.[59]

It is as impossible to reconstruct Colonel Mason's wheat crops from his sales to a single outlet as it is to reconstruct his tobacco crops from his accounts with one or more tobacco factors. The mere fact, however, that he and George Mason V sold 6,128.5 bushels of wheat and 584 barrels of corn to Jenifer and Hooe within a single growing season is sufficient indication that Mason was no longer wholly dependent on tobacco. In this respect, the squire of Gunston Hall acted like many of his neighbors on the upper Potomac who turned marginal tobacco lands into grain fields in the agricultural depression of the 1760s. Alexandria and Georgetown became early centers of the grain and flour trade as they were natural outlets for Frederick County, Maryland, the settlements in Loudoun County, and beyond. John Ballendine and Benjamin Grayson formed a partnership in 1762 to erect merchant mills at the falls of the Occoquan for "the manufacturing of wheat and baking of bread." Some of the wheat and flour from the

upper Potomac went directly to the West Indies, but the South Potomac district never became the great breadbasket of the West Indies
as did the country around Norfolk and the James River in the same
period. John Mason's recollections bear this out:

> In different parts of this tract and detached from each other, my father
> worked four plantations with his own slaves, each under an overseer; and
> containing four or five hundred acres of open land. The crops were prin-
> cipally Indian corn and tobacco; the corn for the support of the plantations
> and the home house, and the tobacco for sale. There was but little small
> grain made in that part of the country in those days. He had also another
> plantation worked in the same manner, on an estate he had in Charles
> County, Maryland, on the Potomac about twenty miles lower down, at a
> place called Stump Neck.[60]

As early as 1768 Mason was experimenting with sheep raising. Perhaps he was encouraged in this undertaking because he received a gift
of a ram and some ewes from his cousin, William Fitzhugh of Rousby
Hall, Calvert County, Maryland, in July of that year.[61] The stock, hogs,
cattle, sheep, and possibly horses, were turned into the woods to find
their own provender, an almost universal custom on American farms
at the time. Again to quote John Mason:

> The isthumus on the northern boundary is narrow and the whole estate
> was kept completely enclosed by a fence on that side of about one mile
> running from the head of Holt's to the margin of Pohick Creek. This fence
> was maintained with great care and in good repair in my father's time, in
> order to secure to his own stock the exclusive range within it, and made of
> uncommon height, to keep in the native deer which had been preserved
> there in abundance from the first settlement of the country and indeed are
> yet there in considerable numbers. The land south of the heights and com-
> prising more than nine tenths of the estate was a uniform level elevated
> some twenty feet above the surface of the river, with the exception of one
> extensive marsh and three or four water courses, which were accompanied
> by some ravines and undulations of minor character . . . and about two
> thirds of it were yet clothed with the primitive wood.[62]

The whole property contained just under 5,000 acres with apparently
some 1,800 acres under cultivation.

While John Mason's recollections (written in 1832) are explicit that
during his boyhood tobacco was the main cash crop at Gunston Hall
and that comparatively little wheat was raised on the upper Potomac
at that time, George Mason was only to some extent dependent on the
price of tobacco on the world market to sustain his prosperity. Like
his father and mother before him, he leased land to small farmers,
receiving from sixty to seventy-five shillings annual rent of one of his

farms in the early 1760s. Even though Mason was concerned about the dangers inherent in the tobacco economy and advised his overseers to diversify his crops, he was never completely dependent on the one-crop economy of the Northern Neck. His inheritance had come from wise investments in land, and it became an obsession with him to leave legacies of land to all his children, as is borne out by the land grants he took up in Kentucky. The tranquility of these years was broken by the death of two women he was very fond of, his aunt, Simpha Bronaugh, at Gunston Hall, on 22 November 1761, and his mother, following a long illness at Chopawamsic on 13 November 1762.[63] With the death of his mother Thomson Mason came into his inheritance.

During the 1758–59 session of the House of Burgesses, where both he and George were serving their initial term, he had married Mary King Barnes of Saint Marys County, Maryland; and at the end of the session he had taken up residence in Maryland, on her father's plantation.[64] Though their first incursion into Virginia politics was a brief one (George Mason did not stand for reelection in 1761), it was of inestimable value to their future careers.[65] It gave them a first-hand experience in the political realities of the Old Dominion and brought them into close association with a distinguished and able group of men.* These men were invariably drawn from among the wealthiest in their counties and had a laudable record of public service in local government behind them. Men such as Col. Richard Bland of Prince George County; George Wythe, representative of the College of William and Mary; Lewis Burwell and Benjamin Waller of James City County; Dudley Digges of York County; and Landon Carter of Richmond County were some of the members of this period. Francis Lightfoot Lee of Loudoun County; Henry Lee of Leesylvania, member for Prince William County; and Richard Henry Lee of Westmoreland County were also serving their first terms in the House of Burgesses.[66] Both George and Thomson behaved with the modesty expected of newly elected members and did not startle their colleagues with bursts of eloquence on the burning issues before the House. They did their duty quietly and unobtrusively, served on minor committees, and presented the petitions and grievances of their own constituents in northern Virginia.

In 1758 the Virginia Assembly was primarily concerned with the

---

* The enthusiastic recognition by the Virginia burgesses of the restoration of Charles II to the throne caused him to grant the colony dominion status. The burgesses adopted the name "Old Dominion," combining their new status with the fact that Virginia was the oldest colony as well as the most loyal of the Stuart settlements (*Dictionary of American History*, ed. James Truslow Adams).

fate of the second Two Penny Act, introduced by Richard Bland, and with the decision whether to employ their own agent in London to defend their measures before the British authorities. The agent they selected was to correspond regularly with a committee composed of members of the Council and the House of Burgesses. The Virginians directed their agent to explain the issue of the additional paper money they had authorized and the Two Penny Act as necessities brought on by the war with the French. He was also to attempt to stave off an increased duty on tobacco, but he was unsuccessful in getting Parliament to understand his clients' case. The Two Penny Act was disallowed in August 1759; the duty on tobacco was increased; and the inflationary issues of paper money in Virginia paved the way for the Currency Act of 1764. Though their efforts were unsuccessful in getting parliamentary approval for the decisions they had made, the experience left a marked effect on the thinking of the House of Burgesses. They had acted independent of London on more than one occasion, and they had formed a Committee of Correspondence that would continue to direct the attention of the London authorities to the rights of Virginia.[67]

The two Masons were on the periphery of these maneuvers. Their initiation into public service followed the usual committee routine. George and Thomson were both appointed to a committee of the House of Burgesses on 19 September 1758 that was concerned with making provision for additional militia to protect the exposed Virginia frontiers. Thomson served on a committee appointed to investigate the case of Capt. John Smith, who had been cashiered after the failure of the joint Cherokee-Virginia expedition against the Shawnees in 1756; on another, concerned with legislation to create new towns in Virginia, particularly with the organization of Winchester in Frederick County; and as a committee of one to bring in a bill for the killing of crows and squirrels [68]—a remarkable variety of assignments to test the abilities of a neophyte!

George took a more active part in the Assembly's deliberations in its February 1759 session. On 6 March he was named to the powerful Committee of Privileges and Elections, and two days later he was put on the larger and somewhat busier Committee of Propositions and Grievances, which contained about a half of the members in attendance in each session of the Assembly and dealt mostly with local matters. He reported on various petitions for the dissolution of vestries, the licensing of ferries, and the establishment of additional warehouses for the inspection of tobacco. His constituents in Fairfax County presented a petition against the appropriation of 22,000 pounds of tobacco to be raised by the county authorities to build a wharf at Alexandria. He and his committee agreed that the town trustees should be authorized to charge wharfage fees and thus repay the county all of the money appropriated.[69]

He also took the lead in the proposals for the division of Prince William County. Petitions and counterpetitions from Fairfax, Loudoun, and Prince William freeholders asked for a division of the back settlements among those counties, an approach favored by the Fairfax family. George Mason succeeded in overcoming this opposition, and in March 1759 the new county of Fauquier was created by the Assembly. To win his point, he had formed an alliance with certain burgesses from counties on the James River and with the Lee family interests. This latter connection was an alliance fraught with importance for the future. It had its roots in the formation of the Ohio Company under the leadership of Thomas Lee, which later entered into competition with the Loyal Company under the direction of the Randolphs. This competition led to the development of the political factions of the Robinson-Randolph interests versus those of the Patrick Henry–Richard Henry Lee group. In the future, Mason and Richard Henry Lee would work closely together in framing some of the most significant legislation passed in Virginia in the next two decades.[70] Opposition from the Fairfax interest may have influenced George Mason's decision not to stand for reelection in 1761.

Thomson Mason's marriage to Mary King Barnes, the daughter of Col. Abraham Barnes, and consequent removal to Maryland turned him from political interests toward a business and legal career. He acted as agent for his father-in-law's commercial interests and succeeded him as manager of the Leonard-Town, Maryland, horse races.[71] He acted as counsel for William Clifton of Maryland, who had tried to withdraw from an agreement he had made with George Washington to sell some land. Feelings ran high on both sides, and what Washington was pleased to call the "Clifton affair" was finally settled at Mount Vernon on 28 March 1760.[72] Thomson's reputation as a successful lawyer becoming well known, he was admitted to the Provincial Court of Maryland during the April term of 1762.[73]

Col. Abraham Barnes had recognized the opportunities opened in Maryland by the passage of the Virginia legislature of regulatory acts in regard to trash tobacco, and in the 1740s he had established himself as a tobacco merchant in Saint Marys County. He had acquired 1,096 acres of land near Leonard-Town in 1744 and had represented the county in the Maryland Assembly from 1745 to 1754. When the Maryland Assembly passed its first Tobacco Inspection Act of 1747, the warehouse of Colonel Barnes near Leonard-town became one of the official inspection warehouses. He was a man of substance in his county: a vestryman of Saint Andrews Parish; a justice of the peace; and a man whose good taste and refinement were reflected in his home, Tudor Hall, still one of the landmarks of southern Maryland. Influential beyond these parochial limits, Colonel Barnes represented Maryland at the Albany Congress in 1754. His business connections with London and Liverpool were substantial. He was a large-scale slave trader during the 1750s and shipped tobacco in these years to the Gildarts of Liverpool. After 1758 he took his son-in-law, Thomson Mason, into partnership, and when he sailed for England in 1761, he left Mason as his representative in America.[74]

Like many other Chesapeake merchants, Colonel Barnes relied on family ties as the most trustworthy kind of partnership. His English partner, John Morton Jordan of London, had married Elinor, daughter of his brother, Col. Richard Barnes, of Richmond County. During the winter of 1761–62, Barnes and Jordan made plans for a very extensive operation in the Chesapeake tobacco trade. Jordan wrote to Robert Carter of Nomini: "I have now entered into Partnership with Colonel [Abraham] Barnes, late of Maryland, and the business of the future will be carried on in our joint Names. We shall have a ship called the *Brunswick* load in James River, another in York [River] called the *Triton*. We have also a ship called the *Brittania* by way of Quebec for Potomack." Jordan and Barnes had another significant association: Jordan was the business agent for Lord Baltimore and later for the province of Maryland. He urged the appointment of Colonel Barnes as receiver general of the province of Maryland in 1763. The governor and the proprietor agreed that Barnes was a man of the highest character and strictest probity, but considerations of practical politics overruled his appointment.[75]

Col. Abraham Barnes considered remaining in England as his two sons, John and Richard, had yet to be provided with adequate means, and he cast about for a prospect of establishing them in business. In 1764 he advanced a considerable sum to his elder son to form the partnership of Barnes and Ridgate to engage in the tobacco trade on the Potomac and Patuxent rivers; they formed an agreement with Osgood Hanbury of London to that effect.[76]

Thomson Mason, acting as the American agent for Barnes, had some interest in these ventures during the 1760s. He engaged in slave trading in this period and had the slaves judged for their ages by the vestry of Saint Andrews Church. He frequently advertised the sale of slaves in the *Maryland Gazette:*

Just imported from the Rivers Gambia and Senegal, on the Coast of Africa, a Cargo of Choice, Healthy Likely Slaves . . . To be sold at his house, near St. Mary's Court House . . . til all are sold.

To be sold Baltimore-Town, a choice Parcel of Slaves . . . most of which Slaves had the Smallpox in their own Country.[77]

To supplement his fees as a lawyer for pleading causes and drawing up caveats, he also engaged in commerce. In 1761 he advertised that the snow *Brent* (a square-rigged brig), plantation-built, 170 tons, mounting seven carriage guns would be sold at auction at the Saint Marys Courthouse in Leonard-town. He also advised that he had a few pipes of choice Madeira for sale. He gave notice to the public in October 1761 that the "Ship Upton, Samuel Pemberton, Master, a letter of marque, carrying seventeen carriage guns, six and four pounders, and four cohorns which will throw six pound shot, now lying in Briton's Bay, will take in tobacco at ten pounds sterling per ton, consigned to James Gildart, Esq., Merchant in Liverpool." In June 1764 he advertised "a large Quantity of Tar and Turpentine" and some few barrels of pork for sale at Leonard-town.[78]

After the death of his mother in 1762, Thomson began to make plans to take up his Virginia inheritance, but it took him some time to close out his Maryland interests. On 27 September 1764 he inserted an advertisement in the *Maryland Gazette:*

For Sale. The Sloop *Nancy* now lying in the Mouth of Chappawamsick Creek, Potomac River, Virginia built, a Prime Sailer, four years old, tolerably well found for Sea, her Rigging half worn, will carry about 3000 Bushels of Grain, or sixty Hogsheads of Tobacco below Deck. Also, a Quantity of Carolina Tar, Pitch, and Rozin, to be sold at the same time. Any person inclinable to purchase may know the terms by applying to the Subscriber at any Time during the Provincial Court, at Mr. Woodward's in Annapolis, and afterwards at his house in Stafford County, Virginia, or to Colonel Abraham Barnes in St. Mary's County.

/S/ Thomson Mason

Another advertisement in the same paper indicated that he planned to cultivate tobacco and hemp as his major crops: "A Person who understands making Hemp; also an Overseer accustomed to make bright Tobacco; each capable of managing ten or twelve hands, who can come well Recommended, will meet with Encouragement, by applying to the Subscriber at any Time during the Provincial Court, at Mr. Woodward's in Annapolis, and afterwards at his house in Stafford County, Virginia. /S/ Thomson Mason." It is of interest that he specified the ability to grow bright tobacco—no trash crop for him.

During this period Thomson's guardianship of his sister's two children involved him in a number of problems. Interesting documents exist of a summons issued to "Thomson Mason of Maryland from Charles Binns, Clerk of the Court, Loudoun County, Virginia, 14 May 1763, for not entering with the Court the quantity of land held by him for the Selden orphans." [79] In 1768 he advertised in the *Virginia Gazette* that Peter Deadfoot, a mulatto slave belonging to Samuel Selden, Jr., had run away. Thomson must have thought highly of the runaway as the advertisement is long and quite specific in describing his qualifications: "In short he is so ingenious a fellow, that he can turn his hand to any thing; he has a great share of pride, though he is very obliging, is extremely fond of dress; and though his holiday clothes were taken from him, when he first attempted to get off, yet, as he has probably passed for a freeman, I make no doubt he has supplied himself with others as such a fellow would readily get employment." [80] Also, in his role of guardian, on 14 May 1769 Thomson paid Martin Cockburn board for Samuel Selden and his own son Stevens Thomson Mason, who were attending classes with their cousins at Gunston Hall.[81]

From 1764 to 1771 Thomson and Mary (Barnes) Mason made their home at Chopawamsic. His advertisement in the *Maryland Gazette* on 1 May 1766 relative to the return of a convict servant named Robin Clarke, whom he had employed as groom and gardener, is further indication he had removed to Virginia by that date, for Clarke had to be returned to his house in Stafford County; the advertisement also attests to his use of convict labor. The petition William Fitzhugh presented to the House of Burgesses on 7 November 1766 complaining of undue election and the return of Thomson Mason to serve as burgess of Stafford County (which he later withdrew) would imply that he was unaware of Thomson's removal from Maryland.[82] Thomson was the last Mason to hold judicial or political office in both the sister colonies of Virginia and Maryland.

During the 1766 session of the Virginia Assembly, Thomson Mason brought in legislation regarding the repeal of the Stamp Act and introduced a bill to separate the office of treasurer and speaker, an office long held by the then late John Robinson to the detriment of Virginia's best interests. He, together with Patrick Henry and Richard Henry Lee, was appointed to a committee to inquire into some of Robinson's suspicious bonds. Later Thomson Mason, Patrick Henry, and George Wythe were authorized to institute suits against Robinson's executors to try to reclaim some of the public funds Robinson had embezzled.

The revelation that the treasurer of Virginia had defrauded the public of nearly £100,000 left the colony thunderstruck. From time to time, the House of Burgesses had called in paper currency and ordered the notes burned. Robinson had loaned these notes to friends and associates with promissory notes as collateral. The recall of these canceled treasury notes by the officials at Williamsburg threatened to plunge Virginia into economic disaster. This scandal overshadowed the deliberations of the House of Burgesses during Thomson Mason's most active years as a member for Stafford County. In the 1767 session he worked on a bill for reforming the procedure of the courts and on legislation having to do with the militia, land transfers, and cattle. He served on a commission under John Blair to inquire into the need for new currency legislation, and a scheme for emitting paper money was reported on the last day of the 1767 session.[83]

He was now acknowledged as a man of ability in a period of economic and political tension and entered upon a career as spokesman for the most revolutionary elements in Virginia. His theories of resistance were tempered, however, by his knowledge of English common law taught him in the Temple.[84] While he gained eminence at the bar and a reputation for farsighted political vision, he was not immune from the effect of financial panic in Virginia. In November and December 1769 he advertised to be sold at Hollingsworth, his plantation near Leesburg, for ready money, a lot of slaves, some of whom were sawyers and coopers, and several valuable blooded horses. Also that December Thomson sold some land at auction, for ready money, in the town of Shockoe (Richmond).[85] In 1770 he advertised for the payment of long overdue legal fees and announced that he would be unable to give legal advice to his clients except on a cash basis:

And that no person may be deceived, they will please to observe that it is my determined resolution to put every such bond in suit which is not discharged within one month after it becomes payable. Every person who favours me with their business upon the above terms will meet with my most grateful acknowledgments, and may depend upon the exertion of my upmost abilities to serve them. With regard to those who, at the time they pretended to be my friends, could cooly sit still and see me reduced to the necessity of selling my slaves to a very great disadvantage, and yet withhold the small sums due to me, which if paid would have removed that necessity, I leave it to their own hearts to determine whether they deserve any farther indulgence.[86]

He was obliged to employ a collector to dun some of his former clients, but three years later Thomson must have questioned the man's honesty, for he placed the following notice in the paper: "I find it necessary to give this public notice, that Jasper Mauduit Gidley was dismissed from being my collector in September last, and that no receipts given by the said Gidley for money on my account, since that time, will be allowed by me." [87]

Upon leaving Maryland to take up his permanent residence in Virginia, Thomson had enlarged his inherited holdings in Loudoun County by purchase of the estate known as Raspberry Plain from Aenas Campbell. By a strange coincidence Campbell had also come from Saint Marys County in 1754 and had become the first sheriff of Loudoun County as well as serving as one of the original trustees of Leesburg with Philip Ludwell, Francis Lightfoot Lee, Thomson Mason, and others.[88] It is thought that Thomson either enlarged the existing house or built a new one about 1771. It was planned as a large handsome house, one befitting a rising young attorney with four children: Stevens Thomson, born in Stafford County in 1760; Abraham Barnes Thomson, born in Saint Marys County in 1761; John Thomson, born at Chopawamsic on 15 March 1765; and Ann Thomson, who was born there 22 February 1769. Before the house was completed, his wife died on 21 October 1771 at the home of the Reverend James Scott while returning from a visit to her father. As was the custom of the times, her eulogy in the *Virginia Gazette* was long and sentimental. It concluded, "Every one of our Readers who had the Pleasure of her Acquaintance will, with sympathizing tears, acknowledge all those amiable characters were united in Mrs. Mary Mason, the Lady of Thomson Mason of Loudon County, Esq." [89] She was buried in the family graveyard at Gunston Hall.

Thomson and his children moved into Raspberry Plain, and while recovering from his wife's death, he undertook to effect some cures of patients suffering from pleurisy. He published his remedy in the *Virginia Gazette*. The wonder is that any person could have survived the treatment, which even in its day must have been considered drastic. Two years later the same newspaper published an article signed "Cleomenes," which refuted the cure.[90] A preoccupation with illness seems to have been almost a family trait, although it could also be argued that death was so large a part of their lives that concern over illnesses and home remedies was almost universal.

In 1762 George Mason was a victim of attacks of erysipelas, which was gradually undermining his health and to which he was "very subject" as well as to chronic gout.[91] The idyllic period of Gunston Hall was drawing to a close. Ann Mason's health was weakened by her many pregnancies as well as the care and nursing of her children, who were not of robust health. In particular the health of their oldest son, George, was always precarious. With Ann's ill health, George Mason probably had to assume more of the guidance of the household than just the overseeing of the household accounts and the hiring of tutors for the children, which were some of the duties of an eighteenth-century gentleman. The first tutor at Gunston Hall was a Mr. McPherson of Maryland, who was employed sometime around 1768. John Davidson, who succeeded McPherson, must have been installed by 1770, as a letter written by Professor Thomas Gordon of King's College, Edinburgh, to the Reverend John Scott dated 23 September says that John "is with Col. Mason before now." [92] This would indicate that George Mason sought assistance in engaging tutors for his children from his great friend and mentor. In addition to their studies young people were instructed in the niceties of conduct and the graces of the dance. The itinerant dancing master was most welcome at the plantation houses. One of the most popular on the Northern Neck was Francis Christian. Though illness brought added cares to the Mason household, Christian was holding classes at Gunston Hall on 18 April 1770. Patsy Custis and Millie Posey attended his class held at Gunston Hall, at which time Nancy Mason was fifteen.[93] Landon Carter records in his diary for Saturday, 7 May 1774: "This day finishes Christeen's dancing in this neighborhood. Young People may be sorry for it but I think School boys will be the better off for every three weeks is certainly too much time to loose two days a time." [94] The young people did enjoy the fun and visiting, and there are many records of Christian's classes, which began after breakfast and lasted until two o'clock in the afternoon.

Mrs. Newman was the only tutoress we know of engaged for the Mason daughters. She came to them about the time of their mother's death and remained in the family for some time. It was she who taught the girls to write and cipher as well as instructing them in all sorts of needlework and in the social graces, such as the correct way to flutter a fan.[95]

Ann Mason's health continued to decline. In December 1772 we find the following entry in the family Bible: "Richard Mason and James Mason Twins were born on Friday the 4th day of December 1772, about eleven o'clock in the Forenoon at Gunston Hall and baptized the same day by the Revd. Mr. Lee Massey but being born two months before their due time (occasioned by a long illness of their Mother), they both died the next morning & were buried in the new Burying Ground at Gunston Hall; being the first of the Family who are buried in that place."

Ann (Eilbeck) Mason never recovered from her long illness, during which she was attended by Dr. Craik. She died on Tuesday, 9 March 1773.[96] All that is known to us of Ann's life is that she married young and, before reaching middle age, died of the strain of continual childbearing.

George Mason had been deeply in love with his wife. His description of her spoke eloquently of his regard:

In the Beauty of her Person, & the Sweetness of her disposition, she was equalled by few, & excelled by none of her sex. She was something taller than the middle size & elegantly shaped. Her eyes were black, tender & Lively; her Features regular & delicate; her Complexion remarkably fair & fresh—Lilies and Roses (almost with a Metaphor) were blended there—and a certain inexpressible Air of Cheerfulness, Health, Innocence & Sensibility diffused over her Countenance form'd a Face the very Reverse of what is generally called masculine. This is not an ideal, but a real Picture drawn from Life. Nor was this beautiful outward-Form disgraced by an unworthy Inhabitant. . . . She was bless'd with a clear & sound Judgment, a gentle & benevolent Heart, a sincere & an humble Mind; with an even calm & cheerful Temper to a very unusual degree Affable to all, but intimate with Few. Her modest Virtues shun'd the public-eye, Superior to the turbulent Passions of Pride & Envy, a Stranger to Altercation of every kind, & content with the Blessings of a private Station, she placed all Happiness here, where only it is to be found, in her own Family. Tho' she despised Dress, she was always neat; cheerful, but not gay; Serious, but not melancholly; she never met me without a Smile.[97]

In this little sketch of his wife, written in 1773, George Mason delineated the virtues that he himself treasured. George and Ann were very happily married, for he shared with her a family-centered life on every level. The regard he felt for her was demonstrated by his hesitancy in remarrying. In a time when a widower consoled himself with a new partner with such haste that sometimes he was condoled upon the death of his first wife and congratulated upon the choice of his second at the same time, George Mason remained a widower for seven years, and his daughter Nancy managed the household. On 2 October 1778 George Mason wrote a young kinsman in London that his eldest daughter, "Nancy, (who is blessed with her mother's amiable disposition,) is mistress of my family and manages my little domestic matters with a degree of prudence far above her years." [98] Quite obviously the father overlooked the fact that she was seven years older than her mother had been at the time of her marriage.

George Mason made the only will he ever wrote eleven days after his wife's death while under the shock of his bereavement. The will is dated 20 March 1773, and it was never amended by a codicil. Most men with an estate to bequeath rewrite their wills, or at least update them with a codicil as they note the development of the characters of their children. Not so George Mason IV. Even though he was well aware of the uncertain condition of the health of his son George, he never made any attempt to appoint another son in his place as executor. It would seem that once having written his will, it was over and done with. Whether the depression he felt over the death of his wife colored all of his reactions and made his dissatisfaction with political life greater it is hard to say, but his admonishment to his sons in his will "to prefer the happiness of independence & a private Station to the troubles and vexations of Public Business" leaves little doubt as to his disillusionment with the political factions of his day. Both George and Thomson had lost their wives and both had suffered political disappointment. But their lives were busy ones taken up with their families, their plantations, their parish interests, the acquisition of land and the improvement of transportation into the wilderness, as well as their financial problems, but above all they had a consuming interest in the problems that were facing the emerging democracy.

Chapter V

George Mason IV: Internal Improvements
and Western Lands

W HILE THE EVENTS THAT CULMINATED in the American Revolution were building to a climax, other issues of
importance to the beginning nation were being discussed in the legislatures of the colonies. The question of internal improvements, such as
roads and canals, and that of the disposition of the lands beyond the
Allegheny Mountains were questions of great moment. George and
Thomson Mason were in the forefront of forwarding proposals for
the improvement of the Potomac River principally by means of a
canal that would open the river to navigation above the Great Falls.
This would link western lands with eastern markets, and the return to
investors on their capital investment would be beneficial not only to
them but to the economy as a whole.[1]

The works projected in the English midlands by Francis Egerton,
duke of Bridgewater, and engineered and carried out by James Brind-
ley in the 1760s demonstrated that canals could be built on a large
scale and could make a handsome return to the investors within a
relatively short time. In 1767 the *Scots Magazine* published a long report on a proposed canal to link the Forth and the Clyde. Shares
priced at £100 each sold at a rapid rate. By February 1767 £15,800
had been raised, John Glassford and John Ritchie pledged an additional £24,200 to complete the subscription. Glassford's interest in the
canal project would certainly attract some comment among the merchants and factors on the Potomac, who were keenly aware of British
business developments.[2]

One of these, John Semple, a proprietor of a complex of flour mills
and iron forges on Occoquan Creek near Gunston Hall, circulated a
series of proposals in 1768–69 for clearing the Potomac River. He
argued that "the opening and making convenient Passage for Vessells
of Ten to Fifteen Tons Burthern; through such particular parts of the
River Potomac, above the Great Falls, as is now difficult, and rather
Tedious and Expensive Portages necessary, has long been considered
as highly meriting the public attention; But as is often the fate of matters wherein many are interested, little has been hitherto done to carry

it into execution." Semple believed that "the vast bodies of land now ceded to us by the Indians must open a new and extensive field of commerce, of which the River Potomac must necessarily be the Principal channell." He suggested that work on the river should begin two miles above the Great Falls, or ten miles above tidewater. From that point to Seneca Falls there was deep water. At Seneca Falls, John Ballendine was building a dam across the channel in order to erect a sawmill. With some minor changes in Ballendine's dam, the level of the water would be raised sufficiently to permit small boats to pass. When the river was high in winter and spring, boats could navigate the Potomac without difficulty for forty miles from Seneca Falls to Payne's Falls, the beginning of the Shenandoah Falls. John Semple maintained that the natural channel at Payne's Falls could be enlarged and deepened at a cost of £250. Two miles further up the river at the Spout, a canal with locks in it would have to be dug; this Semple estimated would cost £800. The longest canal on the river, in the Semple plan, would be just above Harpers Ferry. It would extend more than half a mile and would cost an estimated £2,000 to construct. He proposed another short canal at the upper end of the Shenandoah Falls, which he believed would add £900 to the total estimated cost.[3]

On 5 December 1769 the House of Burgesses "ordered that Leave be given to bring in a Bill for clearing and making navigable the River Potowmack, from the great Falls of the said River up to Fort Cumberland; and that Mr. Richard Henry Lee and Mr. Washington do prepare and bring in the same." On 14 December 1769 Richard Henry Lee reported the bill. It was read twice and ordered engrossed. Writing three days later from Williamsburg, Lee observed that the present session was "a meeting of so much business and great perplexity that an adjournment to the middle of May will certainly take place." The Potomac project was dropped in the press of business before adjournment.[4]

On 18 March 1772 the House of Burgesses entertained a petition from various inhabitants of Frederick County. The petition called for opening the navigation of the Potomac from Fort Cumberland to tidewater, either at the expense of the public, to be reimbursed by tolls, "or for granting the like Tolls to such Adventurers as shall be willing to undertake the Work, at their own expense, or for empowering Trustees to receive and lay out the Money, which Subscribers may voluntarily contribute for that Purpose." The House rejected the proposal for utilizing public money for the project, but gave its approval to the rest. On 3 April 1772 Thomson Mason and others were authorized to prepare and bring in a bill for opening and extending the navigation of the Potomac River. Three days later Mason presented the bill. On the eighth the bill passed the House and Thomson Mason was authorized to carry it to the Council. The Council also gave its approval to the bill but suggested an amendment making damage to property recoverable from the trustees. The proposed amendment was adopted, and the bill went back to the Council to receive its final approval on the ninth. As enacted by the Virginia Assembly, the Potomac bill differed only slightly from the bill passed at the same session for the improvement of the James River. It created a board of managers to supervise a lottery to fund the Potomac project—William Nelson, Thomas Nelson, William Byrd, John Page, Peyton Randolph, Robert Carter Nicholas, Richard Bland, Benjamin Harrison of Berkeley, Benjamin Waller, and Charles Carter of Shirley. Archibald Cary, George Wythe, and Patrick Henry were named as the managers of the Potomac lottery. It would be hard to find a more distinguished group of Virginians or one with fewer personal ties to the Potomac or the Northern Neck. This was obviously the intention of the Virginia Assembly in drawing up and passing the bill. The Potomac and the James River projects were presented as Virginia interests rather than purely local improvements.[5]

On 9 May 1772, after the passage of the James River and Potomac River bills, John Ballendine opened a subscription fund to defray his own expenses for a trip to Europe to obtain the latest information on the technology of building canals. He received the encouragement of the governors of Maryland and Virginia and "most of the principal gentlemen of the said provinces." In the same month Ballendine was in Annapolis consulting with Thomas Johnson and others interested in the project and awaiting "the arrival of Mr. Mason from Virginia," probably Thomson Mason, who had introduced the bill in the Assembly. Johnson was anxious to obtain passage of a similar measure in Maryland, but fear had been expressed in Annapolis that joint action with Virginia would compromise the claims of the lord proprietor to the Potomac River and no bill was passed at this time.[6]

After his return from Europe, John Ballendine made a formal announcement of his intention to open the Potomac to navigation from Fort Cumberland to tidewater in notices published in several newspapers early in September 1774. He called a meeting at Georgetown on September 26 for discussion of the project and for the election of trustees for the Potomac navigation. The trustees who were chosen included George Mason and Thomson Mason. In December another Georgetown meeting gave evidence of further public interest, and a meeting at Alexandria was held in January 1775. By this time John

Ballendine had actually begun work at the Little Falls of the Potomac and advertised for some fifty slaves to be hired as laborers to begin cutting the canal.[7] George Mason of Gunston Hall had assumed the leadership of the Virginia proponents of Potomac navigation and early in 1775 started a bill for that purpose.[8]

John Ballendine traveled between Gunston Hall and Annapolis to consult with Mason and Thomas Johnson. Johnson planned to introduce a bill in the Maryland House of Delegates for the Potomac improvements.[9] Mason was pleased to learn that on nearly every major point his draft would agree with Johnson's bill, but on one issue he had to instruct his Maryland colleague. George Mason restored the most important point in Semple's plan, which had been dropped by Ballendine and his backers. Mason observed:

A sufficient Sum can't be raised by those only who are locally interested; men who are not, will not advance their Money, upon so great a Risque but wth. Veivs of great & increasing Profit, not to depend upon future Alterations: the Tolls, to be sure, must be moderate, such as the Commodities will bear, with advantage to the Makers; it is probable for some Years they will yield very little Profit to the Undertakers, perhaps none; they must run the Risque of this, as well as of the ultimate Failure of the Undertaking, & surely if they succeed they have a just Right to the increased Profits; tho' in process of Time they may become very great.[10]

In March 1775 George Mason informed George Washington that he had completed the bill to be submitted in the Virginia Assembly. He was not sanguine about the prospects of the bill prepared by Thomas Johnson for the Maryland Assembly: "there will be so strong an opposition from Baltimore and the head of the Bay as will go near to prevent its passage through the Maryland Assembly in any shape it can be offered." George Mason's bill "to raise a capital sum of forty thousand pounds sterling by subscription and establishing a company for opening and extending the navigation of the River Potomack" was introduced in the House of Burgesses on 3 June 1775 and received the assent of both houses. However, as Mason had predicted, the Potomac improvements legislation never passed the Maryland legislature. When this became evident, John Ballendine abandoned his Potomac project in October 1775.[11]

George Mason did not abandon the dream of a direct link by water to the lands beyond the mountains. The canal scheme lay dormant through the war years, but in 1784 the Virginia Assembly authorized construction of a canal and other improvements to open navigation on the Potomac River as far west as Cumberland. The Assembly appointed George Mason of Gunston Hall and Alexander Henderson of

Colchester as commissioners of the state of Virginia to meet with commissioners from Maryland to settle disputed rights to navigation on the Potomac and Chesapeake Bay and to prepare for joint action on the canal project.[12] The plan to improve navigation on the Potomac and open the commerce of an inland empire to the Old Dominion was only one part of Mason's tireless effort to develop the lands beyond the mountains. During much of his public life George Mason's vision centered on the western lands claimed by Virginia. An understanding of his western land interest is central to an understanding of Mason's career.

His efforts to obtain lands beyond the crest of the Blue Ridge occupied much of his time and attention. From 1749 to 1779 he was continuously engaged in promoting the Ohio Company proposal for a land grant on the western rivers. In addition to his work with the Ohio Company, Mason sought to obtain grants in his own name to western lands and successfully challenged official British land policy in this effort. When he shaped the official land policy of the state of Virginia, he drew on his own experiences and frustrations of thirty years. Mason fought manfully in the courts to protect his lands in Kentucky and western Maryland from rival claimants in suits that were still unresolved at his death.[13]

George Mason and many of his neighbors had major capital investments in western lands. From the proceeds of these investments they hoped to break out of the cycle of tobacco and slaves, slaves and tobacco. The settlers from Pennsylvania who had begun to move south along the Blue Ridge in the 1730s had given them the vision of a brighter future. They could realize a return on their investments in these western lands by selling or leasing small tracts to farmers whose labor would increase the value of the rented farm and the adjacent area as well. Interest in these lands was evidenced in the first half of the eighteenth century. Sir William Gooch began to receive petitions for grants of land beyond the Blue Ridge from these German migrants in 1731, when Jacob Stauber asked for authority to plant settlements on the upper reaches of the Potomac and along the Shenandoah River. These requests touched off a long discussion in the Board of Trade and Plantations about the limits of the boundaries of Virginia and the Fairfax proprietary in 1747. So long as the western boundaries of the Fairfax grant were in dispute, claims to western land grants also hung in the balance.[14]

The Iroquois Indians had always held title to Virginia west of the settlements. In the time of the first George Mason, they agreed to keep to a path at the eastern side of the Blue Ridge in their expeditions southward. In 1744 the Iroquois sachems again smoked the peace pipe at the Treaty of Lancaster and ceded all the lands as far west as the Mississippi River to the Virginians. With the first rumors of the Lancaster treaty, several schemes were set afoot simultaneously. A group headed by Col. John Robinson, Sr., John Robinson, Jr., and Thomas Nelson, Jr., received a grant of 100,000 acres on the Greenbriar River. William Waller, Benjamin Waller, and others obtained 50,000 acres on the branches of the Roanoke River. Henry Downes, John Blair, Jr., and others secured 50,000 acres west of the Greenbriar. With a grant to Capt. James Patton and his associates, the Council disposed of 300,000 acres in a single day.[15] The members of the Governor's Council were as ready as the chiefs of the Iroquois Confederacy to give title to lands that could only be designated by a vague gesture towards the setting sun.

Governor Gooch was more cautious. In June 1747 he wrote to the Board of Trade and Plantations for specific instructions about dealing with petitions for land beyond the mountains. He repeated this request in November 1747 after the newly formed Ohio Company added their petitions to the lists of demands for land grants.[16] On 20 October 1747 Thomas Lee and others petitioned for 200,000 acres "to be laid out from ye Branche called Kiskamanetts and Buffalo Creeke," tributaries of the Ohio River, somewhere along the east bank of the Ohio from the site of Pittsburgh to near the site of Parkersburg, West Virginia. On 24 October 1747 the members of the Ohio Company, for this was the name adopted by the Lee group, shifted their ground slightly and determined to take the London merchant John Hanbury into their group as a full partner and to request him to present their petition for a land grant to the Crown.[17]

As with so many of the other petitions made by Virginians for grants of land on the western waters, this 1747 petition was offered in the name of several persons who were not active partners but merely lent their names and their influence to the group. By the time the petition to the Crown had been favorably acted upon in 1749, many of the original petitioners had dropped out of the Ohio Company and its affairs. The associates made preliminary moves towards settling their grant, discussed sending for a cargo of trade goods, and entered into correspondence with a Rotterdam merchant about recruiting German Protestant settlers for their lands.[18]

At the general meeting of the Ohio Company at Stafford Courthouse on 21 June 1749, Thomas Lee, Thomas Cresap, Lawrence Washington, Augustine Washington, John Tayloe, Presley Thornton, the Reverend James Scott, Richard Lee, Philip Ludwell Lee, Gavin Corbin, and Hugh Parker agreed to admit George Mason, then present, as a full partner. With the resignations of several inactive members, four shares in the Ohio Company were left open, and each member was assessed £125 toward a cargo of trade goods to be purchased from the English partner, John Hanbury. Mason immediately began to take an active part in the affairs of the Ohio Company. On 25 September 1749 he was appointed the treasurer of the company and held this post until his death in 1792.[19]

The British government directed the Virginia authorities to make the grant of 200,000 acres requested by the Ohio Company associates. Official notification reached Williamsburg in June 1749 and the grant was duly recorded. The Ohio Company was required by the terms of the grant to build a fort and a storehouse and to settle families on its tract. On the same day the Governor's Council approved grants totaling 1,450,000 acres along the Ohio River in modern West Virginia. Many a Virginia gentleman had a share in one or more of these grants. John Tayloe of the Ohio Company joined with the Patton associates in securing a new grant for their claim on the Great Kanawha River.[20]

The Ohio Company set up its first base of operations at Rock Creek Warehouse in Maryland, where the town of Georgetown was soon to be located. Hugh Parker, a member of the partnership, served as their factor. In 1749 they authorized him to take the company's goods to their base camp on the south shore of the Potomac River directly opposite the mouth of Wills Creek. The site of modern Cumberland, Maryland, is directly opposite this base camp and was the location of Fort Cumberland. The company proposed to "clear all such Roads between these places as should be most for the Company's Advantage." From their advanced base at Wills Creek, the factors of the Ohio Company planned to proceed overland to the upper reaches of the Youghiogheny. This river, which flows into the Monongahela, would afford them a water route to the forks of the Ohio and all of the western country, where they planned to set up trading stations.[21]

The dream of Alexander Spotswood to turn the flank of the French would thus be realized. The Ohio Company hoped to secure the trade of all the Indian tribes on the inland rivers and to send pelts back to the wharves at Georgetown to be shipped to Britain. Each of these advanced bases in turn would be the nucleus of a settlement of German farmers, who would be recruited at Rotterdam, following William Penn's example in settling Pennsylvania. They would disembark at Georgetown and go on to Wills Creek. In due time farms would make the advanced settlements more self-sufficient, and eventually

the lands all along the Ohio River from the Kanawha to the Youghiogheny would be prosperous farming country. The fur traders would
then press on to the Mississippi and the Great Lakes. The Ohio Company planned much more than securing a few hundred acres for each
of their associates; they aimed at building an inland empire.

When the members of the Ohio Company gathered for a meeting in
Otcober 1749, they could see both the promise of the future as well
as the more immediate problems that faced them. They were aware
that the Indians beyond the mountains were suspicious and hostile.
They recognized that Virginia and Pennsylvania would have to settle
the western boundary of William Penn's original grant. The members
of the Ohio Company, like most Virginians, assumed that the authority
of Pennsylvania ran no farther west than the crest of the Appalachian
chain and that all the lands beyond the mountains were part of Virginia's jurisdiction. Neither of these problems seemed insoluble. For-
tunately, Thomas Lee of the Ohio Company had been president of the
Council and was the acting governor of Virginia. He took immediate
steps to settle the long dispute with Pennsylvania.[22]

Thomas Penn was also concerned that the boundary between Pennsylvania and Virginia should be scientifically ascertained so as to protect his rights and prevent friction between fur traders from the two
provinces. In June 1749 he instructed Governor James Hamilton to
have a survey made. John Hanbury had meanwhile approached the
Pennsylvania proprietor on the subject. Penn did not want to make
unnecessary concessions. In 1750 Penn and Hanbury were in agreement on the advisability of deferring construction of a fort by the Ohio
Company until the Indians gave their consent to it, "as they may think
we intend to take away their whole Country and share it between us."
The Pennsylvanians sent out their own surveying party and generally
moved with deliberate caution in coming to a settlement of the boundary issue.[23]

The Ohio Company felt no hesitation and sent Hugh Parker and
Thomas Cresap to locate trading posts and convince the Indians along
the upper Ohio of the advantages to be reaped by bringing their pelts
to the Ohio Company store. At the same time Barney Curran, a veteran of many winters in the wilderness, made a long journey among
the tribes beyond the northern banks of the Ohio to tell them of the
fine goods to be had at low costs from the Virginians. One important
problem remained: the Ohio Company could not afford to build and
garrison a regular military fort beyond the mountains. If they had
been able to erect a strong fortified post in the first year of their existence, the Ohio Company might have changed the whole history of

inland America. Unable to take totally independent action, they were dependent on so many variables that they were in effect totally impotent.[24] Moreover, they were harassed by other problems. Mason complained in May 1750 that the trade goods sent by Hanbury for the Ohio Company were still at Rock Creek Warehouse and precious time was being lost. At a later date Mason wrote of these early days as a time when the company was obliged to extend large amounts of credit, most of which was never recovered, to Indian traders for long periods of time.[25]

In January 1750 George Mason, the Reverend James Scott, and James Wardrop of Maryland held a committee meeting of the Ohio Company and determined to petition Lord Fairfax for a grant of land along the south bank of the Potomac in order to strengthen their position opposite the mouth of Wills Creek.[26] For some reason the actual grant was not made until October 1754. The lands were known as the New Store Tract from the fact that the Ohio Company's storehouse was located there. They were divided into lots averaging two or three hundred acres apiece. The Ohio Company obtained title to three lots. George Mason personally took title to lot 1, of 237 acres, and lot 5, of 329 acres. Eventually all of this land plus another 214 acres was resurveyed and title given to Mason. This transaction gave George Mason some 1,649 acres in what was then Hampshire County, Virginia, but is now Mineral County, West Virginia.[27]

In September 1750 the Ohio Company sent Christopher Gist to make a careful exploration of the lands along the Ohio River as far as the falls, the site of modern Louisville, Kentucky. He was ordered to "observe the ways and Passess through all the mountains you cross, and take an exact account of the Soil, Quality, and Product of the Land, and the Wideness and Deepness of the Rivers" and "also to observe what Nations of Indians inhabit there, their Strength & Numbers, who they trade with, and in what commodities they deal." [28] While Gist was on his journey to the western country, the Ohio Company met at Occoquan Ferry in December 1750. The death of Thomas Lee had taken a trusted leader from the group, and in proof of the regard in which Mason was held by the members of the company, he was commissioned to conduct all further negotiations with John Hanbury and the other English partners. After many conferences at the Indian villages in the Ohio country, Gist returned to Roanoke, Virginia, on 19 May 1751 and made his report to the Ohio Company soon afterward.[29]

In 1751 the members agreed to apply, through John Hanbury, to the earl of Granville for a grant of 50,000 acres near the Virginia–

North Carolina boundary and to Lord Baltimore for a grant of 10,000 acres near the Pennsylvania-Maryland line in the vicinity of Wills Creek. They also agreed to petition Thomas Penn for a grant of 10,000 acres near Ray's Town on Juniata Creek in modern Bedford County, Pennsylvania; for 15,000 acres along Loyalhanna Creek and the Kiskiminetas River; an additional 5,000 acres on the Conemaugh River; as well as some four thousand acres at the three forks of the Youghiogheny, a few miles northwest of their base at Wills Creek. They hastened to make clear to John Hanbury, their spokesman in England, that the fort they had proposed could only be a fortified trading post or blockhouse. They also resolved to press construction of a road from Wills Creek to the Youghiogheny and to purchase a tract of about five hundred acres at the mouth of Wills Creek from Governor Thomas Bladen of Maryland.[30]

Trouble was brewing on the western borders. In the summer of 1752 bands of Ottawas with French military advisers devastated the tribes who traded with the English. They fell upon the Twightwees at Pickawillany "an exercised such cruelities in their town as are scarcely credible and at the same time took four Indian traders belonging to Pennsylvania then trading there and sent them prisoners to Canada." The French threat hung a long shadow over the treaty negotiated with the Indians at Logstown in June 1752 by Lunsford Lomax, Joshua Fry, and Col. James Patton, agents for Virginia; Christopher Gist, agent of the Ohio Company; and George Croghan, agent of Pennsylvania. The Indians were informed that "it is the design of the King your father at present to make a settlement of British subjects on the south side of Ohio that we may be united as one people by the strongest ties of neighborhood as well as friendship and by these means prevent the insults of our Enemies." The Seneca chief, the Half King, acknowledged that the French menaced all the allies of the English, "for they have struck our friends the Twightwees. We therefore desire our brothers of Virginia may build a stronghouse at the fork of Monogahela."[31]

In November 1752 John Mercer, Lunsford Lomax, William Trent, and Andrew Montour obtained grants totaling 620,000 acres to the south of the Ohio Company claims, with the provision that each of them was to settle 140 families on his land within three years. The Ohio Company and the Blair-Russell group were operating to the detriment of each other's interest on the upper reaches of the Ohio at the same time.[32]

Until actual settlers could be located on the lands claimed by each of these syndicates, all of their rights were worthless. Efforts to attract

German farmers or other families to the Ohio Company's lands took precedence over other matters and occupied a good deal of the time of the members. George Mason, the Reverend James Scott, and John Mercer of Marlborough corresponded at length in 1753 with the Glasgow merchant John Pagan concerning the problem. Pagan, one of the first Scottish tobacco traders to settle at Alexandria, intended to return to Scotland. He proposed going on to Germany "in Expectation of Engaging a great number of families" to migrate to Virginia "to settle their lands on the Ohio." After outlining the privileges of religious and civil liberty, freedom from quitrents and other levies for ten years, and additional privileges, Mason, Scott, and Mercer promised "in behalf of the said company for the greater Encouragement of such foreign protestants to lay off two hundred Acres of Land for a Town to be called Saltsburg in the best and most convenient place to their Settlement to be divided into Lots of one Acre each, Eight of which to be appropriated for a Fort, church and other public buildings and every Tradesman or other person settling and living three Years in the said Town to have one Lot forever paying the Quitrent of one farthing a Year." The settlement proposed by the Ohio Company as the site of Saltsburg was to be located at the present McKees Rocks, on the Ohio River, just west of Pittsburgh. The Ohio Company planned to build a fort ninety feet square for the protection of the settlers and, among other things, to build a school for the education of Indian children within the town.[33]

George Mason assessed each member of the company to meet the costs of finishing the fort. He wrote to John Hanbury to arrange for the purchase of twenty swivel guns and other arms and ammunition for the fort. In July 1753 Christopher Gist received instructions to lay off the town and survey the lots. This was as far as the Ohio Company was able to advance in its plans for a town on the Ohio.[34]

While John Pagan was attempting to secure settlers for Saltsburg through his agents in Rotterdam and in Germany, some families already in Pennsylvania expressed interest in the lands on the Ohio River. The rival claims of the Ohio Company and the Blair-Russell syndicate overlapped in the area bounded by the Youghiogheny, the Monongahela, and Redstone Creek. Gist contracted with a number of families to settle on the Ohio Company lands, but they were so harassed by the agents of the other groups that they abandoned their plan.

The stream of migration was naturally deflected by the mountain ranges. The Ohio Company tried vainly to encourage the German farmers of eastern Pennsylvania to settle on the company Lands. In

1753 the Moravian Brethren at Bethlehem sent out a group of colonists who founded Salem, North Carolina. Scotch-Irish families were already taking up lands in the Carolina Piedmont. Menaced by French and Indians, thwarted by other speculators with conflicting grants, the Ohio Company had lost its best opportunity to play a decisive role in the establishment of a British colony in the trans-Allegheny west. The Ohio Company's establishment at Wills Creek was only slightly more real in the summer of 1753 than the town on the banks of the Ohio. George Mason had purchased "three likely able Men Slaves who are used to the Country Business and two Negro women" in order to establish a farm at Wills Creek, "for their raising Stock and being supplied with proper Hands for the transporting their Goods and Skins by Water to and from that place." [35]

More trouble on the frontiers in the summer of 1753 caused the English fur traders to flee for their lives. It also spread panic among the prospective Ohio Company settlers. John Mercer reported that, harassed by land speculators and terrified by Indian troubles, "some of the persons who removed from the Northward to settle the companies land not only returned back to their former habitations but stopped the other families that were about to move, and this step with some other instances of the same kind has prejudiced the Northward people to that degree that it is to be feared no promises or offers that the government of Virginia can make will ever be able to remove their prejudice or engage their confidence, and hence it is that some thousands from the Northern provinces have since passed through this colony to procure worse lands and on much worse terms to the Southward." [36]

The Virginia authorities took alarm over these events in the winter of 1753 and attempted to protect the western lands from the incursions of the French and Indians. In December Governor Robert Dinwiddie sent George Washington with a small force to the Ohio Valley and gave William Trent, the Ohio Company factor, a commission as a captain. He advanced from the Ohio Company store at the mouth of Redstone Creek to the forks of the Ohio and began constructing a fort. Trent was back at Wills Creek to arrange for more supplies in April and found Washington there, preparing to advance into the Ohio country. On 18 April 1754 Ens. Edward Ward of Trent's Company surrendered the fort to a French force that outnumbered his own by more than ten to one. Washington pushed on to the Ohio Company storehouse at Redstone Creek. At the Great Meadows, near Farmington, Fayette County, Pennsylvania, Washington and his force hastily threw up the palisade of Fort Necessity on 30 May 1754. Little more than a month later, on 4 July 1754, he too surrendered to an overwhelming French force. The fort at the forks of the Ohio became Fort Duquesne, and a year later Gen. Edward Braddock marched through the forests in a vain effort to retrieve the Ohio country from the French.[37]

The French military success over the British gave them great prestige with the Indians, enabling them to expel the English traders and make the Indians economically dependent on the French. In 1754–55 France controlled everything beyond the mountains. The Ohio Company members might as well have held shares in a gold mine on the moon. The fortunes of war turned slowly against the victors. By the summer of 1758 the French and Indians, who had ravaged as far as Wills Creek and the settlements on the Susquehanna, were themselves routed by the gallant Scotsman Gen. John Forbes and his redcoats. In November the French evacuated Fort Duquesne and retired to a new stronghold on the upper reaches of the Allegheny at Fort Machault. The fall of Fort Niagara in the summer of 1759 turned the French flank, and in August 1759 the French garrison burned Fort Machault and abandoned their efforts to hold the Ohio.[38]

This American spur of the war between the French and English had created new problems for the Ohio Company. When Francis Fauquier arrived as governor of Virginia in 1759, he quickly made clear his opposition to large grants beyond the frontiers.[39] British army posts had taken the place of the hastily constructed Virginia forts and the more sophisticated defensive works of the French. Fort Cumberland stood at Wills Creek, and Fort Pitt dominated the forks of the Ohio. Settlers had followed the army and taken up lands near the forts as the French and Indian menace evaporated. Pennsylvania fur traders established their headquarters at Pittsburgh. Army dependents, soldiers' wives, regimental sutlers, wagoners, and civilian laborers would not be turned out of their homes and stores by the British army at the behest of some land speculators in Virginia. With an eye to political realities the Ohio Company offered a full share to Col. Henry Bouquet, British commandant at Fort Pitt and the most influential man in the trans-Allegheny west. He had the good sense to refuse the offer. In 1761 in line with British policy to cement the loyalty of Indian allies, he began to close the frontier to white settlers, but this did not prevent many of the Ohio Valley tribes from rising against the British in 1763.[40] George Mason attempted to salvage as much as possible from the changed situation. For the time being at least, the lands around Fort Cumberland at Wills Creek were more valuable than those in the Ohio Company's grant beyond the mountains. The title to these lands was in-

disputable, or at least it seemed to be until Dr. David Ross of Bladensburg crossed George Mason's path.

David Ross was a Scottish physician. During the war years he had
served with the British army as commissary and hospital director for
the Maryland troops and was reimbursed by the Maryland authorities
for large sums he had advanced for food and medicine for the Army.[41]
Ross is another outstanding example of the Scottish professional man
who made a fortune in the American colonies. While he continued his
practice of medicine at Bladensburg for many years, he had his hand
in many enterprises. In 1757 he was engaged in the sale of imported
goods at Bladensburg; he was associated with the firm of Stewart and
Armour before 1759 and afterwards with John Stewart and Company
of London. During these years he offered servants for sale, accepted
cargoes of tobacco on consignment, and advertised his mill on Rock
Creek as well as slaves from the Gold Coast.[42] His major interest was
the Frederick Forge Company in western Maryland, at the mouth of
Antietam Creek. In this enterprise Ross was associated with Richard
Henderson, the brother of Mason's friend Alexander Henderson, and
with Samuel Beall, Jr. His interest in western Maryland acreage was
well known. When he learned from a frontiersman in 1759 that a tract
of land near Fort Cumberland was not properly patented, he secured
a warrant for the tract in question, well aware of the value of lands
situated near military posts. The lands had been patented by Governor
Thomas Bladen in 1745–47 and transferred by him to George Mason
as the treasurer of the Ohio Company. In 1756 Mason patented Walnut Bottom, amounting to 500 acres. In 1761 under the threat of
Ross's claims, he obtained a resurvey on Walnut Bottom, totaling 869
acres.[43]

Mason and Ross became involved in a series of lawsuits over disputed land claims. In the midst of this litigation, Mason secured patents in 1763 for Cove, of 510 acres; Hunt the Hare, of 240 acres; and
Welshman's Conquest, containing 260 acres, all located at Wills Creek.
This was obviously a step to forestall Ross, who learned that the patents had not yet been signed by Governor Sharpe but that they were
all made out in Mason's name.[44] Later in 1763 Mason gave Bladen his
bond for the payment of £464 10s. Maryland currency for the total
purchase of 1,310 acres, which included Pleasant Valley, of 300 acres
for which Mason had no patent, and the tracts that he had succeeded
in patenting. The transaction was only finally completed thirty years
later with the payment on 11 January 1792 of £696 10s. currency by
Mason.

Long after the Ohio Company ceased to be an active entity, Mason maintained his interest in these lands on Wills Creek and the Potomac. The legal squabble with Ross was still far from settlement when the Scottish physician-merchant-ironmaster died in 1778 at his ironworks on Antietam Creek. The Ross heirs kept up the suit. In 1783 George Mason purchased from Daniel Cresap a small tract of sixty-three acres on the Potomac near Wills Creek known as Limestone Rock. Later in 1783 he sold Limestone Rock and Walnut Bottom to Thomas Beall; in 1785 he sold Hunt the Hare to James Maccubbin Lingan of George-town for £480 Maryland currency. Lingan was the son-in-law of Richard Henderson, who had been Ross's partner in the Frederick Forge Company. Mason also sold his share of the New Store Tract in Virginia, opposite Wills Creek, to Lingan in 1785. This property contained 1,083 acres and brought a purchase price of £2,166 Maryland currency. After George Mason's death, litigation with Ross's heirs continued to plague the Mason heirs for many years. In 1803 the heirs of George Mason of Lexington obtained £471 5s. 11d. for the Cove tract. Prolonged legal maneuvers for a clear title to Pleasant Valley came to an end in 1821 with a sale by the Mason heirs to the person who had also bought out the Ross claim.[45]

Military necessity blocked the plans of the Ohio Company on the upper Potomac, as it had already halted their efforts to create settlements and trading posts beyond the mountains. When the members of the Ohio Company first published their intention to lay off a town at Wills Creek, they found a great many more purchasers than they had first anticipated. Charlottesburg was to be located at the head of navigation on the Potomac, within seventy-five miles of the Monongahela and linked to it by a good wagon road. Land there promised to be a good investment. Mason gave George Mercer a power of attorney to sell or lease portions of this land for the benefit of the Ohio Company. On 17 February 1763 the Ohio Company advertised lots for sale in a town to be located at Fort Cumberland and also offered to lease their storehouses with dwelling houses, kitchens, stables, meat house, and dairy at the same place. An advertisement in June 1763 explained that "the Ohio Company have ordered 200 Half-Acre lots to be laid off for a Town to be called Charlottesburg on Patowmack River." [46]

The Ohio Company surveyed lots and prepared deeds for the town lots in time for the public sale in June. The first advertised sale had been delayed, partly by the discovery that purchasers were more numerous than expected, partly by a rumor that the British military authorities would not permit settlers to erect a town in the immediate vicinity of Fort Cumberland. To still these reports, the Ohio Company dispatched one of their members (interior evidence points to its being George Mercer) to New York City to discuss the matter with Lord Jeffrey Amherst, commander in chief of British forces in America and to obtain his permission for the opening of the town. The fort was in a ruinous condition with only a storekeeper posted there, but Amherst forbade the Ohio Company to build a town there on their own lands as the pass at Wills Creek might prove important to the military at a later date. As a result the Ohio Company agents had to disperse the people who had assembled at Wills Creek to buy lots in Charlottesburg, even though many of them wanted to remain as squatters and force Amherst to relent. What little the Ohio Company seemed to have left was now taken away.[47]

By right of their land grant of 1754 from Lord Fairfax the Ohio Company held a more certain title to the lands on the southern bank of the Potomac across the river from the proposed town. The summer of 1763, however, was not a propitious time for a real estate boom on the upper Potomac; Pontiac's Rebellion had set the frontiers ablaze with an Indian war. A letter from Frederick, Maryland, in July reported that the terror of the back inhabitants exceeded what had followed on the defeat of General Braddock. "Never was panic more general." The whole western country had been drained of arms by the diligence of the Indian traders, who had bought up everything in sight for the supply of the Indian warriors. Hampshire County had been denuded of inhabitants by fear of Indian raids, and Frederick County, Virginia, was exposed to their depredations. Fort Cumberland still held firm, but an express rider from the fort to Winchester had passed the scalped body of a woman in the road from Fort Cumberland. An appeal went out from the frontier settlements for the Loudoun and Farfax militia to come to their aid. By the end of July militiamen from Frederick County, Maryland, and the five frontier counties in Virginia were advancing on Fort Cumberland.[48] In June Fort Pitt was under seige. Fort Le Boeuf, Fort Venango, Fort Presque Isle had all fallen and their garrisons were dead. Fort Ligonier and Fort Bedford held out, but the frontier settlements were in flames and terrified refugees fled toward the safety of the older towns and villages to the east. In August Col. Henry Bouquet with elements of the forty-second Black Watch and seventy-seventh Highlanders and the Royal American Regiment delivered a mortal blow to the Indian uprising at Bushy Run. It was estimated that 1,500 farms were deserted in that bloody summer along the Virginia-Pennsylvania frontier and at least 2,000 settlers perished. Governor Francis Fauquier argued that the settlers had provoked the Indian troubles and urged the closing of the frontier to settlement altogether.[49]

The firmer stand that the British government now took against further western migration added another grievance to the list that was growing in the colonies against Parliament. In 1763 the frontiers were closed to further settlement and all land grants beyond the mountains were left in abeyance.[50] Governor Fauquier wrote for further information in 1764, pointing out that the Patton grant had been made in proper form and that there were bona fide settlers on his lands on the Great Kanawha. The larger grants to the Ohio Company and the Loyal Company remained unimproved because of the impossibility of locating settlers there under wartime conditions. George Mercer had sailed for England in July 1763 to present a petition to the Crown for confirmation of the Ohio Company's grant. Unable to obtain a hearing for his cause until 1765, Mercer was engaged in protracted negotiations with rival land companies for several years.[51] Thus the possibilities of a vast empire beyond the mountains alternately waxed and waned.

In the ten years that followed the Proclamation of 1763, the Ohio Company's hopes reached ebb water. Their projected town at Fort Cumberland in Maryland was lost to military necessity. Their route to Fort Pitt and the fur trade of the Ohio Valley was blocked. Their title to lands beyond the mountains was in abeyance. They had entrusted their case to an agent in England too busy with other matters or too resentful of their neglect to press their valid claim with the authorities. When George Mercer was at last moved to action, it was only to surrender the Ohio Company claim to the rival Vandalia group.[52]

George Mason summoned the members of the Ohio Company to a meeting to be held in May 1772 at Stafford Courthouse. At this meeting the decision was made to attempt to renew the original Ohio Company grant through a petition to the Governor's Council at Williamsburg. At their session on 27 July 1772 the Council read "a letter from Col. Richard Lee enclosing a Petition from the Ohio Company, wherein they complained of their agent Col. George Mercer's having undertaken without their Consent or Authority to make an Agreement of Copartnership to subsist between the said company and Thomas Walpole Esqr. and others of his Associates in Great Britain with respect to the said Company's grant of Lands on the Western Frontier of this colony, and praying that they may have a Warrant to survey the said Grant." After due consideration, the Council determined "that the substance of the above Representation be entered on the Council's journals, and the Clerk inform Col. Lee that as there is no Precedent of any other Warrant to Survey Lands, then order by which they are granted, and the Company having already such an Order in their Favour, it does not appear necessary for the Board to do any thing further." George Mason chose to interpret the last statement as a confirmation of the Ohio Company grant when he drew up a petition to the Virginia Assembly six years later. The ambiguity of the Council's language could as reasonably be understood as a flat rejection of the Ohio Company petition.[53]

George Mason's own view of the future prospects of the Ohio Company may have grown dim by 1772. An undated "Memorandum for Mr. Lawson" in Mason's handwriting directed Lawson to consult with both Governor Robert Eden and the former Maryland chief executive, Col. Horatio Sharpe at Annapolis. Since Eden did not arrive in Maryland until 1769 and Sharpe sailed for England in 1773, the memorandum must have been drawn up sometime between these dates.

This memorandum is evidence that George Mason was at this time attempting to sell some of the property at Wills Creek. George Mason advised Lawson that from what Colonel Mercer wrote, Colonel Cresap told him that "perhaps Col. Cresap (to whom I have wrote often upon this subject, but never received any answer) may have had the Resurvey made [on the tract known as the Cove, patented by George Mason in 1763] and a proper certificate returned to the Land Office: in that case, Mr. Lawson has nothing more to do than to carry the Certificate from the Land Office to his Lordship's Agent, and pay him the Caution money, at the rate of Five pounds Sterling pr. hundred acres, for the vacant land included therein . . . and there will be no Occasion to trouble either the present or the late Governor with my letters." If no certificate was granted, Lawson was to apply to Governor Eden and Colonel Sharpe at Annapolis. Mason explained that he had applied for patents to Limestone Rock and the Cove in April 1769 but that the warrants were returned in the name of Daniel Cresap. He assured Lawson that "neither of these warrants any way concern my Dispute with Doctor Ross, being quite different Tracts of Land." [54] If Mason intended to sell the property and wanted to give a clear title, the apparent purpose of the Lawson memorandum, he was either unsuccessful or changed his mind, because none of the property was sold.

The Ohio Company title to all of its land in western Maryland was under dispute. In June 1773 Governor Eden granted a warrant to Thomas French for part of the unpatented Walnut Bottom tract, which French duly patented in 1774 as The Brothers. This case was still in litigation in 1788 when Mason wrote to John Francis Mercer regarding "the Ohio Company's title to a tract of land adjoining Fort Cumberland, called the 'Resurvey on Walnut Bottom' fraudulently granted by Governor Eden to one French, a creature of his." [55] With their rights to lands beyond the mountains disputed by the Walpole group and their title to their Potomac lands enmeshed in legal toils by David Ross, Thomas French, and Daniel Cresap, the Ohio Company turned its attention to lands that were indisputably within the gifts of the Virginia authorities. George Mason both in his capacity as treasurer of the Ohio Company and as a private individual began to be concerned after 1773 with efforts to secure lands in Kentucky for himself and his associates.

In 1773 the members of the Ohio Company obtained from the President and professors of the College of William and Mary a special commission appointing William Crawford surveyor of their lands. Crawford had a similar appointment as surveyor to locate the 200,000 acres of land appropriated to George Washington and the officers and men of his regiment under Governor Dinwiddie's proclamation. Washington proposed to join with Crawford "in attempting to secure some of the most valuable lands in the King's part which I think may be accomplished after a while notwithstanding the Proclamation of 1763," which was only "a temporary expedient to quiet the Minds of the Indians" and would eventually be withdrawn. In 1769 Washington raised the question of a grant of land to the Virginia troops who had served under him against the French and who had been promised land near the forks of the Ohio by Dinwiddie. By 1770 these 200,000 acres were definitely located near the mouth of the Great Kanawha River.[56]

William Crawford was occupied with the survey of these military bounty lands and apparently did little or nothing to forward the cause of the Ohio Company. It is doubtful whether he could have legally located lands for the Ohio Company beyond the proclamation line. The Virginian authorities were expressly forbidden to allow any lands beyond the mountains to be taken up other than by veterans of the recent war. On 7 April 1773 the Privy Council instructed the governors of the royal colonies not to issue any warrant or patent or grant licenses for private purchases from the Indians, pending the development of a unified land policy for the British dominions in North America.[57]

In 1774 the Ohio Company obtained a commission for Hancock Lee as assistant surveyor to William Crawford, according to George Mason's account in his petition to the Virginia Assembly four years later, "and they were proceeding down the [Youghiagheny] River, in order to begin their Surveys; but had the Misfortune to have their Cannoes overset, in attempting to pass the Falls of Youghyoughgaina and to lose all their provisions, arms, and ammunition, and have two of their men drowned; which, together with the Indian War that Summer, prevented their further progress." Crawford commanded troops in the campaign. The Ohio Company was forced to shelve its plans for another season.[58]

In the spring of 1773 George Mason and the Reverend James Scott had launched a plan of their own to obtain a grant of lands beyond the mountains. Scott attended a session of Prince William County Court at the Dumfries Courthouse on 5 June 1773 and "made Oath that in the Month of July in the year of our Lord 1742 he imported into this colony fifty nine Persons from Great Britain . . . and that he never before proved or claimed his right to any Lands in the said Colony for importing any of the said Persons." This affidavit was attested by John Graham, Prince William county clerk.[59]

On 6 December 1773 John Graham presented a similar certificate in Prince William County Court. He swore that in 1741 he had imported seventy-four persons into Virginia from Great Britain, whom he listed by name, and that he had imported another fifty-eight persons from Great Britain in 1742, whom he also named, and that he had never "claimed his right to any land in the said Colony of Virginia for importing any of the said one hundred & thirty two persons." On the same day John Graham sold all his rights to land in Virginia arising from this certificate for the sum of £33 to George Mason of Gunston Hall. This deed was witnessed by Henry Dade Hooe, William Carr, and Evan Williams.[60]

Attesting certificates of importation of indentured servants was not part of the ordinary business of a Virginia county court in the 1770s. The Virginia Company of London originally devised the headright system in 1618 as a means of encouraging settlement in Virginia. Every shareholder of the Virginia Company who transported a free person or indentured servant to the Chesapeake acquired a claim to fifty acres for each individual he brought to Virginia. It was open to abuses of various kinds, with shipmasters claiming land for sailors and passengers alike, some of whom would again claim land in their names or, as the servants of some Virginia gentlemen, add to his acreage. The grant of the Northern Neck proprietary ended land claims based on headrights within the territory granted to the proprietors, but Virginians in this area collected headright claims in order to obtain land in other parts of the colony. The headright system gradually fell into desuetude as a quite different abuse became the custom. Planters who wanted to patent larger tracts of public lands often paid a sum of money into the secretary's office. In 1795 this abuse, which already had the force of custom, was codified into statute law. Thereafter Virginians could directly purchase public lands by paying the stipulated fees to the secretary for a patent. The new system had such obvious advantages over the headright system that the latter steadily declined in importance and almost disappeared entirely in the course of the eighteenth century.[61]

Once committed to the program, George Mason acted with vigor. On 21 June 1773 Mason attended the session of Fairfax County Court at Alexandria. Harry Piper, factor for the Whitehaven firm of Dixon and Littledale, produced a list of 377 persons he had brought into Virginia for sale as indentured servants. Piper was one of the major dealers in servants on the Potomac at this time, but he made no reference in his letters to Whitehaven to this rather curious sale of passenger lists. On 20 July 1773 the Fairfax County Court certified a list of 87 persons imported by Robert Adam, an Alexandria merchant, and his assignment of his rights to George Mason.[62] The court record for part of that day's session has been torn out, so that the details of Mason's claim for importing five other individuals are no longer extant in the Fairfax County records.

On 7 April 1773 the Privy Council ordered the colonial governors to make no further grants of land to individuals or to companies. Lord Dunmore sent a vigorous protest against this change of policy to Lord Dartmouth on 4 July 1773, but he did not formally communicate his new instructions to the Virginia Council until 11 October 1773. Word of the alteration in official land policy reached Virginia by June 1773, and the swift action by James Scott and George Mason may well have been prompted by rumors of the impending prohibition of land grants. It is possible that the Scott-Mason plan represented a deliberate test of the new policy. Thwarted at every turn in their continuing effort to obtain western grants, Scott and Mason may simply have hit upon a new approach to their problem and, with the changing situation in London and Williamsburg, found themselves challenging a new governmental policy.[63]

The situation was further complicated early in 1774. The Privy Council expressed a desire for more effective regulation of lands in the royal provinces and directed the Board of Trade and Plantations to study the problem and make a report. In the meantime the royal governors were not to issue any warrant of survey or patents except military land bounties under the Proclamation of 1763, which were to be granted as usual. The Board of Trade made its recommendations late in January 1774, and on 5 February 1774 Lord Dartmouth communicated the new policy to the royal governors. The new system provided for surveys of small tracts of Crown lands and their advertisement and sale at auction at a minimum price; it disallowed all free grants of land. For reasons of his own Lord Dunmore did not choose to promulgate this new land policy until March 1775, although he had received unequivocal instructions on the subject before May 1774. Dunmore's delaying tactics gave Mason and Scott ample time to develop their case. Word of the new development would certainly have come to their knowledge by May 1774, since the new policy aroused considerable comment in London and was officially transmitted to the authorities in Georgia, North and South Carolina, New York, and New Hampshire, as well as to Lord Dunmore.[64]

George Mason made a thorough study of land policy in Virginia in his efforts to protect the Ohio Company's interest and to buttress his own personal claims to lands on the western waters. He marshaled his evidence in his "Extracts from the Virginia Charters, With Some Remarks on them Made in the Year 1773," which he drew up in late 1773 or early 1774. There is some internal evidence that points to the later date for the document. In his fourteenth note George Mason wrote of the Vandalia scheme as a threat to Virginia's charter rights in the past or, at best, as a pattern for future encroachments on the western boundaries of the Old Dominion.* "And tho' the scheme for a new Government on the Ohio, at present seems to be rejected or suspended;" Mason observed, "yet considering how favourably it was entertained by some of the public Boards in England, it may be proper for the General Assembly of Virginia, at this time to assert our rights by a Dutiful Remonstrance and Petition to the Crown." [65] But the Vandalia scheme was very much alive in 1773. The report of the Board of Trade on 6 May 1773 seemingly cleared every obstacle from the path of the Walpole group, and none of the difficulties that arose for the Vandalia proprietors in the course of the summer and autumn could reasonably be considered a rejection or suspension of their claims. These terms more accurately represented the situation early in 1774, when the return of the tea ships and the discovery of Benjamin Franklin's discreditable role in the Hutchinson affair adversely affected his Vandalia associates.[66]

The reference in Mason's twelfth note to the possibility that by some "new Regulation of Government, the Quit Rent of the Crown Lands here should hereafter be raised" would allude to the new

* In 1769 the Grand Ohio, or Walpole, Company, later styled the Vandalia Company, was formed by a group of influential Englishmen and Americans. Thomas Walpole was the most important and active English member; Samuel Wharton and Benjamin Franklin, the Americans. The land they desired encompassed the grant made the Ohio Company in 1749. George Mercer agreed to merge the interests of the Ohio Company with those of the Walpole Company. George Mason and the Virginia shareholders in the Ohio Company repudiated this (Mulkearn, *Mercer Papers,* pp. 667–68) .

measures adopted by the British authorities with the report of the Board of Trade on 25 January 1774. Mason's recommendation that the Virginia Assembly enter a formal protest against the Vandalia project as a caveat to future land speculators strengthened the similar petitions from Augusta, Botetourt, and Fincastle counties in April–June 1774. In this case the reference in Mason's second note to the Virginia Company's order in 1616 establishing the headright system, "which is now no less than 158 years old," is not a slip of the pen but a confirmation that the "Extracts from the Virginia Charters" with the petition he presented to the Governor's Council on 17 June 1774 was compiled, in many instances verbatim, from the "Extracts." George Mason obviously used these "Extracts" with the subjoined observations in presenting his case to the Virginia Council in 1774 and prepared this document for this purpose. It was written in April 1774, rather than 1773, and represented Mason's response to the new land policy adopted by the British Government.[67]

On 11 May 1774 Cumberland Wilson, factor at Dumfries for Colin Dunlop and Company, registered a list of forty persons he had imported into Virginia in October 1772 and a deed selling any claim arising from the importation of these forty persons to George Mason for the sum of five shillings. The extraordinarily low price for a claim to 2,000 acres suggests the lack of faith in the Scott-Mason plan. Cumberland Wilson must have believed it to be worthless. On the same day, and for the same price, Mason acquired all rights to land from the importation of forty-one persons brought to Virginia in August 1773 by Alexander Campbell, another Scots factor at Dumfries. There the matter stood. Mason and Scott had acquired headrights entitling them to considerable acreage, provided they could convince the authorities in Williamsburg of the reasonableness of their case.[68]

George Mason arrived in Williamsburg on 22 May 1774, armed with a thorough understanding of the practice of granting land in Virginia under the headright system. On 27 May 1774 he presented a memorial to the governor and his Council, explaining that "he had purchased a considerable Number of Importation Rights founded on the Charter granted by King Charles the second, whereby he conceived himself to be entitled to fifty acres of land for each Right; and that as this was not a Matter of Favour, but of strict Right, he hoped an Instruction His Excellency may have received for altering the Manner hitherto observed in taking up Lands would not operate." The petition was referred to the attorney general for his advice.[69]

Mason did not lose heart. On 6 June 1774 he purchased importation rights for 137 persons from William Harrison of Dinwiddie County for

£13 4s. Virginia currency. Harrison had purchased the certificate from Thomas Smith of Hanover County, the actual importer, for the same price that Mason had paid him. The gathering of merchants and factors from all parts of Virginia during the Assembly session made it convenient for Harrison to deliver his certificate to Mason, and it was probably at Williamsburg that the transaction was completed, with Mason's friends William Carr of Dumfries and Hector Ross of Colchester as witnesses.[70]

On 17 June 1774 George Mason appeared for the second time before Lord Dunmore and his Council to present a new memorial and petition of his own and a smaller petition from the Reverend James Scott. Mason drew freely from William Stith's *History of the First Discovery and Settlement of Virginia* and rehearsed the entire historical development of the headright system in his closely argued memorial. He cited Stith's conclusion that "that is the Antient, Legal, and a most indubitable Method of granting Lands in Virginia." Mason argued further that the king was bound to observe the grants made by his royal ancestors, and that "the before mentioned Ancient Right to Any vacant or ungranted Lands in this Colony, having been Solemnly continued and Confirmed, by the said Charter from King Charles the Second, in Manner herein before mentioned the same was made thereby part of the Law and Constitution of this country, and hath remained so ever since; and therefore can not be Avoided, injured, invalidated, or in any manner affected, by any Proclamation, Instruction, or other Act of Government; nor subjected to any new Charge, Expense, Burthen, or Imposition whatsoever." Even a claim for western lands had broad constitutional implications in 1774. Mason argued that he had in good faith purchased certificates of rights to large quantities of land from persons who had imported persons from Great Britain and Ireland into the colony of Virginia "and prays that he may be admitted to Entrys for the said Lands, upon the western waters, in the County of Fincastle; upon his producing the usual Certificates and Assignments, [or] that his Excellency the Governor, will be Pleased to Gr[ant your] petition[er his] Warrants for Surveying the same, which Ever his Excellency and this Honorable board Shall Judge most proper." [71]

The members of the Governor's Council considered the evidence and concluded that Mason's allegations were correct and his certificates "such as have been usually received into the Secretary's Office, for which Patents of Land have [been] issued," and consequently that his right to a grant of land was unquestionable. "But his Excellency being restrained by his Majesty's Instruction from granting lands on any of the Western Waters, the Council advised his Excellency to represent the whole Matter to his Majesty, for farther Directions thereupon." [72]

Mason and Scott were by no means stopped by this decision. They had acquired an official acknowledgment from the Council that their claims to land were valid and would have been honored if the royal prohibition had not intervened. They had also obtained an official document from Benjamin Waller, clerk of the secretary's office, attesting that Mason had a valid claim for the importation of 997 persons and the Reverend James Scott for the importation of 59 persons. [73] Since the new land policy had not been officially promulgated in Virginia in June 1774, Mason and Scott had established an indisputable claim to 49,850 acres and 2,950 acres respectively and, moreover, obtained legal sanction for their interpretation of the headright system. This was no small victory.

The affairs of the Ohio Company took a no less hopeful turn. The Ohio Company dispatched Capt. Hancock Lee to the Kentucky wilderness late in 1774 to begin surveying their western land grants under the rather ambiguous authorization of the Virginia Council. John Tayloe of Mount Airy attempted to secure the official appointment of Lee as deputy surveyor of Fincastle County from William Preston. Without waiting for the commission from Preston, Hancock Lee began surveying lands for the Ohio Company in May 1775. He and his party ran the Ohio Company line from a point in modern Scott County to include portions of Scott, Fayette, and Clark counties and almost all of modern Bourbon County. This tract, amounting to some 400,000 acres, took in all of the fertile upper valley of the South Fork of the Licking River and its tributaries. [74]

On 12 March 1776 George Mason wrote from Gunston Hall to Robert Carter to report that Hancock Lee and Daniel Leet had returned from surveying the Kentucky lands, "and are now here making out their returns and settling their accounts, in assisting about which I am closely engaged." Lee had successfully run the survey "in one large tract, upon a large creek called Licking Creek, which falls into the Ohio River on the southeast side, about 150 miles below the Scioto River." The cost of the survey amounted to some £650 Virginia Currency "and I have never received a farthing from the members towards it," except for Richard Lee and John Tayloe. Mason hoped that Robert Carter would pay his proportionate share. [75]

The surveys that Hancock Lee made in Kentucky on behalf of the Ohio Company attracted the hostile attention of some of their rivals for lands on the western waters. Lee held a commission as deputy surveyor from William Crawford, who, in turn, had authority from the

College of William and Mary as well as an appointment as deputy surveyor for Augusta County. William Preston and John May determined to challenge Crawford's authority as a means of striking at the Ohio Company. Rival land companies managed to block Lee's appointment as an official surveyor and by this prevented the Ohio Company from validating its surveys.[76]

George Mason returned to his earlier project of obtaining land by purchasing headrights from merchants. William Ramsay of Alexandria had brought thirty-seven indentured servants from Ireland to Virginia in 1744, and on 20 May 1776 obtained a certificate in Fairfax County Court for their importation, which he sold to George Mason for £9 on the same day. At the Fairfax County Court session on 21 October 1776 John Carlyle and John Dalton of Alexandria presented a list of sixty-six indentured servants they had brought into Virginia in 1745 and transferred their rights to Mason for £16. John Dalton also sold Mason the headrights for six English servants brought over in 1762, and Robert Adam of Alexandria transferred headrights for eighty-four indentured servants. On 14 November 1776 James Dunlop of Caroline County sold his rights to a land grant for seven indentured servants to Mason. By these additional purchases in 1776, George Mason increased his headright claims by an additional 10,000 acres for 200 individuals settled in Virginia. He was entitled altogether to 59,850 acres.

Separation from the British Empire abrogated the policies set up by ministers and agents of the Crown. George Mason took a major role in developing the land policy of the newly independent Commonwealth of Virginia. Virginians now had the opportunity to create their own western land policy. On 13 December 1777 the Virginia House of Delegates, after considering means of raising a revenue, determined that a portion of the unappropriated lands should be disposed of and that the money obtained in this way be "applied in aid of the funds to be provided for discharging the public debt, and that a land office be established for granting waste and unappropriated lands." The aim and purpose is remarkably like that of the Board of Trade proposal in 1774. George Mason was appointed to the committee to draw up the necessary legislation.

On 8 January 1778 Mason introduced a bill for establishing a land office and ascertaining the terms and manner of granting waste and unappropriated lands. Mason's bill went through two readings, but it was then effectively tabled for the remainder of the session by a parliamentary maneuver by his opponents. Aware that the bill would not pass in that session, Mason and his colleagues succeeded in pushing a series of resolutions through the House on the twenty-fourth. These resolves provided that every entry in the country upon the western waters after that date, except for surveys for tracts of less than 400 acres filed with the county surveyor, would be void until the establishment of a land office and that any conditions to be set in the bill would be retroactive. More important, they provided that "all persons claiming any unpatented lands on the said western waters by order of Council, shall lay the same before the General Assembly on or before the 20th day of their next session." [77]

By these resolves the October 1778 session of the Virginia legislature was authorized to adjudicate the claims of the several land syndicates with warrants for tracts beyond the mountains. On 20 November 1778 Mason submitted a petition to the Assembly on behalf of the Ohio Company. At this time eleven shareholders in the Ohio Company resided in Virginia, three in Maryland, and six in Great Britain. With their members so dispersed, the term of their original copartnership expired,

and a War carried on against America by Great Britain, Your Memorialists conceiving it absolutely impracticable for them to comply with that part of the Royal Instruction respecting the Fort and Garrison (originally intended in the Lieu of paying Right-Money) and also that the same is incompatible with the Nature and Constitution of the present Government. Such of the Members of the said company as reside in Virginia and Maryland are willing and desirous to receive a separate Grant or Patent, each in his own Name, for his due share or proportion of the said two hundred thousand Acres of Land, in the common Form, and in Lieu of the Fort and Garrison, to pay for the same the ancient accustomed Right-Money, of ten shillings Sterling per hundred acres; but do not care to advance their money for others; especially for those beyond Sea, in the present Situation of Affairs.[78]

With the reception accorded their petition, the case of the Ohio Company seemed to be reaching a happy outcome.

George Mason and the Reverend James Scott had other claims for lands beyond the Blue Ridge based on the headright assignments that they had acquired after 1773. Scott sent a petition to the Virginia Assembly in May 1778 explaining that he had filed the proper certificates for the importation of fifty-nine indentured servants with the Prince William County Court in 1773 and laid them before the governor and Council in 1774. He would have received his grant of 2,950 acres at that time, but the governor had been enjoined by the king from granting lands on the western waters. Scott asked the Virginia Assembly to make the grant at this time. Mason evidently relied on the general provisions of the land office bill and entered no petition of his own.[79]

On 3 April 1779 Mason wrote to Thomas Jefferson regarding the bills for determining the land policy of Virginia that were still awaiting action by the legislature. "I have, since I came up from the last Session, drawn over again the two Bills for establishing a Land-Office, and for adjusting & setling the Claims to unpatented Lands under the former Government &c. in which I have provided for some Omissions, & Difficultys in the Execution; but have made no material Alterations in the Plan which you & I had agreed on in the Bills in Janry. 1778, except one, in the Land-Office Bill; which I will submit to your Consideration, when we meet, & be governed in it entirely by your Opinion." [80]

Mason's bill for settling titles to unpatented lands was his final answer to the challenge presented by Lord Dartmouth and the Board of Trade in 1773–74 as well as by the Vandalia proprietors and the other land companies since that time. Various and vague claims to unpatented lands covered the greater part of the lands on the western waters, Mason asserted in his preamble, and would discourage purchasers from taking up lands under the proposed land offices act. He proposed therefore

that all Surveys heretofore made by any sworn surveyor, acting under commission from the Masters of William and Mary College, and founded either upon Charter Importation Rights duly proved and certified according to ancient Usage, upon Treasury Rights for Money paid the late Receiver General, upon Entrys made with the Surveyor of any County for Tracts of Land not exceeding four hundred acres, according to Act of Assembly upon any Order of Council or regular Entry in the Council Books, or upon any Warrant from any Governor for the time being, for Military Service in Virtue of any Proclamation either from the King of Great Britain or any former Governor of Virginia, shall be good and valid.[81]

Under Mason's plan, individuals who claimed lands under headrights, or treasury rights, or as military bounty land, but who had not actually located their lands by a surveyor, would be able to obtain warrants for such a survey from the land office. Other lands claimed under orders or entries in the records of the Governor's Council would be granted, but no claim to land founded upon the king of Great Britain's Proclamation of 1763 would be allowed, unless warrants had already been issued by a governor of Virginia or the service had been performed in a Virginia regiment. Mason also sought to protect the interest of actual settlers, who could obtain warrants for tracts of 400 acres on the basis of their settlement and who could preempt in addition 1,000 acres on the terms established by the land office bill.[82]

The Virginia House of Delegates took up the land office bill on 5 June 1779 and passed it on the seventeenth. The Senate made a considerable number of amendments to the bill, altering it to suit the desires of the land companies and large speculators. The lower house concurred in these changes and the bill became law. Mason and Jefferson had intended to make it possible for any county clerk to issue land warrants, but the bill as enacted gave this privilege solely to the land office. The same individuals who had reaped bounteous harvests in the secretary's office at Williamsburg would be able to look after their own interest in the land office, but the small farmer in western Virginia, without friends or influences beyond his county seat, could only patent his claim with considerable difficulty. The original tenor of the bill was further altered by the addition of provisions to quiet titles where surveys had included more land than was warranted. This situation was far from common; the actual survey of the Ohio Company lands was closer to 400,000 acres than to their claim for 200,000 acres. In dealing with this problem, the Virginia Assembly gave every advantage to the land speculator, whose holdings might be doubled or tripled by a faulty survey and made it practically impossible for anyone to challenge the title to the surplus lands.[83]

Mason and Jefferson had failed in their effort to write a land policy for Virginia that could not be twisted by speculators to their own advantage. Mason had also failed to secure lands claimed by himself and his Ohio Company partners. The claims for western lands under Dinwiddie's 1754 proclamation were expressly allowed by an amendment, even though their surveyor (Crawford) did not have an appointment from the county surveyor (Preston). No such special favor validated the Ohio Company claims. Another amendment introduced in Mason's bill provided "that all claims for lands upon surveys under any order of Council's or entry in the council books, shall by the respective claimers be laid before the court of appeals; which shall meet for that purpose on the sixteenth day of December next, and shall adjourn from day to day until the business be finished." [84] Since the Ohio Company survey was tainted by Hancock Lee's failure to obtain a license from the county surveyor of Fincastle, it could not meet the specifications laid down in George Mason's bill. While his bills were under consideration, Mason wrote to Richard Henry Lee about the Ohio Company's struggle with the legislature. This letter suggests that Mason himself introduced the amendment or at least concurred in it:

The Ohio Company were not permitted a special Investigation of their claim, obliged to submit to the Description in a general Bill, and thus in

Fact denied a Hearing; & yet Every Attempt, that art of Cunning cou'd suggest, was made to introduce particular words to exclude them. I have spared no Trouble, nor omitted anything in my Power, to procure them Justice; the only chance now left, is to get their Claim referred to the Court of Appeals, & to preserve to them the right of their Location, by Resurveying the same Lands, if their Claim shall be established upon a hearing before the said Court; & in this I have still Hopes of succeeding; two Days more will determine it.[85]

In the end nothing could save the Ohio Company grants. It may well be that Mason's victorious campaign against the Indiana Company, the heirs of the Vandalia scheme, and the other land speculators exacted this bitter price by uniting Mason's rivals against him.[86]

More successful was the outcome of Mason's fight to validate his headright claims. "My charter rights I believe will be established," Mason told Richard Henry Lee in June 1779, "and my location preserved to me, upon resurveying the same lands, that is upon putting a considerable sum of money out of my pocket into the county surveyor's, for the State will not gain a copper by it." Mason alluded to the opposition that this part of his bill had faced, particularly from "our friend B——n," apparently Carter Braxton, who served on the committee that reported the bill.[87]

The lands that George Mason actually took up were all in western Kentucky, lying along Panther Creek, just south of modern Owensboro in Daviess County. At a hearing held on 25 February 1807 at the Yellow Banks, now Owensboro, William Bailey Smith testified that in 1779 Mason had asked him to locate lands for which Mason had obtained warrants, by surveying land on Panther Creek for him. Smith had not undertaken Mason's survey, but he had given Hancock Lee detailed information about the Panther Creek region. George Mason had evidently changed his mind about the best location for his grant soon after the passage of the bills that had made it possible.[88]

On 12 July 1779 George Mason obtained warrants from the Virginia Land Office for 59,850 acres, divided into five warrants each for slightly more than 8,000 acres, four warrants for tracts of roughly 4,000 acres apiece, and one 2,000 acre tract. The Reverend James Scott obtained a warrant for 2,950 acres on the same day. Their plan to use lists of indentured servants as a means of obtaining land through the headright system had at last come to fruition. On 22 December 1779 George Mason returned his warrants to the land office together with completed surveys of nearly 60,000 acres on the waters of Licking River. He had evidently altered his plans even before he filed his surveys, for when he withdrew these entries on 29 March 1780, Mason already had surveys of the land on Panther Creek that he intended to take up instead. Mason's surveyors had located one tract of 8,400 acres on the east side of Panther Creek, about four miles above the mouth of the west fork. A second tract of 8,300 acres was also located on the east side of Panther Creek, beginning at the upper corner of the first entry. A third tract began at John Smith's upper corner on the west side of Panther Creek and comprised 8,200 acres. This tract included both sides of the Horst Fork of Panther Creek. A tract of 8,100 acres adjoined the tract just mentioned. The mouth of the North Fork of Panther Creek was included in this tract. Adjoining it was a tract of 4,500 acres mostly between the North Fork and Panther Creek. A tract of 4,200 acres ran along Panther Creek. Mason also entered surveys for a tract of 8,000 acres, which he described as "on the Ohio two miles below the mouth of a large Creek running into said River about twenty miles above the mouth of Green River." This 8,000 acre tract was located on the Ohio River on both sides of Yellow Creek. Mason also patented a 2,000 acre tract adjoining this land on Yellow Creek and a tract of 700 acres along Panther Creek upstream from his 4,000 acre tract. Although located in 1780, surveys of Mason's land were not completed until 1783, and the 10,000 acres on the Ohio and Yellow Creek had not been surveyed by December 1785. Mason had exchanged this land for a tract of the same acreage on Panther Creek in an amicable settlement with John May of a disputed title.[89]

The careless methods of Kentucky surveyors involved Mason in almost continual litigation over his lands along Panther Creek. In September 1785 he wrote to Col. George Muter to inform him that Thomas and James Barbour had each separately entered caveats against his surveys of lands above the North Fork of Panther Creek, embracing Mason's tracts totaling 17,500 acres on the upper reaches of the main stream. Mason sent a copy of the caveat filed by George Wilson against him and of his own caveat against Wilson to Colonel Muter. The case of Wilson vs. Mason dragged through the courts for many years after Mason's death.[90]

Although the title to his Panther Creek and Yellow Creek property was still in dispute when George Mason died on 7 October 1792, his children followed his verbal wish to provide a legacy of 4,000 acres of Kentucky land to each of his daughters. None of this property had been mentioned in specific terms in George Mason's will, so that it was bequeathed in general terms to William, Thomson, John, and Thomas Mason. In order to secure the legacy for their sisters and provide a more unified approach to the legal tangle in the Kentucky courts, William, Thomson, John, and Thomas Mason; Rinaldo Johnson and

Ann (Mason) Johnson; Daniel and Sarah (Mason) McCarty; John Cooke and Mary (Mason) Cooke; and William Thornton and Elizabeth (Mason) Thornton turned over all of their claims to Kentucky lands on 21 June 1794 to George Mason of Lexington.[91]

Of all the extensive acreage in Maryland, Virginia, West Virginia, and Kentucky owned by Mason in his lifetime, a portion of the land on Panther Creek in Daviess County, Kentucky, is the only tract that has never been sold out of the family. The great tracts on the Licking River, where the hopes of the Ohio Company settled for a time, had disappeared before 1783. All the exertions of thirty years in behalf of that grand illusion proved in the end to be in vain.

Chapter VI

George Mason IV: Plantation Economy

THE TOBACCO TRADE was an important fact of life for George Mason of Gunston Hall and his neighbors on the Potomac. The commission merchant had given way to the tobacco buyer, who sold goods and purchased tobacco at a fixed place instead of accepting shipments of tobacco on consignment. For men who conducted their business in this way, the official inspection warehouse was the natural site for a store. If the factor had to buy all his tobacco at the warehouse and ship it from there, any other location would simply increase his costs. Glasgow and Whitehaven factors set up shop close to the warehouses, petitioned for a town, and once they were formally organized, drew still more tobacco factors to their community.

Regulation of the tobacco trade in Virginia in 1730 and in Maryland in 1747 set still another pattern in the social and economic life of the Chesapeake-Potomac region. The planter had to carry his crops to an official inspection warehouse where he would normally store his tobacco pending its sale. These warehouses were scattered along the rivers at convenient intervals. In Fairfax County, where most of Mason's property was located, there were warehouses at the Occoquan, at the mouth of Pohick Creek, at Hunting Creek, and at the falls of the Potomac. The principal warehouse in Prince William County was on Quantico Creek. When Maryland followed the example of her sister colony, inspection warehouses were set up at similar intervals along the Potomac as far up river as the mouth of Rock Creek, just below the Little Falls. There was no need for warehouses above the fall line, as the impossibility of shipping from there set an effective boundary on expansion beyond the falls.

The inspection and grading, buying and selling, and actual shipping of tobacco were now all localized by act of Assembly at the warehouse. No more convenient place could then be found for the tobacco merchant to conduct his business. The tobacco buyer and the consignment merchant both loaded their ships at the inspection warehouse. The Scottish retailers found it an ideal location for their stores. After 1730 the commercial life of the Potomac gradually settled around the inspection warehouses, and every warehouse became the nucleus of a small town. These tobacco towns of the Potomac sprang into being to serve the needs of trade and were already commercially important when the Assembly gave them legal status.

The development of these commercial centers gave an added importance to the ferries across the Potomac and the lesser rivers. As Rock Creek Warehouse drew merchants and factors in the tobacco trade, the Rock Creek Ferry over the Potomac gave access to a thriving town. On 11 May 1749 the Assembly passed almost identical bills for the creation of a town at Quantico Creek on the land of John Graham, near the public warehouses, and for the creation of a town on land owned by Philip Alexander and Hugh West, situated on the Potomac River near the mouth of Great Hunting Creek. The town on Quantico was to be called Dumfries, presumably in compliment to John Graham and the other factors from that Scottish city. The town at the Hunting Creek Warehouse was to be known as Alexandria, in honor of the Alexanders.[1]

Since the two enabling acts are almost verbally identical, the Dumfries and Alexandria promoters were clearly of one mind on the advantage to be reaped from creating a town. The sixty acres included in each townsite were to be surveyed and laid out in streets and lots of equal size. The lots were then to be sold at auction. No one purchaser might own more than two lots at any one time. The total purchase price was to be paid to the landowner, in the one case Graham, in the other West and the Alexanders. Everyone who purchased a lot was obliged to improve it within two years by erecting a house of brick, wood, or stone at least twenty feet square, or his lot would be forfeited to the trustees of the town.

The advantage to the original landowner is obvious, but it was the merchants, not the landowners, who initiated the movement for the establishment of towns. The landowners actually seem to have been in opposition to the proposed town in the case of Georgetown, planned by the Maryland Assembly in 1750 to be located at Rock Creek warehouse.[2] What did the tobacco factors at Dumfries gain that they did not already possess when they opened their stores at Quantico warehouse? The answer seems to lie in what these enabling acts did not provide. Each of these tobacco towns was to be laid out in lots and the lots auctioned by a board of trustees, who were appointed by the Assembly initially, but who were thereafter to fill up vacancies in their own number without reference to anyone else. These self-perpetuating boards of trustees had full control over such matters as building wharves, marketplaces, public landings, and so on.

There was nothing democratic about the organization of these town boards. While the law limited membership to actual lot owners, in practice membership was narrowed still further to influential merchants or local magnates. Inhabitants of the town had no claim under that title to take part in local elections, since the boards were self-perpetuating, nor in the election of representatives to the Assembly, since none of these towns were entitled to a representative of their own, apart from the burgesses chosen by each county. The Maryland legislation explicitly stated that these tobacco towns were not being chartered as borough towns and could claim no special status.

George Mason served on the town board of both Dumfries and Alexandria. Unfortunately, the loss of the Dumfries trustees' records makes it impossible to know any details of his service on this board, but apparently he had resigned before 1761.[3] Though he was not one of the original trustees of the town of Alexandria, he was chosen to fill a vacancy in 1754 and served on the Alexandria board thereafter until 1779, when the town of Alexandria became a self-governing municipality.[4]

In the original division of Alexandria property, Mason acquired lot 53, situated at the northeast corner of King and Fairfax streets, and lot 55, situated at the northeast corner of King and Royal streets. The deed to George Mason, from William Ramsay and John Pagan, trustees of Alexandria, dated 28 March 1752, adhered to the requirements concerning the erection of a house on the property, and Mason evidently built the necessary structure to improve his lot.[5] On 20 July 1762 George and Ann (Eilbeck) Mason conveyed lot 53 in Alexandria, together with the houses, buildings, and other improvements, for £114 4s. 6d. to Richard Arell of Alexandria, merchant.[6] On 15 October 1762 he sold lot 55 with its improvements for £120 Virginia currency to David Young of Alexandria, baker. This deed was witnessed by Harry Piper and Hector Ross, both merchants in the tobacco trade. George Mason also acquired lot 54, which fronted on Royal Street, when it was forfeited by its original patentee, and conveyed it, evidently still unimproved to George Mercer of Fairfax County, Gentleman, for £10 on 18 August 1756.[7]

The trustees of Alexandria made every effort to develop the nascent town. In 1760 they proposed a public lottery to raise money for repairing the public wharf and erecting a grammar school in Alexandria. The managers of the lottery were to be George William Fairfax, William Ramsay, John Carlyle, Gerard Alexander, John Dalton, George Johnston, George Mason, Robert Hunter, John Muir, and Robert Adam, all of whom were authorized to sell tickets for the Alexandria lottery.[8]

Keeping wharves in repair and providing for public warehouses and other public buildings were among the most important concerns of the town trustees, for if trade moved elsewhere, grass would again grow in the streets of Georgetown and Alexandria. Their deliberations were always taken with an eye to the tobacco and wheat trade that provided their town with its lifeblood. The merchants of Dumfries and Colchester had a similar sense of priorities.

The Maryland tobacco merchants gradually came to see the value of Sir William Gooch's legislation for the regulation of the staple. When the Virginia shore of the Potomac enjoyed a new burst of commercial enterprise as a result of the building of towns, credit and commerce fled from the Maryland shore. In 1747 the Maryland Assembly bowed to the inevitable and passed an act for the inspection of tobacco on the model of the 1730 Virginia legislation. When the initial act came up for renewal in 1753, few correspondents of the *Maryland Gazette* saw any reason to return to the system, or lack of system, that prevailed before 1747.[9]

The Maryland legislation created an inspection warehouse in 1745 at the mouth of Rock Creek, on the land of George Gordon.[10] As noted, the Virginia warehouse sites formed the nuclei of towns, and it could be expected that the Rock Creek inspection warehouse would do the same if the Scottish and Whitehaven factors in Maryland followed the pattern set by their neighbors in Virginia. George Mason could not have been unaware of this fact when he petitioned in 1748 for the right to the Rock Creek Ferry. He had chosen Gordon's Warehouse at Rock Creek as the spot to store the goods of the Ohio Company before Georgetown came into existence. As early as 1749 the company ordered its factor, Hugh Parker, to send goods up the Potomac. The company's enterprise at Rock Creek is mentioned in Mason's correspondence with John Pagan in 1753 as the point of embarkation for settlers moving west.[11]

The bitter rivalry with which some of the Occoquan landowners viewed the possibility of a town at Dumfries or Alexandria counted against them and led town builders to ignore the site of the old Prince William Courthouse on the broad expanse of the Occoquan River. In 1753 the Virginia lawmakers remedied the situation by creating the town of Colchester on Doegs' Neck opposite the ferry landing on the Mason property at the courthouse. Its site included twenty-five acres of land owned by Peter Wagener on the northern bank of the Occoquan.[12] It is curious that no Mason appeared as a founding father of a town almost surrounded by their lands. Colchester was born after Alexandria, Georgetown, and Dumfries had begun to flourish and never rivaled the older towns.

No one thought seriously of the town as a place in which to live. It was primarily a place to make money and then to return to the more agreeable surroundings of the countryside. Large planters, such as Mason and Washington, had an office in Alexandria. Tobacco factors needed to reside above their stores or next door to them, but they were generally bachelors, dreaming of the soft mists of Ayrshire and the girls they left behind. When some fair Virginian or Marylander won their hearts, they set about improving the acres they had bought up river as a hedge against the future and took their brides to plantations christened Cross Basket, Gosforth, or Burlieth, after the villages they might never see again.

These Scot factors were the dominant voices in the tobacco towns on the Potomac. They had called them into existence, and the proud little river ports now served only an ancillary role in the tobacco trade. The Scottish and West Cumberland factors made their presence felt to an increasing degree in the years between the French and Indian War and the American Revolution. Writing in 1765, William Lux of Annapolis observed that Glasgow merchants were competing everywhere for the Patuxent and Potomac trade. In a series of reports to his employers in the 1760s, the Whitehaven factor Harry Piper noted sourly that "the Scotch grasp at everything." [13]

The Glasgow merchants did not have it all their own way once they gained the lion's share of the tobacco trade. In 1764 James Lawson of Glasgow sent his nephew Alexander Hamilton, factor at Port Tobacco, an explanation of the costs that had to be calculated in setting the price of tobacco in Maryland:

A Note of the Charges Discounts & Allowances on Tobacco calculated to cost 7/- pr Ct in Maryland . . . . Vizt.

To one Hhd Tobacco con[tainin]g 1000 lbs at 7/- Stg pr Ct.	£3.10. 0
To 4 per Cent for Cask	0. 2. 9½
To Inspection in Maryland	0. 2. 6
To Impost in Maryland	0. 2. 3
To Craft hire in Maryland	0. 2. 6
To Freight Home at £6..10 per Ton	1.12. 6
To Insurance on do. at 3½ per Cent	0. 2.10
To Import & export Charges here 6/ per hhd	0. 6. 0
To Interest on Subsidy & Celler Rent	0. 3. 6
	£6. 4.10½
One Hhd by manifest	1000 lbs.
Shrinkage on do	70
	930
Nailage at Exportation	4
	926 lbs.

4 per Cent discount for payment ⎱
3 months after shipping which is ⎰ 37 lbs.
the present case on all that is ⎰
lately sold

889 lbs. at 1½d. per lb.   £5.17. 9½

Loss   0. 7. 1

N. B. The above is the justest Calculation I can make on the hhd. and by which you may easily calculate whether it is best to settle the Accounts in Tobacco or in Currency. This Specimen will serve for a Cargoe as one Hhd. You will know whether the Charges with you in Maryland are more or less than mentioned above. Tobacco just now in Holland does not neat above ½ per lb. and here it will not sell at any price. God pity those who are Concerned in such a Trade. I am really feared it will not sell at any price, there is so much of it made, and it certainly will be the case while the Planters continue making so much as they have done for some years past. I wish to God I was out of the Trade for undoubtedly we must all be ruined while it Continues in this dismal situation There being large quantities lying upon hand here, London, Holland, and in short Every Market in Europe.[14]

While this letter reflects the depressed conditions of the market at the close of the Seven Years War, the problem of fixed charges to be calculated and the effects of overproduction on tobacco prices remained a constant. The factor had to be a man the company could depend on to act wisely and decisively, when consultation with the home office required the lapse of many months.

The factors did what they could to keep prices down on the Virginia rivers. They met each year at Williamsburg during the session of the General Court to set a mutually agreeable policy on wholesale and retail prices. The Scottish houses needed some brake on tobacco prices, since they rarely could fill their ships with tobacco brought in by their retail stores and necessarily bought large quantities of tobacco on the open market. The Scots were retail merchants by preference, selling dry goods and hardware for tobacco, and had to balance with great accuracy the wholesale price of tobacco in Virginia and in Scotland with the wholesale and retail prices of Sheffield needles and Kilmarnock shoes.

The consignment merchants had a different set of problems. Some of the principal consignment merchants, such as Samuel Martin of Whitehaven, dealt with retail storekeepers and employed their own factors. The majority of them kept clear of sending out goods to the Chesapeake.

The tobacco grower could play off one set of traders against the other. If the Glasgow buyers offered too low a price on the Potomac, the grower could ship his crop on consignment to a merchant in London. If the consignment merchant gave him no inducement to ship, he could sell his crop in Virginia and be done with it. The consignment merchant might promise a better price than the market would permit and advance cash or credit to the planter on that basis. The Glasgow factor might raise his price to keep the planters from shipping. Both would discover that the market would not support their optimism.

The planters distrusted the merchants, and frequently combined to hold back crops to force prices to rise. (George Mason was rumored to be the leader of one such combination.) The Glasgow merchant had already sold last year's merchandise against this year's crop and sent out other goods to engage next year's crop while his factors collected last year's debts. With money nearly as scarce in Glasgow as on the Potomac, neither group could break out of this cycle.

The wheat trade was an important element in the commercial life of northern Virginia. When Nicholas Cresswell visited Alexandria in 1774 he was told that "they exported 100,000 bushels of wheat and 14,000 barrels of flour from this port, last year." The wheat brought from the back country was "as good wheat as I ever saw" but he had a poor opinion of Virginia farming methods.[15] By 1775 there were four Alexandria firms engaged in the wheat and flour trade for every tobacco merchant in town.[16]

Virginians clung tenaciously to the agricultural methods of their grandfathers, to the detriment of their fortunes. The few gentlemen farmers with a bent for scientific agriculture were the exceptions that proved the rule. J. F. D. Smyth, who spent some years in Charles County, Maryland, contrasted the handsome country seats of the great planters with their ill-tended fields and badly managed crops. More casual visitors to the Potomac carried back the same tale. Poor farming methods invariably meant a poor yield. However, a Scottish factor at Colchester on Occoquan Creek thought the wheat fully equal to that grown on the James River and, like many British merchants, favored the wheat trade over the tobacco business because it was exclusively a cash trade with none of the long credits usual in the tobacco trade.[17]

As the Scots began to gather a greater share of the tobacco trade into their hands, they gathered with it a great deal of the available credit on the Potomac. These resident-agents of British firms invested heavily in land in Virginia and Maryland, sometimes as speculators, sometimes as developers of iron and other mineral interests, and sometimes as shareholders in the vast enterprises of the Ohio Company and the Principio Company. They also invested in the smaller merchant mills, iron forges, and even snuff manufactories that developed in the Chesa-peake in the middle years of the century.[18]

Money was scarce in Virginia for a number of reasons, not least of which was that tobacco so greatly dominated the economy. Planters necessarily sank a great deal of their capital into land and slaves. It was in this way that the Chesapeake economy was expanding. Over-production, brought about by this expansion, tended to cheapen the market value of the principal cash crops. Careless farming methods had a similar tendency to reduce the market value of farm acreage. Large and small planter alike operated on a narrow margin in the best of times and slid easily into debt. Tobacco growing was not un-profitable by any means, but it was called upon to support far too high a standard of living in the case of the large planters. While they were men of more than simple means, their fortunes in most cases were not of the amplitude to cover the costly possessions with which they sur-rounded themselves, and they ran deeply into debt.

Credit with his British correspondent enabled the Virginia planter to live far more lavishly than he could have if he were obliged to pay cash for every nail and for every bolt of calico. Extensive credit and the extravagant tastes of the Virginia gentlemen contributed to an unfavorable balance of payments against the Chesapeake colonies. The value of the tobacco and other products exported from Maryland and Virginia did not equal the value of the imports of goods from Britain and slaves shipped by British merchants. Planter debts shifted the burden of extravagant living onto the shoulders of the businessmen and bankers of Glasgow and Whitehaven. When British firms ex-tended long-term credits to Marylanders and Virginians, they were in effect investing in the expanding plantation economy. When the planter used credit to buy cloth and nails, fine furniture, or fashion-able gowns or to send his children to Saint Bees or Marischal College, he was able to turn the cash received for his tobacco into more slaves and more land. The merchant was, consequently, enabling the planter to expand by giving him credit. The unfavorable trade balance tended to raise the rate of exchange, and this unfavorable balance was due, in large measure, to the extravagant purchases made by planters who enjoyed long-term credit from British merchants. To this extent, the British merchant was himself the cause of the misery he suffered from the high exchange rate of the early 1760s.[19]

The Glasgow factor on the Potomac also suffered from the rising exchange rate. His debts and obligations, as well as those of his princi-pal at home, were all in sterling, but their store accounts and small currency loans were all payable in paper. The factor in Virginia was therefore obliged to send home bills payable in sterling. The merchants lost money whenever exchange rates rose beyond expectations between the time a debt was entered in Virginia and the time it was paid. One Virginia tobacco trader complained in 1762 that the Scottish traders had all been "amazingly infatuated for some years past by giving too extensive Credits to our Customers in consequence of the Credit we ourselves had with our friends at home . . . and now in Order to Assist our friends which we before neglected are obliged to remitt at a very high Exchange Such as no trade can afford." [20]

The exchange rates turned on the balance of payments. These reflected the fluctuating trade relations between an underdeveloped agricultural economy with little capital and an advanced industrial one. When British firms restricted credit, in effect withdrawing their investment in an expanding plantation economy, the rate of exchange rose sharply. In 1761–62 many British firms were compelled by the situation at home to tighten credit and demand remittances from their factors and correspondents. This pressured the factors, who were forced to dun their customers for payment in depreciated currency in order to send their remittances home at a ruinous exchange rate. [21]

Tobacco factors were caught between the home office and the planters and between falling commodity prices and soaring exchange rates. The planters were so deeply in debt that they could settle with only some of their creditors; the rest would be put off and forced to go to law. With the tobacco market grossly oversupplied, the merchant did better to take currency in settlement of his account than tobacco, despite the high rate of exchange.

The debt-ridden planter had several weapons in his own arsenal. The real buying power of 500 pounds of Little Frederick tobacco at Pohick Warehouse depended on the price that the British merchants would pay for it. The Virginia legislators normally could do little or nothing to influence the price of tobacco on the world market. They were, however, able to set the rate at which tobacco notes could be converted into Virginia currency. The celebrated Two-Penny Acts gave Virginians the option of paying their debts in cash or tobacco at the rate of twelve shillings sixpence the hundred pounds, or roughly twopence a pound, when the market price of the meanest variety was approaching twenty-five shillings the hundredweight. This legislation was swiftly disallowed, of course, by the authorities in London. Without this artificial interference the value of tobacco fluctuated with the demands of the European markets. The Two-Penny Acts of 1755 and 1758 represented one kind of direct relief that was most profitable to the larger planters. The continued emission of paper currency during the war years represented another form of relief. As the first money depreciated in value, the rate of exchange for Virginia currency to be converted into sterling began to rise from this source.[22]

There were other causes, many of them beyond the control, or even the foresight, of any of the merchants on the Potomac. The Maryland Inspection Act had expired in 1770 and was not renewed. The issue of regulation of the tobacco trade was inextricably confused with Maryland politics, with the controverted rate of exchange for tobacco into currency, and with the fees paid in tobacco to various officials of church and province. To meet the crisis, Potomac tobacco buyers agreed to purchase tobacco only at existing inspection warehouses between 1 November and 1 July of each year. They set the hogshead at 900 pounds and would take smaller quantities only at a 6 percent reduction. They appointed county committees of merchants to deal with new problems as they arose. Barnes and Ridgate were among the twenty-five signers of this agreement.[23] Private inspection sprang up under the patronage of local tobacco merchants. "An Honest Planter" protested in the columns of the *Maryland Gazette* against a self-interested group establishing law by fiat and compared the merchants to the North Carolina Regulators.[24] The effect of all this uncertainty was reflected in the tobacco prices current on the Potomac. James Brown, a Glasgow factor, tried to sell his store goods on a one-price scale, rather than discounting goods for tobacco, and there is considerable evidence that the tobacco factors were dissatisfied with the state of the market. All the worst features of the trash tobacco era were revived. Debtors had no reason to be concerned about the quality of their crop when any grade of tobacco could pay their rent or their bills. Consignment merchants could take the dregs of the market if the Glasgow factors refused. The price of Maryland tobacco naturally fell in Great Britain, and the Potomac shopkeepers were the real sufferers.[25]

The tobacco trade could be highly profitable, however, for those firms who had the staying power to survive a bad season. John Glassford of Glasgow greatly expanded his interests during the 1760s and consolidated his hold on the Potomac trade.[26] Other British firms collapsed during the same decade, sometimes dragging down their Virginia correspondents. The failure of Peter How and Company of Whitehaven caused litigation that was far from settlement in 1778. Robert Bogle and Scott, of Glasgow, and Perkins, Buchanan and Brown, of London, went bankrupt in the early 1770s. Both firms had been active on the Potomac for more than ten years.[27]

Richard Henry Lee observed in 1773 that sending out goods had been the ruin of many firms trading on the Potomac and urged William Lee to attend strictly to the business of a consignment merchant.[28] Businessmen seem to have been an optimistic lot even in the worst of times, and for every failure in the tobacco trade, there were new partnerships forming in Glasgow and London and on the Chesapeake itself. John Barnes and Thomas How Ridgate, comparative latecomers to the Potomac tobacco trade, seemed determined to lose no time in gaining a large share of the market. They quickly expanded their operations along the Patuxent and on both sides of the Potomac and made large investments in land, particularly in town lots in Georgetown and Carrollsburg.[29] While many a Glasgow factor was content to supervise one or two branch establishments, Barnes and Ridgate maintained stores in Georgetown, Port Tobacco, Newport, Benedict, and Nottingham in Maryland, and at Colchester and Dumfries in Virginia.[30] The firm went into bankruptcy after prolonged litigation in 1771. They had considerable assets, including goods worth £5900 and houses and lots in Benedict, Newport, and Georgetown, which were offered for sale in 1773 to meet the demands of their Maryland creditors. George Mason offered goods from Barnes and Ridgate's Colchester store for sale in 1773 in advertisements in the *Virginia Gazette*.[31] Mason had apparently advanced a considerable sum of money to Barnes and Ridgate during their expansive years. On 19 May 1773 John Barnes and Thomas How Ridgate transferred all the debts due to them for transactions at their Colchester store with their factor, Edward Sprigg, Jr., to George Mason and Martin Cockburn, acknowledging their indebtedness to Mason and Cockburn in the deed. John Rogers, Thomas Stone, and Philip R. Fendall acted as receivers for Barnes and Ridgate in Maryland. Mason gradually recovered his losses from the ruin of Barnes and Ridgate. Martin Cockburn, himself a merchant, did much of the actual collecting. His ledgers record the recovery of many small sums between 17 September 1774 and 31 December 1778 under the heading "Colonel George Mason on account of Barnes and Ridgate." [32]

The affairs of Barnes and Ridgate occupied a surprising amount of Mason's tme. Promissory notes from Frederick Nicholls and Edward Smith in the Gunston Hall archives preserve the record of two debtors who came to an early agreement with Mason in May and July 1773, respectively. In the September 1773 term of the Fairfax County Court, Mason and Cockburn were obliged to sue others for small sums owed to the defunct firm. Some of the other claims dragged on for years, as such cases often did. A paper in the hand of Martin Cockburn, now in the possession of the Virginia Historical Society, records the final settlement of the affairs of Barnes and Ridgate: on 17 May 1790 Barnes and Ridgate still owed George Mason the sum of £183 17s. 6d. sterling or £217 13s. 7d. Virginia Currency. Their debtors had paid £123 13s. 7d., and Barnes and Ridgate agreed to pay Mason £93 9s. for the balance.[33]

The failure of Barnes and Ridgate and the losses that John Barnes had brought on his father and his Mason kinsmen caused Col. Abraham Barnes to disinherit his elder son in his will. Richard Barnes, the second son, was his principal heir together with his Mason grandchildren.[34] Richard inherited the Tudor Hall plantation at his father's death in 1778. After the failure of Barnes and Ridgate, John Barnes turned to developing lands in western Maryland and emerged as a popular leader in Washington County, Maryland. He developed the estate known as Montpelier. Both men made their nephew John Thomson Mason their heir, on condition he assume the surname Barnes, so that all of the Barnes property in Maryland eventually came into the Mason family.

The reasons for Barnes and Ridgate's failure can only be surmised. They followed a pattern of rapid expansion of new outlets in a trade that subsisted on long-term credits and made capital investments in goods, houses, and lands before their business could begin to make a substantial return on their first investment. They attempted to set up the kind of enterprise that Stephen West had developed over a longer period. Barnes and Ridgate probably moved too fast and outdistanced their own concern. Like John Semple and John Ballendine, they relied on the kind of credit buying utilized by planters and poured cash returns into new efforts while staving off their British creditors. Barnes and Ridgate would seem to be one more example of the chronic shortage of investment capital in the Chesapeake colonies and its unfortunate results for individual entrepreneurs and businesses. The fact that their assets paid an annual dividend to the creditors in receivership and ultimately repaid all the sums advanced to them suggests that Barnes and Ridgate would have shown a substantial profit if the day of reckoning with their creditors could have been postponed.

Barnes and Ridgate had entered into the tobacco trade as consignment merchants, but they dealt also in African slaves and British convict servants at a time when the Chesapeake legislatures frankly aimed at crushing the slave trade by the burdensome purchase tax. Both slaves and servants were costly to maintain; if unsold, both had to be paid for in cash, whether resold or not.[35]

Slavery made the cost of labor to the planter very high, as slaves and indentured servants formed the greatest part of the work force and had to be hired from their masters, rather than hired as individuals. John Mercer of Marlborough wrote in 1768 that he had "hired Mr. Semple 21 negro men, 1 woman & 3 boys & 2 white servants, the man at £12, woman at £6, & boys at £5 the year. He allows each 6 lb. of meat a week, finds them bedding tools, &c. pays their levies & taxes & is to return them completely cloathed. I shou'd have been glad I cou'd have got clear of all the rest upon as good terms, for I am sure those I keep, tho the best will not yield as much profit." Mercer went on to observe that "few people keep regular accounts & therefore don't know what their crops stand them in, & they often imagine them clear gains, after the overseer's share deducted, when if everything else, that ought as properly to be deducted, was so, they wou'd find, they did not amount to the interest of their money. Every negroes cloaths, bedding, corn, tools, levies & taxes will stand yearly at least in £5." Semple was charged £297 for the lease of his laborers in addition to a minimum of £125 for their subsistence, free laborers could have done the same work for £200 or less.[36]

George Mason relied on the labor of a large number of slaves for the operation of a nearly self-sufficient tobacco plantation. He also publicly criticized the entire system of African slavery as he knew it in Virginia. The paradox was not without its own significance. Like many another Virginian of his generation, Mason's experience with slave labor made him hate slavery but his heavy investment in slave property made it difficult for him to divest himself of a system that he despised. He helped end the slave trade with his nonimportation resolves and, later, by direct legislation. Writing to the Fairfax County burgesses in 1765 Mason stated:

The Policy of encouraging the Importation of free People & discouraging that of Slaves has never been duly considered in this Colony, or we shou'd not at this Day see one Half of our best Lands in most Parts of the Country remain unsetled, & the other cultivated with Slaves; not to mention the ill Effect such a Practice has upon the Morals & Manners of our People: one of the first Signs of the Decay, & perhaps the primary Cause of the Destruction of the most flourishing Government that ever existed was the Introduction of great Numbers of Slaves—an Evil very pathetically described by the Roman Historians—but 'tis not the present Intention to expose our Weakness by examining this Subject too freely. That the Custom of leasing Lands is more beneficial to the Community than that of setling them with Slaves is a Maxim that will hardly be denied in any free Country; tho' it may not be attended with so much imediate Profit to the Land-holder: in Proportion as it is more useful to the Public, the Invitations from the Legislature to pursue it shou'd be stronger:—no Means seem so natural as securing the Payment of Rents in an easy & effectual Manner: the little Trouble &

Risque attending this Species of Property may be considered as an Equivalent to the greater Profit arising from the Labour of Slaves, or any other precarious & troublesom Estate.[37]

Mason acknowledged that these ideas formed a digression from his subject. He had promised to send them a suggestion for remedial legislation on writs of replevin. The introductory section on slavery touched only indirectly on the problem of tenants who could not pay their rent and the legal redress available to the landlord. Mason admitted frankly, "The first Part of it has very little to do with the Alteration proposed, & only inculcates a Doctrine I was always fond of promoting, & which I cou'd wish to see more generally adopted than it is like to be." [38] Mason was a convinced opponent of slavery and had offered his thoughts on the subject to the members from Fairfax in hopes that the issue would be taken up by the House of Burgesses.

By 1765 slavery was as firmly fixed in the Chesapeake economy as tobacco. Men of vision who sought to break out of the cycle of tobacco and slaves, overproduction and low prices, agreed with Mason that Virginia should discourage the importation of slaves. The number of slaves in the Chesapeake colonies would always be augmented by natural increase, and the constant importation of fresh laborers from Africa could only presage an enormous slave population at a future date. The slave trade was profitable to the African chief as well as to the Liverpool merchant, and so long as Virginians continued to pay a high enough price the slave trade would go on as long as it remained profitable to all concerned. The very volume of this African trade had a tendency to oversupply the market. Governor Francis Fauquier of Virginia reported in 1763 that the considerable increase in population was due "in part to the great yearly importation of Negroes." Fauquier noted that the balance of trade ran strongly against the Chesapeake colonies, due in part to the African slave trade.[39]

George Mason blamed the "avarice of British merchants" for the refusal of the British government to permit Virginia to put a stop to "this infernal traffic" and urged the Virginia legislature to do something to remedy this situation. Virginia already taxed the slave trade by an act passed in 1752 imposing "a Duty of £5 per cent on all slaves imported upon the price for which they were sold." This tax was renewed from time to time and the money raised applied to Virginia's war debt. The act expired in 1763 and was reenacted. In 1766 the same bill was again renewed, and an additional bill placed a similar duty on slaves brought into Virginia from Maryland, North and South Carolina, and the West Indies.[40]

In 1767 Arthur Lee published an article on slavery in William Rind's *Virginia Gazette.* Essays on different topics had flowed freely from his pen since his return to Virginia.* In his essay, addressed to the members of the House of Burgesses, he proposed to discuss both "the Abolition of Slavery and the Retrieval of Specie, in this Colony," but only the first part of his essay was printed. His article appeared in the Williamsburg paper 17 March 1767. On the twenty-eighth his brother, Richard Henry Lee, introduced a bill in the House of Burgesses to impose an additional tax on slaves imported into Virginia. Lee's bill passed in April and the Virginia Assembly requested its agent to obtain the king's assent. The royal consent was not forthcoming, and in 1768 the Virginia House again discussed the possibility of imposing additional duties on slaves brought into the colony and using the revenue to redeem its paper currency. In November 1769 Richard Henry Lee reported another bill in the Virginia House of Burgesses that would impose a duty of £5 on every slave brought into Virginia from Africa.[41]

The Virginia bill had a predictable effect in England. The merchants of Liverpool and Lancaster engaged in the African trade petitioned the Lords of Trade and Plantations to set aside the objectionable legislation. The merchants pointed out that the additional duty would impose a prohibitive 15 percent tax on the purchase of slaves and charged that the bill was intended for the "Private Emolument only of the Lawmakers whose Estates (the most considerable in that country) would rise in value for the present in proportion as the number of Negroes is diminished." The British government admitted that the Virginia act was within the legitimate power of the House of Burgesses and did not infringe any British law, but determined that it was not then "expedient in point of Commercial policy to approve so high a duty on the importation of a considerable article of British Commerce.[42] The Virginia act was consequently suspended by the Crown.

Rind's *Virginia Gazette* published two spirited essays condemning the slave trade and the trade in convict servants as equally injurious

---

* Arthur Lee had written a number of essays in the Williamsburg newspapers on a rather wide variety of subjects. After George Mercer's resignation as stamp agent for Virginia in 1765, there was a residue of bitter feeling between John Mercer and the Lees. In a letter written in 1767 to his son, John Mercer of Marlborough had few kind words for the "F. R. S. Doctor": "His Vanity & itch of scribbling still continue & our prints are yet disgraced with his performances; his essay on honour, has been answered by an essay on pride which has produced other performances of authors to me unknown, & when they will end, God only knows" (Mulkearn, *Mercer Papers,* pp. 203–4). The original manuscript of Lee's published essay has survived, although no copy of Rind's *Va. Gaz.* for 17 Mar. 1767 is known to be extant.

to the commonweal. Neither writer believed that an increase in the number of slaves and white servants could serve any useful purpose. The Virginia legislation did apparently increase the market value of slaves already in the colony, as the Liverpool merchants alleged it was intended to do. Harry Piper, a Whitehaven factor at Alexandria, wrote in 1770: "I believe Slaves have been high on James River, especially Country born & will still continue so, while commodities are high. I believe the Duty on Imported Slaves is now 20 pr.ct. which amounts almost to a prohibition." [43]

The Virginians adopted an Address to King George III asking him to permit them to curtail the importation of slaves. The Address was dated 1 April 1772. It stigmatized the African slave trade as a "trade of great inhumanity." The Burgesses declared that "some of your Majesty's subjects in Great Britain, may reap emoluments from this sort of traffic; but, when we consider that it greatly retards the settlement of the Colonies with more useful inhabitants, and may, in time, have the most destructive influence, we presume to hope, that the interest of a few will be disregarded. . . ."

The Address to the Crown from the House of Burgesses, requesting that the governor be permitted to promulgate the new legislation, was transmitted to the king in Council in July 1772, together with a letter from Governor Dunmore expressing his views on the subject.[44] Predictably, the legislation was once again disallowed.

One last effort was made by the Virginia Assembly with a bill introduced by Richard Henry Lee in May 1774. When Lord Dunmore dissolved the House a few days later, it was left in abeyance. Finally presented to him for approval in June 1775, it was rejected, but this was now an empty gesture and did not retard the foes of the slave trade.[45]

As early as 1769, when the first nonimportation association was adopted by Virginians, George Mason and Richard Henry Lee included in it an article by which the subscribers pledged themselves "not to import any slave, or buy any imported." The second Virginia nonimportation association met at Williamsburg in June 1770 and agreed to exclude African slaves along with other articles sold by British merchants.[46] The intention of these agreements was primarily to bring pressure on Parliament by distressing the merchants. In 1771 an anonymous writer proposed in the *Virginia Gazette* that the existing agreement not to buy slaves until certain laws were repealed should be extended indefinitely, so that the importation of slaves would never be permitted again in the Old Dominion.[47]

This proposal proved the means of ending the slave trade to Virginia. When Dunmore dissolved the House of Burgesses in May 1774, the delegates agreed to meet in an extralegal convention. Elections were held in each county and instructions drawn up by the voters to guide their representatives. George Mason prepared the resolves adopted by the Fairfax County freeholders. They agreed "that it is the opinion of this meeting, that during our present difficulty and distress, no slaves ought to be imported into any of the British Colonies on this continent; and we take this opportunity of declaring our most earnest wishes to see an entire stop forever put to such wicked, cruel and unnatural trade." By August 1774 when the delegates came together for the Virginia Convention, a large majority voted for an immediate end to the slave trade.[48] This action was ratified by the Virginia State Legislature in 1778.

George Mason carried his crusade against the slave trade to the Constitutional Convention in 1787, and in unambiguous terms he condemned slavery as an institution, although he never advocated the emancipation of the slaves already in Virginia or their acceptance as fellow citizens. When the opening phrase of George Mason's Declaration of Rights—"That all men are born equally free and independent" —caused some alarm in the Virginia convention as suggesting that slaves might have equal rights with their masters, Mason accepted a compromise. Edmund Randolph recalled that Mason agreed with his critics "that slaves not being constituent members of our society could never pretend to any benefit from such a maxim." Mason made no objection when his original words were so modified as to exclude slaves from the compass of natural rights.

Philip Mazzei, who actively supported our independence, remembered that Mason had convinced Thomas Jefferson of the inexpediency of emancipation until the blacks had first been educated to prepare them for freedom.[49] Mason did not sign the petition circulated in Fairfax County by Gen. Daniel Roberdeau in 1785 asking the Virginia Assembly to take immediate steps to abolish slavery. In 1788 Mason voted for a bill that would have required manumitted slaves to leave Virginia within twelve months or forfeit their freedom. In his address to the Virginia Ratifying Convention in 1788, Mason depicted as equally menacing the constitutional protection of the slave trade for twenty years and the lack of security for slave property against a federal emancipation act. "They have done those things which they ought not have done, and they have left undone those things which they ought to have done."[50] George Mason was an outspoken critic of the slave trade and of slavery itself, but he saw no possible remedy for slavery in his generation.

Chapter VII

George Mason IV: Civic and Parish Interests

THE VESTRY AND THE COUNTY COURT served as a preliminary training for those men who went on to represent their county's interests in the House of Burgesses at Williamsburg. A man would
not ordinarily stand as a candidate for the Virginia Assembly who had
not already demonstrated his abilities as vestryman and justice. When
George Mason took his seat for the first time in 1758 as the member
from Fairfax County, he had had ten years' experience in settling disputes and meeting the needs of the members of his parish and the residents of the county. When one of the county gentry had his name put
forward as a candidate for the Assembly, his neighbors asked whether
he had demonstrated his ability as a vestryman or a member of the
county court. They also asked how openhanded he was in buying cider
and rum punch for the voters.

The Virginia county courts concerned themselves with a wide range
of social and economic problems, from the maintenance of ferries,
bridges, and highways to the collection of private debts and the suppression of crime and immorality. The county courts functioned with
the parish vestries as the local government of Virginia and had much
broader responsibilities than did the vestry, with its primary obligation to questions of religion and social welfare. The duties and privileges of vestry and county court had so many points of contact, that it
was perhaps inevitable that their membership would be very nearly
identical. Court and vestry alike served the interests of the local landowners and scarcely provided a check on one another's power.[1] The
vestry and county court were so closely interlocked that on occasion
Dissenters, even Quakers and Roman Catholics, sat on the Anglican
vestry. The vestry was "packed" with members chosen in excess of the
legal limits, so as to include all of the local gentry. The Reverend
Charles Green of Truro Parish complained bitterly of these illegal
elections.[2] These county oligarchies represented at once an effective
control of all forms of local government by the larger landowners and
an equally effective school of public service. The country gentlemen
controlled the courts, the militia, and the vestry, managed the busi-

ness of the county, and influenced the lives of their neighbors on every
level.

When George Mason first took the oath as a justice of Fairfax
County on 22 April 1749, his colleagues on the bench were all men of
considerable real property. Mason, John Colvill, Richard Osborne,
William Payne, William Henry Terrett, George William Fairfax,
Daniel McCarty, John Carlyle, William Ramsay, Charles Broadwater,
and Anthony Russell were named in the king's commission of peace
for Fairfax County, which then included all of Loudoun County, and
among themselves accounted for a high proportion of the landed
interests in their jurisdiction.[3]

Mason and other landowners attended the Fairfax court sessions
very irregularly, sometimes sitting on the bench for only a few hours
in the course of a year. Members of the great landed families normally
held a majority of seats on the county bench, but in actual practice
merchants and factors tended to dominate the county courts. Unless
the large planter was himself involved in litigation or driven by an
unusually strong sense of civic duty, he would normally find more
pressing business outside the courtroom. While many of these gentlemen justices had to travel great distances to attend court, the Prince
William County Courthouse at Alexandria was conveniently situated
for the merchants. Only four or five of the eligible justices attended
court sessions, and it was not unusual for a court composed entirely
of Glasgow factors to determine a series of cases involving debts to
British firms. Mason averred that merchants similarly dominated the
general courts held at Williamsburg in the same decades. In 1783 he
wrote to Patrick Henry, "It is notorious that the Custom of giving
Interest upon common Accounts was introduced by the Partiality of
the Merchants, of whom the Jurys at the General Court were chiefly
composed for several Years before the late Revolution."[4]

Criminal matters took up comparatively little of the county court's
time, partly because its jurisdiction was limited. After a preliminary
hearing persons indicted for serious crimes had to be remanded to the
General Court at Williamsburg. They were passed on as swiftly as
possible from the sheriff of Fairfax County to the Prince William sheriff, who would conduct the criminal to the next county, and so on,
until the criminal was safely lodged in the Williamsburg jail.[5] In dealing with social problems, whether unwed mothers or unorthodox
preachers, the county court usually followed the lead of the churchwardens. Cases of runaway slaves and indentured servants turned up
with great regularity. The court certified expenses for taking up fugi-
tive slaves and added the runaway time and the cost of recapture to

the indenture of white servants. One man was fined for not allowing his slaves the Sabbath rest, but little was said about the treatment of slaves and servants.[6]

More than any other Virginia institution, the county courts had a direct bearing on the tobacco trade. The gentlemen justices chose the tobacco inspectors, with nomination tantamount to appointment; saw to the upkeep of the public warehouses; maintained standard weights and measurements in the tobacco inspection; and enabled the merchant to collect from defaulting debtors. The greater part of the court's sessions, especially in the 1760s and 1770s, was taken up with the claims of British firms against local planters.

The appointment of Glasgow factors, like Alexander Henderson and Hector Ross, along with large landowners, like George Mason and Daniel McCarty, to committees of the county magistracy that dealt with tobacco trade matters is an indication of the considerable influence Scots merchants exercised on the county bench in the last decades of the colonial era. Suits for debt by British merchants formed a large part of the ordinary business of the courts. After 1760 the suits filed by John Glassford and Company against Fairfax County debtors constituted part of the agenda of every court session, and other firms did not lag far behind. In 1768–74 the affairs of John Glassford and Company and Glassford and Henderson occupied more of the court's time than those of any other litigant.

Sydenham and Hodgson engaged Mason in prolonged litigation in 1763. A jury headed by John Copithorne, a Bristol merchant, found in Mason's favor and awarded him damages. In another case in 1770 Mason appeared as plaintiff against Philip Sewell in an action for a debt of 1,260 pounds of tobacco. Sewell was bankrupt and the court seized his entire property consisting of one bed, two blankets, a rug, a hog, a gun, two plates, a basin, an iron pot, some earthenware, a chest, some pewter spoons, a water pail, a frying pan, one pair of flesh forks and two or three old knives and forks, the whole valued at only twenty-one shillings threepence in partial payment. The debtors who found themselves accused before the county magistrates were generally men of little substance, but occasionally a planter or entrepreneur who had overextended himself was haled into the courtroom to hear the particulars of his downfall. Besides enabling the merchant or other creditor to compel payment of just debts, the county court audited and notarized the shop ledgers kept by the British factors.[7]

The ordinary business of the court was more concerned with the petty debts run up by small farmers at the store kept by a Glasgow factor than with any other single item on its agenda. The personnel of the county bench reflected this increasing interest on the part of the merchants. Although justices like Alexander Henderson, William Ramsay, John Carlyle, and other Alexandria businessmen were assiduous in the attendance at court sessions, chronic absenteeism was the rule for many of the justices of the county court. The notion that the courthouse at Alexandria was the peculiar preserve of the commercial interests of the town was reflected in the tug-of-war between town and county over the location of the county seat between 1752 and 1792, as well as in the composition of the court and the jury.[8]

The vestry conducted much of its most important business through the churchwardens. The two churchwardens were supposed to bring forward all persons leading a disorderly life and all masters and mistresses who failed to catechize their children and servants. They were also expected to keep the church buildings in good repair, see to the supply of the elements and the communion cloth for the communion service, and, finally, to make certain that all was done in accord with the precepts and order of the Book of Common Prayer. The churchwardens had immediate responsibility for the care of the needy and infirm within the parish, and they were authorized to bind illegitimate children to serve as apprentices and learn a useful trade.[9]

Truro Parish was divided on 10 June 1749 by the creation of Cameron Parish. At George Mason's first vestry meeting, the division of the parish was completed. There were 1,240 tithables in Truro Parish's new boundaries and 707 tithables in the new parish. The Truro Parish that George Mason knew had the same boundaries as modern Fairfax County. Within the Truro vestry itself there was a nice balance of family interests: Masons, McCartys, Fairfaxes, Wests, and Washingtons succeeded one another on the vestry as if inheriting a family property. On 9 October 1749 Hugh West and Jeremiah Bronaugh were chosen as the churchwardens for the following year. On 19 February 1749 / 50 "George Mason, Gentleman, was appointed Churchwarden in the room of Jeremiah Bronaugh, Gentleman, Deceased." As warden or vestryman, Mason was continuously associated with Truro Parish after his first election as a member of the vestry in October 1749.[10]

Within the new limits of the parish there were only two church edifices. Pohick Church was located near the ford over Pohick Creek, some two miles closer to Gunston Hall than the present church building. The Upper Church, as it was termed in the vestry proceedings, was located at the crossroads above Mason's Ferry, at the same site as the present Falls Church.

At a vestry meeting on 19 February 1750 it was determined to repair and shingle Pohick Church and to build a new vestry house adjacent to it. Daniel McCarty agreed to undertake this project, but at the vestry meeting in October 1750 he acknowledged that he had not fulfilled his agreement. The old church was still in need of repairs in 1752, and Daniel French agreed to carry out McCarty's original contract. At the same time the vestry agreed to sell the old glebe lands to William Ramsay and to purchase 176 acres from the Reverend Charles Green for a glebe.* They further agreed to build the necessary farm buildings on the new glebe lands. Mason, Hugh West, and Daniel McCarty were appointed a committee to inspect the new glebe buildings when some of them were nearing completion in 1753. West and McCarty accepted the buildings and instructed the vestry to pay Thomas Waite £39 13s. for his work, but George Mason desired that his dissent might be entered on the vestry record. He was apparently justified in his demurral, for a second inspection by the vestry brought a unanimous decision that Waite's work was shoddy and that his brick walls should be pulled down. In 1759 the vestry refused to pay anything to Waite, as he had not fulfilled his contract, but authorized in 1760 the payment to William Buckland of £93 2s. of the money set aside for Waite. Buckland was steadily gaining a reputation as a gifted architect and builder. Though his indenture time was not complete when he finished Gunston Hall, Mason released him on 8 November 1759 to allow him further scope for his talents as an architect. The glebe house contract was undoubtedly arranged by Mason to help his former servant establish himself in his profession.[11]

In 1751 the Alexandria trustees raised money to build a church in the town through a public lottery. At a vestry meeting in 1756 George Mason ordered that seats should be provided for the church at Alexandria at the vestry's expense. This church, later named Christ Church, Alexandria, was the nucleus for the division of Fairfax Parish from Truro Parish in 1765.[12]

The Truro vestry set about building a new brick church in the upper part of the newly divided parish. They leased a tobacco house from Samuel Littlejohn and authorized John Robertson, Jr., to fit it up for divine worship, with six benches the length of the building and two at the ends, a reading desk, and a communion table. As churchwarden, Mason had overall supervision of the project. In November 1765 the vestry agreed to make contracts with workmen on the first Monday in February for building the new church. On 4 February 1766 they staked

---

* A glebe was a farm attached to the parsonage to provide a residence and partial support for the incumbent minister.

out the site for the new edifice on the middle ridge near the Ox Road, not far south of the present Fairfax County Courthouse.[13]

The new church was finally completed and officially accepted by the vestry on 9 September 1768. Col. George Mason was then authorized to pay Capt. Edward Payne for the costs of construction.[14] Payne's Church, as it was commonly called, stood for almost a century, but fell into ruins during the Civil War.

The parish church proper was somewhat neglected during these years, evidently falling into disrepair. In 1769 the vestry determined to build a new Pohick Church rather than try once more to repair the old building. Mason led the group of vestrymen who favored constructing a new church at the same site; but the decision was made to erect the new Pohick Church at the crossroads leading from Hollis's to Pohick warehouse, or some two miles northwest of the original site. Mason was a member of the vestry committee supervising the construction, while Daniel French was entrusted with the contract to build the new church.[15]

Daniel French spared no expense in making Pohick Church as handsome as any in Virginia. On 2 August 1770 Harry Piper of Alexandria wrote to John Dixon and Isaac Littledale, merchants in Whitehaven, England: "Inclosed is an order from Daniel French for 110 square yards of Flaggstones. They are to lay the Aisles of a new Church. I was unwilling to take this Order, as I find they are much dearer than formerly and is attended with a good deal of trouble; of this I informed Mr. French, but he begged you might send them, and charge whatever you think is reasonable." Daniel French died in 1772 before Pohick Church was completed, and it fell to George Mason to finish the project. On 15 February 1774 he presented the new church to the vestry and it was duly accepted. He purchased pews 3 and 4 at £14 11s. each, and on 2 February 1774 the vestry gave him title to the pews.[16]

The duties of the wardens and vestrymen involved much more than maintaining the fabric of the parish church and, when necessary, building new chapels of ease.* A large part of the tax levied by the parish on every tithable was expended in the support of the poor and disabled. At Mason's first vestry meeting in 1749, money was allowed to Dr. John Robertson and Dr. John Hunter for the expenses incurred in caring for the sick poor.

At a vestry meeting in November 1754, it was "ordered that the Churchwardens give notice for the impotent people of this parish to

* A chapel of ease was subordinate to the parish church and was built for the convenience of the parishioners who lived far from the church. It also served to "ease" the work of the rector.

appear at the vestry the second Monday in May and also for any person that would undertake to board them." In a rural community, where everyone knew his neighbor, this form of home relief apparently worked to general satisfaction. The churchwardens preferred to pay a sum of money or tobacco to some respectable householder who was willing to take an aged widow or an orphan into his home, rather than to allow the needy person to draw money directly from the parish, but direct payments were made frequently. The system was designed to provide relief for the disabled and the aged who were unable to provide for themselves at all, but it did not make ample enough provision for those who were in need because of crop failures or shortage of provisions. From time to time the vestry set aside a portion of its levy for such emergency cases, but the winter of 1775–76 found the poorer people on the Potomac in almost unprecedented want of food and clothing.[17] In part, this scarcity of necessary supplies was a direct result of the nonimportation and nonexportation agreements adopted in 1774. The correspondence of a number of Mason's neighbors on the Potomac included references to the hard times and scarcity of goods that bore most heavily on the poor.

In order to support these works of charity, maintain divine worship, and pay the minister's salary, the parish levied a tax on every tithable. The parish levy varied considerably from year to year. In 1750 it amounted to thirty-two pounds of tobacco for each tithable, but in 1755 the levy was only twenty-five pounds. In 1767 it rose to forty-one pounds, probably as a result of falling prices on the tobacco market, and in 1772 again increased to forty-seven pounds. Since there were 1,260 tithables in Truro Parish in 1772, the levy for that year totaled 59,220 pounds of tobacco. The annual parish budget in Mason's time normally varied from forty thousand to sixty thousand pounds of tobacco.

The parish levy was normally sold to one or more merchants in the parish. In 1768 William Gardner, the parish collector, presented the vestry with notes for the crop and transfer of tobacco for the 1767 levy, which was then in the hands of George Mason. In his turn Mason sold the parish tobacco to Alexander Henderson, factor at Colchester for Glassford and Henderson of Glasgow. Thereafter, until the dissolution of the vestry, the Truro Parish levy went to Glasgow consigned to Glassford and Henderson.[18]

Not all the tobacco was sold by the churchwardens, for part of it was due to the minister in lieu of a glebe. After Parson Green died in 1765, Truro Parish was without an incumbent for more than a year. The Reverend James Scott, George Mason's old friend and mentor, filled the pulpit at Pohick Church. He was again paid for six sermons at Pohick in the parish account for 1768, but on 14 January 1767 the vestry presented the Reverend Lee Massey to the living of Truro Parish. They agreed to allow him an additional 4,000 pounds of tobacco in lieu of a glebe, having just advertised the glebe lands for sale.[19] Massey, the pastor and close friend of George Mason, had originally planned a career as a lawyer. He married Nancy Burrell, the daughter of a Glasgow tobacco factor, and many years after her death married George Mason's cousin, Elizabeth Bronaugh.

The issue of religious liberty came up again and again during the years of George Mason's active public service. The Church of England was established by law in Virginia. The handful of Quakers and other Dissenters in the colony had always enjoyed a full measure of toleration, although as Virginia taxpayers they were obliged to pay their share of the expenses of the Anglican vestry. The Great Awakening gave a tremendous impetus to the growth of Presbyterian congregations in Virginia in the 1750s, notably in the Northern Neck. Every session of the Virginia Assembly received petitions and counterpetitions on religious freedom. The Baptists began their growth in Virginia with a series of revivals in the 1760s. The Ketocten Baptist Association organized itself in 1765 from churches in Loudoun and Fauquier counties. Baptist preachers soon began to form congregations in Fairfax and nearly every other Virginia county. Baptists and Presbyterians joined with Quakers to press the authorities in Williamsburg for greater freedom of worship. At the same time litigation over the Parsons' Cause, the attempt of the clergy to collect the salaries that the Two-Penny Act had reduced to a pittance, and quarrels between patriot leaders and the clerical gentlemen at William and Mary created some bitterness against the established church.[20]

George Mason was presiding as a justice of the county court in 1773 when a Baptist preacher was obliged to post heavy bond not to expound the gospel without a proper license. Jeremiah Moore, a lay reader who was converted at a revival meeting at Dumfries, had been a lay reader under the Reverend James Scott of Dettingen Parish. He continued to preach without a license and was soon imprisoned in the Alexandria jail.[21] Mason, who knew him personally, regretted this sentence, as he was aware that Baptists worshipped in the courthouse at Leesburg without hindrance from the Loudoun County justices. The inconsistencies, as much as the inequities, of the existing system presaged a major overhauling of the religious establishment, whatever other changes separation from England might bring.[22]

The imprisonment of fellow Christians because of their religious beliefs created considerable stir in Virginia. A letter in the *Virginia Gazette* suggested that a lack of civility, rather than religious convictions, had brought these lay preachers into the toils of the law, but Virginians seem to have been heartily ashamed of the situation.[23] The House of Burgesses responded in 1772 with a bill that pleased nobody and offended everyone.

The whole tone of the new legislation seemed to imply that only Anglicans were trustworthy citizens and that Dissenters were to be tolerated, in the strict sense of the word. They were required to keep their churches unlocked and permit the justices to inspect their books and meetings for worship at all times. They were strictly forbidden to hold evening meetings of any kind and to baptize or instruct slaves. Blacks played an important part in the religious awakening in the 1760s and 1770s. One could hardly preach to slaves during their hours of labor, and watchnights were familiar to English Wesleyans as a means of evangelism, but prayer meetings by torchlight raised specters of insurrection. Petitions against the Dissenters generally stressed the dangers inherent in nocturnal gatherings and missions to slaves.[24]

The bill for religious toleration was still pending in the Virginia Assembly when troubles between Great Britain and her American colonies reached the breaking point. In his draft of the Virginia Declaration of Rights in 1776, George Mason wrote:

That as Religion, or the Duty which we owe to our divine and omnipotent Creator, and the Manner of discharging it, can be governed only by Reason and Conviction, not by Force or Violence; and therefore that all Men shou'd enjoy the fullest Toleration in the Exercise of Religion, according to the Dictates of Conscience, unpunished and unrestrained by the Magistrate, unless, under Colour of Religion, any Man disturb the Peace, the Happiness, or Safety of Society, or of Individuals. And that it is the mutual Duty of all, to practice Christian Forbearance, Love and Charity towards Each other.[25]

George Mason was named chairman of a committee in the Virginia Assembly that drew up a bill of relief for Dissenters in 1776. The measure was adopted on 9 December 1776. It repealed all previous acts that might be construed as restraints on the free exercise of religious liberty and exempted Dissenters from contributions of any kind to the support of the established church. It further provided that the salaries already voted to the clergy of the established church should be held in abeyance until June 1777. This provision was extended by successive acts to prevent any public money from being applied to the support of the Anglican Church. The preamble to the act stated clearly, in words that echoed Mason's earlier statement of principle in the Declaration of Rights, that the bill was introduced because there are within this commonwealth great numbers of dissenters from the church established by law who have been heretofore taxed for its support, and it is contrary to the principles of reason and justice that any should be compelled to contribute to the maintenance of a church with which their consciences will not permit them to join, and from which they can derive no benefit: for remedy whereof, and that equal liberty as well religious as civil, may be universally extended to all the good people of this commonwealth.[26]

The act of 9 December 1776 effectively destroyed the vestry system by removing its power to tax Dissenters. The Truro Vestry continued to hold meetings through 1778. The Fairfax Vestry also continued to meet and to supply the needs of the poor throughout the war years.[27]

The vestry system for relief of the poor did not satisfy everyone by any means. On 3 November 1775 the vestry of Truro Parish ordered that "George Mason, Esquire, Colonel Daniel McCarty, Captain Martin Cockburn, Captain Thomas Pollard, the Reverend Lee Massey, and Mr. Alexander Henderson do prepare a plan for the Employment of and providing for the poor of the parish and report to the next vestry." Mason was at this time engaged in the affairs of the Virginia Convention, and his extant correspondence provides no clue to the deliberations of this committee. The vestry meeting on 6 May 1776 made some minor changes in the method of collecting the parish levy but did not discuss the report of the committee.

During the troubled years of the Revolution, elections for vestrymen had not been held. On 21 November 1783 some Fairfax County freeholders sent a petition to the Virginia Assembly, asking for the dissolution of Fairfax Vestry. They argued that "the Power exercised by the Vestries of filling up their own vacancies is attended with many Inconveniences, and [is] inconsistent with the Principles of Republican Government . . . [and] that the mode prescribed for making Provision for the Parish Poor, as by Law now directed, by Vestries and Churchwardens to be chosen from among those of one Profession only, deprives many good people of rights and privileges essential to Free men." [28] The document was signed by a number of Presbyterians, Quakers, and at least one Roman Catholic. In December 1784 the Assembly incorporated the Protestant Episcopal Church as the successor to the Church of England, legally entitled to its churches, land, glebe houses, and so on, in Virginia.[29]

By taking away the revenues that had supported their activities, the Virginia Assembly had dealt the vestry system a mortal blow, but they had not killed it, nor had they provided any other means of caring for the poor and carrying out the other secular duties of the vestry. In

1785 a bill came before the legislature to restore the vestry system under a new name. The bill for the support of teachers of the Christian religion received a good deal of backing in the House of Delegates, but Mason prevailed on James Madison to draw up a remonstrance against the proposal. A series of letters opposed to the proposal to support Christian ministers of all denominations with funds raised by taxes appeared in the *Virginia Journal and the Alexandria Advertiser* over the signature "Vigilarius," and "A friend of the Bill of Rights" endorsed a counterproposal introduced by Thomas Jefferson.[30] Mason had copies of Madison's remonstrance printed at his own expense and wrote to friends in different parts of Virginia urging them to circulate petitions against the bill establishing provision for teachers of the Christian religion. In a letter to Robert Carter of Nomini Hall of 5 October 1785, George Mason wrote:

> I take the Liberty of inclosing you a Memorial & Remonstrance to the General Assembly, confided to me by a particular Friend, whose Name I am not at Liberty to mention; and as it accords entirely with my Sentiments upon the Subject (which is a very important one) I have been at the Charge of printing several Copys, to be dispersed in the different Parts of the Country.
>
> You will easily perceive that all manner of Declamation, and Address to the Passions, have been avoided, as unfair in themselves, & improper for such a Subject, and altho' the Remonstrance is long, that Brevity has been aimed at; but the Field is extensive. If upon Consideration, you approve the Reasoning, & the Principles upon which it is founded, I make no Doubt you will endeavour to promote the Subscriptions in your Part of the Country: if they can be compleated, & the Remonstrance sent down to the Assembly, by the first or second Week in Novemr. I presume it will be in good Time.[31]

Petitions poured in from Dissenters and others who wished the vestry system abolished once and for all. George Mason himself drew up the petition signed by a large number of Fairfax County voters, and the issue received a full hearing in the local newspapers.[32] Mason and his associates triumphed at the session of the Virginia legislature in December 1785. In a swift series of actions the representatives of the people rejected the proposal for public support of all denominations equally; they abolished the vestry system and replaced it with freely elected overseers of the poor, who, of course, had no special religious qualifications; and, finally, they enacted Thomas Jefferson's Act for Establishing Religious Freedom.[33] With these legislative actions the historic links between the Anglican vestry and the organs of local government were broken apart.

Chapter VIII

George Mason IV: The American Revolution

GEORGE AND THOMSON MASON both helped direct Virginia through the crises that led finally to independence for all the colonies. Their mutual concern for the economic development of Virginia is also reflected in their proposals for legislative reforms in this period, particularly in the first years of the conflict. George Mason formulated his generation's ideas about separation of church and state and the abolition of slavery. In his Virgina Declaration of Rights and in his revision of the laws of Virginia, he made a lasting contribution to the American tradition of individual liberty and limited government.

George Mason's earliest extant political writing is a sketch of a bill for altering the method of replevying goods under distress for rent, which he sent to George William Fairfax and George Washington, the Fairfax County burgesses in December 1765.[1] Mason's bill afforded a means of collecting overdue rents without using the stamped paper required by the hated Stamp Act.

Early in 1766 Thomson Mason signed the Articles of Agreement of Association by the citizens of Westmoreland, binding the subscribers to import no British goods until the Stamp Act was repealed. Among the 125 gentlemen of the county who signed the agreement were six Lees and three brothers of George Washington.

In June 1766 Mason addressed a reply to a committee of London merchants in the American trade who had advised the Americans not to "seize the yielding of Parliament [on the Stamp Act] as a point gained over Parliament authority." Mason retorted that it made little difference "whether the Oppression comes from a British Parliament, or a Turkish Divan." He did not deny the authority of Great Britain over its colonies, but he insisted that authority be exercised without partiality. The Stamp Act was only one objectionable measure. Great Britain had made an odious distinction between the colonists and their fellow subjects at home by depriving them of the ancient right of trial by a jury of their peers living within the same vicinity as those accused. "In crossing the Atlantic Ocean, we have only changed our Climate, not our Minds . . . We are still the same People with them, in every Respect."[2]

Tempers ran high in Williamsburg over the Stamp Act. A cousin of the Masons, Col. George Mercer, had accepted an appointment in London as stamp agent for Virginia, thinking to find it only a profitable sinecure. Instead he found himself a focal point of the resentment felt in Virginia over the passage of the act.[3] When he was hanged in effigy and excoriated in the *Virginia Gazette,* he promptly resigned the appointment. Dr. Arthur Lee, newly chosen Fellow of the Royal Society, who returned to Williamsburg in 1766 from medical studies at Edinburgh and Leyden, viciously attacked George Mercer and his relations in the Williamsburg newspaper. Col. James Mercer sprang to his brother's defense. The dispute became so violent that Lee finally challenged Mercer to a duel. Mason assumed the thankless task of intermediary and peacemaker between the two hotheads. Long afterwards old John Mercer of Marlborough was still bitter toward the Lees. Mason managed, however, to keep on intimate relations with his Mercer relatives as well as with the Lee family, both of whom were important links in his public career.[4]

After the Stamp Act crisis had subsided, relations between Great Britain and its American colonies were strained again by the passage in 1767 of the Townshend Acts, which placed a tax on glass, lead, paint, tea, and paper; reorganized the customs service; and suspended the New York Assembly until it complied with the mutiny act. Thomson Mason was a member of the House of Burgesses for Stafford County on 14 April 1768 when the House adopted a series of memorials to the king, the House of Lords, and the House of Commons protesting the Townshend duties and the suspension of the New York Assembly. He served on the committee that presented these petitions to the Governor's Council.

In August 1768 Bostonians adopted a nonimportation agreement and called on Philadelphia and New York to follow their lead. The Virginia House of Burgesses, however, only condemned the Townshend duties as unconstitutional and hinted at a boycott of British goods. The planting colonies depended too greatly on imported goods to take such an abrupt action against the tobacco traders.[5]

George Mason gave serious thought to the measures adopted to coerce the British merchants into bringing pressure on Parliament, but he was cautious in his optimism about nonimportation. This action would certainly have its effect; "yet it is plain that in the Tobo. Colonys we can't at present confine our Importations within such narrow Bounds as the Northern Colonys, a Plan of this kind, to be practicable, must be adapted to our Circumstances; for not steadily executed, it had better have remained unattempted." Rather than attempt a total embargo on British goods, Mason suggested, "We may retrench all Manner of Superfluitys, Finery of all Denominations, & confine ourselves to Linnens Woolens &c, not exceeding a certain Price: it is amazing how much this (if adopted in all the Colonys) wou'd lessen the American Imports, and distress the various Traders & Manufacturers in Great Britain." He went on by warning Parliament that Virginians were in earnest and that "it may not be amiss to let the Ministry understand that untill we obtain a Redress of Grievances, we will withhold from them our Commoditys, particularly refrain from making Tobacco, by which the Revenue wou'd lose fifty times more than all their Oppressions cou'd raise here." [6]

A boycott would work more harm in Virginia than in England if it were not unanimous, and a total embargo on British manufactures would have no chance of success. Nonimportation agreements might vex British businessmen, but nonexportation was a much stronger weapon in the Virginian arsenal. Mason observed "with Anxiety That the Debt due to Great Britain for Goods imported from thence is very great, and that the means of paying this Debt in the present situation of Affairs is likely to become more and more precarious." [7] He suggested that the debts owed to British merchants by Virginians, or, in reality, the investments made by British capital in the tobacco economy of Virginia, should be used as a weapon to bring pressure on Parliament.

George Washington forwarded a copy of the Philadelphia resolves on nonimportation of British goods to Mason in April 1769 and asked his opinion on the course Virginia ought to follow in the crisis. Mason had already received a copy from Dr. David Ross of Bladensburg. He told Washington that the session of the General Court or the Assembly would be the proper time for a meeting at Williamsburg to discuss similar action in the colony. In the meantime Mason recommended an article be published in the *Virginia Gazette* to prepare public opinion for such action and mentioned that he had already begun an essay on the subject. Late in April 1769, when Washington was about to set out for Williamsburg, Mason sent him a corrected draft of a nonimportation agreement adopted at Williamsburg. Historians have generally assumed that Mason wrote the original draft and made the corrections and additions he sent to Washington. It is more likely that Richard Henry Lee, Mason, and possibly others worked together on the document. [8]

On 16 May 1769 the House unanimously adopted four resolutions asserting their right to be taxed only by their own representatives, to petition the king for redress of grievances without any recourse to Parliament, and their ancient right to trial by jury in their own vicinity. Thomson Mason was appointed to draw up an address to the governor, Lord Botetourt, on the views of the House of Burgesses with regard to the transportation of Americans beyond the seas for trial in cases of riot and treason. He also served with John Blair, Jr., Patrick Henry, Richard Henry Lee, Robert Carter Nicholas, and Benjamin Harrison on a committee to draw up an address to King George III setting forth their grievances.[9]

When Thomson Mason presented Governor Botetourt with the resolutions of the House of Burgesses on 17 May 1769, the governor dissolved the Assembly. The delegates adjourned to Anthony Hay's tavern, the Raleigh, in Williamsburg. The meeting adopted all of the Mason-Lee resolves with one significant exception. George Mason had offered a draft resolution:

That if the Measures already entered into should prove ineffectual, & our Grievances & oppressions should notwithstanding be continue'd; then & in that case, the Subscribers will put a stop to their exports to Europe of Tar, pitch, Turpentine, Timber, & Lumber, & Skins and Furs of all sorts, and will endeavour to find some other Employment for their Slaves and other Hands than cultivating Tobacco, which they will entirely leave off making, & will enter into such Regulations as may be necessary with Regard to Rents & other Tobacco Debts (due to them).[10]

An agreement to stop the exportation of forest products and of furs and hides as a temporary measure to obtain redress for grievances was within the realm of possibility. A sudden stoppage in the tobacco trade would ruin Virginians, since the Chesapeake economy depended so completely on the sale of tobacco overseas, but a "farm holiday" would be a different matter. By diverting land and laborers into other kinds of agriculture, the planters could sell all of the tobacco on hand at a profit and let the bankers of Glasgow and London contemplate the effects of a tobacco famine on the British economy. Since rents, taxes, and many kinds of public and private debts were payable in tobacco, the Virginia authorities would have to commute these obligations into money at a specified rate. The words "due to them" were added by Mason in a letter to Washington to make it clear that he meant debts payable in Virginia tobacco, not debts to British merchants per se.[11]

One of the resolutions adopted at the meeting held at the Raleigh tavern put an end to the African slave trade until the Townshend Acts were repealed. Another put a halt to the importation of an enumerated list of articles from Great Britain or any part of Europe. By this agreement the members of the House of Burgesses strictly bound only themselves and their families to abide by its provisions. They would have to rely on moral suasion to bring all Virginians into agreement on this mode of action.[12]

Enforcement of a voluntary curb on the importation of goods proved nearly impossible. Every county had its committee of associators, but it had no real power to obligate either factor or planter. In June 1770 Mason wrote to Richard Henry Lee: "I am glad to hear that the Members below intend to establish some further Regulations to render the Association effectual, & I know of none that will answer the End proposed, but preventing by all legal & peaceable Means in our Power (for we must avoid even the Appearance of Violence) the Importation of the enumerated goods." Experience had shown that once landed in the country, the goods would find a buyer. Mason urged that importers and purchasers alike be blacklisted and violators subjected to social pressure by ostracism.

"The non-Importation Associations here are at present in a very languid State," Mason wrote in December 1770.[13] All of this uncertainty put considerable strain on the merchants and factors in Virginia, and the burden of nonimportation fell on those firms whose representatives on the Chesapeake adopted its provisions. Glassford and Henderson could hardly be expected to shoulder the burden of fighting Virginia's battles while Virginians cheerfully bought imported goods from their competitors. Mason discussed the subject with neighboring merchants and found them ready to do whatever should be necessary for the preservation of liberty. Alexander Henderson assured Mason "that he will cheerfully order to be packed up such goods as are contrary to the Association in any of the stores he has the direction of (and you know he is concerned for one of the greatest houses in the tobacco trade), and either store them until our grievances are redressed or reship them."[14]

In 1771 Alexander Henderson and William Balmain (a Glassford factor at Alexandria) approached George Mason with grievances of their own. They declared "that they found so little regard paid to the association by others, and such quantities of goods imported into different parts of the colony diametrically opposite both to the spirit and letter of the articles entered into, that they should think themselves obliged for the future, in justice to their constituents (however contrary to their own sentiments) to send their orders in the same manner with other importers; restraining themselves only from importing tea, and other taxed articles, which they were still determined to adhere to." George Mason drew up a statement on the situation that was signed by George Washington, Peter Wagener, John West, and John Dalton and published in the *Virginia Gazette;* his statement appealed to the other associators to adhere to the same principles as Virginia regarding the imports from England.[15] The repeal of all the objectionable taxes except that on tea enabled Virginia quietly to drop the nonimportation scheme. Commerce returned to its normal channels until the Boston Tea Party provoked a new crisis.

The first reports of the reaction in England to the Boston Tea Party suggested that officialdom would regard the dumping of 340 chests of tea into Boston harbor on the night of 16 December 1773 as but one more riot in that tumultuous and troublesome town. News of the passage in May 1774 of the so-called Intolerable Acts came as an unexpected shock to the American colonies. The Virginia Assembly was in session. "Infinite astonishment, and equal resentment, has seized everyone here on account of the war sent to Boston," one member reported from Williamsburg. On 24 May 1774 the House of Burgesses voted to set aside 1 June as a day of prayer "to implore the divine interposition, for averting the heavy calamity which threatens destruction to our civil rights, and the evils of civil war." [16] Though not a member of the Assembly at this session, George Mason was in Williamsburg on personal business. He wrote to Martin Cockburn that his children should also observe the day. "Should a day of Prayer and fasting be appointed in our county, please to tell my dear little Family that I charge them to pay strict Attention to it, and that I Desire my three eldest sons, and my two eldest daughters, may attend church in Mourning, if they have it, as I believe they have."

Mason had traveled to the capital in connection with his charter rights to some western lands. At this time he met Patrick Henry, and the two men formed the friendship that would remain unbroken until Mason's death. He informed Martin Cockburn that "whatever resolves or measures are intended for the preservation of our rights and liberties, will be reserved for the conclusion of the session. Matters of that sort here are conducted and prepared with a great deal of privacy, and by very few members; of whom Patrick Henry is the principal. At the request of the gentlemen concerned I have spent an evening with them upon the subject." [17]

On 27 May 1774 after Governor Dunmore had dissolved the Virginia Assembly, eighty-nine members met in the long room of the Raleigh tavern and adopted a series of resolutions, declaring "that an attack made on one of our sister Colonies, to complet submission to arbitrary taxes, is an attack made on all British America." They agreed not to use tea or "any kind of East India commodity whatsoever, except saltpetre and spices" and to recommend the boycott against the East India Company to their constituents. Their resolves went no further than to suggest that it might soon be necessary "to avoid all commercial intercourse with Britain."[18]

The door was now open for George Mason's plan of putting a halt to all exports to Great Britain. Nonimportation agreements had proved unsuccessful. Dr. Arthur Lee wrote from London in April, urging the same course of action. "The shipping, manufactures, and revenue, depend so much on the tobacco and Carolina colonies, that they alone, by stopping their exports, would force redress."[19]

Nonexportation was in the air. A factor for a Glasgow firm wrote in May 1774: "It is said the Bostonians have strongly recommended to the Southern Colonys to distress as much as they can the trade from Scotland, giving for Reason that the Scots members in the House of Commons were unanimous against them, but it is suspected that this is done to terrify the trade of Glasgow and force them to petition the Parliament for a Repeal of the Tea Act."[20] Stopping exports was not a step to be taken lightly. If the prosperity of Glasgow and Whitehaven largely depended on the tobacco trade, the prosperity of most Maryland and Virginia counties was equally dependent on the price of tobacco.

On Sunday afternoon, 29 May 1774, the postrider galloped into Williamsburg with copies of the resolutions passed by the Annapolis townspeople against the Intolerable Acts. They had resolved "that the inhabitants of this city, will join in an Association with the several counties of this Province, and the principal Colonies of America, to put an immediate stop to all exports to Great Britain, and that after a short day hereafter to be agreed on that there be no imports from Great Britain till the said Act be repealed, and that such Association be on oath."[21]

Peyton Randolph, moderator of the dissolved House of Burgesses, had no sooner read the Annapolis resolves than he called a meeting of those delegates who were still in Williamsburg. The hastily summoned deputies decided on that Sunday afternoon that the issue was too important for them to settle by themselves. They sent riders speeding to the homes of those members who lived near Williamsburg, informing them of developments and urging them to attend a meeting the next morning. When they gathered on Monday, they "unanimously agreed to refer the further consideration of this matter to the first day of August next; at which time it is expected there will be a very general attendance of the late members of the House of Burgesses, and that a non-importation agreement will be then entered into, as well as resolutions to suspend at some future day, exporting any of our commodities to Britain."[22]

Thomson Mason emerged as the most outspoken opponent of the suggestion that Virginia stop exporting tobacco. In a series of articles in the *Virginia Gazette,* over the signature "A British American," Thomson Mason analyzed the dispute between Great Britain and the colonies. He argued that the proposal to force the repeal of the objectionable legislation by interfering with Anglo-American trade was a more radical measure than its proponents realized. Rather than rebel in favor of the Americans, the British workers would almost certainly enlist as soldiers to put down the rebellion that caused such needless suffering in the manufacturing districts. So far as America was concerned, experience had shown beyond cavil that some men would make pecuniary sacrifices in the name of liberty, but that others would turn the nonimportation agreement to personal profit. They could not be made to comply with the boycott except by force, and if force were to be employed against factors on the Rappahannock, why not against Parliament?

Thomson Mason had no patience with equivocations: nonimportation was rebellion under a softer name. If the colonies were not to import manufactured goods, they must then manufacture their own, but this would violate statutes of the British Parliament they had always accepted. Far from solving the problem, the next session of Parliament would produce more stringent laws forbidding colonial industries, which would provoke a new crisis, and so on. He concluded, "to enter, therefore, into associations against importing British manufacturers, any farther than a rational attention to your circumstances, is surely no moderate measure, but must, at last, end in a humiliating submission, or oblige you to have recourse to that force which the proposers of this Plan would wish to avoid."

The plan to put a stop to all exports to Great Britain found even less favor with Thomson Mason:

This plan, if it means anything, is to distress Great Britain. But surely you cannot more effectually do this than by lessening your imports, and increasing your exports, as much as possible; for by selling your commodities to the British merchants, and by taking none of theirs in exchange, you will increase your own wealth by exhausting that of Britain. But as is objected, we are at present largely indebted to the British merchants: The more incumbent it is upon you to export all the commodities you can, to pay them as soon as possible; for you ought to have more gratitude than to attempt to ruin the families of those who have been kind enough to furnish you not only with the elegancies, but the necessaries of life.

He dismissed the argument that stopping the export of tobacco would materially injure the revenue. The tax was paid, after all, by

British consumers, not by the ministry personally; if the tax on tobacco showed a decline, a new tax would be levied on some other commodity to make up the difference. Mason was not opposed to voluntary reduction of the tobacco crop, but he thought it senseless for Virginians to withhold their supplies of wheat and corn, or even tobacco, to enable a few to profit by the misery of the many.[23]

The freeholders of Loudoun County met on 14 June 1774 in Leesburg "to consider the most effective method to preserve the rights and liberties of North America," and Thomson Mason and Francis Peyton, Esquires, were appointed to represent the county at a general meeting to be held at Williamsburg 1 August 1774.

When Governor Dunmore dissolved the House of Burgesses in May 1774, he had set the first of August as the date for a new assembly. County elections were held in the intervening weeks, and by August the issue of withholding exports and imports was fully aired. Prince William County, in the Potomac tobacco region, accepted the stoppage of imports and exports, but added that "the courts of justice in this Colony ought to decline hearing any civil causes until the said Acts are repealed." These resolutions were drafted by George Mason.[24] By the hasty dissolution of the Assembly before the passage of a supply bill, the civil courts simply died a natural death. Planters opposed reopening the courts to civil suits after a nonexportation plan went into effect as they would have no ready means to pay their creditors.

The business community looked with horror on proposals to close the courts. Harry Piper, a Whitehaven factor, wrote from Alexandria, "It is also proposed to stop all proceedings in the Courts of Justice with regard to the recovery of Debts, so that you can see the Merchants are to be distressed at all events in order to make them active in getting the Acts repealed." William Reynolds expressed the fear that without recourse to the courts, "the situation of the trading people will be truly distressing, no recovering debts, which will of course prevent our paying those whom we owe." [25]

The freeholders and inhabitants of Fairfax County met on 18 July 1774 at the Courthouse in Alexandria. They also adopted a set of resolutions on the subject of nonimportation written by George Mason. The resolutions, which were printed each week in the *Virginia Gazette,* showed substantial agreement on stopping imports but opinion was divided on halting exports.[26]

The delegates assembled at Williamsburg on 1 August 1774. William Reynolds, a Yorktown factor, reported he had attended "the Meeting two days and was really fearfull they would resolve against Exporting to take place immediately but am happy to find Moderation has guided their counsels so far as to postpone it till August next, by which time we may have it in our power to pay off or at any rate lessen our debts in England." [27]

The whole dispute resolved itself into the question of whether the British Parliament had the right to legislate for the American Colonies. If it did, then any act of resistance was illegal; if it did not, then any act of submission was immoral. Rather than vex the merchants and manufacturers in a vague hope of forcing the repeal of certain legislative acts, the Americans should simply disobey them. If the act closing the port of Boston was illegal, merchants and shipmasters should proceed as if it had never been enacted; if the British authorities chose to enforce it by violence, then they, and not the Americans, had brought violence into the constitutional dispute.

The Virginians agreed not to import goods from Great Britain or British manufacturers from the West Indies after 1 November 1774. Delegates from the Norfolk area had succeeded in keeping the West Indian trade open. The final resolve left more than a year for exports to continue, in hopes that the threat would be enough to arouse the merchants of Britain without impoverishing the planters of Virginia. The convention further recommended that tobacco be curtailed and that hemp, flax, and other "articles as may form a proper basis for manufacturer's should be cultivated." [28]

The unhappy experience with earlier nonimportation agreements led the delegates to require all merchants to sign the association as a prerequisite to doing business in Virginia. Planters, as well as merchants who sought to enrich themselves by the artificial scarcity would be penalized. Only one member refused to vote for these measures. "All signed but Thomson Mason," Landon Carter recorded in his diary, "and because with all his Patriotism he was against any nonimportation Scheme at all, he would not sign." [29]

Thomson retired to private life, his ill health aggravated by the tensions and disappointments of public life. Writing to John Dickinson on 17 June 1775, he gave his reasons for his withdrawal:

It ever was and still is my Opinion that if all America had united in declaring at once, that they would not suffer any Act of a British Parliament to be enforced in America, and like New England had put themselves into a Posture of Defense, the Parliament of Britain would not have attempted to enforce her Claim to a Jurisdiction, unjust in itself, and subversive of American Liberty. But for giving this advice to my Country, and for dissuading them from stopping their imports, and Exports till they were provided with Necessary Means of Defense, I was thought too violent a Man, as such excluded from being one of the delegates to the Congress held in your

City last Fall, and the Non-importation and Non-exportation Plan was recommended as the more moderate Measure.[30]

The Chesapeake colonies severed all their commercial ties with Great Britain when they adopted the Association in 1774, and of necessity the Virginians had to create a new economy. Their tobacco would no longer be purchased by British merchants and carried to European markets in British ships. The objects of everyday use that had come in the holds of every British vessel that entered the Chesapeake would no longer be imported.

When the Fairfax Committee of Safety was organized in the summer of 1774, George Mason became a member and was made the chairman in August. As chairman he prepared measures for the enrollment of an independent militia company in Fairfax County and supervised the operations of the nonimportation agreement when it went into effect.[31] The committee also collected relief supplies for the people of Boston, who were suffering from the effects of the Boston Port Bill.

Neighbors urged Mason throughout the summer of 1774 to offer his name as a candidate for the Virginia Convention. They had long relied on his judgment in private and believed he would contribute more to the commonwealth in a public station. On the eve of their departure for the Continental Congress in 1774, Edmund Pendleton, Patrick Henry, and George Washington met with Mason to discuss the political situation and Virginia's position in regard to it.[32] But Mason still preferred to shun political life as much as possible without shirking his public duty.

After the death of his beloved wife, Mason had spent weeks at a time visiting Richard Henry Lee and his family. Then in February 1775 Mason and his daughter, Nancy, went to Mrs. Eilbeck's in Maryland, in order to be with her at the time of her operation for cancer. But his long-standing friendship with Richard Henry Lee and George Washington drew him more and more into Virginia politics and the storm center of the revolutionary movement. Mason's most active public service coincided almost exactly with the war years. On 17 April 1775 Mason and George Washington rode together to Alexandria for the election of deputies from Fairfax County to the Virginia Convention. Washington had resigned in order to take his seat in the Continental Congress as a delegate from Virginia. The Fairfax County freeholders selected George Mason to take his place in the Provincial Congress at Richmond.[33]

Early on the morning of 19 April 1775 a party of Massachusetts militia stood their ground on Lexington common and attempted to dispute the passage of a column of British regulars. When the rebels finally dispersed, eight minutemen were dead and ten others lay wounded on the village green. The long-expected war had come in earnest. Within a few days Virginia was startled by the news from Lexington. George Mason impulsively gave the name of the Massachusetts town to the thousand-acre plantation on Mason's Neck that he had set aside for his eldest son.* Lexington marked a break with the past and a new beginning.

Virginia had its own independent militia companies, the equivalent of the minutemen drawn up on Lexington green, and George Mason had been the prime mover in the formation of the Fairfax County company. He presided at a meeting of Fairfax County freeholders held at Alexandria in September 1774 to form such a body. Those present pledged

that we will form ourselves in a Company, not exceeding one hundred Men, by the Name of the Fairfax independent Company of Voluntiers, making Choice of our own Officers; to whom, for the Sake of Good-order & Regularity, we will pay due submission. That we will meet at such Times & Places in this County as our said Officers (to be chosen by a Majority of the Members, so soon as fifty have subscribed) shall appoint & direct, for the Purpose of learning & practising the military Exercise & Discipline; dressed in a regular Uniform of Blue, turn'd up with Buff; with plain yellow metal Buttons, Buff Waist Coat & Breeches, & white Stockings; and furnished with a good Fire-lock & Bayonet, Sling Cartouch Box, and Tomahawk. And that we will, each of us, constantly keep by us a Stock of six pounds of Gunpowder, twenty pounds of Lead, and fifty Gunflints, at the least.[34]

The hand of George Mason of Gunston Hall can be seen in everything the Fairfax company represented. It was a regular militia company, loyal to King George, determined to defend the colony against foreign invasion or hostile Indian incursion. It was raised without any reference to the representatives of royal government in Virginia, and Governor Dunmore had no authority over it. Naturally the governor and his Council could not be asked to issue commissions in regular form for the officers of the company. Direct election of officers by the men of their company answered this difficulty, but George Mason intended much more than a pragmatic solution in pressing for the election of officers. His abiding distrust of a regular military establishment was so great that he strongly advised his son, George Mason of Lexington, not to join the standing army. "When the Plan for the Minute-Men is completed, if he has a Mind to enter into that I shall have no Objection;

---

* On 15 Mar. 1776 George Mason leased 1,000 acres on Doegs' Neck "for about two years past in the possession of the said George Mason, Jr." for an annual rent of one ear of Indian corn (Fairfax D.B. M-1, fols. 236–39).

as I look upon it to be the true natural, and safest Defence of this, or any other free Country." [35] He believed that militia officers should be elected by their men and then be returned themselves into the ranks at the end of a year's service and new officers elected. If it should be objected that the militia would lose the experience of veteran officers, Mason retorted that this was a small price to pay for removing the danger inherent in an elite corps of professional military officers:

We came equals into this world, and equals shall we go out of it. All men are by nature born equally free and independent. To protect the weaker from the injuries and insults of the stronger were societies first formed; when men entered into compacts to give up some of their natural rights, that by union and mutual assistance they might secure the rest; but they gave up no more than the nature of the thing required. Every society, all government, and every kind of civil compact therefore, is or ought to be calculated for the general good and safety of the community.

But when we reflect upon the insidious art of wicked and designing men, the various and plausible pretences for continuing and increasing authority, the inordinate lust of power in the few, we shall no longer be surprised that free-born man hath been enslaved, and that those very means which were contrived for his preservation have been perverted to his ruin.[36]

Thus he argued that the most effective check on the ambition of those in government "is frequently appealing to the body of the people, to those constituent members from whom authority originated, for their approbation or dissent." Mason was an advocate of democracy, not because he held some romantic notion of the inherent goodness of man, but because he feared the inherent tendency to evil in every man, a tendency most dangerous in those who held power by reason of their public office.

Mason's Fairfax constituents did not always share his enthusiasm for militia units. His colleagues on the Fairfax Committee wrote to Mason to "recommend the raising of Regulars" since "daily Experience evinces, that the Minute System is very inadequate to the Design." They believed that regular troops should be stationed wherever danger existed of an attack and armed vessels should patrol the principal rivers.[37]

In July 1775 George Mason was busy with the work of preparing an ordinance for raising an armed force for the defense of Virginia. The problems he and his colleagues faced were enormous: "To raise forces for immediate service—to new-model the whole militia—to render about one-fifth of it fit for the field at the shortest warning—to melt down all the volunteer and independent companies into this great establishment—to provide arms, ammunition, &c.—and to point out ways and means of raising money, these are difficulties indeed!" When the bill was finally submitted to the Convention, it provided for the appointment of line officers of the several Virginia regiments by the Committee of Safety of Virginia, a major departure from Mason's philosophy. In all, three thousand regulars were to be raised in Virginia and formed into three regiments. Each county would raise a company of fifty men. Mason considered this a needless expense. He was more enthusiastic about the militia section of the bill and was obviously its author. "The Minute-Plan I think is a wise one, & will in a short time furnish 8,000 good Troops, ready for action, & composed of men in whose Hands the Sword may be safely trusted." [38] Military necessity never modified Mason's deep distrust of a regular army.

In order to insure an adequate supply of food to the armies raised by the American colonies for their own defense, he introduced a bill in July 1775 in the Virginia Convention to put a stop to all exports of wheat and flour. It provided that "no flour, wheat, or other grain, or provisions of any kind, be exported from this colony, to any part of the world, from and after the fifth day of August next" and that "no quantities of the said articles, more than are necessary for the use of the inhabitants, be brought to, collected, or stored in the towns or other places upon or near the navigable waters." [39]

Patrick Henry, Thomas Jefferson, and more than two-thirds of his colleagues in the Virginia Convention urged him in August 1775 to accept a place in the Virginia delegation to the Continental Congress. He was adamant in his refusal and publicly asked his colleagues not to force the honor upon him but to send Francis Lightfoot Lee in his place. "But my getting clear of this Appointment has avail'd me little," Mason confided to Martin Cockburn, "as I have been since, in spite of every thing I cou'd do the Contrary, put upon the Committee of Safety." The Committee would have immediate charge of the defense of the colony and acted as the executive council of Virginia after the Convention broke up at the end of August. [40]

George Mason's ill health delayed his return to Williamsburg until 18 May 1776, but he remained for the rest of the Convention. During this session Patrick Henry was chosen the first governor. The 5 July 1776 issue of the *Virginia Gazette* reported the following by Patrick Henry: "To the Honourable President of The House of Convention Gentlemen: The vote of this day appointing me the Governor of this Commonwealth has been notified to me in the most polite and obliging manner by George Mason, Henry Lee, Dudley Digges, John Blair and Bartholomew Dandridge esqrs."

The rivers and tidal estuaries that had brought ships in the tobacco trade to the planters' dooryards exposed the heart of Virginia to the ravages of seaborne raiders. During 1775–76 John Murray, Lord Dunmore, the last royal governor of Virginia, directed a series of expeditions intended to plunder and intimidate the rebellious colony. In January 1776 Mason attempted to secure cooperation from the Maryland authorities in the common defense of the Potomac. He wrote to the Maryland Council of Safety: "Being empowered & directed, by the Committee of Safety for this Colony to build two row gallies, one to carry a 24 & the other an 18 pounder, & provide three arm'd cutters for the protection of Potomac River, we think it proper to inform your board that this measure will be carryed into execution with all possible expedition, & that we hope to have your co-operation, in adopting some similar plan, for the same purpose." [41] The Maryland Council of Safety indicated an inability to follow the lead of Virginia, as they had already committed themselves to build a larger ship for the protection of Chesapeake Bay. "The Powder necessary for this Ship and for Fortifications which we are building, will diminish our Stock so much, as to prevent us from attempting an Increase of our Marine, till we receive a Supply of that necessary Article, more than sufficient for our Troops & Militia on whom we chiefly rely for Protection." [42]

The arms and ammunition necessary to equip the soldiers guarding the Virginia Coasts from Lord Dunmore's raids were in short supply. "God knows what will become of you even if you have your 9 Battalions Raised," Benjamin Harrison wrote in February, "for I understand you have not Arms for a Quarter part of them." Efforts to fill military demands with home-front industry brought only the smallest results. "Would you believe it, that we have not yet erected one Powder Mill at the public Expense," John Page observed in April 1776.[43] Despite Mason's efforts to protect the Potomac plantations, British ships cruised up and down the river almost at will. In July 1776 "Lord Dunmores fleet went up Potowmack untill they found the Water fresh enough to drink, [and] they landed about ten Miles below Dumfries. The Poltroons, the Militia of Stafford, run, but 30 of the P. William Militia happily arriv'd, advanc'd with good Countenance, and drove him on board." [44]

On 23 July 1776 two small boats attached to the *Protector,* a row galley commanded by Capt. Robert Conway, were stationed at Sandy Point on the Maryland shore of the Potomac watching the movements of Dunmore's expedition. The Virginians informed a party of Maryland militia under Col. William Harrison that the British were manning their boats. The enemy rowed over to the Virginia side with two tenders, one gondola, and ten rowboats; landed and burned William Brent's house. Harrison's militiamen numbered more than three hundred; but when ordered to the beach to protect the Virginia navy, all ran away except Harrison. The *Protector's* crew of seven were forced to haul their own boats into a marsh to save them from Dunmore. At times the militia proved scarcely more welcome than the British. Thomas Collis complained that the Prince William militia stationed on his plantation in July 1776 "to oppose any descent that might have been made from the Enemys ships of war" destroyed his crops, valuable furniture, and other household goods." [45]

Martin Cockburn answered the call to the colors when Dunmore's fleet threatened the Potomac planters. In the daybook kept by Martin Cockburn £43 10s. 11d. is recorded as "by Cash received from Colonel Mason on Acct of the Common Wealth to pay off the Militia that were under me in Dogue Neck when Lord Dunmore came up the River in July 1776." Young George Mason V was active in the defense of American liberties, commanding a Minute Company sent to Hampton in 1776 to protect the coast against Dunmore's ravages. According to tradition the girls of the Mason family and their slaves fled Gunston Hall when the British fleet menaced the area. Slaves in particular were casualties of such raids. They often ran off or were carried away by the British. Richard Graham wrote from Dumfries in 1777 that "the Ships in the Bay have taken above 300 Negroes. . . . Several of the people in Lancaster & Northumberland have lost every slave they were possessed of." [46]

With the remembrance of the bitter experience of the July 1776 alarm, Mason attempted to secure two cannons to mount for the defense of Alexandria: "If the Congress is pleased to indulge them with such an order, the sooner it can be granted the better; as the fortifieing of the said Town will be very advantageous to the Trade of great Part of Virginia and Maryland, and give considerable encouragement to foreign Adventurers, by affording them Protection at a good Port, where they can speedily procure Cargoes of Country-produce." [47]

Mason realized that defense of Virginia's rivers and harbors was a prime requisite for the importation of foreign manufacturers, and he was much concerned in the plans and discussions for effectively putting such a program into action. Offensive operations against British shipping to the West Indies would provide one source of finished goods. Direct trade with France, Spain, and Holland would earn hard credits with Virginia tobacco to pay for the weapons of war and the luxuries of peace. In all of these areas of concern Mason had much to say and do. Dunmore's fleet aimed at stifling the efforts of the

Chesapeake colonies to obtain the supplies they needed. He had informed the British authorities of the number of vessels from Virginia sent to the West Indies to secure gunpowder for the use of the colonists. His raids on the Virginia rivers led to the capture of a number of ships that were bringing contraband to the Virginians or carrying provisions to the American army in New England.[48]

When the tobacco exportation ended, many of the merchants and factors in Virginia settled their accounts, packed their ledgers, and sailed for Glasgow or Whitehaven to await more peaceful times. With family and friends in Britain, as well as on the Chesapeake, those who elected to remain in Virginia faced a cruel dilemma. George Mason introduced legislation in the Virginia Convention to encourage them to remain: "A very sensible Petition from the Merchants who are Natives of Great Britain has been put into my Hands, and will be presented today or to-morrow, praying that some certain line of Conduct may be prescribed to them, and a recommendation to the people from the Convention, respecting them. As I drew the ordinance for a general Test, I have endeavoured to make it such as no good man would object to; the Merchants here [Richmond], declare themselves well pleased with." [49] Virginia did not give up tobacco during the war, for it was soon evident that tobacco was the only American export that would bear the costs of shipping and insurance in wartime.

Direct trade with the tobacco buyers of France and Holland was a hope fostered by Mason and other Virginia leaders in the early days of the war. In April 1776 he wrote to Washington, "Large Ventures have been lately made for military Stores; for which Purpose we are now loading a Ship for Europe, with Tobo. at Alexandria; her Cargo is all on float, & I hope to have her under sailing in a few Days." [50] Mason's enterprise was to open a new door to the Virginia tobacco trade. He strove earnestly to help Virginia break out of the stagnation imposed by the rending of commercial ties with the British tobacco houses. Perhaps no single effort on Mason's part was more consequential than his patronage of Richard Harrison.

Harrison, a member of a well-known family in Charles County, Maryland, was a partner in the firm of Hooe and Harrison, wheat purchasers of Alexandria. Robert Townshend Hooe, his partner and cousin, had been a member of the firm of Jenifer and Hooe. Richard Harrison, twenty-five years old and ambitious, was a young man with the ability and the courage to undertake a complicated and dangerous mission. At the instance of George Mason, and with the commissions of the Maryland and Virginia committees of safety to be filled, the young merchant of Alexandria sailed for the West Indies in 1775. His mission was to arrange for the flow of arms and ammunition through the French island of Martinique to the Chesapeake patriots and for the passage of the produce of Virginia to markets in the West Indies and Europe.[51]

In December 1775 Robert Townshend Hooe loaded a cargo of flour on the sloops *Molly* and *Batchelor* and sent both of them down the Potomac from Alexandria bound for Martinique. His letter of instructions to the master of the *Batchelor* explained: "If any accident should have prevented Mr. Harrisons getting to the Island, you are in that case to open his Letter, sell Your Cargoe at the very highest Prices you can get; the Money arising from the Sales you must lay out in Gun Powder if you can get it, if not, in Musketts & if they are not to be had, Salt Petre & Sulpher & if you cannot get those Articles, then lay out the whole in Strong coarse Linnens." Hooe purchased wheat and flour for the West Indian market and shipped the cargoes to Harrison, who sold them to the French merchants, who, in turn, supplied the military needs of the Chesapeake colonies. The firm was allowed a commission of 5 percent for their contracts with Maryland. In January 1776 the Maryland Council of Safety sent the brig *Sam* to Martinique with 1,386 barrels of bread and 4,000 staves, with instruction to the *Sam's* skipper to deliver the goods to Richard Harrison. Largely through Harrison's agency, commercial ties with the Dutch island of Saint Eustatius, and thus with the merchants of Holland were being forged by Virginians and Marylanders. Trade with this tiny island reached such proportions that within thirteen months 3,182 vessels sailed between Saint Eustatius and the American coast, carrying the material of war or the cargoes of tobacco, flour, and staves that built up the purchasing power of the American rebels.[52]

Congress created a Secret Committee to enable the American colonies to develop a means of trading with foreign powers and thus bring in the supplies needed to carry on the war. Robert Morris of Philadelphia became a member of that committee in the winter of 1775 and within a short time its most influential member. He dispatched the Philadelphia merchant William Bingham to Martinique early in 1776. By shipping tobacco, flour, and other produce to Bingham in the West Indies, Morris was able to order French products from Silas Deane, his agent in Paris, and have them sent out to Bingham at Martinique. The Chesapeake colonies were ahead of Morris in this trade because of the efficient work of George Mason and Richard Harrison. Mason had long stressed the primary importance of overseas trade to supply Virginia with the necessary sinews of war. Discussing the possibility of a European alliance with Richard Henry

Lee, he observed, "We want but two things—a regular Supply of military Stores, and a naval Protection of our Trade & Coasts—for the first we are able & willing to pay the Value in the Produce of our Country."

In order to supply its military needs as the war dragged on, the state of Virginia became a major purchaser of tobacco for export. George Mason acted for the commonwealth in expediting the purchase of the needed tobacco and loading it on board the vessels that would carry it to a French port. In 1777 Mason explained to Governor Patrick Henry that difficulties in the inspection of the tobacco due to the epidemic of smallpox had caused some delay in deliveries and recommended that the state authorities give earlier notice of their intention to purchase large quantities of tobacco. He included a careful list of the amount bought from each planter, the grade of the tobacco, and the price paid. By such shipments of tobacco to Europe, Virginia obtained the credits needed to buy arms and ammunition.[53]

In addition to purchasing tobacco for the state, Mason directed the purchase of flour at Alexandria until April 1777, when he turned over the direction of the flour purchase to a business associate, William Herbert, an Irish merchant of Alexandria. The Virginians had to compete with purchasers for the Continental Congress. Five vessels were taking on flour at Alexandria in 1777 to be sold abroad to enable Congress to make needed purchasers of weapons and equipment.[54]

Besides bringing the means of defense to the Potomac, the West Indian trade brought many of the essentials of everyday life to the planters of the Northern Neck. In February 1777 Jenifer and Hooe offered for sale at Alexandria the schooner *Anne Maria* and its cargo of salt, linen, and clothing from the West Indies. In June 1777 they advertised hardware, stockings, shoes, sacking, waistcoat patterns, blankets, and molasses, lately imported from Martinique in the *Molly;* and coffee, rum, sugar, strong duck, and medicines, brought to Alexandria by the *Lucy.* Alexandria's prosperity during the Revolution lay in its trade in grain and in the possession of enterprising local merchants. Dumfries, its principal colonial rival, had a more specialized interest in tobacco and declined during the war. Alexandria was the natural depot for Virginia state supplies imported during the war from Maryland and the North. Moreover, the flour needs of the state and of Congress helped make Alexandria an important center for collecting articles of public use. In 1776 and 1777 Virginia required flour to send to Richard Harrison at Martinique for his military purchases. Because of both public and private demands, Alexandria became one of the important wheat-exporting centers of Virginia. By 1781, when Alexandria merchants asked for a state flour inspection there, they argued that "the Manufacturing of Wheat has been for some years past carried to such an extent by the Inhabitants of the Western Counties as to render Flour and Bread Staple Commodities of the State." [55]

Alexandria's interest in the tobacco trade was also stimulated by state activities. A public commissary was stationed there to collect tobacco for French shipments. Private purchasers were numerous. Hooe and Harrison's business was largely in tobacco, which they shipped to the West Indies on many occasions for the state of Maryland, as well as to Cadiz after 1779, when Richard Harrison established a branch of this house there. They also shipped flour to Spain in 1779 for Robert Morris, and they frequently disposed of goods for William Bingham, who in turn did work for them in the West Indies.

George Mason had difficulties with this West Indian trade. He wrote to William Bingham at Martinique:

Some time in the Summer 1777 Mr. Richard Harrison remitted from Martinique Bills of Exchange on London for the Sum of £310 Sterling to Mr. Andrew Lemozin Mercht. in Havre de Grace, upon my Acct., transmitting him, at the same time, by my Directions, an Invoyce of Goods (not fully equal to the Amount of the Bills) to be purchased with the proceeds of the said Bills, & ship'd to Martinique, from whence Mr. Harrison was to forward them to me in Virginia. Mr. Lemozin acknowledged the Rect. of the Bills, & Payment for them, & wrote Mr. Harrison that he was purchasing the Goods; but complaining of the Trouble, on Account of the Variety of Articles; altho' I well know that such an Order, or one of much greater Variety, wou'd have been executed, with the greatest Ease in London, Bristol, Liverpoole, or any other considerable trading Town in Great Britain. [56]

Mason and Harrison had called on Messrs. Schweighauser and Dobree, merchants in Nantes, to obtain satisfaction from Lemozin. He had insisted that he had been unable to send the goods because of high wartime insurance rates and returned the money to William Bingham. By this time Harrison had gone on to Holland and Mason was at the end of his tether because Bingham claimed he had never received the money and could not repay Mason.

The goods that Mason ordered were "intended for the use of my own Family." It is worth noting that Mason anticipated an order of British goods and regretted the absence of British commercial method in filling his order. Although the Virginians would be obliged to trade of necessity through France and Holland during wartime, they never lost their taste for British manufacturers. A number of ventures in the tobacco trade in the postwar era would founder on that rock.

Trade with neutral Holland provided a means of obtaining British manufactured goods after France and England went to war in 1778.

American authorities winked at the importation of British manufacturers by way of Holland and Saint Eustatius, which Marylanders and
Virginians preferred to Continental goods. The British navy took a
dimmer view of this trade with the enemy at one remove and seized
large amounts of British property as contraband when they captured
Saint Eustatius in 1781.

George Mason had many business dealings with Richard Harrison
over a period of years. In 1778 he wrote to his friend that he had sent
him "a few silver dollars, to discharge the little balance you was so
kind of advance to me, in the goods purchased and sent me by [Captain
John Sanford of the sloop *Flying Fish*] from Martinique." Mason
added that he was "uneasy at not hearing anything respecting the goods
you ordered for me last year from France," as he was afraid that the
outbreak of war between France and Great Britain would imperil any
shipments then on the high seas. Richard Harrison returned to Alexandria with the French entry into the war in 1778. Mason had written
him promising to look after Harrison's interest in Williamsburg and
complaining of the conduct of Andrew Lemozin, their correspondent
in France.[57]

In 1779 it was decided that Mason's son George should go to Europe
for a year or two in an effort to find a climate that would improve his
health. He had never recovered from the rheumatic condition he had
contracted in 1775. It seems to have been a decision of desperation,
because Mason wrote George Washington at his army headquarters:
"Whether he will fix his Residence in France Spain or Italy must depend on the advice of the Physicians in Paris . . . and as I have no
Acquaintance, & he will be an utter Stranger in France, you will oblige
me exceedingly by giving him Letters of Introduction, as the Son of
a friend of yours, to the Marquis De la Fayette & Dr. Franklin, at Paris;
whose Notice will be a great Satisfaction and Advantage to him." [58]
Washington replied quickly to his friend's request that it gave him the
opportunity to "testify the sincerity of my regard." The letter Washington wrote from Camp Middlebrook in March of 1779 to Benjamin
Franklin is exactly the pleasant letter that any parent at any period in
history would be pleased to have had written for his son.

Dear Sir:

This letter will be delivered to you by Mr. G. Mason, son of George
Mason Esqr. of Virginia, a Gent. of future and influence in that State—a
zealous & able supporter of the liberties of this Country—and a particular
friend of mine.

The young Gentlemans bad health induced him to try some other clime,
preferably the air of Montpelier, while inclination may lead him to Paris, in

which case, I take the liberty of recommending him to your friendly countenance & civilities. . . .[59]

George sailed in early April 1779 in one of the ships of Hooe and Harrison bound for Cadiz, Spain. These merchants had by this time entered both the tobacco trade at Amsterdam and the wheat trade in Cadiz. His father had given George "credit upon a House in Nantes," but he didn't expect that George would go there immediately upon his landing in Spain.[60] No letters seem to exist from George Mason V, telling of his impressions of Europe or where he spent his first year, but he eventually settled in Nantes, where he entered the tobacco trade without becoming involved in the tangled affairs of his father.

George Mason of Gunston Hall was part-owner of an American privateer, the *General Washington* of Alexandria. His partners in this venture were Robert Townshend Hooe, Richard Harrison, William Herbert, and Josiah Watson, all of Alexandria. In July 1779 the *General Washington* arrived safely in the Potomac after capturing a British privateer on its homeward passage from France. It brought a rich cargo of civilian goods to Alexandria, including linen, calicoes, cambrics, thread, silk, handkerchiefs, bohea and green tea, loaf sugar, spices, claret, brandy, knives, forks, combs, scissors, china, and salt.[61] The firm of John De Neufville and Son of Amsterdam shipped a similarly diffuse cargo of European goods to Mason on the *General Washington* in 1780.

In 1780 Mason recommended Richard Harrison to James Madison for appointment as the Consul in Spain:

This Gentleman is a native of Maryland, but along the Beginning of the present Troubles, removed to the Island of Martinique, where He resided about two Years, learned the french Language, & transacted a good deal of Business for Virginia & some other of the United States, in a Manner that gave general Satisfaction. . . . I have always been cautious in giving Recommendations for public Offices; but my Knowledge of Mr. Harrison's Diligence, Integrity & commercial Knowledge, from a personal Acquaintance with him, convinces me He will discharge such an Office with Reputation to himself, & Advantage to the Commercial Interest of America.[62]

The transatlantic passage was fraught with dangers, even to armed vessels. George Mason V lost a cargo of goods shipped on the schooner *Isabella* from Nantes in 1781. The *General Washington* arrived safely from Amsterdam earlier in the year, but the British blockade of the Chesapeake forced it to put into a New England port, where the sale of its cargo did not produce half of what it would have brought in Virginia. George Mason had more than £200 of goods on his private account on the *General Washington,* "which still remain in New England; from which I am not likely to get them soon, if ever. By these Disappointments the Family are in great want of Necessarys." [63]

Tobacco prices reached phenomenally high levels in Great Britain and on the Continent. In some cases the profits were so immense that British companies were able to cover their losses in goods, real property, and debts in America from the sale of tobacco imported in 1775. In 1778 the supply of tobacco in England had been nearly exhausted. British annual consumption of tobacco amounted to some twelve thousand hogsheads, according to William Molleson, and by February 1778 there were fewer than four thousand hogsheads of tobacco in the British Isles. Prices advanced from tenpence halfpenny the pound to three shillings the pound.[64]

Neil Jamieson of Norfolk, a loyalist refugee, argued in a letter to Sir Henry Clinton in 1780 that there was a direct relation between the tobacco export and the economic stability of the entire United States. "Since the taking of Charlestown So. Carolina and the buying up and exportation of Tobacco and Indigo by the people in rebellion is put a stop to, their paper money has depreciated from 60 to 75 & 80 for one—on account of General Leslie's arrival in Virginia it immediately got to 110 & 120 for one." Jamieson explained that the capture of Charleston had blocked the export of indigo, so that "there is only the Colony of Virginia and province of Maryland where there is any commodity that will bear exportation and this is the article of Tobacco." [65]

The European market fluctuated considerably during this period of wartime shortages. The outbreak of war between Britain and the Dutch in December 1780 had caused a considerable increase in tobacco prices. In February 1781 Maryland tobacco stood at 85 livres and Virginia tobaccos varied between 90 and 100 livres. In March 1781 Joshua Johnson, an American merchant in Nantes, reported that there was not a hogshead of tobacco to be had at any price, but the capture of the Saint Eustatius fleet left the market glutted in June of the same year. The Atlantic voyage was no less precarious. Chesapeake Bay was infested with small privateers and peckaroons, while larger British vessels preyed on the Atlantic sea lanes.

A letter written by Joshua Johnson to George Mason of Lexington in February 1781 enclosed the invoice of goods and bills of lading for a cargo valued at 5,431 livres on board the *Lady Lee,* Capt. R. Dashiell. Johnson had purchased the goods on Mason's account and hoped "that the sales may equal your most sanguine expectations." The firm charged him no commission or fees "being richly paid for our trouble by the confidence you have placed in us." The *Lady Lee* arrived at

Bordeaux with a cargo of Mason's Chesapeake tobacco, which had
been sold through the Irish merchants V. and P. French and Company
at 80 Livres per hundred pounds. Otter skins, rice, and beeswax
formed part of the cargo. The entire shipment brought the firm some
£6,000.[66]

George Mason V dispatched certain goods from Nantes early in
1782 for his father and for Van Bibber, the Baltimore merchant. His
father also had direct dealings with Joshua Johnson in Nantes. Johnson wrote to him in October 1782 to inform him that the firm had
purchased the goods he had ordered and notified his own partners in
Annapolis that he was shipping them goods valued at £2,306 17s. for
Mason's account, "which you will receive and dispose of according to
former Orders." [67] The Mason accounts represented a significant portion of the total business done by Wallace, Johnson and Muir.

In July 1781 Joshua Johnson sent his partners in Annapolis the
invoice for "a parcel of goods, ship'd you by order of Mr. George
Mason, and for this acct., amounting to £2,377 5s. which you will
please to receive and pass to his credit the proceeds. He is now at one
of the Watering places for his Health which deprives him of writing
you tho' as he hinted to us a Desire that you wou'd forward us Sales
& Remittances, we have to beg you will not disappoint him." In December 1782 Johnson wrote to the home office, "We formerly pointed
out to you a Method of Remitting Mr. Mason and Every other whom
we have shipped goods for and hope You have adopted it particularly
Mr. Mason's as we have been advancing for him." [68]

George Mason did everything in his power to encourage home manufactures during the war years. But there was little enough that any
man could do to transform an almost completely agricultural nation
into one capable of producing its own needs in a period of wartime
shortages and financial distress. The *Maryland Gazette* and the *Virginia
Gazette* occasionally carried notices of projected cloth factories, cannon
foundries, and other proposed factories, often mere visionary schemes
without backers or workmen. In 1777 Mason found a skilled craftsman
who had worked in the sailcloth factory at Hull in Yorkshire and was
"master of every part of the business, from breaking the hemp to
finishing the said cloth" and recommended him to the managers of the
state-run sail manufactory. The Virginia Convention supported the
Scottish engineer John Tait in his plans to create a saltworks near
Williamsburg. Salt was one of the most difficult commodities to obtain
during the war, and the various schemes for making it more plentiful
occupied a good deal of Mason's time.[69]

Mason's principal involvement with manufacturing in Virginia brought him into contact again with an old friend and neighbor, John Ballendine, with whom he and other Virginians had been associated in planning the Potomac Canal project. Ballendine had developed a series of industrial complexes, iron forges and furnaces, and gristmills, first on the Occoquan, then at the Little Falls of the Potomac and at a point near Harpers Ferry on the upper Potomac. In October 1775 he transferred his operations to the falls of the James River, began the construction of a canal, and projected an ironworks of considerable magnitude.

In May 1776 the Virginia Assembly had determined to erect a foundry at Westham, on the James River, and had purchased three and a half acres adjacent to Ballendine's canal. They had also acquired the right to draw water from the canal, and to operate a boring mill and the right to unrestricted navigation on the canal. The state authorities advanced additional money to Ballendine to help him finish his canal. The Assembly also advanced £5,000 to Ballendine and his partner, John Reveley, repayable in pig iron, to erect an iron furnace. In 1777 Ballendine took the ground that he was the only legal representative of the board appointed in 1772 to open the James River and that he had exclusive rights to improvements erected for that purpose. In 1778 Mason offered a bill authorizing the state to purchase iron from Ballendine and Reveley, despite the fact that their original contract had not been met.

In 1779 George Mason headed a committee charged with settling Ballendine's accounts and transferring the operations of the foundry to the French concern Pierre Penet and Company. It was not an easy task. "Ballendine has got Possession of the Key to the Navigation of James River, & is acting exactly the Part of the Dog in the Manger," Mason observed. In June 1779 Mason offered a bill to authorize the Virginia Assembly to give 3,000 acres on the James River to Penet and Company for the erection of a foundry and other necessary works. He also introduced a bill to arrange a final settlement with Ballendine. It took considerable time for Mason to arrive at an amicable settlement, but it was finally determined that Ballendine owed the state of Virginia over £2,000. Ballendine, for his part, insisted that he had spent ten times that amount on the canal alone and demanded that the sole right to collect tolls on the James River be vested in him and his heirs. Thomas Jefferson offered a bill in October 1779 to circumvent Ballendine entirely and rid the state of this troublesome business.[70]

Penet and Company proved more reliable than Ballendine. Pierre Penet returned to France in March 1780 to arrange a loan for Virginia to obtain skilled artisans for the Westham foundry, but without success. In June 1780 Mason called for a full investigation of the foundry business. The state had placed its operations under Turner Southall and John Reveley, and some progress was made before the British army laid the place in ashes in 1781. The British invasion of Virginia in 1781 was in answer to American "King Tobacco" diplomacy. As tobacco exports kept the American army in the field, a British strike at the Chesapeake would have been a telling blow to the American economy. In May and June 1781 British units crossed and recrossed Virginia at will as the militia could do little to restrain the invaders, who burnt tobacco warehouses, destroyed or carried off military supplies of every kind, and put the torch to shipyards, foundries, and furnaces. Mason was bitter because of the failure of the French fleet to keep the English navy out of Chesapeake Bay, thus offering protection to the British forces on land. He acknowledged that many Virginians thought the allies were spinning out the war to their own advantage, regardless of the hardships suffered by the Americans.[71]

The surrender of Cornwallis at Yorktown and the vote in the British Parliament to end offensive operations in America effectively released the United States from dependence on France and Spain. With no need for a French fleet to protect their coasts or a French army to force Cornwallis into a pocket, Virginians grew restive. Mason prepared a petition directed against Governor Thomas Nelson's continuance of certain economic restraints under emergency powers given him during the British invasion. Mason principally objected to the continued requisition of supplies for the French army, when it would be more profitable for Virginians to have the French buy provisions at market prices and pay cash for them. He also protested the continued embargo of Virginia exports.[72]

Mason struggled with the specter of mounting inflation throughout his term of service in the Virginia Assembly, but it was a losing battle. In the month after Yorktown brown sugar sold at eighteen pence the pound in silver, a bushel of salt cost eight silver dollars, needles were two shillings a dozen, and men's hats sixteen dollars each—all in hard money. In 1775 George Mason sold 275 pounds of Bohea to Richard Harrison for three shillings sterling the pound. In 1780 Martin Cockburn bought a pound of Bohea from George Mason for £36 Virginia currency. By the end of the war Virginia paper money was nearly worthless. Late in 1781 a silver dollar could buy $1,000 in Virginia currency.

In 1777 John Parke Custis wrote to George Washington, informing him that "our Neighbour Colo. Mason is preparing a remedy against the Depreciation of our Money, which I think will do him great Credit.

He is preparing a Bill for a general Assessment on all Property by which he will draw in 500,000 £ pr. ann.; his Valuation of property is very low, which will render his plan very agreeable to the People." Custis also thought highly of Mason's plan for raising an army, but he feared that neither measure would carry in the Assembly if George Mason should be too unwell to argue his own case. Mason's constituents in Fairfax County were of the same mind, instructing him to press for a general assessment as a means of raising the taxes needed and, at the same time, giving some real backing to the paper money in circulation. They were already suffering from rising prices and cheapening money.[73]

Mason introduced legislation to prevent individuals from holding back supplies needed by army contractors and civilians in order to force prices higher. In December 1777 he proposed laws for an increased duty on tobacco exports, the sale of public lands, and a tax on horses. In January 1778 Mason brought to the Assembly his plan for a general tax of ten shillings on every hundred pounds of assessed valuation of land, slaves, money, horses, and plate. A similar tax of ten shillings on every hundred pounds was levied on salaries and offices of profit within the commonwealth. As part of his overall plan, Mason introduced legislation for a Virginia Land Office and the sale of western lands.

In December 1779 Mason introduced a new series of taxes aimed principally at avoiding "the ruinous expedient of future emissions of paper money." This noble intention was not enough to save the tottering economy. It placed a general poll tax of £3 on every free male above twenty-one years of age, £4 on every slave, and a special tax on carriages. Merchants were to collect a 2.5 percent sales tax and a similar 2.5 percent tax on the goods they had in stock. This provision caused a storm of protest from the traders and shopkeepers, and Mason modified it by amending his bill. Less than six months later the state was again bankrupt. In July 1780 Mason introduced a bill authorizing the printing of paper dollars up to the value of £2 million. He attempted to secure some sort of backing for this new emission of paper by levying a window tax of one shilling on every glass window. The window tax had been one of several proposals made by a group of large planters in Lancaster County who considered the poll tax on slaves an unfair burden and a species of class legislation.[74]

George Mason's most significant contribution to the commonwealth during the years of the American Revolution was unquestionably his role in forming a permanent government for the independent state of Virginia and in securing the liberties of its citizens. In May 1776 Mason had reported to Richard Henry Lee that the Virginia Convention had committed itself to independence from the British Empire. "We are now going upon the most important of all Subjects—Government." Mason feared that his colleagues would present "a Plan form'd of heterogenious, jarring & unintelligible Ingredients." George Mason himself very swiftly became the dominant figure on the committee entrusted with preparing a draft. Various plans were indeed offered. "That proposed by George Mason swallowed up all the rest, by fixing the grounds and plan, which after great discussion and correction, were finally ratified." [75]

Mason's original draft of the Virginia Declaration of Rights stressed the fact that all men are born equally free and independent and possess certain inalienable rights, "Life and Liberty, with Means of acquiring and possessing Property, and pursueing and obtaining Happiness and Safety." All power is vested in the people. Magistrates are their trustees and servants. Governments are instituted to secure the common benefit and safety of the people, and when they fail to do so, the people have the inherent right to alter or abolish them. Hereditary offices are repugnant to this principle. The legislative and executive bodies should be at all times distinct from the judiciary. Mason believed that public officials of every description should be returned to a private station after a brief set term in office and replaced by other men chosen in free elections. No man could be deprived of his property without his consent, nor are the people bound by laws they have not ratified. Trial by jury is a fundamental right. No man could be obliged to give witness against himself, and imprisonment on mere suspicion, unsupported by legal evidence, was repugnant to human liberty. No man should be coerced in matters of religion, and all men should enjoy the fullest toleration, unless under color of religion they act against the common good. Trial by jury should be had in civil suits, as well as in criminal cases. Liberty of the press should be enjoyed to the fullest extent. Ex post facto legislation is always dangerous and should be avoided.

The committee made some minor changes in the wording of Mason's resolutions, but scarcely altered the meaning of a single phrase of the original. Two major additions introduced ideas that were fundamental to Mason's thought. He may have added them himself. A well-regulated militia was declared to be "the proper, natural, and safe defence of a free State," a phrase he had used in a letter to Martin Cockburn. Excessive bail and cruel and unusual punishments were reprobated in the final version. Mason's draft was the model for similar bills of rights in other state constitutions and for the ten amendments added to the United States Constitution.[76]

In June 1776 immediately after the adoption of the Declaration of

Rights, George Mason offered a plan of government for the newly independent state of Virginia. It began with the characteristic insistence on the separation of the legislative, executive, and judicial branches. The legislative branch was to be composed of two houses. The lower house would be composed of two delegates from every county, each delegate a bonafide landowner in that county with property worth at least £1,000. The upper house would be made up of twenty-four delegates elected from twenty-four electoral districts, not by the direct vote of the people, but by a body of twelve electors chosen by the voters of each county. Members of the upper house would need to own at least £2,000 worth of land in their electoral district. Mason's qualifications for voting were quite liberal. Men who rented farms and men who had lived a year in the county would be eligible in addition to the freeholders of the county. The governor would be elected annually by the two houses of the General Assembly. He would be assisted by a Council of State similarly elected by the vote of both houses, from their members or from any citizens of the state. These councillors could then serve only three years in succession and would be ineligible for reelection until another three years had passed. The General Assembly would elect all judges, who would then serve during good behavior. The governor would appoint justices of the peace and confirm the nominations of minor court officials made by the respective county courts. The governor, councillors, judges, and all public officials could be impeached by a regular trial by the lower house. Thomas Jefferson added a preamble to the final draft of Mason's constitution. Other changes were mainly verbal or were explanatory of the original meaning. The high property qualification for election to the House of Delegates or the Senate was dropped, but the property qualification was restored for all voters. In this form the Virginia Constitution was adopted on 29 June 1776.[77]

In January 1777 George Mason served with Thomas Jefferson, Edmund Pendleton, George Wythe, and Thomas Ludwell Lee on a committee to revise the existing laws of Virginia. The principles they set down for their own guidance are instructive. English common law was not to be meddled with unless absolutely necessary. The statutes were to be revised and digested, "the Diction, where obsolete or redundant, to be reformed; but otherwise to undergo as few Changes as possible." Where several acts had been passed on the same subject at different times, they were to be combined for clarity's sake.

Thus a group of men, entrusted by their fellows with a mandate to rewrite the laws of the land, free to draw on every new and heady idea bruited about by the Enlightenment, free to begin with a tabula rasa

and draw on it the schematic outline of a perfect society, did nothing
of the sort. They contented themselves with introducing a comma here,
changing an archaic spelling there, but carefully preserving every jot
and tittle of the laws passed by the Virginia Assembly and sanctioned
by the British Crown. Local government under the United States
would not differ in any significant way from local government under
George III. The constitution of Virginia is slightly more innovative.
In Mason's draft it interposed an upper house composed entirely of
county magnates between the governor and an elective council, but
neither of these bodies would be directly elected by the people. The
real distinction between the Governor's Council of 1774 and that of
1776 would try the ingenuity of a scholastic philosopher. The governor
yielded some power to the Assembly, power that it had always held in
practice. Fundamentally, the House of Delegates differed little from
the House of Burgesses. The same men would be elected by the same
land-owning electorate. As for the Declaration of Rights, were these
not the rights of Englishmen that pamphleteers and preachers had
been asserting in a loud voice as far back as living memory?

The greatness of George Mason of Gunston Hall is not dimmed by
suggesting that he was setting up a traditional form of government
based on traditional English liberties. The British ministry and their
supporters in Parliament had been the innovators. The men who made
the American Revolution were conservatives, clinging to traditional
ways and ancient rights. George Mason and his colleagues were men
experienced from early manhood in the uses and limits of power. They
knew from experience the nature of men. They did not waste their
time legislating for a society of men who could not exist outside the
imagination of a political philosopher. Again and again George Mason
returned in his writings to his low opinion of his fellow patriots, men
who masked their avarice and their lust for power "behind pretty
speeches replete with Patriotism and Moral cant."

The year 1779 opened propitiously for the American cause with the
capture of Vincennes by George Rogers Clark in February, securing
the Northwest Territory from British control. Mason was active in the
government of Virginia, though he was plagued with attacks of gout.
The attack he suffered in April, although "a most dangerous one in
my stomach," did not keep him from attending the election in Williamsburg in June, when Thomas Jefferson became governor of Virginia, succeeding Patrick Henry. On his arrival he suffered another
severe attack that hampered his activities. When he was able at last
to attend sessions, the bill to remove the seat of government to Richmond was passed over his opposition. He was appointed chairman of

two committees: one to report on "Kitt's [a Negro's] emancipation, and the other to prepare a bill for settling the rate of exchange." [78] On 19 June he was still in Williamsburg, and on 16 July he wrote Thomas Jefferson from Cartwright's Ordinary, which was located west of the town.

If he went home for part of the summer, he was back in the fall, for on 18 October 1779 a bill prepared by George Mason "for providing a Great Seal for the Commonwealth" was passed by the House. This bill also provided that the seal designed and reported to the Convention on 5 July 1776 "be henceforward called the lesser Seal of the Commonwealth." He was also active in other capacities during that session, which did not close until 24 December 1779.

James Mercer of Fredericksburg records, in a letter dated 8 January 1780, that George Mason was staying at his home "because bad weather prevented his traveling on to Gunston Hall from Williamsburg." Mason wrote to James Mercer on 5 February 1780 following his long visit, and a trace of his sense of humor, little of which has come down to posterity, is evident in his letter: "This cold weather has set all the young Folks to providing Bedfellows. I have signed two or three Licenses every day since I have been at Home. I wish I knew where to get a good one myself; for I find cold Sheets extreamly disagreeable." A little more than two weeks later, on 26 February, he wrote to his cousin, William Fitzhugh of Rousby Hall, Calvert County, Maryland, "My brother desires his Compliments to you and your Lady & Family. He was in Williamsburg a good while last Session, in better health than I have ever seen him for many years. Matrimony seems to agree with him so well that it has almost inclined me to try what it will do for my Constitution. I wish you cou'd recommend some Widow or old maid to me; she must be tolerably Handsome tho' goodnatured & Sensible." [79]

George Mason had matrimony very much on his mind after seven years of being a widower, but his second marriage was one of convenience rather than one of affection, as shown by the marriage agreement.[80] Also, family tradition has it that he wore mourning for Ann, his first wife, until his death. Very little is known about his second wife, Sarah Brent. She was an "old maid," about fifty-two years old, and, as no portrait has been found, it may be assumed she was "tolerably handsome." She would of necessity have been a "sensible" woman to undertake the management of his household, with eight children still living at home.

On 11 April 1780 George Mason and Sarah Brent were married in Dettingen Parish, Prince William County, by the Reverend James

Scott. Sarah was the eldest daughter of George and Catherine (Trimingham) Brent, of Woodstock, and a descendant of Giles Brent, who had patrolled the Indian frontiers with the second George Mason. It is of significance that Sarah's father was a Roman Catholic. The following note concerning him is most interesting: "It also appeared to your Committee that George Brent, Gent., voted at the said Election for Mr. Lee, whose vote the Petitioner objected to, as being a Roman Catholick; but it not appearing to your Committee that the said George Brent, is a Recusant convert Resolved, That it is the Opinion of this Committee that the said George Brent had a good Right to vote for Burgesses at the said Election." [81] This would indicate that an unobtrusive practice of their religion, service as guardians of the frontier, and the transportation of settlers into Virginia had secured for the Brents a practical toleration; their services were too valuable to the colony for them to be harassed by the enforcement of anti-Catholic laws.

Since the Woodstock family were firm adherents of their church, Sarah was probably brought up by her parents as a Roman Catholic, but her religion did not prevent her being married in the Anglican Church. Following her marriage, Sarah brought her ten-year-old nephew, George Graham, with her to Gunston Hall. He was the eldest son of her sister, Jean, and her brother-in-law, Richard Graham of Dumfries, with whom she had made her home. George Graham and Thomas, the youngest son of George Mason, were the same age, each having been born in May 1770. The Mason children became very fond of George Graham and looked upon him as a brother.[82]

Thomson Mason had remarried three years before George. While a widower he had maintained a reputation as a generous and hospitable host. Guests to his home at Raspberry Plain received a warm welcome. One of those whom Thomson befriended was Nicholas Cresswell, a fun-loving young Englishman who was visiting in Virginia with the idea of becoming a plantation owner. He dined with Thomson on 24 April 1776 and many times later. Thomson was kind to the impoverished traveler who was having difficulty in obtaining funds because of the beginning of the war. Fear of having to take up arms against his country made Cresswell so despondent that Thomson gave him a letter to the governor of Virginia asking his help in enabling him to return to England. On 18 April 1777 Nicholas Cresswell left Leesburg and eventually succeeded in reaching his home in Derbyshire.[83]

Social life as a single man was not Thomson's idea of a happy life. On 22 September 1773 he wrote Daniel of Saint Thomas Jenifer at Annapolis:

And now my old friend, how have you been this long time? Words cannot express how glad I should be to see you; for I look upon you to be a kind of Phenomenon, and *honest* courtier. But what are you doing? Making money fast, I know; upon which, and your several promotions, I sincerely congratulate you. But do you not think, that it would now be a good Way, to employ some of your leisure hours in making of Children, to give that money to? Believe me, if you could form any Conception of the ———, the heartfelt Satisfaction of being the Father of a promising son; you would be a married man in less than a week, but if you are obstinately bent agt. tasting the pleasures of Matrimony yourself, for God Sake recommend me to some amiable Maid or Widow of your Acquaintance for I like you at Present live upon the Public, and am heartily tired of it; but as the Lady I marry must be very handsome, moderately rich, exceedingly good natured, sensible etc., etc., etc., I expect to hug a Widower's pillow the remainder of my life which in that case, I shall most ardently pray may be no longer than till my sons come of age, for the solitary Life I lead at present, by no means suits a Man of my social disposition.[84]

Thomson married his second wife, Elizabeth (Westwood) Wallace, at Elizabeth City on 23 November 1777. They had known each other years before, but circumstances blighted their romance. When Thomson heard that Elizabeth was widowed, he resumed his courtship and won the hand of the lady, who had "a liberal, improved & benevolent mind, and entertaining flow of vivacity, a sweet and even temper, and elegant economy." According to the *Virginia Gazette* of 5 December 1777, the lady apparently met all of Thomson's requirements. Although no longer a young woman and the mother of eleven children, Elizabeth bore Thomson three sons and one daughter.

Thomson had been elected to another term as a burgess from Loudoun County in 1776; in 1777 he served in the General Assembly with his brother George. On 23 January 1778 he was elected a judge of the General Court. The Act of 1777 which established the court stated that there should be five judges. "Joseph Jones was elected initially, then John Blair, Thomas Ludwell Lee, Thomas Mason and Paul Carrington, in that order."[85]

The territorial dispute between Virginia and Pennsylvania and the Mason-Dixon line were important issues in Virginia at this time. George Mason's desire for harmony in the new country is expressed in a letter of 27 July 1780 to Joseph Jones, who had served with him on the committee to draft a declaration of rights: "I think it the duty of a staunch whig, and friend of his country, to do every thing in his power to remove any cause of ill will or disagreement with a sister state; and therefore (though I clearly saw from the proceedings that our commissioners had been overmatched by those of Pennsylvania) I labored the ratification of the agreement, as heartily as I ever did any subject in my life."

On 6 October of that year he ⸻ his son William to Monticello to deliver some peach stones and a letter to Thomas Jefferson. In it he said, "As my very ill Health, at present, makes my attendance at the next Session of Assembly rather uncertain I take this Opportunity, by my Son of sending you a few of the Portugal & best kind of rare-ripe Peach Stones." The letter also gave direction for their planting and this caution: "They shou'd be secured from the Moles by Slabs." Unfortunately, he proved unable to go to Richmond, and on the twenty-fourth his excuse of nonattendance was read before the General Assembly.[86]

George's mother-in-law, Sarah (Edgar) Eilbeck, died of cancer on 11 December 1780 following a long and painful illness. She was buried in the family graveyard at Mount Eilbeck next to her husband, William, who had died 26 July 1764. Their headstones may be seen today. Her grandson, William Mason, named for her husband, inherited all of her considerable property in Maryland. He was twenty-three at this time and a member of the Fairfax militia under Henry ("Light-Horse Harry") Lee, who commanded the southern armies. William must have served well enough to be commissioned an officer. His uncle, Martin Cockburn, referred to him by the title of captain in his day-book: "January 21, 1779, paid Captain William Mason for 21 pounds of corn." It appears from his father's letter to General Lee dated 13 December 1780 that William was offered a post on Lee's staff. George Mason rejected the offer: "I have ever intended him for civil and private life; his lot must be that of a farmer and country gentleman, and at this time there is a particular domestic circumstance which will require his return as soon as his present term of service expires." William returned to Gunston Hall sometime before 3 June 1781, for on that date both he and his father wrote letters to George, who was still in France. We have no means of knowing whether William was pleased with the decision his father made for him, but he seems to have accepted it.

Virginia was tense in the spring of 1781. British frigates were advancing up the Potomac as far as Alexandria, looting and destroying property along the way. George Mason described these hardships in the letter he wrote to his son George on 3 June. "This family has not lost any Tobo, slaves or other Property by the Enemy," but added that they expected to share the same fate as their neighbors. He also wrote of the damage to their furniture caused by having to move it back and forth from Virginia to Maryland two or three times "upon different

Alarms" and noted that "yr Brother Thomson, & yr Sisters" are now in Maryland.

The letter Mason wrote on ⌐ ⌐ ⌐e 1781 was received by George Mason V on 30 August at Paris. The father commented upon how many letters had miscarried and then embarked upon a great deal of family news. He asked the whereabouts of William Lee, with whom he was in litigation, and then continued: "I am sorry to hear you made so slow Progress in the French Language; it is oweing to your conversing too much among your own Countrymen, & to your not accustoming yourself to write french; I hope however, you will not be discouraged; but will still endeavor to make yourself Master of it." Mason also found him negligent in some business transactions that probably caused the son some losses, "tho' very deservedly: if ever you send any more Goods, pray be more methodical and exact." Further admonishment continued:

I presume this will find you in Paris or as I rather hope in the South of France. I can not but think you judged extreamly ill, in spending as much time in Nantes; where you cou'd expect no great Improvement, either in Health, Knowledge, or Manners. I think it will also be very imprudent in you to return to America, without trying the Effect of one Summer either in South of France, Italy or Spain; as the best physicians in Paris may advise you. The Recovery of Health should be considered as your primary Object; for without that, you will have incurred much Expense & Loss of Time, to little Purpose.

In a second letter written on the same date the father closed on an idealistic tone: "God bless you, my dear Child! and grant that we may again meet in your native Country, as Freemen; otherwise, that we may never see each other more is the Prayer of Your Affectionate Father." [87]

Young Mason stayed at the Hotel de L'Empereur rue de Grenelle while in Paris. Early in September he wrote William Temple Franklin to ask if William's grandfather had received "a letter of Gm's which Capt. Robeson left with him some days since." Mason felt that if his son made proper use of his credentials and his acquaintances, particularly Dr. Franklin, he could secure his passage home on one of the French ships of war. He followed this note with another of 12 September 1781 asking for a passport permitting him to embark for Italy. The Count de Vergennes had just become secretary of foreign affairs, and France was in the financial crisis that in a few years precipitated the French Revolution. The instability of the French government may have prompted Vergennes to close the frontiers, an act that necessitated George's asking for a passport "to go into the South of this Kingdom as far as Marseilles—I am told I shall meet with difficulty in quitting the Kingdom from one of those remote parts unless I have a passport from the Count de Vergennes." [88]

Nothing more is known of his travels for a year until he wrote his father 31 July 1782 from the French spa Saint Amand, where he had gone for the mud baths following his visit to Amsterdam. He was back in Nantes in September but was again in Paris by 25 October 1782, as the mercantile firm in Nantes of Wallace, Johnson, and Muir forwarded him some letters from his father. On this visit to Paris George was concerned about his health and asked William Temple Franklin his opinion of a doctor who had recently become famous because of "some very extraordinary Cures he has performed at the Hospital of Invalids." George had already been to see "M. Bonsart, Docteur en Medicine, Medecin-Consultant de leurs Altesses, les princes de Liege et de Stavelot," who thought George's "Disorder curable in the course of four or five months." But George did not wish to put himself in the doctor's "clutches" until he knew more about him.[89] George may have undergone the cure, because he was still in Paris where his father's letter of 8 January 1783 had been forwarded to him. It contained a great deal of news and a suggestion that George might have been frittering away his time:

As to the Money you have spent in Europe, provided you can satisfy me that it has not been spent in Extravagance, Dissipation or idle Parade, I don't regard it. It is true I have a large family to provide for; & that I am determined, from Motives of Morality & Duty, to do Justice to them all . . . and all my views are center'd in the Happiness & well-fare of my children; you will therefore find from me every Indulgence which you have a right to expect from an affectionate parent.

I have been for some time in Retirement, & shall not probably return again to public Life; yet my Anxiety for my Country, in these Times of Danger, makes me sometimes dabble a little in Politicks, & keep up a Correspondence with some Men upon the public Stage; you know I am not apt to form Opinions lightly, & without due Examination; and I can venture to say that the french Court & Nation may confide in the Honour & good faith of America; we reflect with gratitude on important Aid France has given us; but she must not and I hope will not attempt to lead us into a War of Ambition, or Conquest, or trail us round the mysterious Circle of European Politicks. . . .

George wrote his father from Paris on 20 February 1783 and concluded by saying, "I wish America wou'd put her Trust only in God, and herself and have as little to do with the Politicks of Europe as possible." [90] This comment is of interest as it was made soon after preliminary articles of peace were signed between Great Britain and France and hostilities had ceased. Upon the result of these negotiations the American commissioners opened formal peace meetings with the British representative, Richard Oswald. As George Mason V was on speaking terms with Franklin, Jay, and Adams, it must have been an exciting time for him to be in Paris. It was during the same visit that George saw his father's friend Philip Mazzei, who was in Europe to obtain loans for the state of Virginia.[91]

In April 1783 George was making preparations for his return trip to Virginia. On the twelfth he wrote a note to William Temple Franklin: "You said yesterday that you would do me the Honor to call on me on Monday [with] your Grandfather's dispatches. I will thank you for a Line by the petite poste informing me about what Hour you call that I may be at Home for I have a thousand little Affairs that call me out." He also had one more favor to ask: "If your Grandfather will do me the Honor to give me a letter of Introduction to Mr. Morris he will oblige me exceedingly for I shall be as much a Stranger in Phila. as an European." Robert Morris was a partner in the counting house of Charles Willing of Philadelphia, who had been sent to Martinique in 1776 as an American purchasing agent, but he also did business on his own account for American and European customers. It has been said that the success of the American Revolution owed as much to the financial operations of Robert Morris as to the negotiations of Benjamin Franklin. As Morris was president of the Bank of North America, Mason may have wanted to consider a banking career upon his return home.

From another note Mason wrote to young Franklin later in April it is learned that the dispatches were delivered:

I found your packet last night on my coming Home. Today Mr. Jay & Mr. Ridley * sent theirs nearly as large. I am afraid from the number and [size] of the packets that I shall meet with some Difficulty at the Barrier of Britany where they are often very strict. In case they should offer to open them shall I suffer it or shall I desire them to Detain them. I have very little Baggage of my own—only a few old clothes—can carry your packet with the greatest convenience and only fearful they may meet with some difficulty in entering Britany. I will thank your Grandfather for a passport perhaps his mentioning in it that I have packets for America may remove any difficulties at the Barrier.

By 30 April 1783 George had arrived in Nantes from Paris and was awaiting passage to America on the *Hannibal,* having missed by just

* Matthew Ridley was a Maryland merchant representing Maryland abroad. He later became Jay's brother-in-law (Richard B. Morris, *The Peacemakers* [New York, 1965] p. 317).

two days the sailing of the *Prince de Liege,* on which he had intended to make the voyage. He was still in Nantes on 20 June, and he apparently did not arrive in Philadelphia until late August or early September, as George Fox * wrote to William Temple Franklin from Philadelphia on 1 October 1783, "Mason and Hoops arrived here before me but they had not the most agreeable, altho a very safe passage." [92] Apparently George had remained in Philadelphia.

His father wrote to Dr. Arthur Lee in 1783, glancing in retrospect at the Revolution and its achievements:

I once thought that we ought to risque a long War, in order to bring the remaining British Colonies into our Union; but Time & Reflection have altered by Opinion. I have seen that Lust of Power, so natural to the Mind of Man, prevailing in Congress, at a much earlier Period than cou'd well have been expected. I have seen some of the States, from partial, local, temporary Views, conniving at, and fostering Principles, which wou'd inevitably end in their own Destruction. I have seen our Legislatures trampling under Foot the Obligations of Morality & Justice; and wantonly invading the sacred Rights of their fellow-Citizens. It may not be amiss to have some rival power at their door, some powerful Motives to restrain them within the Bounds of Moderation. It will at least be a comfortable Reflection, that if our Governments shou'd grow intollerable (which, judging of the future from the Past, is neither impossible, nor improbable) a Man wou'd have some place of Refuge, the Means of sheltering himself from Anarchy, Ignorance, & Knavery." [93]

Meanwhile in Virginia the year 1783 had brought acclaim to Thomson Mason, whose ability as a lawyer had brought him many cases and who was considered by many to be one of the outstanding lawyers of Virginia. He and his brother had well-earned reputations for their abilities in public service and in private life. While each of them suffered long bouts of illness, which must have been extremely painful and enervating, they continued, nevertheless, to serve the public weal.

Thomson died at his home, Raspberry Plain, 26 February 1785, leaving a large family for whose well-being and future upbringing he expressed concern in his will. He wanted his two younger sons to grow up in the tradition of the Mason family in the Potomac area, and in his will directed "that neither of my younger sons, Westwood Thomson Mason, nor William Temple Thomson Mason, shall reside on the south side of the James River or below Williamsburg before they respectively attain the age of twenty-one years, lest they should imbibe more exalted notions of their own importance than I could wish any

---

* George Fox was a great friend of William Temple Franklin, who bequeathed to Fox the greater part of his manuscripts and letters ("Biographical Sketch of Joseph Fox," *Pennsylvania Magazine of History and Biography* 13 [1908]:196–97).

child of mine to possess.[94] This was no doubt a reaction to the inordinate pride of Elizabeth Westwood in her Howard ancestry and her unwillingness to consider Loudoun County other than the rough frontier.[95]

He further directed that he be interred on the plantation of his son, Stevens, "so that the foot of my Coffin may touch the head of my Son George's" and that Stevens should remove the remains "of his Mother from the family burying Ground at my brother's" in order to be reinterred alongside him. He set aside land and ordered his executors to set up a town, resurveying at the request of his son Stevens Thomson Mason four acres as a situation for a public house. His books were divided between his first and third sons. His second and third sons were named his executors with his second wife.[96]

Neither George nor Thomson left a bequest to the other or appointed the other as an executor of his will. George, however, released Thomson from money owed him. In his will dated 20 March 1773 George appointed his ailing eldest son his executor and left his five sons an equal fifth of his estate, his books included, and advised them that "from my own experience in life, to prefer the happiness of Independence and a private station to the troubles and vexation of publick business, but if either their own inclinations or the necessity of the times should engage them in public affairs, I charge them on a father's blessing never to let the motives of private interest or ambition induce them to betray, nor the terror of poverty and disgrace, or the fear of danger or of death, deter them from asserting the liberty of their country and endeavoring to transmit to their posterity those sacred rights to which themselves were born."[97]

Following their deaths, the families of each brother became involved in law suits over their legacies. The wife of Thomson relinquished all rights in her husband's estate, but she and Abraham Barnes Thomson Mason made "sundry claims and demands against each other which required court action to settle all matters in controversy between them in an amicable manner."[98] The heirs of George Mason were involved in court battles over the western lands that had been left to them in their father's will. The suits were endless and went on for years. As late as 27 March 1824 George Graham gave a deposition at the Land Office in Washington that he could vouch for the persons involved as he had known them since childhood.[99] After the final court action few of the immense tracts that George Mason IV had labored so hard to put together for his descendants were left to them.

Chapter IX

George Mason IV: The Sage of Gunston Hall

WITH THE SIGNING OF THE TREATY OF PARIS and the threat of invasion past, the normal flow of paying visits and entertaining guests became general once more along the Potomac. In September 1783 George Mason and his son William paid their respects to Gen. Nathanael Greene, who was ill in Alexandria. The general referred to William as "an amiable youth" who "carried off Major Hyrne on a visit to Mr. Mason's where one of the young ladies made a great impression on his heart." The heavy rains of December 1783 caused much flooding, but in spite of this James Madison was able to visit Colonel Mason and wrote to Thomas Jefferson of his evening's conversation. George Mason spent Christmas at Mount Vernon. Among the other guests was a Miss Lewis of Fredericksburg, who wrote that George Mason was "slight in figure, but not tall, and has a grand head and clear gray eyes." [1]

At the close of the American Revolution the Masons were among the largest planters on the Potomac and, within their own county, stood second only to George Washington. In a 1785 property listing Gunston Hall plantation had one dwelling house and thirty other buildings, while George Mason of Lexington had no dwelling house on his property but six other buildings. [2] Their estates seem to have been more productive than most of the others in their area. No doubt this was due to George Mason's interest in the advanced farming ideas of his time.

Potomac planters were gleaning the meager harvest sown by a century of poor farming methods and neglect. James Mercer wrote in September 1783 that without six month's notice £600 could not be furnished from any estate in Virginia. The cornfields on his plantation were scattered and irregular, tobacco fields a prey to the cankerworm. Mercer was better off than many of his neighbors, but his Marlborough lands would produce only 400 bushels of corn, 12 hogsheads of tobacco, and 250 bushels of wheat, and the wheat would be almost totally lost to the weevil. There was not a single building in repair on either property, except for the overseer's house and one Negro cabin at Marlborough. The stock was uniformly wretched, the cornhouse unfit for use, and the windmill in dire repair. Yet James Mercer considered the Marlborough plantation as fairly fixed as any in Virginia.[3]

According to the 1782 tax list George Mason of Gunston Hall listed more black tithables than any other person in Fairfax County except George Washington. Mason had 128 while George Mason V was taxed for 24 blacks.[4] The war had seriously depleted the labor force of the tobacco plantations. Many slaves had availed themselves of the opportunity to run away when Dunmore's raiders landed at their master's wharf or Tarleton's cavalry galloped to a halt in the farm-yard. But there are enough complaints about the excessive numbers of idle hands in some Northern Neck counties to suggest that this is only part of the story.[5]

The Mason estates had suffered little from the depredations of the British, and in January 1783 they had a large stock of tobacco on hand, according to a letter Mason wrote to his son George:

I have at this time two year's Rents (you know mine are all Tobo.-Rents) in Arrear, & two Crops uninspected, so that if a Peace happens, it will find me pretty full handed in the Article of Tobo. which will then be very valuable. Your Brother Thomson has lately sold Wheat from your plantations to the amt. of abt. £230 Specie, & there will be a good deal of Indian Corn to spare from this year; which (the Crops being generally short) will sell for a pretty good Price. He means (unless you direct him otherwise) to invest the Money in Tobo. for you; which, in the Event of Peace, will be very profitable. You have two or three years crops of Tobo. uninspected; your Brother & myself thinking it safer in your own Tobacco-Houses than in the public Ware houses until an Opportunity should offer of disposing of it to advantage. Your Stocks of Horses, Cattle &c have encreased, and your estate is in good Order; except that you have had some Losses in your Slaves.[6]

But the most sweeping change in American commerce after the American Revolution was the drastic decline of tobacco exports to Britain.[7] Methods of agricultural production throughout the Chesapeake region contributed to the decline of tobacco, and the shift to new markets for the tobacco export disrupted the flow of Chesapeake commerce. The amount of American tobacco exported to Great Britain in the prewar decade had varied considerably from year to year but it averaged out to 99,899,144 pounds per year. In 1783 only 19,579,581 pounds were exported to Great Britain. In 1784, the first year of peace, the export figures rose to 43,492,302 pounds, but they never reached the prewar level or even approximated it. An average of the years 1771 through 1773 indicated that the American colonies absorbed £3,064,843 worth of British goods and exported goods valued at £1,322, 532; by contrast the United States exported goods to Great Britain in 1784 valued at only £701,189 and imported goods from Great Britain valued at £3,359,864. Since tobacco constituted from a third to a half of the total value of American exports, the great imbalance in favor of Great Britain was due in large part to the failure of the tobacco grower to maintain his markets while buying roughly the same amount of British goods he had previously been accustomed to purchase.[8] The results of this changeover were not immediately apparent, and those planters who had weathered the war and had stocks of tobacco on hand looked forward to its sale at the end of the war for a good price.

With the balance so clearly running in favor of British merchants, their factor and agents on the Potomac quickly resumed their former important place in the commercial life of Virginia and Maryland. Several British firms reorganized as soon as the definitive treaty of peace was signed and prepared to recapture their former markets. Others dispatched special agents to collect debts and wind up their American affairs as quickly as possible or called on influential friends in Virginia or Maryland to help them settle their accounts. John Pagan of Glasgow, who at one time had been a merchant in Alexandria, asked Mason to aid him. Mason had some correspondence with Alexander Hamilton of Piscataway, Maryland, regarding a parcel of linens sold by Hamilton on Pagan's account. He had dealings with some of Pagan's other American debtors and assisted Pagan's son in settling their Virginia accounts.[9]

George Mason faced the issue of British claims on American citizens in a frank letter to Patrick Henry in 1783: "Had it been in the power of the American Commissioners (which it certainly was not) to have abolished the British Debts here, it would have been but short sighted Policy to have done so." He argued that foreign merchants would not venture their effects in America if on the occasion of every national quarrel they were liable to confiscation. Further, he said that he "could have wished indeed that some reasonable time had been allowed for the Payment of British Debts, and that the Interest on them had been relinquished. As to the first, the Desire of the British Merchants to reinstate themselves in their Trade here, will probably prevent their pressing their Debtors." [10]

During the war both Maryland and Virginia permitted debtors to pay into the state treasury or the continental loan office any debt owed to British subjects, thereby discharging it. The implication of this policy was that prewar debts had been sequestered by the states along with other forms of alien property. The advantage was that debtors could use rapidly depreciating paper currency to settle sterling accounts, and some five hundred Virginians availed themselves of the opportunity. The firm of Barnes and Ridgate settled their debt of £437 12s. 2d. to Colin Dunlop and Son of Glasgow in 1781 by paying this sum in continental currency into the Maryland Treasury.[11] When the definitive treaty of peace was signed in 1783, the problem of British debts once more became acute. The wartime legislation was disallowed by the treaty, which stipulated that there should be no legal impediment to the collection of debts owed to British subjects. With the legality of the wartime payments called into question, the problem arose of repaying those individuals who had paid British debts by depositing an identical sum in the state treasury. Should they receive the same amount in continental notes, which had now depreciated far below their value in 1778–80, or should their repayment be adjusted to the real value of the notes at the time? Many Virginians opposed making any concession to the British debtor, even in the face of the specific treaty provision, and sought to lay snares in the way of the British debt collector by special legislation; others feared too great a concession to the individuals who had paid their sterling debts with nearly worthless paper. George Mason took the latter view: "The People here too are greatly alarm'd, at a prevailing Notion, that those Men who have paid British Debts into the Treasury, in depreciated Paper-Money, instead of making up the real Value to their Creditors, will now attempt to throw the Difference upon the Shoulders of the public, and levy it by Taxes upon the people." [12]

He put the case forcefully in the Address and Instructions from the Fairfax County voters to their representatives in the House of Delegates, Alexander Henderson and Charles Broadwater, who probably needed little instruction from their constituents on this particular point. The Fairfax freeholders directed Henderson and Broadwater to "oppose to the utmost of your power, the smallest infraction of the late Treaty of Peace, either with respect to the payment of debts, or in any other matter whatsoever, whereby the public faith, solemnly pledged by the American Commissioners duly authorized, may be violated, and this country again involved in the calamities of war, or the danger of reprisals." They were also instructed to obtain a law "for repayment of the principal and interest to each and every individual, who hath paid paper money into the public treasury in discharge of debts due to British creditors, according to its real value as specie, to be adjusted by the legal scale of depreciation, at the time each sum was respectively placed in the Treasury." [13]

Thomson Mason issued a similar address to the freeholders of Stafford County, who had elected him to the Assembly, explaining that he believed that the moneys paid into the treasury for payment of British debts on loans should be accounted for at the real depreciation at the time it was paid in. He expressed his firm conviction that the treaty should be observed and the debts paid, but he "wished also to suspend all executions on judgements obtained for debts contracted before the war, so as to issue for one fourth or fifth part of the debt annually, till the whole was discharged, in order to place the debtor as near as we could in the same flourishing situation that he was when the debt was contracted." The instructions from the Fairfax voters specifically excluded any such scheme: "We desire and instruct you that you give not your assent to, and that you oppose, any further occlusion of the Courts of Justice, as likely to loosen the bonds of society and create needless confusion." In a letter of 3 May 1783 to Madison, Jefferson wrote of Thomson Mason as "a meteor whose path cannot be calculated." [14]

Debt collection was not an easy task for British firms. Most of their debtors owed small sums, almost too trifling to collect, but amounting to a considerable sum in the aggregate. In many cases their largest debtors were not planters but other merchants. The problem of debt collection did not deter British firms from sending large shipments of manufactured goods to the Chesapeake. In January 1784 Alexander Hamilton reported that British goods "are in greater estimation and preferred to any other European manufactors." He noted that tobacco had sold on the Potomac in 1783 from 30 to 35 shillings the hundred-weight, "yet the peoples expectations are very sanguine that it will be higher when the great quantity of shipping arrives that is expected from Europe, and that business will be carried on in the same manner it was during the former connection with Britain and goods as cheap as they have been sold." [15]

Many planters whose hopes hinged on even higher tobacco prices were soon disappointed. The European market could not sustain such price levels in America. "The prospects of Tobacco as a remittance are gloomy," Alexander Henderson wrote from Colchester in 1784 advising his Glasgow correspondents to consider changing to the importing of wheat from Alexandria.[16]

The domestic troubles that the planters faced were further aggravated by the lower prices paid for American tobacco on the world market. Two causes combined to drive down tobacco prices after 1785. Great Britain imposed an additional tax of one shilling threepence a pound on tobacco imported for the home market; this tax had a natural tendency to reduce tobacco consumption when it was passed on to the consumer in the form of higher prices. The French Farmers General negotiated a contract with Robert Morris to give him a monopoly on supplying the French market with Chesapeake tobacco. This contract forced tobacco prices from 40 to 22 shillings and cost Maryland and Virginia £400,000 in a year.[17]

In attempting to sell his wartime tobacco at the highest possible price, Mason found himself dragged down in the financial ruin that inevitably overtook careless speculators like Thomas Rutland. The story was a familiar one on the Chesapeake in the 1780s, and many another planter and merchant were caught in the same trap when prices began to decline in 1784.[18]

Mason had kept his tobacco off the market in 1784, waiting for sufficiently higher prices, as had many other large planters. In August 1784 Mason received a letter from Thomas Rutland, an Annapolis merchant associated with the firm of Yates and Petty of London. Rutland had learned from Richard Sprigg that Mason had a large quantity of tobacco on hand, and he informed him that he would be interested in buying it for cash or good bills of exchange in London, if they could agree on price. Mason's reply is not extant, but sometime in August 1784 both Mason and his son George of Lexington sold their entire stock of tobacco to Thomas Rutland at the same price per hundredweight. Rutland had promised to send a ship with manufactured goods to Dumfries but reported it had been delayed. He was also unable to give George Mason of Lexington the cash payment previously agreed upon. Rutland also made large tobacco purchases from Robert Fergusson of Henderson, Fergusson, and Gibson and found the same difficulty in paying him. Rutland confided to Fergusson that he had bought far more tobacco than he actually needed to make remittances to his London correspondents.[19]

By May 1786 Thomas Rutland could only beg George Mason for a further extension of time to meet his obligation, offering his real estate as security and complaining of his London associate John Petty. Mason himself was hard pressed for money at this time. A letter to William Carr in 1786 indicated that he was obliged to a forced sale of his snuff in order to pay his Maryland taxes. In May 1786 Mason obtained a judgment against Rutland.[20]

In August 1786 Rutland promised a deed of mortgage on all of his real property to George Mason of Gunston Hall, regretting that this would make it impossible for him to do justice to his other creditors. Rutland himself had had an attachment for £1,400 served on Stephen West of West and Hobson and hoped to be able to pay Mason in full as soon as West paid him. The mortgage was not actually delivered until May 1787. By this time West's real estate was under attachment. Rutland lost the most valuable part of his Annapolis property and his dwelling plantation in Anne Arundel County to the state of Maryland in payment for the arrears of import duties.[21]

Thomas Rutland's letters indicate a woeful lack of business ability in a period of commercial depression that would demand more than ordinary skill to keep a firm from bankruptcy. By 1788 Rutland was insolvent. Mason wrote to John Francis Mercer in May 1788, inquiring whether Rutland's new store, warehouse, and wharf were among the portions of his effects advertised for sale to settle another creditor's demands. He feared that Rutland had permitted the lands already mortgaged to Mason to be attached by the Maryland authorities and hoped that Mercer could secure some of Rutland's other property in Frederick County to settle the judgment against him.[22] A letter written by Rutland in July 1788 expressed some annoyance at Mason's impatience to obtain his money. "When Colo. Mason considers what an amazing price I gave for his Tobo., how old a great deal of it was, & how much damaged, he should not be surprised at the outcome of his venture." Rutland finally offered a tract of 430 acres on the James River, two miles below Petersburg, in settlement, but through some error Mason did not learn of the existence of this property until after Rutland's death. In May 1792 Mason had still not received any part of the money Rutland owed him.[23]

Since Mason was hard pressed for money during the last years of the eighteenth century, the vexing business with Rutland caused him considerable distress. When the case dragged on beyond reason, Mason urged John Francis Mercer to foreclose on Rutland's mortgage as the arrears of rent on his Annapolis property would otherwise increase Mason's loss. Mason suspected that Rutland had a hoard of certificates that he might give up in settlement if pressed hard enough. At the same time Mason was making every effort to settle his accounts with Stephen West, "altho upon the Score of old Acquaintance and good will, I should be very loth to serve an Execution on him." Mason had informed West that he would accept only cash in payment of his claim. He was simultaneously trying to obtain payment of another outstanding obligation due to the estate of Sarah Eilbeck from William Molleson of London. Molleson's agent in Maryland was Robert Young of Nottingham, Prince George County, who had taken charge of his affairs from his former agent, Thomas Contee.[24]

The 1780s were a period of agricultural depression and commercial stagnation in many parts of Virginia. This was reflected in the drift of trade away from old commercial centers. The decay of Dumfries can be traced in the petitions forwarded to the Virginia Assembly by Prince William County Court. In 1779 William Grayson petitioned for authorization to convert twelve town lots in Dumfries into farmland, and a number of citizens of Prince William County asked for the removal of the courthouse from Dumfries. The passage of the Five Ports Bill in 1786 sealed the fate of the already declining town. This law limited trade to a single port on each of the major rivers, making Alexandria, Tappahannock, York, Bermuda Hundred, and Norfolk the only ports of entry for the entire state. Petitions against it immediately appeared from Dumfries, Colchester, and other towns that had not met with the official favor.[25]

Mason raised his own complaint against the Five Ports Bill in some queries to the Virginia Assembly:

Will not the Port Bill be particularly hurtful to the revenue and trade of Virginia in Potowmack river, by inducing many vessels, which would otherwise enter & load in both States, to enter & load only in the state of Maryland? And will not the inhabitants of the counties of Prince William, Stafford, King George, Westmoreland & Northumberland, have just cause to complain of the unnecessary charge of freight to Alexandria, on their Indian corn and other bulky produce of their lands; & instead of the convenience they have always heretofore enjoyed, of supplying their families with West India goods, salt, and other heavy articles, at their own doors; be compelled to buy them in future, burthened with the charge of freight to and from Alexandria, or running the risk of smuggling them from Maryland? [26]

The high tariff levied by the Virginia Assembly in 1782, and raised again in 1787, brought protests from Virginians, especially from Alexandria. A printed petition against the 1782 levy bore the signatures of nearly every businessman prominent in the commercial life of Alexandria. George Mason suggested that an unwise policy of taxation had created the situation that the Virginia Assembly attempted to remedy with the Five Ports Act.[27]

The observant French traveler Jacques Brissot de Warville recorded his impressions concerning the effects of the Virginia taxation program on the growth of towns in Maryland and, in particular, Georgetown, when he stopped there on his way to visit Mount Vernon in 1788. He observed, "Regulations and Taxes foolishly imposed on commerce by the state of Virginia have brought to Georgetown a large part of the trade which would have normally gone to Alexandria, eight miles farther down the Potomac." He found that "superb wharfs and vast warehouses" had been constructed at Alexandria after the war, in the belief that the city would become the commercial center of the Potomac, but trade was stagnant there, and although some trade was carried on in 1788 to the West Indies and New Orleans from the port of Alexandria, many residents were moving away from the town.[28]

In an endeavor to repair their fortunes, Virginians turned to a greater extent to the manufacture of tobacco products in the 1780s. George Mason wrote to Col. William Cabell in 1783 to ask his assistance in obtaining a protective duty on foreign snuff imported into Virginia: "One of my Sons & one William Allison have lately erected a Snuff Manufactory in this County, and have already made a large Quantity of Snuff; which they intend to send soon into different parts of the Country." [29]

Tobacco factories began to spring up in Virginia at this time, but their early history is conjectural. The export figures for the United States after 1790, when the export of tobacco was declining, indicate a steady growth in the amount of manufactured tobacco sent to foreign parts. The manufactured tobacco rose from 15,350 pounds in 1790 to 173,343 pounds in 1793, a phenomenal growth in four years.[30]

The establishment of commercial houses at home and abroad appeared to Virginians to be another means of bolstering their declining fortunes. With this in mind George Mason determined that his fourth son, John, should go into business; his early training as an apprentice to a wheat trader in Alexandria and the connections John had established at that time could now be developed to his advantage.

George Washington had returned to Mount Vernon and the two friends resumed their friendship. In Washington's Diary of 1785 there are many entries relating to George Mason. In March he grafted two varieties of Mason's cherries, and he spent a night at Gunston Hall. On the twentieth he sent his carriage to Gunston Hall to take Colonel Mason to a meeting of commissioners at Alexandria to settle regulations for the commerce of the Potomac River. The outcome of these meetings was known as the Mount Vernon Compact.[31] George Mason remained in Alexandria to preside at a court held for the county of Fairfax. George Washington dined in Alexandria on the twenty-third and returned to Mount Vernon. The next day he sent his carriage for Colonel Mason "according to appointment, who came in about dusk." On the twenty-sixth George Mason V and Dr. Brown dined at Mount Vernon and returned. On the twenty-ninth Washington noted that several gentlemen left before breakfast and "Colo. Mason (in my carriage) after it; by return of which he sent me some young shoots of Persian Jessamine and Guilder Rose." In April, Mason sent his neighbor some watermelon seeds. On 7 May Washington recorded that most of his transplanted trees had a sickly look but that the Guilder Roses were just in bloom on the thirteenth. Although no more visits were recorded until 25 November, when Washington dined at Gunston Hall, many letters were exchanged between them. One letter dated 3 October expressed Washington's concern for Mason's indisposition.[32]

On the fourteenth George Mason was visited by George Augustine Washington and Burwell Basset to obtain a marriage license for the former, whose wedding was to take place the next day at Mount Vernon.[33] It was a small wedding of intimate friends, but one of the guests who provoked interest was Jean Antoine Houdon the French sculptor who was staying at Mount Vernon preparing the model of the statue of Washington ordered by the state of Virginia. Early in November George Mason sent his friend a side of venison. On 8 December Washington "sent to Colo. Mason's Quarter and got young Crab Trees for the Shrubberies"; and on the twelfth the fox hunt "killed up in an open field of Colo. Mason's, every rider and every Dog present at the Death." [34] The names of the hunt members were not recorded.

George Mason was at all times deeply concerned with the establishment of good government for his country. Not the least of his concern was the jurisdiction and navigation of the Potomac River. He worked hard on this problem, and it must have been a great disappointment that his ill health prevented him from going to Richmond on 13 December 1785 to present the Mount Vernon Compact to the speaker of the House of Delegates. He must forcibly have been reminded that it had been his ill health that earlier had prevented him from presenting the nonimportation resolutions. The compact was signed, but as he indicated in a letter to his cousin William Fitzhugh on 26 February 1786, he felt that most of the session had accomplished little or nothing.[35]

At a session of the House of Delegates held on 21 January 1786, George Mason was appointed one of the commissioners to a national conference on trade and the regulation of commerce, which was to be held in Annapolis in September. His main personal concern at this time was his lack of ready cash. On 3 March he sent his son William to Dumfries to collect money from William Carr for the sale of snuff so he could pay his Maryland taxes. He was disappointed at the manner in which Ridout, a Bordeaux merchant, had filled his order for china. When notified that the shipment had arrived in Alexandria, he sent his own boat for it, only to find the china not to be what he and his wife had expected. Ridout's firm failed and Mason spent considerable time trying to settle his accounts with him.[36]

April of 1786 opened with a hard frost and enough snow to cause drifting, but by the seventeenth the weather was normal when elections for delegates to the Assembly were held in Alexandria. George Mason had declared he would not serve and remained at home. But even though he was not a candidate, still he was elected—an indication of the respect with which he was held by the voters. In August he suffered a severe attack of convulsive cholic, and on a plea of illness he was excused from attending the October session. On 3 September Monroe wrote to Madison from New York, "I consider the Convention of Annapolis as a most important era in our affairs. Prevail, I beg of you, on Colonel Mason to attend the convention." There was no way he could fulfill either obligation because the attack was a particularly virulent and long-lasting one, and he was still lame when he wrote John Fitzgerald in Alexandria on 28 November 1786.[37]

On 6 December 1786 Edmund Randolph wrote him of "the tottering condition of the United States" and urged him to accept his appointment as a delegate to "a Convention proposed to be held in the city of Philadelphia in May next for the purpose of revising the federal constitution," his health permitting.[38]

Christmas of 1786 must have been spent very quietly for no comments can be found about it other than the mention of George Mason of Pohick having called at Gunston Hall.

The year 1787 opened uneventfully. Charles Little, who was the tax assessor for Mason's district, came to Gunston Hall on 2 April, at which time the tithables were noted as "9 blacks over 16; 13 under; 11 horses; 34 black cattle; and 4-wheels [meaning a coach or chariot]. Since the first census taken in 1782, the number of cattle and horses that Mason owned varied considerably from year to year, but no tax list indicates he paid a tax on a horse at stud. Some years no "wheels" were recorded, which must have been the reason that he together with George William Fairfax, George Washington, and others were once summoned before the grand jury and indicted for "not reporting their wheeled vehicles, according to law." On 12 April he wrote to Edmund Randolph that he was so short of money, due to the nonpayment of tobacco he had sold and the payment of taxes, that had the treasury not been able to advance him the money to attend the forthcoming convention in Philadelphia, he would have been unable to go.[39]

His health must have improved as there are no comments upon it. On 16 April 1787 he was able to attend the election of delegates held in Alexandria to represent the county of Fairfax at the next General Assembly. He was accompanied by his two sons George and William and his son-in-law John Travers Cooke. George Washington, too, went to Alexandria to vote, and they all returned with him to Mount Vernon for the night. Once again Mason was returned to office by his fellow citizens, who knew that if he were unable to represent them personally in the Assembly, his influence would be felt in Richmond and his advice sought by his colleagues.[40]

Although Washington and Mason were both attending the convention, they did not travel to Philadelphia together. Washington left

Mount Vernon on 9 May. George Mason and his son John left Gunston Hall about that time to make the trip by way of Baltimore, where he wrote several letters. During his absence Sarah (Brent) Mason stayed in Dumfries with her sister, Mrs. Richard Graham. Although the opening day set for the convention was 14 May, the Masons did not arrive in Philadelphia until the evening of the seventeenth. Delegates from other states arrived even later, as George Mason found only the states of Virginia and Pennsylvania fully represented when he arrived. Mason and his son were fortunate in having a room to themselves at the old Indian Queen on Fourth Street.[41]

On 15 May 1787 Richard Henry Lee wrote George Mason a very agreeable letter regarding Mason's and Washington's attendance at the convention, setting forth some of his views on questions to come before the convention. He hoped that from their efforts "alterations beneficial will take place in our Federal Constitution." The long letter closes with a warmth that clearly shows the friendship that existed among these able men. Richard Henry Lee also suffered from gout and had declined to serve as a delegate, giving his poor health and his service in the Continental Congress as his reasons.[42]

In his first letter from Philadelphia to his son George on 20 May, Mason makes some interesting observations about the Roman Catholic service he had attended that morning with the other Virginia deputies, "more out of Compliment than Religion, and more out of Curiosity than Compliment." He was struck with the "Solemnity of the Aparatus, & cou'd not help remarking how much everything was calculated to warm The Imagination & captivate the Senses. The Church Musick was exceeding fine." Although he "had been in a [Roman] Catholic Chappel before," presumably with his wife Sarah, he was struck by its differences from the Anglican celebration, which normally consisted of three services: Morning Prayer, the Litany, and Holy Communion, including a sermon of one-and-a-half hours, all of which would take three hours. The congregation was silent, except for the amens after prayers, as only a few parishes could afford prayer books. Even the Lord's Prayer was repeated phrase by phrase after the clerk. He also would not have been used to music as part of the service since hymns were not permitted in the Anglican worship until the end of the eighteenth century, except for chants, which were sung only by the choir. He was "disgusted with the frequent Tinckling of a little Bell which put [him] in Mind of the drawing up of the Curtain of a Puppet-Shew." [43]

As early as 27 May, Mason was "heartily tired of the etiquette and nonsense so fashionable" in Philadelphia. But having made the decision to serve as a member of the Virginia delegation at this important time in the formation of the new country, he was determined to take an active role in the political discussions and to aid in reaching logical conclusions, if that could be accomplished. There is no need to comment on his role in the Constitutional Convention. That has been documented thoroughly by eminent historians. Since few personal letters have been found from this most interesting period in his life, we lack his own observations except for his comments in a letter to Thomas Jefferson of 26 May 1788 that the newspapers had printed his "Objections" very incorrectly and "without my Approbation or Privity." These objections, he told Jefferson, "were Written Upon the most mature Consideraton I was capable of, and from Motives of sincere Patriotism, I was under the Necessity of refusing my Signature, as one of the Virginia Delegates; and drew up some general Objections.[44] A copy of them was enclosed in the letter.

On 17 September, the day of the final leave-taking of the delegates, Mason wrote Beverly Randolph that Robert Morris had advanced him some money. He left Philadelphia in a coach accompanied by Dr. James McHenry "in an exceeding ill humor indeed," which was not helped by the overturning of the coach near Baltimore, injuring both men. The account he submitted of his expenses, incurred on Federal Business, "including time of going and returning from 13 May to 27 September," indicates the day of his return to Gunston Hall.[45]

George Mason was opposed to ratifying the new Constitution because it lacked a bill of rights. Whether this objection encouraged the local politicians, who were protesting certain laws and acts, to engage in personal attacks on him in newspapers can only be surmised. It was a time of suspicion and rumor George Mason was unable to accept lightly. During the 1787–88 session of the Virginia Assembly, he succeeded, however, in getting legislation passed in spite of the friction over the tax levies by the local justices. Opposition to Mason increased with the result that he was not selected by Fairfax County as a delegate to the Virginia Convention to ratify the Constitution. He was, however, so highly regarded in general that Stafford County petitioned him to become a delegate. Although "warmly opposed by Colo. Carter and Mr. Fitzhugh," he won the election.[46]

This expression of confidence should have raised his spirits, but his personal affairs were still of grave concern; his crops were short; and his attending the Assembly in Richmond from October through December had made it impossible for him to remain at Gunston Hall long enough to resolve the problems there, nor had he had time to settle some old business of the Ohio Company. He was, moreover,

trying to recover a long overdue debt. He had engaged the services
of his cousin John Francis Mercer to act as his attorney in this affair
and to help him complete the settlement of Mrs. Eilbeck's estate, of
which Mason was executor.[47]

He returned to Richmond on 2 June 1788, the day the Virginia Convention opened, to consider the ratification of the proposed Federal
Constitution. This was one of the few times that his political persua-
sions took priority over his family problems, and his attendance in the
face of these family obligations stresses his firm opposition to ratification. Nothing but his steadfast conviction that his presence was essential at Richmond would have taken him from home when he was
faced with so many personal problems and the departure of his son
John for a long stay in Europe. He wrote him on 12 June from Richmond, closing with a postscript: "Let me hear from you often, & in a
most particular Manner; especially as soon as possible after your arrival
at Bordeaux. Not having time to give you the Convention-News, I
must refer you to your Brother George." [48] This suggests that George
Mason V may have accompanied his father to Richmond. To the dis-
may of George Mason and Patrick Henry, Virginia finally voted to
ratify the Constitution. "Two of the leaders," Madison wrote to Washington on 25 June 1788, "betray the effect of the disappointment so
far as it is marked in their countenances."

The crushing blows Mason had undergone politically, the aspersions
against his honesty—one newspaper had intimated that he had used
his political influence to increase his landholdings—and his continuing
financial difficulties, all doubtless contributed to the severe fit of gout
that struck him in July, when he wrote to Jefferson in Paris of his
weakened condition. From now until his death, the attacks came more
frequently and lasted longer. He withdrew more and more into his
close family circle, but those engaged in the new government continued to keep him informed.

The permanent seat of government was the most discussed issue, as
it had been since 1783, when it had divided Congress. It fomented
major sectional differences. Because large sums of money were involved, every member of Congress wanted the capital in his area.
Thomas Jefferson estimated that the choice of a Potomac site would
enrich the area by a half million dollars yearly.[49]

Later the battle became one between the North and the South, and
it eventually became involved with the controversy regarding the question of the assumption of debts. The meetings, countermeetings, and
bargainings finally ended with a dinner arranged by Jefferson in New
York on Sunday afternoon 20 June 1790.[50] Alexander Hamilton, in

consultation with James Madison, agreed to exert his influence to secure enough northern votes to assure the location of the federal city
along the Potomac in return for Madison's pledge to obtain a sufficient
number of southern votes to effect passage of the assumption of debts
bill. Jefferson had written Mason on 13 June predicting a compromise,
whereby assumption and residence would be resolved. The bill was
passed 10 July, fixing the site of the projected national capital in a
district ten square miles along the Potomac, the precise area to be
selected by a three-man commission. Washington had always hoped
for a Potomac site; so he must have been pleased to sign the bill into
law on 16 July 1790.[51]

Instead of putting the matter in the hands of the commissioners,
Washington decided to make the decision himself. Recent studies show
that he was anxious to have Mason's opinion regarding the best location.[52] Jefferson called on Mason at Gunston Hall to discuss it and then
wrote Washington the following from Fredericksburg 17 September
1790:

In the course of the visit we made the day we left Mount Vernon, we drew
our host into conversation on the subject of the federal seat. He came into
it with a shyness not usual in him. Whether this proceeded from his delicacy
as having property adjoining Georgetown, or from what other motive I cannot say. He quitted the subject almost as soon as he could. He said enough
however to shew his decided preference of George-town. He mentioned
shortly, in it's favor, these circumstances. 1. It's being at the junction of the
upper and lower navigation where the commodities must be transferred
into other vessels; (and here he was confident that no vessel could be contrived which could pass the upper shoals and live in the wide waters below
his island.) 2. The depth of the water, which would admit any vessels that
could come to Alexandria. 3. The narrowness of the river and consequent
safeness of the harbour. 4. It's being clear of ice as early at least as the canal
and river above would be clear. 5. It's neighborhood to the Eastern branch,
whether any vessels might conveniently withdraw which should be detained
through the winter. 6. It's defensibility, as derived from the high and commanding hills around it. 7. It's actual possession of the commerce, and the
start it already has.

He spoke of Georgetown always in comparison with Alexandria. When
led to mention the Eastern branch he spoke of it as an admirable position,
superior in all respects to Alexandria.

I have committed to writing a Memorandum for Mr. Carroll of the kind
of conveyance, I suggested to him, and which I had not the opportunity then
to put on paper. I inclose it open for your perusal, and take the liberty of
asking you to put a wafer onto it, when you are done with it, and forward
it to Mr. Carroll.[53]

Early in 1791 Washington appointed the three federal district com-missioners: Thomas Johnson and Daniel Carroll of Maryland and David Stuart of Virginia. The last two were friends of George Mason; Stuart was a political colleague. The most southerly portion of the specified area, going three miles south of the Eastern Branch (the Anacostia River), was selected "so that when the line was taken across the Potomac into Virginia, Alexandria would be included in the district." On 16 April 1791 Mason wrote to his son John, who was still in Europe, in detail about the permanent seat of government and its boundaries, which included "all my tract of Land there of about 2000 Acres." He went on to say, "The Alexandrians, as usual, are very much buoyed up, on the Occasion, and Think their Fortunes made for ever; altho' it is evident to any cool impartial sensible Man that if the Inland Navigation of Potomack & Shanandoe is effectually compleated, & the Seat of The Federal Government fixed near the Harbour of The Eastern Branch, Alexandria must become a deserted Village." [54]

As disappointment, old age, and ill health exacted their toll, George Mason probably became more difficult to get along with. In 1789 his coachman wanted to leave him and applied to Washington for a posi-tion. Perhaps it was something of a coincidence, but it was at this time that aspersions were being cast on Washington's character, and rumor had it that George Mason had promoted the stories. The letters of Tobias Lear, the president's secretary, to John Langdon, 31 January 1789, and Lund Washington, March 1789, to George Washington re-flect this attitude. The change of regard is most evident in the letter of Lund Washington, who had long been an admirer of Mason. Later in the year, when President Washington was very ill in New York, George Mason's letter to him on behalf of the appointment of Joseph Fenwick as consul in Bordeaux was acknowledged in a most imper-sonal, businesslike way by Lear.[55] Although the estrangement between these two friends never healed, Washington sought Mason's opinions and continued to be influenced by him. Otherwise, there is no good explanation for the appointment of Fenwick as consul and Washing-ton's desire to know how Mason felt about the location he had chosen for the federal city.

George Mason depended more and more on his overseers to manage his farms. Following John's return from Europe in August 1791, he turned over to him all of his business transactions. September of 1792 was a very sickly season, and all the members of the family at Gunston Hall were ill or just recovering from "the fever of the Season." Mason was annoyed "with an exceeding Troublesome Cough," from which he probably never recovered. It kept him in the weakened state in which Jefferson found him on the thirtieth.[56]

The following week, on 7 October 1792, the sage of Gunston Hall died. No letters or diaries have been found to give us an account of his last illness, and the issues of the *Virginia Gazette* for that date are missing. His obituary was carried in the *Maryland Journal* and the *Baltimore Advertiser* on 2 November 1792, at which time the date of his death was given incorrectly as the fourteenth instead of the seventh.[57] His death went virtually unnoticed, perhaps because his national politics had been so strongly anti-Federalist.

Chapter X

George Mason IV: Siblings and Progeny

G EORGE MASON IV had endeavored to leave all of his children
well endowed, with enough land to provide them with security
and position. He was a patriot who expended much of his life in the
service of his country, but even a cursory reading of his papers and
letters shows how great was his concern for the future of his children—
their physical well-being, their social advancement, and their financial
stability. So careful was he not to endanger the structure of their lives
that he made it a principle not to involve himself in speculative ventures. He wrote to his cousin John Francis Mercer on 26 August 1791,
explaining why he was unable to purchase Marlborough plantation:
"I have made it a Rule thro' Life, never on any Consideration whatever, to embarrass, or subject myself to Difficulties; and the Payment
of my Daughter's Fortunes, the building for, & setling two of my Sons,
and raising Capitals in Trade for two others' has required, & will require, all the Money I am able to command, and puts any large Purchase, at present, out of my Power." [1]

Of the twelve children born to George and Ann (Eilbeck) Mason,
nine reached maturity. Mason's will, written in 1773 just after the
death of his wife Ann, is a long document. The copy in Will Book F
of Fairfax County covers twenty-four pages. His concern that all of
his children should be well provided for is mirrored in this document.
The harmony that prevailed among his heirs at his death and the
concern of the brothers for their sisters' interests indicate that George
Mason had achieved his goal of building a strong family unit whose
care and concern were first for the members of it.

During his lifetime, as his children reached maturity or married,
he gave each of them substantial gifts of land. He devoted a great deal
of time to the advancement of his sons. Mason was keenly aware of the
advantages to be gained through the favors of acquaintances and was
never hesitant in seeking help for his sons in the careers he had chosen
for them.

He provided a generous bequest of money and personal property for
each of his daughters. Each had inherited money and a slave from their

grandfather, William Eilbeck; and at the death of their grandmother, Sarah (Edgar) Eilbeck, each inherited slaves, jewelry, and £100 "over and above the money by me heretofore lodged in their Father's Hands for the use of the three youngest." His eldest daughter, Ann, or Nancy, as she was called, acted as his hostess after the death of her mother. George Mason speaks of her accomplishments in this respect in a letter of 2 October 1778. This letter also contained the news of the first of his children's marriages, that of his second daughter, Sarah, to Daniel McCarty, Jr., the son of his neighbor, who lived at nearby Cedar Grove, which was situated on a point of land jutting into Pohick Bay. The young son-in-law, a lieutenant in the Revolutionary War, had taken part in the battles of Brandywine Creek and Germantown. There were six children of this union. Daniel McCarty III married Ann Matilda Margaret Snoden Magruder before he came of age. Ann was the daughter of Dennis and Anne (Contee) Magruder of Charles County, Maryland, where the young couple settled, and lived an apparently uneventful life.[2]

William Mason McCarty was born at his family's plantation, Cedar Grove, about 1789. He was tutored at home until he attended the College of William and Mary in 1813 and 1814. He studied law and was admitted to the Virginia bar. His first wife was Emily Rutger Mason, the daughter of Stevens Thomson Mason, whom he married 24 October 1816 at her father's plantation, Raspberry Plain. He practiced law in Virginia until he moved to Florida in 1824 and became active in the administration of the newly acquired territory. On 3 March 1827 President John Quincy Adams appointed him secretary for the territory and acting governor in the absence of Governor Duval. He returned to Virginia in 1830 and settled in Loudoun County to resume his law practice. He was elected to the Twenty-sixth Congress in 1839 when his cousin, Charles Fenton Mercer, resigned.[3] He inherited Cedar Grove, where his niece, Emily Virginia Mason, visited him in March 1846, presumably after the death of his wife. She wrote to Catherine Mason Rowland:

Uncle McCarty met us with the greatest affection and seemed delighted to see us—sending instantly for the boys [James Ball McCarty and William Thornton McCarty], who have each a large plantation of his own, house servants & all & each lives by himself! . . . They teach a Sunday School for the poor children in the neighborhood at old Pohick Church, where has been no minister since the time of Washington & George Mason . . . & have no neighbors but Mrs. Mason of Gunston & Mt. Vernon (five miles off both).

. . . Now to return to Cedar Grove. I must tell you that it is in a great state of dilapidation (the house) & but little left to remind us of Aunt Emily. The old pictures of our Grandparents, the old Raspberry Plain silver, her piano, guitar &c. were all in the house.[4]

His second wife, whom he married in Richmond, was Mary B. Burwell, the daughter of Lewis and Judith (Kennan) Burwell of that city. William Mason McCarty sold Cedar Grove in 1852 when he moved to Richmond. He died 20 December 1863 and was buried in Shockhoe Hill Cemetery.[5] Only one son married, and no living descendants have been located.

John Mason McCarty is remembered for the duel he fought with his cousin Armistead Thomson Mason, whom he killed 5 February 1819, at Bladensburg, Maryland. Both were spirited young men who were unable to reconcile their political differences following the congressional campaign of 1816, during which party differences ran high. McCarty was a member of the House of Delegates in 1818–19, and Mason was a United States Senator from Virginia, serving from 8 January 1816 to 3 March 1817. The year after the duel McCarty married Lucinda Lee, the daughter of Thomas Ludwell and Fanny (Carter) Lee, and they removed to Charles County, Maryland. Tragedy followed these two families. Each man had only one son, each of whom died an early death. Stevens Thomson Mason, the son of Armistead Thomson Mason, was killed in the Mexican War, and John McCarty's son died in a hunting accident. These branches of the Mason family became extinct because of these tragedies.[6]

On 19 May 1873, fifty-four years after the Mason-McCarty duel, another McCarty duel took place between William Page McCarty a nephew of John Mason McCarty, and John D. Mordecai, who were rivals for the hand of a charming young lady. Both were injured, but Mordecai died. The emotional effects of this tragedy caused William Page McCarty to become something of a recluse, and he never married. For some years he was editor of the *Richmond Times*. He was the last known McCarty to have inherited the magnificent Irish silver that had been handed down through seven generations of McCartys.[7]

The only daughter of Sarah and Daniel McCarty was Ann Eilbeck Mason McCarty, who married her cousin John William Bronaugh, son of William and Margaret (Strother) Bronaugh. Little is known of the descendants of Ann and John Bronaugh.[8]

Three marriages took place at Gunston Hall in 1784: Mary Thomson Mason to John Travers Cooke, Thomson Mason to Sarah McCarty Chichester, and George Mason V to Elizabeth Mary Ann Barnes Hooe.

Mary Thomson Mason's wedding to John Travers Cooke of West Farms, Stafford County, took place on 18 November. He was the son of Travers and Mary (Doniphan) Cooke, whose second husband was William Bronaugh, a first cousin of George Mason. Four of the eleven children of Mary Thomson and John Travers Cooke married. Sarah Mason Cooke, born 14 September 1791, married a family connection. Her first husband was Wilson Cary Selden of Salvington, the son of Samuel Selden and his second wife, Sarah Ann Mason Mercer. Her mother, who was Catherine (Mason) Mercer, was the aunt of George Mason IV.[9] Sarah (Cooke) Selden's second marriage took place on 15 March 1825. Her second husband was Robert Osborn Grayson, the son of Benjamin and Ann (Bronaugh) Grayson. This, too, was an intra-family marriage, as the parents of Ann (Bronaugh) Grayson were William and Mary (Doniphan) Bronaugh. This is the line from which the distinguished admiral Cary Travers Grayson, physician to President Woodrow Wilson, is descended. Million Cooke married John Williams Green of Culpeper County, Virginia, who served with distinction on the Virginia Supreme Court of Appeals.[10] There are many descendants of this marriage. Nancy Cooke married Sydney Wishart, but no information about this family has been forthcoming.

John Travers Cooke bought Marlborough, the Mercer family plantation and took an insurance policy on the house in 1806. In it, as tenant, he set up his half brother, John William Bronaugh, who had married his wife's niece, Ann Eilbeck McCarty.[11]

Thomson Mason's marriage to Sarah McCarty Chichester of Newington, Fairfax County, took place in 1784. In his boyhood he was tutored with his brother John and his cousin John Thomson Mason by the Reverend Robert Buchan, rector of Aquia and Potomac churches, who lived on Passapatanzy Creek on the plantation that Dr. Edward Maddox bequeathed to the parish as a glebe.[12]

Thomson served in 1781 in the militia and conducted himself "with proper Coolness & Intrepidity." His period of service must have been short; in January 1783 he was managing his brother George's estates, because his father wrote to George in France that Thomson was doing well with his plantations. Thomson was endeavoring, with his father's help, to establish himself; in the same year he engaged in the manufacture of snuff with William Allison. He was probably engaged in this business at the time of his marriage, although it seems to have been a venture of short duration. He and his wife lived at Gunston Hall, where their first children, Thomson Francis and Ann Eilbeck, were born in 1785 and 1787, respectively. They were building their own house by 1787 on the estate given Thomson by his father. He named it Hollin Hall, after one of the estates of his Thomson ancestors in Ripon, Yorkshire, England. He and Sarah moved into their new but unfinished house in 1788 in time to celebrate Christmas. In 1789 their daughter, Elizabeth, was born there. The house must have remained incomplete for several years, as in May 1792 George Mason was interested in ordering "Cypress Scantlin, for the Collumns, Rails Ballusters &c of the piazzas and steps to your brother Thomson's house"; and in August of the same year he was concerned with ordering chimneypieces for them. Sarah bore nine children, all of whom grew to maturity, married, and had families, except one son.[13]

Thomson Mason was collector for the Port of Alexandria, and he was the only son of George Mason to serve as a justice of Fairfax County. He carried the honorary title of "General." Elijah Fletcher, founder of Sweetbriar College, who had lived for a while with the Masons, referred to him in his letters by this title. One of the last duties he is known to have performed was that of administrator in 1815 of the estate of Sarah Barnes (Hooe) Mason, widow of his brother, Thomas.[14]

Thomson Mason died at Hollin Hall on 11 March 1820, it is said, of a fit while shaving. His will was not admitted to probate until the following November. Hollin Hall passed out of the Mason family in 1852, when it was occupied by Edward and Eliza (Troth) Gibbs, who in turn sold it to Theron Thomson. Some of the original outbuildings, among them Little Hollin Hall, still stand, but the hall itself burned in 1824.[15]

On his return from France, George Mason V married Elizabeth Mary Ann Barnes Hooe on 22 April 1784. She was the daughter of Gerard and Sarah (Barnes) Hooe of Barnesfield, King George County, Virginia. The Reverend William Stuart, rector of Saint Paul's Parish, King George County, officiated at the ceremony. The young couple set up housekeeping at Lexington, the plantation on Doegs' Neck that George had been given by his father when he came of age in 1774. It was named Lexington in 1775 to commemorate the battle in Massachusetts that rallied the colonies to the standard of liberty and independence. Their first child was born there on 9 March 1785.[16] They were on visiting terms with their illustrious neighbor George Washington, for on 20 March 1785 he wrote in his diary, "Mr. G. Mason Jnr. and Dr. Brown came, dined and returned"; on 29 November Washington recorded that he "went out after breakfast with my hounds from France and two which were lent me yesterday by young Mr. Mason."

During the summer of 1787 George and Elizabeth (Betsey) were renovating or enlarging Lexington and considering the use of wall-paper as a cheap way of finishing a room. They were informed by George's father, who wrote them from Philadelphia on 1 June, that they were "mistaken in thinking Paper will be as cheap as plaistering; because nothing will be saved by the Paper, but the third coat of plaister; however as you prefer it, I will endeavor to procure it.[17] Another entry in Washington's diary mentions George Mason, Jr., as attending Pohick Church on 28 October 1787 and then going on to Mount Vernon, where he spent the night.

On 1 April 1791 Betsey's fourth child was born at Gunston Hall. A smallpox epidemic was feared, and inoculations were given at both Gunston Hall and Lexington at the end of May. The chronic ill health that continued to plague George Mason, Jr., made him decide to try the cure again at Augusta Springs. On 10 July he and his brother William set out for the springs. That winter George kept well, better than his father had expected, for the weather was very severe in January of 1792.[18]

George Mason V and Martin Cockburn were executors of the will of George Mason IV, which was admitted to probate at Fairfax County Court on 5 December 1792. George Mason V inherited the "Mansion house and Seat at Gunston" and the "lands thereto belonging . . . being between five and six thousand Acres." He also received his father's gold watch, a large "Silver Salver, which being an old piece of family plate, I desire may remain unaltered; also a large silver Bowl given him by my Mother, in which all my children have been christened, and which I desire may remain in the family unaltered for that purpose," and a fifth of his father's books.

It is not clear what happened to Gunston Hall after Mason's death. The tax lists of 1792 through 1796, when George Mason V died, are not helpful in determining who occupied the mansion or maintained the estate. It appears that during the minority of George Mason VI the estate was under the supervision of a hired manager. An account book of Martin Cockburn records dealings with James G. Smith, "Manager of George Mason's dec'd Estate" as late as 1807. But Sarah (Brent) Mason did not claim the 500 acres of her choice on Mason's Neck, as was stipulated in the marriage agreement; instead she and George Mason V arrived at a financial settlement. This must have been much more satisfactory to Sarah as she seems never to have enjoyed living at Gunston Hall when her husband was away. She and her sister Jean (Brent) Graham were very close, and there is every reason to believe that Sarah returned to Dumfries whenever she could. Also she was not in good health, as in a letter to his son John 10 September 1792 not long before his death, Mason refers to her as being "still unable to walk a step, tho, I think she begins to gather strength in her leg and foot." As Mason died the following month, on 7 October, it seems likely that she would return to her sister's for the nursing care she would require after her illness. This assumption is strengthened by the date of her will made at Dumfries 29 October 1794 and witnessed by her brother-in-law Richard Graham.[19] The watch she left to her sister Jean Graham was probably the one sent her by George Mason V in 1783 while he was in France. The only Mason stepchild mentioned in her will was Mary Thomson (Mason) Cooke, to whom she left "a mourning ring I had from her father."

George Mason V drew up his will on 7 April 1795.[20] He stated that he was to be buried "without pomp or parade in a plain unornamented coffin in the family burying ground at Gunston" and that neither his family nor friends were to wear mourning "unless it be a scrap or some such trifling badge." He bequeathed to his son George VI "my gold watch which was given me by my Father also a large Silver Bowl and a large Silver Salver both of them old pieces of Family Plate. I also confirm unto him the gift of a Silver beaker given him by his grand Father Collo. George Mason." The will also stipulated where the money was to be found to pay Sarah (Brent) Mason the £35 he had agreed to pay her annually for the rest of her life. The first codicil directed "that the House at Gunston be kept in Decent repair & the Garden enclosed & the Expense paid of the Money arrising from the profits of my Estate." (This was undoubtedly written because his son, the sixth George Mason, who inherited Gunston Hall and its dependencies, was a minor aged ten, and his father wanted to be certain that the Gunston Hall estate would be properly maintained until his son came of age and could assume its responsibilities.) The second codicil was concerned with the lots that he owned in the new Federal City of Washington. These lots were located on what is now the southeast corner of Nineteenth and I streets, four and one-half blocks from the White House and one block off Pennsylvania Avenue, now site of the Columbia Medical Building. The city had 4,500 lots, the price of which varied according to the advantage of the situation, from forty-five cents per foot down to eighteen or even fifteen cents per foot. At this same time lands in Fairfax County sold from ten dollars to twenty dollars per acre.[21] George left the five lots to his daughters, Betsey, Nancy, and Sally, to be improved or not at the direction of his executors, one of whom was his brother John, who was a merchant in Georgetown. The inventory of his estate filed 16 December 1799 not only included the very elegant furnishings of Lexington but the simpler household equipment of the Pohick and Hallowing Point quarters, occupied by his overseers. His widow, Betsey, continued to reside at Lexington, where her posthumous son was born 16 January 1797.[22] There are many descendants of this couple, for their children had large families of their own.

On 16 July 1803 Elizabeth Mary Ann Barnes (Hooe) Mason made a second marriage. She married George Graham, who had come to live at Gunston Hall at the time of the marriage of his aunt, Sarah (Brent) Mason, where he was raised with the Mason children, whom he knew intimately. George Graham was an adviser to James Monroe and held various political assignments, one of which was commissioner of the General Land Office. It was while serving in this capacity that he signed the deposition in regard to the Mason family land suits in Kentucky.[23]

Elizabeth Mason, the last daughter of George Mason IV, married William Thornton, son of Francis and Sarah (Fitzhugh) Thornton of Society Hill, King George County, Virginia, at Gunston Hall in 1789. No adequate study has been made of the Thornton family. In the absence of fuller records, it would appear that the progenitor of the family was William Thornton, of the Hills, Yorkshire, England. His son, Francis, had a son, Francis of Fall Hill, Spottsylvania, from whom was descended the William Thornton who married Elizabeth Mason. Their two sons died without issue.

Ann Mason, who so capably managed Gunston Hall for her father, even after his marriage to Sarah Brent, had inherited from her grandmother Eilbeck the tea chest with silver canisters that was first mentioned in the will of William Eilbeck as a "shagreen tea chest with silver cannisters."[24] On 6 February 1789, at Gunston Hall, Ann married Rinaldo Johnson. The bride and groom were both thirty-four years old. He was the son of Thomas and Anne (Riston) Johnson of Pleasant Grove, or Pleasant Green, Middlesex Hundred, near Baltimore. Rinaldo is said to have been romantically named for the hero of Tasso's *Jerusalem Delivered,* an epic poem dealing with the capture of Jerusalem during the First Crusade. It seems more likely that he was named for Rinaldo Monk, the stepfather of Anne (Riston) Monk. Charles Willson Peale was commissioned by Rinaldo Johnson in 1788 to do portraits of his parents, and a miniature of himself was begun at the same time.[25] He and Ann lived at Aquasco, Prince Georges County, Maryland, although Rinaldo died in Baltimore and was buried in Springfield, Baltimore County, Maryland. The *Pennsylvania Gazette* carried a notice of his death on 18 November 1811. Nancy's death occurred in 1814.[26]

There were many descendants of this couple. Their son, Thomas Rinaldo Johnson, married a cousin, Sarah Ann Mason, daughter of Abram Barnes Mason, and had five children, all of whom married. Their daughter, Ann Eilbeck Mason Johnson, made her home at Analostan with her uncle John Mason from the time of her mother's death in 1814 till her marriage on 20 May 1817 to Cecilius Coudon Jamison. Thirty years later he married Catherine, daughter of John Mason, as his second wife.[27] There are descendants from both of these marriages.

William Mason did not marry until he was thirty-four years old. On his father's death, he had inherited all of his lands in Charles County, Maryland, and a silver watch. These were adjacent to the lands he had inherited from his grandmother Eilbeck. His marriage to Ann Stuart took place on 11 July 1793. She was the daughter of the Reverend William and Sarah (Foote) Stuart, the heiress of Richard Foote of Cedar Grove Plantation, King George County. William Stuart had studied theology in London, where he was ordained, and upon his return to Virginia acted as assistant to his father, the Reverend David Stuart, whom he succeeded as rector of Saint Paul's Parish, King George County.[28] William Stuart was very popular with his parishioners and officiated at many rituals of the Mason family.

Through this alliance with the Stuarts, William became connected with other important Virginia families, and it would seem that his respectability was established beyond any doubt. Nevertheless, a legend still persists that he married a girl of Spanish origin while he was with the militia in South Carolina and that his father refused to acknowledge the marriage. Be that as it may, letters have been received by the keeper of the records at Gunston Hall asking for verification of a William Mason, son of William, son of George Mason IV. William and Ann (Stuart) Mason had four children who married. The sons were George and Edgar Eilbeck, whose sons died without issue. But in the family Bible is the following notation: "William Stuart Mason d. March 7, 1854." For some reason his birth is not recorded, but with the name Stuart, it is almost impossible for him to be a son of an earlier marriage. It is known that he attended William and Mary College and that he left before graduation to serve as a volunteer at the age of seventeen in the War of 1812. He appeared before the Charles County, Maryland, Court on 8 December 1818 to present his father's will for probate,[29] and in the *Alexandria Gazette* of 17 November 1840 he is mentioned in an advertisement for the sale of the Mason fisheries, which lists "cotton seines and ropes, two boats, twenty oars, twelve capstans, eighty stands, and other articles appertaining to the Mason fisheries." A fragment of his headstone can be seen in the family grave-yard at Gunston Hall. This background makes it most unlikely that another son, William, could have been born of a previous marriage by his father. Both daughters of William and Ann (Stuart) Mason married and have living descendants.

William and Ann (Stuart) Mason's heirs became involved in the dissolution of the Mason family's Virginia properties. His second son, George Mason, purchased Lexington, the estate of his uncle, and he in turn left the property to his son, George Mason of Springbank, who died without issue in Portland, Oregon, on 19 April 1888, of typhoid fever. It is he who left the "Declaration of Rights" Table to the Virginia Historical Society, which they have lent to the Board of Regents of Gunston Hall who have placed it in Col. George Mason's "little parlour" for all to enjoy. It is most probable that only the notes or redrafts of the Declaration of Rights were actually written on this table, as many people took part in its compilation and final form.

Thomas, George Mason IV's youngest child, had been tutored by the Reverend Robert Buchan until 1788, when he and George Graham attended the Fredericksburg Academy. George Mason's cousin James Mercer was an enthusiastic supporter of the school and in May 1786 had been made a trustee. Following his appointment he wrote to James Madison a glowing description of the academy. "This place is the most fit, being most healthy, the cheapest for maintenance, and the Inhabitants being of the middle Rank, a class the best fitted for a voyage through Life. Williamsburg is already too gay, Prince Edward too rustic. I see Richmond is only solicitous for instructing the heels and fingers. Where then are we to look for that change you and all good men wish for? If not at Fredericksburg!" Later Thomas was sent to Alexandria to a Mr. Hodgson to be trained as a merchant, "upon the same terms you [John] were with Mr. Hartshorne. He boards at Patrick Murray's, and seems pleased with his situation, both as to Mr. Hodgson and the family he boards in." Following this training, his father established him in business in Richmond, Virginia.[30]

George Mason IV spent a good part of the last year of his life worrying about Thomas. He received a letter from Thomas on 22 May 1792, but in July he complained to John that Thomas owed him a letter. George Mason continued to express his displeasure:

He wrote me a Letter, some time ago, expressing his great Desire of being established in some Business upon his own Account; at the same time expressing much Disgust at the Business & Profession of a Merchant; which after the time he has spent in the pursuit, and which too was his own choice; shewed a Fickleness of Disposition, & want of Steadiness, that may prove highly injurious to him. He can't be more desirous of being established in Business, than I am of establishing him, as soon as it is in my Power. The Money (if not the whole, the greater part of it) which I intended for his capital, has been remitted to your House in Bordeaux; that it might be ready for him, as soon as he was ready for it; indeed I wished him to spend a Year or two in your Counting House at Bordeaux, in order to acquire some Knowledge & Experience in Shipping, & foreign Business.

Thomas seems to have felt that the parental hand was being laid upon him with greater firmness than he desired, and Mason's disillusionment is evident because he went on:

To tell you the Truth, I am almost out of Conceit of sending another Son to Europe; for Fear of giving him a Distaste of his own Country. This is generally the Case with such Americans as have spent much time in Europe; it is, in some measure, the case with yourself; I see it with great Concern (and it is the only thing I have to regret in you) for in my Opinion, there can hardly be a greater Misfortune, than a Man's having a Distaste to the Country, in which all his connections are, and in which he is to spend his Life.

Your Knowledge & Experience in mercantile Affairs enables you to judge better than I can, what will be the most advantageous Prospects; where there will probably be the most favourable opening, and what will be the best, within my Power, to be done for your Brother Tom. I wou'd have you, with him, consider the Subject; and assure him, nothing on my Part, consistent with my circumstances, & Justice to his Brothers & Sisters, shall be wanting; for in my time of Life, my only satisfaction and Pleasure is in my Children; and all my Views are centered in their Welfare and Happiness.[31]

The girl Thomas chose to marry in 1793 was Sarah Barnes Hooe, sister of the wife of his oldest brother, George. It was probably because of this relationship that the wedding took place at Lexington plantation.

Thomas inherited from his father "all my land upon the lower side of Occoquan River, together with the right and benefit of keeping the ferry over Occoquan from both sides of the river, which has been vested in me and my ancestors from the first settlement of this part of the country and long before the land there was taken up or patented."[32] Thomas named the estate Woodbridge after the toll bridge he built in 1795 to replace the ferry. He secured the services of a man who was soon to be recognized as the foremost civil engineer of the day. Theodore Burr designed a bridge on the plan known as the Burr truss, consisting of semielliptical wooden arches carried by a wooden truss. The first toll was six cents, which was raised to 8 cents on 31 December 1804 upon the request of the administrators of the estate of Thomas

Mason, who had died 18 September 1800 while serving as a member from Prince William County to the Virginia House of Delegates.[33]

From the following, written in 1800 by her sister Elizabeth to Martin Cockburn, it appears that Sarah's fourth child, and second son, was born unexpectedly while she was visiting at Lexington. It was addressed to Cockburn at nearby Springfield, which adjoined the Lexington plantation.

My dear Sir,

My sister earnestly desires (if you have no objection) that you will ride over and christen her little boy. She says she is well acquainted with your piety, virtue, and knowledge of religion, and that if you will do it for her, she shall be as well satisfied as if it had been done by an Ordained Minister. She is anxious for Sister McCarty to be surety for her little Tom. Mrs. McC. is also desirous of returning to Cedar Grove as quick as possible on account of sending for Daniel, therefore if you will come we wish you to come to dinner. My valuable friend and neighbor I hope will come with you, if she is not fearful of rain.

Saturday noon.   Yours in haste, E. Mason [34]

Sarah's first child to marry was Leannah, who married William Barron of Kentucky on 11 May 1817. Thomas Mason, Jr., her youngest brother, married Martha F. Berry and lived at Goose Bay, Charles County, Maryland. Their two sons died unmarried. Her older brother, Gerard Alexander Mason, married Ann Mary (Wisenbaker) Triebner on 4 February 1818 at Jerusalem Lutheran Church, Effingham County, Georgia. She was a descendant of the Saltzburgers, a group of people as dedicated to the rights of man as were the forebears of her husband. Hers, however, had immigrated to Georgia from the Palatinate. Of this marriage there was only one son, Richard Alexander Thadeus Mason. His mother died when he was ten, and it is not known whether Richard returned to Virginia with his father or remained with his mother's family in Georgia. Gerard was in Virginia in the 1830s, and on 1 August 1832 George Mason of Springbank gave to Gerard and William Mason McCarty, for the sum of $1 each, a lien on his fisheries as security for a debt of $400 he owed to Gerard. Gerard seems to have been a difficult person: 19 December 1849 he was killed by a slave he had mistreated. Richard moved at some unknown date to Scotia, South Carolina, where he married and where his descendants continue to live.[35]

Although George Mason IV was perhaps closest to his son John, he did not let his affection alter his determination to treat all his children with equal consideration and justice; each one absorbed his attention as his or her needs required it. It is from John Mason's "Recollections" that we have some of the most vivid pictures of life at Gunston Hall and of the Mason family. He was the eighth living child of George and Ann (Eilbeck) Mason and was born on 4 April 1766 at the home of his maternal grandparents, the Eilbecks, in Charles County, Maryland.[36] Although he was only six and a half years old when his mother died, he retained a lasting impression of her final days throughout his own life. He received his early schooling from the tutors at Gunston Hall; later he studied under the Reverend John Buchan of Passapatanzy before he was apprenticed to a prominent Quaker merchant of Alexandria, William Hartshorne, a member of the firm of Harper and Hartshorne, who were active in the wheat trade before the war. Hartshorne was the first treasurer of the Potowmack Company in 1785 and became one of the first directors of the Bank of Alexandria, whose chartering in 1792 was due in great part to his efforts.[37] These early associations no doubt led to John Mason's later participation in the canal-building efforts of the Potowmack Company and in the development of the Bank of Columbia at Georgetown.

John accompanied his father to Philadelphia for the convention. While there Mason made a point of introducing him to some of the important men of the times who might help further his career as a merchant. It appears that he met Elbridge Gerry, because on 20 October 1787 George Mason wrote to Gerry that John would be making a trip to Boston on one of Hartshorne's vessels and asked him to introduce "him to some of Your Friends of Reputation in the commercial line, as an act of the greatest Friendship." He expected that John would eventually "settle in trade probably in Georgetown, or the Situation opposite to it, on the Virginia Side; where the Land belongs to me, for about three miles upon the River, in such Manner as to command all the deep Water on that Shore." [38] It would be useful to the young man in his future career to know men in Massachusetts.

As Mason's duties as a delegate to the convention occupied most of his time, young John made the best of the opportunities offered in Philadelphia, even though the Masons were somewhat strained for money at this time. Their room at the Indian Queen cost them twenty shillings a day Pennsylvania currency, which included a room for their servant and stabling for their horses. They also had the luxury of a room to themselves in the overcrowded city. Provided their expenses could be kept within the per diem allowed each delegate, John could enjoy himself as he chose, using the horses and coach to call on the young ladies and other friends in the city and to take them out driving.[39]

John returned to Alexandria before the convention was over to resume his training under Hartshorne and so was not in the coach accident with his father. He remained with Hartshorne until the spring of 1788 when he entered the mercantile trade as a partner with James and Joseph Fenwick of Maryland, who were planning to open a firm in Bordeaux. It is possible the Fenwick brothers were influenced in their choice of Bordeaux by Robert Fenwick, who was already established there. He was married on 27 May 1762 to Marie Duret, the daughter of Louis-Abraham Duret. The Durets were one of the leading Protestant French families in the Bordeaux trade active in West Indian commerce. When Joseph Fenwick came to be married, it was Robert who was one of the witnesses to sign his marriage contract with Catherine Eleonore Menoire; they were married on 9 November 1792 in the church of Saint Dominique, Bordeaux.[40]

Mason continued his efforts on the behalf of John's business ventures and wrote many letters to friends and associates during the winter of 1787 and the spring of 1788. One of these letters was to Robert Carter of Nomini Hall, which John delivered personally on 8 May. Another similar letter John delivered to Richard Henry Lee at Chantilly, wth the pleasing result of Lee's consigning to John some tobacco to sell in France.

John Mason's partners were men little older than himself. They were sons of Col. Ignatius Fenwick, member for Saint Marys County in the first Maryland Convention. Their kinsman, Capt. Ignatius Fenwick, was an officer in the Maryland navy during the war and was active in overseas comerce. He provided the young Fenwick brothers with an inspiration and some of the capital needed to establish a commercial house in France. He had had business associations with Joshua Johnson in the wartime tobacco trade and had discussed the establishment of an American firm at Bordeaux with Johnson as early as 1782. After his marriage to the widow of Charles Carroll of Carrollsburg, Captain Fenwick devoted much of his time to managing the estates of his stepsons but did not neglect his commercial interest. Capt. James Fenwick, when he married Catherine Ford in 1778, was already a shipmaster commanding vessels in the transatlantic trade. He played an important part in the postwar development of the port of Georgetown. Joseph Fenwick was apprenticed to a Georgetown merchant in April 1784 and launched on his business career in 1785.[41]

When Joseph Fenwick arrived in France early in the summer of 1787, he established an independent American tobacco firm. The price of Virginia and Maryland tobacco was low because of the manipulations of the Farmers General, who held a monopoly on the sale of tobacco in France. After unsuccessful attempts to obtain control of the American export trade, the Farmers General signed a contract with Robert Morris of Philadelphia on 10 April 1785. By its terms Morris was to supply 20,000 hogsheads of tobacco a year and the farmers agreed to buy American tobacco only through Morris. The contract covered the years 1785–87. As a direct result of this monopoly, the price of tobacco fell from forty to twenty-two shillings the hundred-weight.[42]

On his way to Bordeaux, Joseph Fenwick consulted with the American minister in Paris, Thomas Jefferson, regarding the future prospects of the tobacco trade in France. Jefferson believed that after the contract with Morris expired at the end of 1787, "the Farmers will be precluded from purchasing American Tobo. at the English or any foreign Markets and that there will be no stipulation in the prices nor any new contracts made." He expressed no doubt that after January 1788 the French market for Chesapeake tobacco would be as good as any in Europe. Joseph Fenwick's journey to Bordeaux represented a direct effort by the merchants and planters of the Chesapeake to end the monopoly and develop competitive trade after it expired. He reported soon after his arrival in France that "various are the opinions here respecting the price Tobo. will be after the contract with Mr. Morris elapses, tho' it is probable the change will not be great." He had no difficulty in disposing of his initial cargo of tobacco to the Farmers General at the same price that Morris had contracted for, as Morris had fallen short of the stipulated quantity. During these first months at Bordeaux, Fenwick carried on some business as a commission merchant through Forrest and Stoddert of Georgetown.[43]

John sailed for Bordeaux on 22 June 1788, bearing a letter written by his father to Thomas Jefferson at the Court of Versailles, saying that John would be paying his respects in person, "as soon as he can conveniently go to Paris. I flatter myself you will find him a modest, chearful, sensible young man; and that his Integrity & Diligence will merit the Confidence of those who may favour the Copartnership, in which he is concern'd, with Consignments or other Business in their Line. The Firm of the House will I expect upon his Arrival in Bordeaux be changed to Fenwick Mason & Compy. Any good offices which you may do to the said House, or any Advice, which you may be pleased to give my Son, I shall esteem as the highest Mark of your Friendship." [44]

Capt. James Fenwick had the direction of the business in America from his office in Georgetown. George Mason was one of the firm's major customers. His account with Fenwick and Mason in May 1789 is an indication both of the kind of business undertaken by the firm and of George Mason's considerable shift to wheat on his farms by this date. He shipped 726.5 bushels on the *Maryland,* and Thomson Mason shipped 273.5 bushels on the same vessel. The elder Mason shipped 910.5 bushels on the *Becky,* and William Mason shipped 388 bushels, a total of 2,298.5 bushels from the several Mason plantations. In addition to the wheat shipped on these vessels, Mason had sent thirteen hogsheads of tobacco on the *Becky* in 1789 and thirty hogsheads on the *Union* in 1788. In return, George Mason ordered six half hogsheads, amounting to 180 gallons, of good cordial brandy; half a gross of claret; half a gross of white wine; two gallons of olive oil; a piece of silk, dress pattern, and trimmings to make a dress for one of his daughters, and he asked to have sent to him a few young trees of the best kinds of pears and plums as well as a few young grape vines. The shipments of wheat and tobacco were to be credited toward John Mason's capital of £1,000 in the new firm. His father hoped that the remittances made that autumn would bring the sum to the stipulated total.[45] He did everything possible to advance the interest of his son's firm, whose prospects seemed bright enough.

Fenwick and Mason had received a large cargo of whale oil, whalebone, rice, and tar from Boston. From it they sold 5,000 livres worth and dispatched the vessel with a cargo of salt and micellaneous French goods. They sold the entire shipment on board the *Union* to the Farmers General at 32 livres the hundredweight and believed that they would net 200 livres on every hogshead.[46] The two young men were getting along well together, and Joseph Fenwick had a high opinion of John Mason's ability. It would seem from all points of view that George Mason had chosen wisely in the partnership for his son. On 12 June 1788 Mason thought it prudent to give his son some advice that is as good today as it was then:

If you persevere steadily in your plan of giving no Credits what ever in America, & in never either paying Bills or sending goods for a Livre more than the certain Value to the Effects in your Hands & avoid being drawn into any dangerous Connection with french or other foreign Merchants, it may contract your Business at first; but it will rise upon safe & solid Foundations. Some Patience & Firmness will be necessary in such a Situation, & Mr. Jo. Fenwick & you are both Young Men, & consequently can't yet know much of Mankind. I entreat you to let no flattering Prospects whatever induce you to a Departure from this plan; for in my Opinion, almost inevitable Ruin wou'd be the Consequence. Confide as little as possible in the Merchants of the Place; at least never so far, as to give them the Power of hurting you; for they will look on your Success with a Jealous & Evil Eye. Live in a frugal Style, without parade or Ostentation, avoid all unnecessary

Expence, & do as much of your Business your selves, as you can; when it exceeds this Compass, look narrowly into the Conduct of those you employ. Attend with Diligence & Strict Integrity to the Interest of your Correspondents & enter into no Engagements which you have not the almost certain Means of performing. With an Observance of these Maxims you will deserve to be rich; and you will be rich; and in the Progress, you will possess Safety & Ease, unmingled with Fear or Danger.[47]

In May 1789 he warned him to use extreme caution in dealing with Carter Braxton and to be careful of advancing credit to Stephen West, although the old merchant could be a valuable friend and ally. James McClurg of Richmond had shipped eight or ten hogsheads and might be instrumental in securing a portion of the trade of the James River for Fenwick, Mason and Company. Daniel Brent of Richland and his brother, Richard Brent, had done a great deal to promote the company's interests.[48]

The political crisis in France did little to improve the state of trade between Bordeaux and the Potomac. Planters and merchants alike were increasingly cautious about committing themselves. In May 1790 George Mason wrote to his son that Capt. James Fenwick had been obliged to charter the ship *Confidence* at a very low rate rather than send it back in ballast—"which has been the fate of many of the ships sent out to America for wheat or flour, and has reduced freights this year lower than they were ever known before." Mason did not know when the *Washington,* Fenwick and Mason's own ship, would be able to sail and indicated that it would be very difficult to obtain a cargo: "for the confusion and uncertain state of affairs in France makes people cautious of venturing their property there, which together with the low price of tobacco at that market last fall, discourages everybody from shipping thither." Tobacco was selling in Virginia from eighteen to twenty shillings Virginia currency per hundredweight and was expected to go higher. With the exchange on London at 15 to 20 percent, it would be suicidal for Fenwick, Mason and Company to buy tobacco on their own account for shipment to France.[49]

George Mason was trying to encourage trade with France, as opposed to England, and to break the habit of the colonists' insatiable demand for British goods. The British merchants were encouraging these demands in order to make up for the unpaid war debts.

Late in the autumn of 1787 John received a letter from his father that criticized the goods shipped to him from France. "The chintzes dear, the Cambric very bad at the price, I would have imported better at the same Prices from London." Thus, the superiority of English manufactured goods over those of France made it difficult to establish this type of trade. He also advised John that as "Mr. [Benjamin] Franklin's intimacy's" had been more with the literati than with the merchants, he should "cultivate a Correspondence with the American minister, Mr. Jefferson; which I think will be servicable to you & give Credit to the House."

When Joseph Fenwick asked George Mason's help in securing the position of American consul at Bordeaux, Mason felt that such an opportunity would be of great advantage to Fenwick, Mason and Company and agreed to do what he could. He felt, however, that "as the President of the United States has the nomination to offices, I thought there was some impropriety and indelicacy in making application before General Washington has accepted the office of President." He concluded his letter with some comments that the long-standing friendship between himself and Washington might become strained on account of their political differences. But as much as he valued the friendship, "I would not forfeit the approbation of my own mind for the approbation of any man, or all the men upon the earth." [50]

George Mason did write to President Washington on 19 June 1789, recommending Joseph Fenwick as American consul in Bordeaux, as mentioned earlier. Washington granted the appointment, and Joseph served in this post from 1790 through 1798.[51]

Earlier in the year John had had a severe attack of his "old Disorder, the convulsive Cholic," which delayed him from going to Paris to present his respects to Thomas Jefferson until February 1789 and to discuss with him ways and means to increase trade with the French. About this time it seemed probable that Jefferson, after many delays, would be returning to America; so the conference did not accomplish its goal. When Jefferson was able to announce his departure in September, John offered him passage on one of his ships.[52]

His father was much upset by the news of John's illness and wrote him, "I am afraid this Complaint is, in some Measure, constitutional in you, as it has been, almost thro' Life, in me; and without great Care, will become habitual." The letter continued with admonitions concerning business transactions and warned that although he had always heard a very good character of Fenwick, he regretted noting "a Softness and Milkiness of Temper" that John should guard against. He urged John and Fenwick to go into "Housekeeping" as they had many people to whom to show civilities. "I can't think House-keeping will be any great addition to your expenses . . . besides that it must be much more agreeable than living in a boarding-House." He continued with comments about the quality of the brandy Fenwick had sent him the year previously, "which tho' at a very high Price is exceeding bad; the Man who furnished it must have been a Knave; for I make no Doubt that Mr. Fenwick expected it was good and paid a price accordingly. The Peice of silk ordered is for your Sister Betsey and I expect you will chuse it yourself." George Mason must have had a low opinion of French food, for he sent John a barrel of eight hams, a barrel of hominy, and some smoked beef. John's brothers sent him a female and one male opossum with which "to puzzle" the French! [53]

Following his sojourn in Paris, John went to London, where he met Joshua Johnson. He gave John a copy of the order George Mason had sent him that he might "have the arms thereon described engraved on his plate that he had ordered." Joshua was a younger brother of Thomas Johnson, the first governor of Maryland, and in 1783, following the Treaty of Paris, he had been appointed one of the trustees to act for Maryland in London to settle controversies in regard to commercial privileges and bank stock transactions left over from the Peace Treaty. He remained in London, where he acted as agent for his family and friends. As he was a friend of Capt. Ignatius Fenwick and a cousin of Joseph, with whom John Mason was associated, he was a logical agent for George Mason to have selected to administer his London orders.[54] The plate to which the memorandum referred was the tea services that George Mason had ordered to be made for each of his four daughters. The maker was John Denziloe, a son of William Denziloe of Bridport, Dorsetshire, a member of the Haberdashers Company, who apprenticed him to Charles Wright, citizen of London and goldsmith, for a term of seven years from 9 January 1765 for the sum of £20. Denziloe's mark was recorded at the Assay Office on 27 October 1774.[55] As his daybooks or ledgers have not yet been found, it is impossible to say who selected him as the silversmith to execute George Mason's order. Nor do we know what Denziloe charged the planter across the seas. Several pieces of these services may be seen at Gunston Hall today.

According to John's "Recollections," he remained in London about a month before returning to Bordeaux. As both of his partners were in America, the management of the whole business was in his hands. The French Revolution had begun, and in July 1789 there was considerable agitation in Bordeaux. This must have increased John's responsibilities. He was assisted by M. Menoire, the father of Joseph Fenwick's fiancée, who was not only a winegrower but a merchant in brandy. Undoubtedly, he supplied the brandy that called forth those scathing comments of George Mason. John must have improved in his knowledge of liquors because later in Georgetown he became a well-known importer of wine and brandy. In 1793 Fenwick, Mason & Company supplied Thomas Jefferson with fourteen cases of wine from Bordeaux, "bottled in the strongest bottle to be had here—and we hope the quality which you described—it is the vintage of 1788."[56]

In the meantime John kept the business going while France was unsettled. In spite of the coolness between his father and George Washington, he was pleased to have George Washington place an order on his behalf with Fenwick, Mason and Company on 12 October 1789.[57]

John was ill again during the winter but was recovered by March of 1790. He wrote his father on 11 May that there had been demonstrations in Bordeaux against the king. The letter gives an eyewitness account of the revolution as it affected him and his life in that city.[58] About this time he took "the oath under the new French Constitution." His position in the city must have been helped by his close connection with the Menoires, who were people of influence. Later that summer he was invited to become a member "of the friends to the Constitution Club." He wrote his father, "I felicitate myself very much of having been admitted a member." George Mason in turn wrote Thomas Jefferson on 10 January 1791: "My son John was admitted, about the End of last Summer, a Member of the great Constitutional Committee for the City of Bordeaux; an Appointment with which I am very well pleased; not only as it shews that he is well known & esteemed in the City, but as it will make him acquainted with some of the first Characters in that Part of the Kingdom, and will be the Means of much Information and Improvement."[59]

Despite the gathering clouds Joseph Fenwick's visit to the United States was successful in securing new business for the company. Besides renewing important contacts in the South and on the Chesapeake, Fenwick traveled through New England. The Masons had used their influence with Washington and Jefferson to have Fenwick appointed the American consul at Bordeaux. In October on his return to Bordeaux in that capacity, Fenwick wrote to many of the merchants with whom he had made contact during the summer. In a letter to Christopher Champlin of Newport, Rhode Island, for instance, he quoted prices on many different commodities. American pork was in demand and commanded sixty-five to seventy livres per barrel. Wheat brought five shillings American currency the bushel, rye two shillings, Indian corn one shilling sixpence, and flour twenty-four shillings. War seemed inevitable and would certainly raise the price and demand for American foodstuffs.[60]

John was relieved to have Fenwick back. The strain of handling the business alone had undermined his health and he was tired and discouraged. His physicians recommended "a small trip to Sea," but in his "Recollections" he indicates he visited Montauban, Toulouse, Carcassone, Montpelier, Marseilles, Avignon, and Nimes, in the south of France. Upon his return to Bordeaux he took the necessary time to settle his affairs and to say his adieux to the hospitable Menoires.[61]

It is interesting that Victor duPont met Eleonore Menoire after her marriage to Joseph Fenwick and wrote the following description of her: "Mrs. Fenwick is one of the most extraordinary characters; full of life, wit, and sport, she is an excellent companion. Honni soit qui mal y pense is her motto. She has given up long ago all claims to the reputation of a prudent woman; and certainly she is far superior to her reputation, which is much more than many ladies from Paris can say for themselves."[62] John and Victor continued their acquaintance, as several years later Mrs. William Thornton, the French wife of the architect of many of the buildings in the new Federal City, recorded in her diary on 9 July 1800 "that Mr. duPont a French gentleman from New York called with a letter from Mr. Mason of Georgetown."[63]

John sailed from Bordeaux in June 1791 in the *Louis XIV* Captain Roux, Master, and had a disagreeable passage. It took seventy days, but evidently the long sea voyage was good for his illness as he was perfectly restored to health when he landed at Norfolk in August. He first settled at Richmond because he considered it best for the tobacco trade, but by spring 1792 he had established himself in Georgetown, doing business under the firm name of Mason and Fenwick. Insurance policies indicate that his warehouses were built of stone and brick. One was situated on the north side of Water Street between Frederick and Fayette streets; it measured sixty-three feet front by thirty-five feet deep, and was four stories high; the other one, slightly larger, was on the southwest corner of Frederick and Key streets.[64] While John was busy getting established, he had the sorrow of losing his father and of realizing that his oldest brother was incurably ill.

Some difficulty in obtaining consignments of tobacco held John Mason's ships on the Potomac far into the winter of 1791. His father came forward in this emergency with a consignment of sixty-five hogsheads of his own tobacco for Fenwick, Mason and Company. Mason hesitated to ship this tobacco to France, as it was "common, ordinary, light Tobacco, and I was dubious of the Quality answering the french Market, now that the Emulation among the individual Manufacturers will occasion a demand for Tobaccos of superior Qualities, though considering the present low price and unflattering Prospects here, I think I can hardly lose by shipping in french Bottoms."[65]

There are indications that George Mason grew only an inferior, light tobacco on his plantations. Writing to John Mason in April 1791, he described the varieties that he had grown in 1787–91 in more detail than usual:

The six Hhds marked GDM are part of my Crop at Dogues Run; it is little Frederick Tobo. (as all my own Crops are) consequently the leaf broad, & the Stem small; it is also neatly handled; Yet I think the Quality but indifferent, the Tobo. being rather weak; the five Hhds. GDM are part of Green's Crop at Hallowing Point, little Frederick also, neatly handled, strong & of good Substance, much such Tobo. as that of mine which you carried out with you in the *Union,* in the Year 1788, the eight Hhds. GDM are my crop on the plantation next to Gunston, made by the same Overseer (a very neat Planter) & on the same Land, with six Hhds. ship'd you, under the same Mark, per the *Washington* last Fall which you sold at 40 Livres, the Quality much the same, tho' not quite so large. These last mentioned thirteen Hhds. marked GHM and GPM I hope may suite the British or Irish smuglers.[66]

Little Frederick tobacco was a strain of the Oronoco variety, and enjoyed great popularity among eighteenth-century Virginia tobacco growers. Tobacco shipped to Bordeaux found its way in large part to the British and Irish market, which preferred this variety to the stronger and darker kinds favored on the domestic French market.

John Mason also arranged for the sale of wheat raised on his father's Little Hunting Creek quarters and sold it to William Wilson of Alexandria. The French market had raised Alexandria wheat prices from $0.80 to $1.25 a bushel in the course of 1790, so that, as Joseph Fenwick pointed out in April 1791, the American market had raised prices higher and faster than the French market on which it partially depended. Prices began to dip again, and by December 1791 Mason feared a continuing downward spiral.[67]

Political conditions in France remained in an unsettled state, and preparations for a general war in Europe were apparent on every hand. In May 1792 the exchange stood at three French livres for sixteen English pennies, with paper money depreciated from 50 percent to 60 percent below the specie equivalent. With the exchange rate so unfavorable it seemed wise to liquidate the firm in Bordeaux. A printed notice so stating was issued there on May 1793. John Davidson and John Woods were to act as Mason and Fenwick's agents in Bordeaux.[68]

When John Mason became head of Mason, Fenwick and Company in spring 1792, it was a moment of international crisis. The French Republic was approaching a state of war with England and looked to the United States for military and economic assistance. Edmond Genet arrived in America early in 1793 to promote an alliance between the two young republics and to arrange for the purchase of needed supplies using French credits in America. In order to facilitate these purchases, John Mason offered his firm's services to the president in April 1793. He received a courteous reply stating that "it is not the intention of the Government of the United States, to have any agency in supplying the French with the productions of this country further than to furnish such agent or agents as may be duly authorized by the French Government therefor, with the means of making the purchases, out of the Debt due from the United States to France." [69] Washington's Neutrality Proclamation effectively dashed Genet's hopes of American involvement.

The outbreak of war between Britain and France could only complicate matters for neutral shippers like Mason, Fenwick and Company. The British Orders in Council in June 1793 authorized the seizure and preemptive purchase of all neutral cargoes of foodstuffs to ports under French control. In November 1793 the British determined to seize and detain any ship carrying the produce of a French colony or bringing supplies of any kind to it. The French retaliated with measures of their own. One of Mason's ships, the *Maryland,* was boarded by a British frigate on the outward passage and had to run a British blockade to slip into Bordeaux in August 1793. It left that port for the French island of Mauritius in the Indian Ocean. Homeward bound to America, the *Maryland* was taken into Bermuda by a British warship. John Mason dispatched Jesse Dewees to Bermuda as his agent to save the ship and its cargo from condemnation. The *Maryland* sailed from Bermuda for Georgetown in July 1795, but Dewees had not been able to save the cargo or obtain a license to take on goods in Bermuda.[70]

The case of the *Maryland* was no isolated problem. The *Pigeon* had scarcely left Chesapeake Bay when it was captured by British cruisers off Cape Henry. The chartered Danish ship *Susannah* was carried into Saint Kitts by a British privateer. One of Mason's skippers wrote from Montserrat in the British West Indies, "We are very much at a loss to know whether there is really a war between Great Britain and America or not. I find they make it a point to Capture all Vessels under the American Flag without paying any kind of respect to where they are bound." Another friend warned Mason that "the Combined Powers now take every thing of ours, bound to a French Port or not." Jesse Dewees found evidence in Bermuda that Mason, Fenwick and Company were on a blacklist circulated to a privateers of firms trading with the enemy.[71]

Shipment in wartime sea lanes posed constant dangers. Joshua Barney sent $31,000 in silver ingots in the ship *Pomona* to John Mason as part payment for produce shipped to France. British cruisers captured the ship on the high seas and took it into Halifax in 1795. Mason's silver hung in the judicial balance until 1803. Mason, Fenwick and Company fared no better at French hands. In January 1794 three of Mason's ships were among over a hundred American vessels trapped at Bordeaux by a general embargo. The *Molly* of Georgetown was taken by a French privateer but escaped loss when it was discovered that both prize and captor were partly owned by Joseph Fenwick.[72]

John Mason came to Georgetown as a merchant in the tobacco trade, but European wars and the declining price of tobacco in the 1790s gradually led Mason, Fenwick and Company into other ventures, such as banking, international commerce, the organization of foundries, and navigation and turnpike companies, as well as the flour and wheat trade and land investment. Most important was his connection with the Bank of Columbia, chartered by the state of Maryland in 1793. He served on its first board of directors and became president in 1798. The bank served in its early years as the financial agent of the commissioners of the newly formed District of Columbia. The men who organized the bank aimed to extend financial assistance to the commissioners, who had the difficult task of creating a capital city from tobacco fields, woods, and swamps. They needed money and had no means of obtaining credit until the Bank of Columbia filled the gap. The commissioners became stockholders in the new bank. When they needed money or credit, the bank provided it; and when they needed land, the bank's directors sold them their private holdings. The directors, as stockholders, had first claim on the loan facilities of the bank. They were all considerable landowners in the District and its immediate environs. All of them wanted the new capital city to expand and grow, for its expansion and growth would make their real estate more valuable. The directors of the Bank of Columbia gave first priority to land in advancing bank credit and sank nearly all of its resources in real estate rather than in commerce and industry.[73]

John Mason owned a good deal of land within the new federal district as well as in Georgetown, and his city lots were primarily a speculation. In June 1793 Mason purchased two lots in Carrollsburg confiscated from British factors during the war. In 1798 he obtained from the Virginia Assembly a bill incorporating a speculative town of his own, to be called South Haven and located on his own Fairfax County lands. His connections grew, and with his appointment in 1807 as the superintendent of the Indian Trade, with offices at Georgetown, he became more and more involved in government service.[74]

In February 1796 John married Anna Maria Murray, daughter of James and Sarah (Maynadier) Murray, of Annapolis, Maryland. The license is dated the eleventh. Mrs. Benjamin Stoddert of Georgetown, in writing of the new Mrs. Mason, said, "She is a charming woman— not so much in her face, as in her whole deportment—her face tho' quite pretty enough for she has charming eyes and fine teeth—and plays delightfully and sings really sweetly—her face as I before began to say is not as pretty as I expected, but she has sufficient reason to be satisfied with it. I know I should if I had such a one—her sister I imagine is more a beauty to please the Ladies than Mrs. Mason is, for Miss Murray looks all amiability, very pretty too." [75] There is a charming portrait by Bouchet of Mrs. John Mason and her sister, Mrs. Edward Lloyd, wife of the governor of Maryland, still in possession of the Lloyd family.

Following his marriage John built his plantation house on Analostan Island, which became the scene of many elegant festivities. The island was a part of his inheritance of 2,000 acres, which came to be included in the area that George Washington selected for the site of the federal city. The mansion must have been completed by 1798, as the Masons gave a lavish entertainment there for Louis Philippe, the Duc d'Orleans.[76] John Mason also had a residence in Georgetown on the corner of twenty-fifth and L streets and Pennsylvania Avenue, which became the site of the Columbia Hospital in 1932. John retained his interest in France through his friendship with David Bailie Warden and Joel Barlow, although he never returned there. When he sent his son John to school in Paris, he was under the care of the former, and he named his youngest son after the latter.[77]

Following a congressional order that the federal city should have a militia similar to those of Virginia and Maryland, he was appointed a brigadier general by President Jefferson in May 1802. Later he became commissioner general of prisoners during the War of 1812. John was a man of many parts and with diverse interests too numerous to include here in the general family biography, but it is interesting to note that in August 1817 he was elected president of the Potowmack Company, founded in 1774 with George Washington as the first president and his father as treasurer. He held the office eleven years and was the last president.[78]

In 1801 John Dickinson expressed the hope that John Mason would stop in New Castle, Delaware, on his next trip; he wanted to meet him because he had been intimate with his father, "for whom I had a sincere friendship." John Mason did a lot of traveling, even going as far afield as Nova Scotia.[79]

Two interesting letters of John's, written in 1805 to President Jefferson, reveal a considerable intimacy:

George Town 13 May, 1805

Dear Sir

Enclosed I take the Liberty to hand you for your consideration my Friend Hodgson's Invoice of the two glasses which I mentioned to you some time agoe; you will be pleased to remark, that in estimating these plates, by the square inch, the Frames are included, which are said to be remarkably elegant large, and richly ornamented.

I do myself the Pleasure also to send you herein a Sketch of the country and roads from this Place to Occoquan; which I have made out roughly from recollection, but which you will find accurate enough, I flatter myself, to serve as a guide in your proposed excursion. From Ward's Tavern, opposite to Colchester, to Piscataway, there is no Tavern. I have noted Mr. Graham's in Dogues Neck—and my Brother's [William Mason's] on the Plot, both are near your Rout and will be extremely happy to see you.

With great Respect
I have the honor
to be Sir
your very Obt. Sevt.
J. Mason

The President

The second letter is actually addressed to a Mr. Barnes, secretary to Thomas Jefferson and concerns the fact that John had discovered an error in the amount the president was charged for the cases of wine he purchased in 1793, and he enclosed a check for $15.50, the sum the president had overpaid. This circumstance came to light when John was settling up his "old commercial" concerns.

Later in the same year John received this letter from the president:

Dear Sir   Washington, Dec. 17, 1805

Mr. Barnes my factotum in money matters is on a journey to Baltimore, and in his absence a pressing call is made on me, which renders it necessary for me to get a Thousand Dollars from the bank of Columbia. I have not another mercantile or monied acquaintance in the place. In this dilemma, I venture to ask the favor of you to indorse & put in the enclosed for me as the rules of the bank require an indorser a resident. I trust it is unnecessary for me to assure you it shall be duly taken up. Accept my friendly salutation & assurances of great esteem & respect.

Thos. Jefferson [80]

John transacted the business and asked the president to command him "on all similar occasions."

John and Maria (Murray) Mason were popular in Georgetown and became noted for their gracious hospitality at their home on Analostan Island. The parties they gave were memorable ones, particularly one given for their son John in 1811 before he left to attend school in Paris. The marriage of their daughter, Anna Maria, to Sydney Smith Lee in 1834 intertwined still further the Mason and Lee family ties that had begun in the days when George Mason IV and Richard Henry Lee were drawn together as political allies and as neighboring planters sharing similar problems. Anna Maria gave a spectacular party on the return of her husband from Japan. He served as a fleet captain under Commodore Perry on the historic occasion of Perry's voyage to Japan for the signing of the peace treaty on 8 March 1854 that opened the ports of Japan to foreign trade. The island was hung with Japanese lanterns that Lee had brought back and the gaiety went on far into the night.[81]

They were equally well known for their kindliness and friendliness to those in need. Their daughter often said that her father's "love for his fellowmen was just as important in the history of the world as George Mason's knowledge of history and constitutional government." She was known also to have said, "Watch any member of the family who has been blessed with and accepted the creed of John Mason. He will soon be noticed, soon succeed, and will leave a blessing to his kin." [82]

John Mason was caught up in the enthusiasm of the period for agricultural and domestic improvements. He was a member of both the Agricultural Society of Georgetown and the Columbian Agricultural Society. Both he and his wife entered various classes held at these societies. At the various shows and exhibitions he entered his Merino sheep while she exhibited her skill in producing cloth from domestic materials. Both won prizes.[83]

It was John Mason who was the most interested in perpetuating the memory of his father. In 1811 he commissioned copies of the portrait of his father for each of his brothers and sisters. He also made an effort to preserve his father's papers. In his search for them he wrote a letter on 6 March 1844 from Clermont, where he had retired following his financial reverses, addressed to his nephew's widow, "Mrs. Eleanor Anne C. Mason of Gunston Hall near Occoquan, Prince William County, Virginia." The name of the county on the envelope appears added as an afterthought, and it is surprising that he should have located Gunston Hall in the wrong county. It has been suggested that perhaps Occoquan was the nearest post office. He told Mrs. Mason that he had "some of his [George Mason's] original letters . . . to Mr. Cockburn but none of those to Mr. Massey" and went on to solicit her help in suggesting to his "good friend Mrs. Triplett,* that she look among her papers for any letters "of a public character, emanating from my Father." On this same subject there is an interesting letter of Emily Virginia Mason's to Kate Mason Rowland, Washington, D.C., 7 June 1844: "Old General Mason has been ill—something like paralysis—Papa is going down to see him to get the papers for Mr. Sparks who is preparing a life of the old George Mason." [84]

John Mason died 19 March 1849 at Clermont, where he had been living since September 1833, and was buried in Christ Church graveyard, Alexandria. [85] His widow survived him by ten years and lived with her daughter, Sarah Maria (Mason) Cooper, at Cameron, until her death on 29 November 1859. She was interred next to her husband. The John Masons had ten children, all of whom married well and about whom there is information available in the library at Gunston Hall.

John Mason reflected the changing economic outlook of the Potomac area and, as a farsighted entrepreneur, helped to give it direction. Tidewater Virginia could no longer depend on the tobacco trade with Europe as the sole support of its economy. New enterprises were needed at home, and the potential riches of the American West called out to the venturesome. John Mason, businessman of Georgetown, represented a new generation on the Potomac, prepared to face and conquer new challenges. Following his precedent, every generation of the Mason family has associated itself with active enterprises, to the continued prestige and distinction of the family.

---

* Ann (Massey) Triplett inherited Springfield near Gunston Hall and was the last member of the family to live there.

Chapter XI

Notes on Later Masons

AMONG LATER DESCENDANTS of Ann and George Mason was Richard Barnes Mason, who was born at Lexington on 16 January 1797. Nothing is known of his childhood, but when he was twenty years old he accepted an appointment as second lieutenant in the Eighth United States Infantry, in the city of Washington, 2 September 1817.[1] "His reputation of stern character, deemed by some as harsh and severe," was begun by an incident while he was a captain when he boxed the ears of an impudent soldier who retaliated by shooting Captain Mason, who had returned to his tent. He recuperated from the wounds in Virginia. He wrote a letter from Pohick Run, Fairfax County, Virginia, 30 April 1821 to the secretary of war asking that he might study military science at West Point, but his request was not granted, and he was sent west to participate in the Indian Wars, where he earned a reputation as great as that of his redoubtable ancestor George Mason II. He overcame several charges of "conduct unbecoming a gentleman and a Commanding Officer" to assume the position of the first military governor of California in 1847. In October Kit Carson arrived in Monterey to deliver dispatches to Governor Mason. It is not to be wondered that such a hotheaded man as Mason should threaten John Charles Frémont, another well-known Indian fighter and explorer, with a duel when the two men were members of opposing factions at the time of the "Bear Flag" episode.[2] Mason seems to have been a better soldier than businessman. In October 1822 he sold to Robert Triplett of Owensboro, Kentucky, for the small sum of $5,000 three thousand acres of land in Daviess County, Kentucky, which he had inherited from his grandfather George Mason IV. A part of this land has since become some of the most valuable real estate in Owensboro.[3] Mason was also reluctant to believe the reports of John A. Sutter and William Tecumseh Sherman of the prodigious amount of gold to be found in California, and he was "disgusted with the crass commercialism and wealth hunger that were stampeding soldiers into desertion."[4]

This stern warrior asked to be relieved as military governor in 1849, and he was given command of Jefferson Barracks, near Saint Louis.

William Tecumseh Sherman later wrote, "I parted with my old commander, Colonel Mason, with sincere regret. To me he had ever been kind and considerate, and while stern, honest to a fault, he was the very embodiment of the principle of fidelity to the interest of General Government. He possessed a strong native intellect and far more knowledge of the principles of civil government and law than he got credit for." [5] In 1859 George Mason Graham appointed Sherman superintendent of the Louisiana State Seminary of Learning at Baton Rouge because he was aware of the affection his half brother, Richard Barnes Mason, had had for Sherman during their military service in California. [6]

Unfortunately, General Mason contracted cholera soon after his arrival at Jefferson Barracks, where an epidemic was in full force, and he died there 25 July 1850. He was survived by his widow, Elizabeth (Hunter) Mason, and two daughters, Emma Twiggs and Elizabeth Ann Sally. The elder, Emma Twiggs Mason, married Gen. Frank Wheaton, whose first wife was her cousin Sarah Maria Cooper. The descendants of this couple have also pursued military careers.

A colorful young man was Alexander Macomb Mason, son of John and Catherine (Macomb) Mason, who left the United States Naval Academy in 1861 to join the Confederate army. He was captured and confined at Johnson's Island, Ohio where he wrote a letter to Major Linell, superintendent of prisons, requesting that he be allowed to receive articles of underclothing from his aunt, Mrs. Devereaux Williams, Detroit, as he was "perfectly destitute." [7]

After the Civil War, Mason was an officer of the Chilean navy, then he accepted an invitation to join the forces of the Khedive of Egypt and serve as military governor of Massawa. He was also a member of Gordon's staff and was active in Abyssinia and the Sudan during 1871–97. He was often referred to as Colonel Mason Bey. He and his American wife, Sophia (Hurry) Shreve, whom he married in Berlin in 1890, lived in Cairo, but he died 17 March 1897 in Washington, D.C., while on one of his infrequent visits to his native land. [8]

Although James Murray Mason, son of John and Anna Maria (Murray) Mason, is more often remembered in connection with the Trent Affair of the Civil War, he was a lawyer who began his practice in the office of Benjamin Watkins Leigh of Richmond. He soon moved to Winchester, Virginia, where he established his own practice in 1820. While he was in England as Confederate commissioner to Great Britain he visited Gunston Hall, the Fowke estate that formerly belonged to his ancestors on the maternal side. Reference is made to this visit in the *Wolverhampton Chronicle*. [9] He also visited Lord Beresford

Hope of Bedgebury Park, Kent, who had been billeted with the Masons on Analostan Island in 1812.[10]

James Murray Mason's son, George, also graduated in law from the College of William and Mary and first practiced law with his father in Winchester. But like other younger Masons, he felt the lure of the Southwest and removed to Texas in April 1854, where he was admitted to the bar. In 1861 he was appointed district attorney of the Confederate States of Texas. After the Civil War, he resumed his law practice in Galveston until his death on 3 February 1896.[11]

George Mason V has living descendants in Texas, among whom are Homoiselle Randall (Haden) Fay and Sarah Mason (Eastham) Chapoton. Descended from Thomas Mason of Woodbridge is Elizabeth (Evans) Young.

His Mason descendants in Kentucky are numerous, too many to mention individually, but Leannah Mason, who married William Henry Barron in 1817 is their forebear. Their son, Thomas Mason Barron, married Penelope McFarland of Utica, Kentucky, and it is through their offspring that many residents of Daviess County, can trace their ancestry to George Mason IV.

The only son of Thomas Mason Barron and Penelope (McFarland) was William Thomas Barron II, who married Mary (Mulligan) Barron. Their daughter Mary was the first wife of Conrad Nicholson Hilton, who named one of their sons Barron to perpetuate the Kentucky connection. It is this Barron Hilton whose business acumen has developed a hotel chain of international fame.

Among the Masons interested in education was Laura Lee Dorsey, the daughter of John Thomas Beale and Catherine Chew (Mason) Dorsey. Mrs. Dorsey had taught school in Alexandria with such success that she was asked to open a school in Georgetown in 1887. Amusing anecdotes of this change of residence from Alexandria to Georgetown have been recorded by Ruth Putnam Chase.[12]

Laura Lee Dorsey assisted her mother in the school and later operated Saint Mary's Hall at San Antonio, Texas, from 1915 to 1923 and Saint Anne's School at Charlottesville, Virginia, from 1923 to 1929.

Her cousin, Beverly Randolph Mason, who had served in the Black Horse Troop under Gen. Robert E. Lee, married Elizabeth Harrison Nelson 18 August 1875 and returned to Fairfax County, where he built a small house on land originally owned by his ancestor, George Mason. Later they moved to Georgetown and founded Gunston Hall School for their children and those of their intimate friends. Under their guidance the school continued to expand and flourish. One of their early pupils was Adelaide Specht, whose parents bought Gunston Hall from Edward Daniels in June 1891. Margaret Truman Daniel was a member of one of the last classes at Gunston Hall School, and when she graduated in June 1942, her father, then Senator Truman, delivered the graduation address. The Board of Regents of Gunston Hall has in its archives the records of this school.[13]

Kate Mason Rowland, the early biographer of George Mason IV, visited Gunston Hall about 1890. She found that the old mansion revealed few signs of the ravages of time, although only the old schoolhouse remained of the thirty outbuildings familar to George Mason. From the mansion she passed down the boxwood alley to the terraced gardens where one looked down "from a considerable elevation, on the beautiful river, on wood, and field, and pastures dotted with sheep. . . . The old public road has been long disused, with its chariots and horsemen, making the long overland journey north and south, but the river is changeless, an immortal highway."[14]

The river had carried the first Masons to new lands on Aquia and Accokeek and to the neck of land in the Potomac Freshes named after the Doegs. They had prospered on its shores and shipped their cargoes of tobacco and wheat to England and France. It bound together these transplanted Englishmen who lived on its either shore and helped them to develop their own way of life. It was their highway over the mountains to other new lands, and it carried the produce of the western farms back to Alexandria and Georgetown. The tobacco fields and the pastures have gone back to jack pine and honeysuckle, but the river remains.

And so the same river, only slightly changed by industry and overpopulation, flows by Gunston Hall, now owned by the state of Virginia and administered by a Board of Regents appointed by the National Society of Colonial Dames of America. Serving in the capacity of regent have been several women with the proud heritage of Mason blood, who cherish the thought that through the preservation of the plantation of George Mason they are helping the present generations to understand and appreciate the legacy of disciplined freedom left them by that individualistic thinker and dreamer George Mason IV.

Genealogical Tables

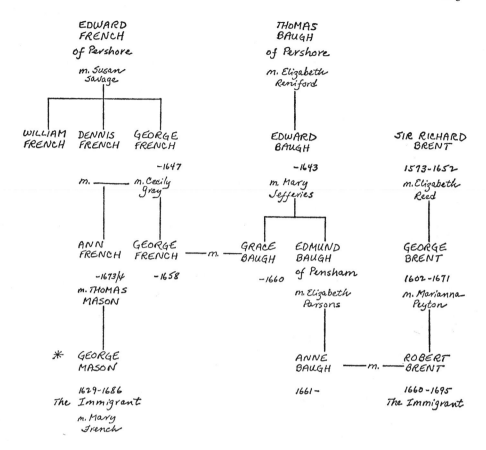

*baptized 10 June 1629 at Holy Cross Church, Pershore, England

Table 2. Baugh-French-Mason connections

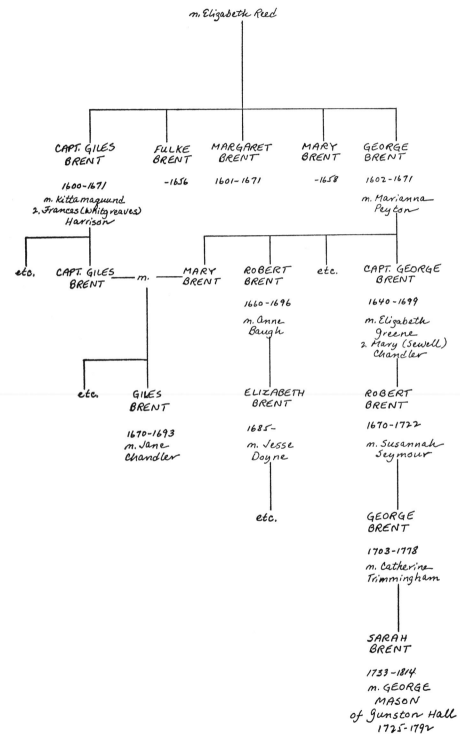

SIR RICHARD BRENT
Lord of Stoke and Admington
1573-1652

m. Elizabeth Reed

CAPT. GILES BRENT
1600-1671
m. Kittamaquund
2. Frances (Whitgreaves) Harrison

FULKE BRENT
-1656

MARGARET BRENT
1601-1671

MARY BRENT
-1658

GEORGE BRENT
1602-1671
m. Marianna Peyton

etc.

CAPT. GILES BRENT ___ m.

MARY BRENT

ROBERT BRENT
1660-1696
m. Anne Baugh

etc.

CAPT. GEORGE BRENT
1640-1699
m. Elizabeth Greene
2. Mary (Sewell) Chandler

etc.

GILES BRENT
1670-1693
m. Jane Chandler

ELIZABETH BRENT
1685-
m. Jesse Doyne

etc.

ROBERT BRENT
1670-1722
m. Susannah Seymour

GEORGE BRENT
1703-1778
m. Catherine Trimmingham

SARAH BRENT
1733-1814
m. GEORGE MASON
of Gunston Hall
1725-1792

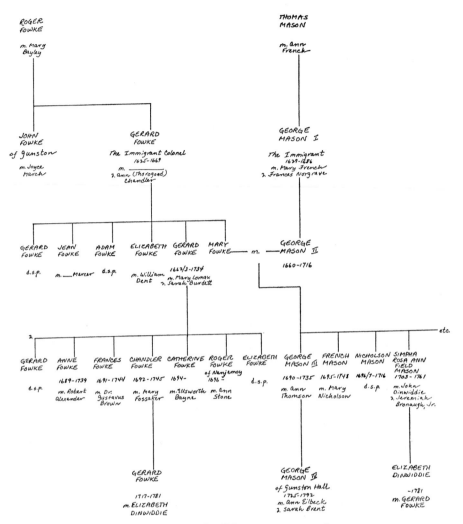

Table 4. Fowke-Mason connections

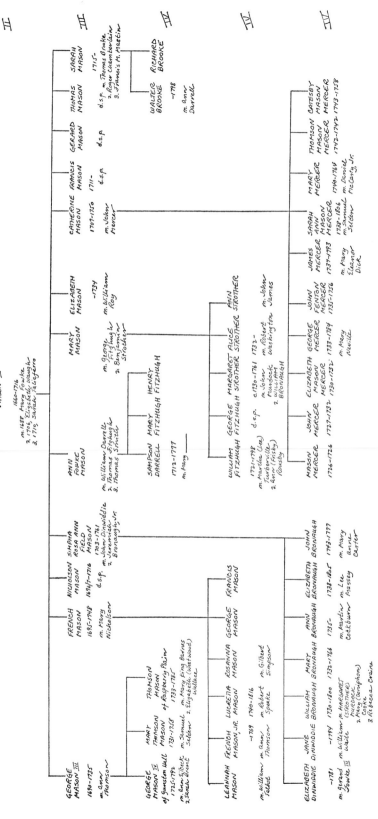

Table 5. Descendants of George Mason II (1660–1716)

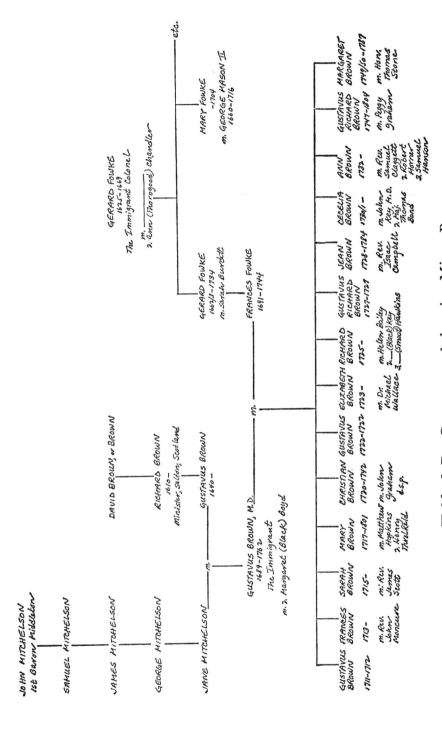

Table 6. Dr. Gustavus and the nine Misses Brown

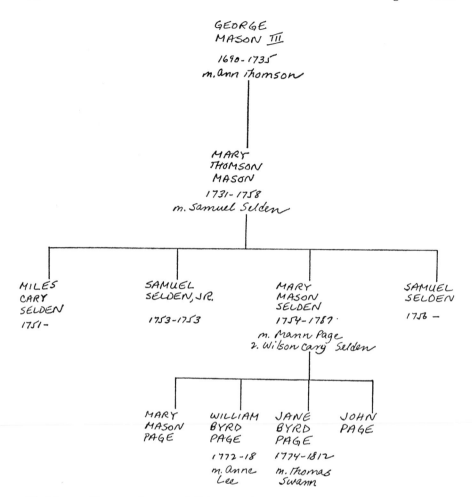

Table 7. Descendants of Mary Thomson Mason (1731–1758)

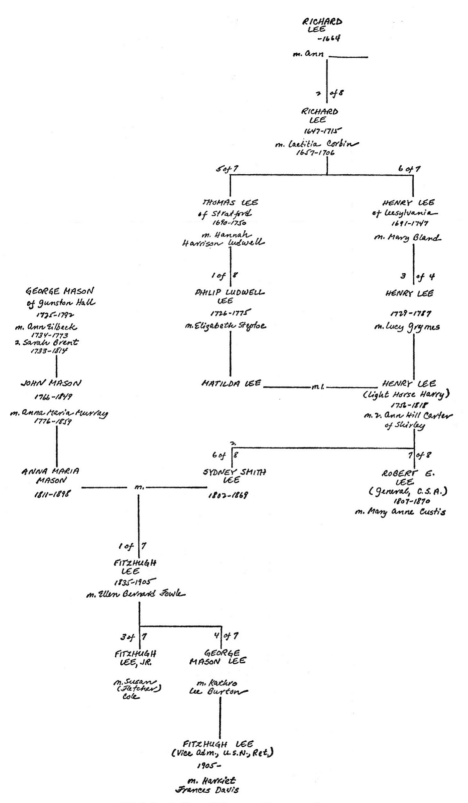

RICHARD
LEE
-1664

m. ann _____

2 of 8

RICHARD
LEE
1647-1715
m. Laetitia Corbin
1657-1706

5 of 7

THOMAS LEE
of Stratford
1690-1750
m. Hannah
Harrison Ludwell

6 of 7

HENRY LEE
of Leesylvania
1691-1747
m. Mary Bland

1 of 8

PHILIP LUDWELL
LEE
1726-1775
m. Elizabeth Steptoe

3 of 4

HENRY LEE
1729-1787
m. Lucy Grymes

GEORGE MASON
of Gunston Hall
1725-1792
m. Ann Eilbeck
1734-1773
2. Sarah Brent
1733-1814

JOHN MASON
1766-1849
m. anna Maria Murray
1776-1859

MATILDA LEE _____ m.1. _____ HENRY LEE
(Light Horse Harry)
1756-1818
m. 2. Ann Hill Carter
of Shirley

ANNA MARIA
MASON
1811-1898 _____ m. _____

2.

6 of 8

SYDNEY SMITH
LEE
1802-1869

7 of 8

ROBERT E.
LEE
(General, C.S.A.)
1807-1870
m. Mary anne Custis

1 of 7

FITZHUGH
LEE
1835-1905
m. Ellen Bernard Fowle

3 of 7

FITZHUGH
LEE, JR.
m. Susan
(Fletcher)
Cole

4 of 7

GEORGE
MASON LEE
m. Kathro
Lee Burton

FITZHUGH LEE
(Vice adm., U.S.N., Ret.)
1905-
m. Harriet
Frances Davis

Table 8. Lee-Mason Connections

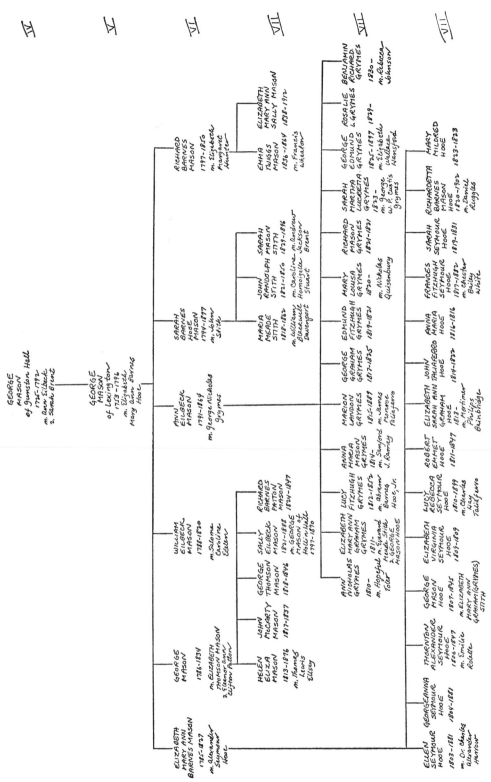

Table 9. Descendants of George Mason of Lexington (1753–1796)

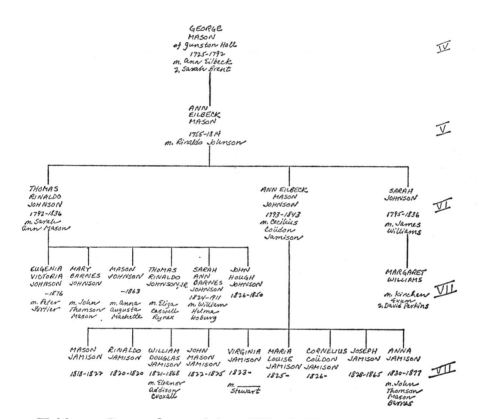

Table 10. Descendants of Ann Eilbeck Mason (1755–1814)

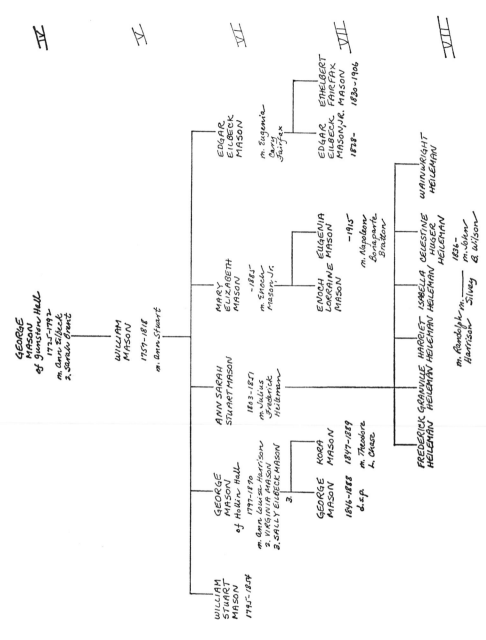

Table 11. Descendants of William Mason (1757–1818)

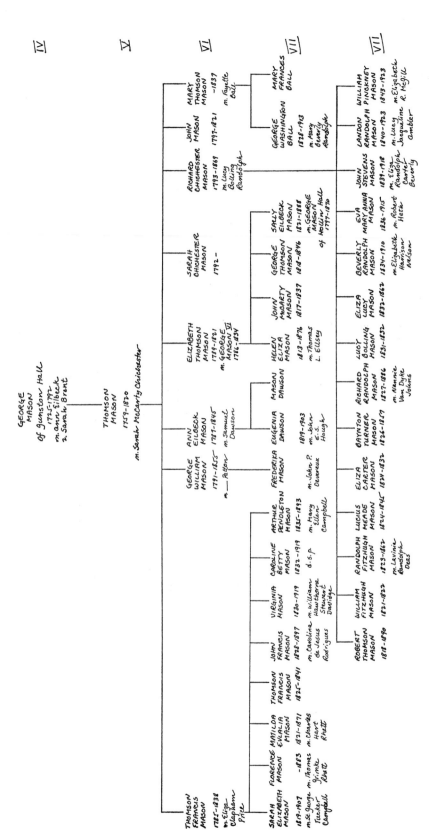

Table 12. Descendants of Thomson Mason (1759–1820)

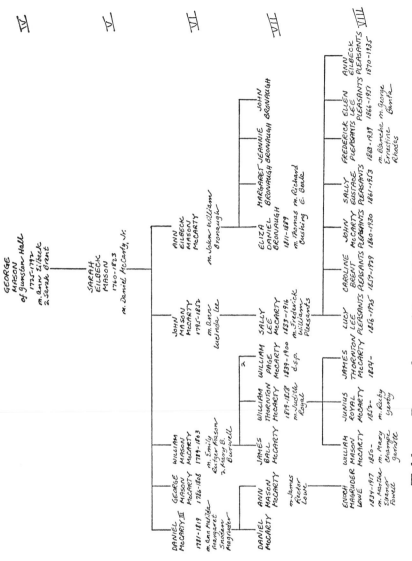

Table 13. Descendants of Sarah Eilbeck Mason (1760–1823)

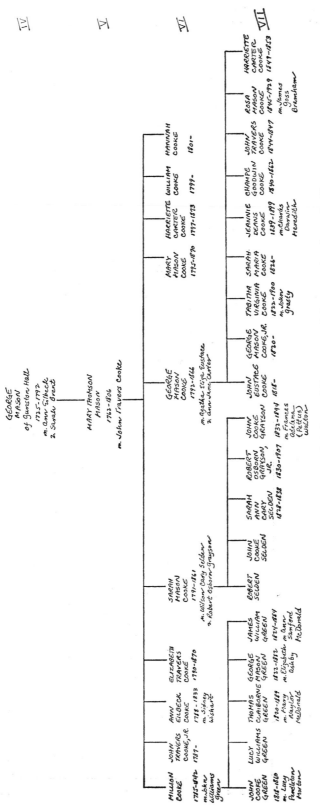

Table 14. Descendants of Mary Thomson Mason (1762–1806)

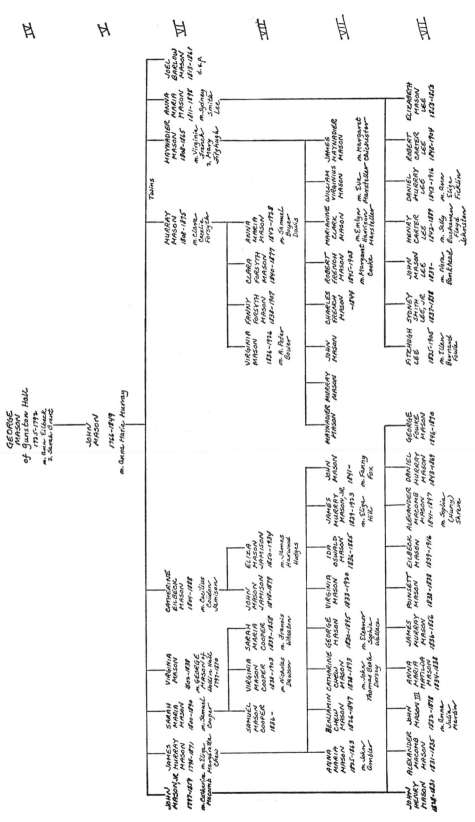

Table 15. Descendants of John Mason (1766–1849)

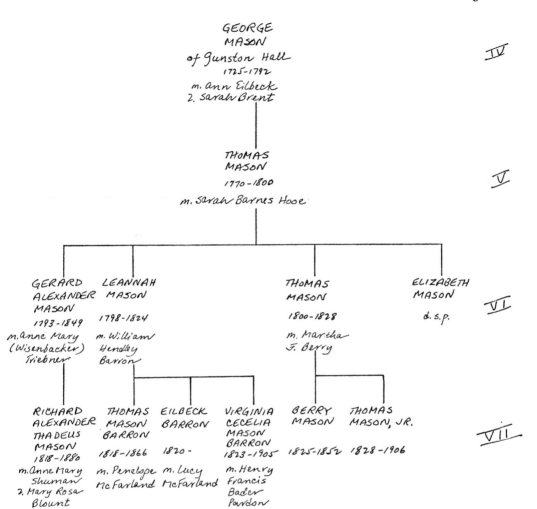

GEORGE
MASON
of Gunston Hall
1725-1792
m. Ann Eilbeck
2. Sarah Brent

IV

THOMAS
MASON
1770-1800
m. Sarah Barnes Hooe

V

GERARD
ALEXANDER
MASON
1793-1849
m. Anne Mary
(Wisenbacker)
Triebner

LEANNAH
MASON
1798-1824
m. William
Hendley
Barron

THOMAS
MASON
1800-1828
m. Martha
F. Berry

ELIZABETH
MASON
d. s. p.

VI

RICHARD
ALEXANDER
THADEUS
MASON
1818-1880
m. Anne Mary
Shuman
2. Mary Rosa
Blount

THOMAS
MASON
BARRON
1818-1866
m. Penelope
McFarland

EILBECK
BARRON
1820-
m. Lucy
McFarland

VIRGINIA
CECELIA
MASON
BARRON
1823-1905
m. Henry
Francis
Bader
Pardon

BERRY
MASON
1825-1852

THOMAS
MASON, JR.
1828-1906

VII

Table 16. Descendants of Thomas Mason (1770–1800)

Notes

Notes

Chapter I Colonel George Mason I

1. Anthony Richard Wagner, "Mason Pedigree," Pamela C. Copeland Mason Family Research File, Gunston Hall Library, Lorton, Va.

2. W. E. Tate, *The Parish Chest: A Study of the Records of Parochial Administration in England*, 3d ed. (Cambridge, Eng., 1969) , pp. 2–5.

3. Francis Baugh Andrews, "Notes on Pershore Abbey at the Time of the Suppression," pp. 232–43.

4. J. W. Willis Bund, ed., *Worcestershire County Records Calendar of the Quarter Sessions Papers, 1591–1643* (Worcester, Eng., 1899–1900) , 1:695.

5. Will of Thomas Mason, Worcestershire County Archives, Worcester, Eng.; Will of Grace French, Principal Probate Register, Somerset House, London.

6. Thomas Nash, *Collections for the History of Worcestershire* (London, 1781) , 2:249.

7. Bund, 1:700.

8. Walter C. Metcalfe, ed., *The Visitation of the County of Worcester, Begun by Thomas May, Chester, and Gregory King, Rouge Dragon, in Trinity Vacacon, 1682* (Exeter, 1883) , pp. 11–12; *Victoria History of the Counties of England—Worcestershire* (London, 1924) , 4:156.

9. Nash, vol. 2, App.

10. John Amphlett, ed., *The Churchwardens' Accounts of St. Michael's in Bedwardine, Worcester, from 1559–1603* (Worcester, Eng., 1896) contains a valuable monograph by Amphlett on the duties of Worcestershire churchwardens.

11. Tate, pp. 13–25, 243–50.

12. Ibid., p. 17, and passim.

13. Worcestershire County Archives, Worcester, Eng. Documents from the adjacent hamlets of Eckington and Birlingham provide a fair picture of the operations of a court baron, notable being the 1628 view of frankpledge with Court Baron of Francis Hanford, Manor of West Green Comberton and Birlingham (BA950 / 705 / 154) , a similar view of frankpledge for 1633–35 (BA950 / 705 / 164) , and an abstract of Orders at Court Leetes for 1640 (BA950 / 705 / 173) .

14. J. H. Gleason, *The Justices of the Peace in England, 1558–1640* (Oxford, 1969) pp. 47–67, and passim.

15. C. H. Karraker, *The Seventeenth Century Sheriff: A Comparative Study of England and the Chesapeake Colonies, 1607–1689* (Chapel Hill, N.C., 1930) , pp. 24–28, and passim.

16. Philip Alexander Bruce, *Institutional History of Virginia in the Seventeenth Century*, 1:15.

17. Ibid., 1:484–96.

18. Annie L. Jester, comp. and ed., in collaboration with Martha W. Hiden, *Adventurers of Purse and Person, Virginia, 1607–1625* (Princeton, N.J., 1965) , p. 6.

19. Chester H. Brent, *The Descendants of Col. Giles Brent, Capt. George Brent, and Robert Brent, Gent.* (Ruthland, Vt., 1946) , pp. 37, 39, 42–45, 50, 56, 81, 83.

20. Ibid., pp. 56, 83.

21. Ibid., pp. 39, 43.

22. Northumberland County Patent Book no. 4, 25 Mar. 1656, Virginia State Library,

Richmond, shows a patent of 900 acres in Northumberland County, but the headrights are omitted. The blank space between this patent and the succeeding one would indicate that the clerk intended to fill in the names subsequent to the recording of the patent.

23. Northumberland County Court Order Book no. 2, fol. 7, VSL.

24. Fairfax Harrison, *Landmarks of Old Prince William*, 1:37–39.

25. Westmoreland County Court Order Book no. 1, fol. 15, VSL.

26. Bruce, *Institutional History*, 2:19–21.

27. Westmoreland County Patent Book no. 3, fol. 301, VSL.

28. Louis B. Wright, *The First Gentlemen of Virginia* (San Marino, Calif., 1940), pp. 46–48.

29. The Reverend Anthony Fowke was the son of John and Dorothy (Cupper) Fowke (Horace E. Hayden, *Virginia Genealogies*, p. 744); Will of Dorothy Fowke of Gunston, 1651, Principal Probate Registry, Somerset House, London).

30. Hayden, p. 154.

31. Westmoreland O.B. no. 1, fols. 82–84; John Mercer Land Book, VSL.

32. Westmoreland O.B. no. 1, fols. 82–83, 85.

33. Stafford County Court Order Book, 1664–68, fol. 2, VSL. Stafford County was created in 1665 from the upper portion of Westmoreland County.

34. Northern Neck Proprietary of the Grants, bk. 2, fol. 33, VSL; George Harrison Sanford King, *The Register of Overwharton Parish*, p. 73.

35. Stafford O.B., fols. 9, 16, 20, 76, 87.

36. Henry R. McIlwaine, ed., *Minutes of the Council and General Court of Colonial Virginia*, pp. 205, 240.

37. Wesley Frank Craven, "Indian Policy in Early Virginia," pp. 77–79.

38. King, *Register of Overwharton Parish*, p. 173.

39. Henry R. McIlwaine and John P. Kennedy, eds., *Journals of the House of Burgesses of Virginia* [1619–1776], 6:14–19; Westmoreland O.B. no. 1, fol. 75; William Waller Hening, *The Statutes at Large*, 2:149–154.

40. Gerard Fowke to Richard Hope, 7 Sept. 1664, Richard Hope to Ann Fowke, 18 Sept. 1672, Fowke Family Papers, in possession of Mrs. Elsie Fowke Jackson, Alexandria, Va.

41. Sigismunda Mary Frances Chapman, *A History of Chapman and Alexander Families* (Richmond, 1946), pp. 47–48.

42. Stafford O.B., fols. 7, 10.

43. Wesley Frank Craven, *The Colonies in Transition, 1660–1761* (New York, 1968), pp. 125–28.

44. Thomas Mathew, "The Beginning, Progress and Conclusion of Bacons Rebellion in Virginia, in the Years 1675 and 1676," Peter Force, comp., in *Tracts and Other Papers Relating Principally to the Origin, Settlement, and Progress of the Colonies in North America*, 1, no. 8 (Washington, D.C., 1836), 12. On the identity of Thomas Mathew, see Wilcomb E. Washburn, *The Governor and the Rebel* (Chapel Hill, N.C., 1957), p. 183, 17n.

45. Washburn, pp. 24, 34–39.

46. Mathew, p. 18.

47. "The History of Bacon's and Ingram's Rebellion," in *Narratives of the Insurrections, 1675–1690*, ed. Charles M. Andrews (New York, 1915), pp. 72–73.

48. Mathew, p. 18.

49. Harrison, 1:123–5.

50. *Jour. H.B.*, 6:120, 189, 234.

51. Westmoreland O.B. no. 1, fols. 82–83.

52. King, *Register of Overwharton Parish*, pp. 173, 247.

53. *Jour. H.B.*, 6:265.

CHAPTER II   Colonel George Mason II

1. Gerard Fowke, "Colonel Gerard Fowke of Virginia and Maryland from 1651," p. 5.
2. Ibid., p. 11.
3. Philip Alexander Bruce, *Economic History of Virginia in the Seventeenth Century* (New York, 1896) , 1:375.
4. Fowke, "Colonel Gerard Fowke," p. 5; William Armstrong Crozier, *Virginia Heraldica, Being a Registry of Virginia Gentry Entitled to Coat Armor with Genealogical Notes of the Families* (Baltimore, 1965) , pp. 12, 13.
5. Charles County Wills, bk. 1, fol. 100, Maryland Hall of Records, Annapolis.
6. Westmoreland County Patent Book no. 5, pp. 437, 521.
7. Maryland Historical Society, *Archives of Maryland*, 24:325.
8. Charles County Wills, bk. 3, fol. 480.
9. George Harrison Sanford King, "Notes from the Journal of John Mercer, Esquire (1704 / 5–1768) of Marlborough, Stafford County, Virginia," pp. 99–109. King, *Register of Overwharton Parish*, p. 248.
10. *Archives of Maryland*, 15:403.
11. Charles Campbell, *History of the Colony and Ancient Dominion of Virginia* (Philadelphia, 1860) , pp. 274–75; John T. Scharf, *History of Maryland*, 1:410.
12. Robert Beverley, *The History and Present State of Virginia*, ed. Louis B. Wright (Chapel Hill, N.C., 1947) , p. 94.
13. Bruce, *Economic History*, 1:401, 402; Campbell, pp. 332, 333.
14. Harrison, 1:129–30.
15. Richard B. Morris, ed., *Encyclopedia of American History* (New York, 1953) , p. 6.
16. Scharf, *History of Maryland*, 1:310, 315–18, and passim.
17. *Jour. H.B.*, 6:288–90, 310; Henry R. McIlwaine, ed., *Legislative Journals of the Council of Colonial Virginia*, 1:519.
18. Kate Mason Rowland, *The Life of George Mason 1725–1792* (New York, 1892) , 1:19.
19. *Archives of Maryland*, 8:93.
20. Michael G. Hall, *The Glorious Revolution in America* (Chapel Hill, N.C., 1964) , pp. 143–46; Michael G. Kammer, "The Causes of the Maryland Revolution of 1689," pp. 293–333; Bruce E. Steiner, "The Royal Province of Maryland in 1692," pp. 123–68.
21. Richard Beale Davis, ed., *William Fitzhugh and His Chesapeake World 1676–1701*, p. 286; Harrison, 1:132–33.
22. Davis, pp. 284–88, 294–95.
23. *Jour. H.B.*, 6:334–35.
24. Davis, p. 287.
25. Stafford O.B., 6 Oct. 1691, 13 Dec. 1692, 6 April 1693; Bruce E. Steiner, "The Catholic Brents of Colonial Virginia," pp. 387–409.
26. Davis, pp. 296–99; Stafford County Court Records, p. 311, VSL.
27. *Leg. Jour. Council*, 302 ff.; N.N. bk. 2, fol. 33.
28. Hening, 2:469, 498.
29. Harrison, 1:80.
30. Henry R. McIlwaine and Wilmer L. Hall, eds., *Executive Journals of the Council of Colonial Virginia*, 1:206.
31. Stafford O.B., 22 Dec. 1691 and 9 Mar. 1691 / 92.
32. Ibid., 11 Mar. 1691 / 92, 9 Oct. 1691, 13 Nov. 1691.
33. *Exec. Jour. Council*, 1:278–79; *Jour. H.B.*, 6:405.
34. *Leg. Jour. Council*, 3:1508.
35. *Jour. H.B.*, 7:3, 6, 12; *Leg. Jour. Council*, 1:214; *Jour. H.B.*, 7:14, 17–18.
36. *Exec. Jour. Council*, 1:347; *Jour. H.B.*, 7:65, 69, 73, 76.
37. *Archives of Maryland*, 8:270.

38. Ibid., 23:182–84, 226.

39. *Exec. Jour. Council,* 1:368–69; *Jour. H.B.,* 7:105–6, 109.

40. Harrison, 1:96–97; *Archives of Maryland,* 23:295.

41. *Jour. H.B.,* 8, 123, 159, 191; *Leg. Jour. Council,* 3:1517; Harrison, 1:97; *Jour. H.B.,* 8, 158–59, 191.

42. *Exec. Jour. Council,* 1:445, 2:10, 56.

43. Mason to Nicholson, 15 June 1700, C.O. 5 / 1312, fol. 17, Public Record Office, London.

44. Mason to Nicholson, 18 June 1700, C.O. 5 / 1312, fol. 8, PRO.

45. Nicholson to Mason, 2 July 1700, C.O. 5 / 1312, fol. 18, PRO.

46. Mason to Nicholson, 18 July 1700, C.O. 5 / 1312, fol. 19, PRO.

47. Ibid., 17 Aug. 1700, fol. 70, PRO.

48. Ibid., 20 July 1700, fol. 20; Nicholson to Mason, 23 Aug. 1700, C.O. 5 / 1312, fol. 72, PRO.

49. *Exec. Jour. Council,* 2:104, 113, 125; *Leg. Jour. Council,* 1:290; *Jour. H.B.,* 8:239–40.

50. C.O. 5 / 1312, fol. 261, PRO.

51. Rowland, *Mason,* 1:376.

52. *Exec. Jour. Council,* 2:357, 389, 404–5; *Jour. H.B.,* 8:275, 9:171, 178, 244.

53. Warren M. Billings, "The Causes of Bacon's Rebellion: Some Suggestions," pp. 409–35; Bernard Bailyn, "Politics and Social Structure in Colonial Virginia," in James Morton Smith, ed., *Seventeenth-Century America: Essays in Colonial History* (Chapel Hill, N.C., 1959), pp. 90–115.

54. Harrison, 1:45–46.

55. Stafford O.B., 8 Oct. 1691; N.N., bk. 2, fols. 33 and 58.

56. Stafford O.B., 10 Feb. 1692–93.

57. *Leg. Jour. Council,* 3:1508; Stafford O.B., 10 Feb. 1692–93 and 18 May 1693.

58. N.N., bk. 2, fol. 33; Mercer Land Book, fols. 103–4. This was a deed of gift to Thomas and Mary Barbee, son and daughter of Andrew Barbee, deceased.

59. Avery O. Craven, *Soil Exhaustion as a Factor in the Agricultural History of Virginia and Maryland 1606–1860,* p. 57.

60. Bruce, *Economic History,* 1:410; ibid., pp. 402–3, 407–8; Davis, p. 254.

61. Davis, pp. 303–4, 308.

62. Stafford County Deed Book W–Z, fol. 203, VSL.

63. Harrison, 2:360–62.

64. Hening, 3:53; Stafford O.B., 10 June 1691, 13 Nov. 1691, 9 Oct. 1691.

65. Stafford O.B., 9 Oct. 1691; Mercer Land Book, fol. 28; Malcolm C. Watkins, *The Cultural History of Marlborough, Virginia,* Smithsonian Institution Bulletin no. 253 (Washington, D.C., 1968), p. 12. George Mason to William Robinson, 14 Apr. 1708, Stafford D.B., W–Z, fol. 407; Mercer Land Book, fol. 36.

66. Hening, 3:108.

67. Ibid., p. 404; William P. Palmer, ed., *Calendar of Virginia State Papers . . .* [1652–1869], 1:137–38.

68. George Larkin to the Board of Trade and Plantations, 22 Dec. 1700, C.O. 5 / 1312, fol. 91, PRO.

69. Wesley F. Craven, *The Southern Colonies in the Seventeenth Century, 1607–1689* (Baton Rouge, La., 1949), pp. 400–401.

70. Davis, p. 20; Harrison, 1:168–69; Nicholson to the Board of Trade and Plantations, 22 Sept. 1705, C.O. 5 / 1314, p. 66; C.O. 5 / 1441, p. 361, PRO.

71. *Jour. H.B.,* 9:257–58, 264.

72. Campbell, p. 383.

73. William Byrd, *The Secret Diary of William Byrd of Westover, 1709–1712,* ed. Louis B. Wright and trans. Marion Tingling (Richmond, 1941), p. 263.

74. King, *Register of Overwharton Parish,* p. 180.

75. N.N., bk. 5, fol. 43; Harrison, 1:285.

76. Mason to Nicholson, 21 Oct. 1704, C.O. 5 / 1314, fol. 476, PRO. The Reverend John Frazier was rector of Overwharton Parish in 1702, which ran from Potomac Creek up river to the limits of settlement (C.O. 5 / 1312, fol. 187, PRO).

77. Two copies of this will are extant, in the Mercer Land Book, pp. 248–251 and in the Fairfax County Land Causes, Book no. 1, 1812–1832 [13–15], VSL. The original has been lost. The existence of a will in Stafford County as late as 1845 made by a George Mason, who made bequests to his wife Mary and his sisters Margaret Bennett and Ann French Mason, remains a puzzle to genealogists (Rowland, *Mason,* 1:376); Prince William County Deed Book A, fols. 280–81, VSL; "Field Notes upon a Survey Made of Dogues Neck, February 1754," Ms. Div., Library of Congress.

78. "The Fitzhugh Family," pp. 317–19.

79. R. A. Brock, ed., *The Official Records of Robert Dinwiddie,* 1:xxiii; Hayden, p. 534. Elizabeth Mason married William Roy (Rowland, *Mason,* 1:30). Catherine Mason married John Mercer of Marlborough (James Mercer Garnett, "James Mercer," p. 85).

80. Mercer Land Book, fol. 252. The implication of this will is that George Mason died after 29 Jan. 1715 / 16 and before 13 Feb. 1715 / 16.

81. Prince William D.B. B, fols. 485–88.

Chapter III Colonel George Mason III

1. Stafford D.B. W–Z, fol. 390.

2. *Exec. Jour. Council,* 3:338, 371, 420. The original commission is in Gunston Hall Library.

3. *Jour. H.B.,* 4:121, 123, 127, 147.

4. Hugh Jones, *The Present State of Virginia,* pp. 66–71.

5. John Fontaine's journal of the expedition over the mountains has but a solitary reference to Colonel Mason, who kept the party at Germanna on their return homeward (Ann Fontaine Maury, *Memoirs of a Huguenot Family* [New York, 1853], p. 268). Their quest was the subject of a Latin poem, *Expeditio Ultramontana,* of which John Mercer of Marlbourough possessed a copy in 1726 (Earl G. Swem, ed., *Mr. Blackamore's Expeditio Ultramontana Rendered into English Verse by the Reverend Mr. George Seagood* [Richmond, 1960]); John Mercer Ledger, bk. 8, fol. 20.

6. Harrison, 1:224.

7. Harrison, 1:107, 223–26; Edmund Bailey O'Callaghan, ed., *Documents Relative to the Colonial History of the State of New York* (Albany, 1846), 5:637–39; Rowland, *Mason,* 1:36.

8. *Jour. H.B.,* 4:205–6, 226, 251, 258, 361.

9. Watkins, p. 14; *Jour. H.B.,* 4:336, 373.

10. *Jour. H. B.,* 4:408.

11. The tradition that George Mason III was married earlier and left no children by his first wife is cited in Rowland, *Mason,* 1:39.

12. Nicholson to Board of Trade, 31 May 1704, C.O. 5 / 1314, fols. 106–7; C.O. 5 / 1313, fols. 128, 130; C.O. 5/1360, fols. 369–97, PRO. Photocopies, GHL.

13. Marriage license dated 5 May 1665, Saint Mary Magdalene Bermondsey, County Surry, Eng. P.C.C. Mason File. Mary Stephens (or Stevens) came from a family of landowners in the parish of Broadway, Worcestershire. William Stevens of Broadway, Gent., paid a fine for not accepting knighthood at the coronation of Charles I, as did William Stevens, Jr., of Broadway, gent. (R. Sydney Glazebrook, *Heraldry of Worcestershire* [London, 1873], 2:711).

14. Will of Sir William Thomson, Kt., 1696, Bond fol. 103, Principal Probate Registry, Somerset House, London, photocopy P.C.C. Mason File.

15. *Middle Temple Records,* 3:1285, 1385; *Calendar of Inner Temple Records,* 3:454;

Register of the Temple Church, London, fol. 108, MS. The burial place of Sir William Thomson in the north aisle is not marked by any stone.

16. Parish Register of Saint James, Aldgate, London.

17. C.O. 5 / 1360, fols. 403–5, PRO.

18. *Exec. Jour. Council*, 2:349.

19. *Exec. Jour. Council*, 3:372. This entry disproves the death date of Dorothea (Tanton) Thomson as 2 July 1713, as stated in "Colonial Attorney-Generals," pp. 140–41.

20. Ann Thomson Mason to John Thomson, c. 1743 (draft), Mason Papers, the Library of the College of William and Mary, Williamsburg, Va.

21. Mason Family Bible (transcript), owned by the Reverend Melvin Lee Steadman, Virginia Beach, Va.

22. Fairfax County Deed Book Q-1, fols. 249–54, VSL.

23. Bessie Wilmarth Gahn, *Original Patentees of Land at Washington Prior to 1700,* (Washington, D.C., 1936), pp. 48–49.

24. William Woodford to Col. George Mason, 25 Nov. 1723, 4 Dec. 1723, William Woodford Letter Book, Margaret I. King Library, University of Kentucky, Lexington. A memorial to William Bladen is at Saint Anne's Church, Annapolis, Md.

25. Charles County Deeds, bk. 2, fols. 341, 348, MdHR. Another 211-acre portion of Christian Temple Manor was owned by Matthew Mason, Gent., of Saint Marys County, Md., who bequeathed it to his son John Mason in his will dated 12 Feb. 1722 and probated 27 Mar. 1729. This portion of Christian Temple Manor passed into the Smallwood family of Charles County before 1732. It is now Smallwood's Retreat State Park.

26. Louis B. Wright, ed., *Letters of Robert Carter 1720–1727: The Commercial Interests of a Virginia Gentleman* (1940; reprint ed., Westport, Conn., 1970), p. 50.

27. Stafford D.B. L, fols. 47–50.

28. Prince William D.B. B, fols. 296–97.

29. Edmund Bagge Account Book, fols. 9, 50, 99, 122, Research Department, Colonial Williamsburg, Williamsburg, Va.

30. Jones, *Present State of Virginia*, pp. 77–78.

31. Arthur P. Middleton, *Tobacco Coast*, pp. 98–99, 107–8.

32. Outports are English ports other than London. Wright, *Letters of Robert Carter,* p. 5; Middleton, p. 110.

33. John Bowman to George Mason, 2 Mar. 1720, Chicago Historical Society, Chicago, Ill.; Scottish Record Society, *Burgesses and Guild Brethern of Glasgow, 1573–1750* (Edinburgh, 1911), p. 347.

34. Harrison, 2:380–84.

35. Woodford to Jonathan Forward, 27 Aug. 1728, Woodford Letter Book. Jonathan Forward had a contract for shipping convicts to the Chesapeake colonies.

36. Ebenezer Cook, *Sotweed Redivivus: Or the Planters Looking-Glass* (1730; rpt. Bernard C. Steiner, *Early Maryland Poetry*, Baltimore, 1900). Richard Lewis, *Muscipula* (Annapolis, 1728). Col. George Mason was a subscriber to this volume.

37. William Gooch Papers, transcripts in the Library of Congress and typewritten copies in the Virginia Historical Society, Richmond; Jones, *Present State of Virginia*, p. 192; Hening, 4:247.

38. Great Britain, *Calendar of State Papers, Colonial Series, America and West Indies, 1732,* pp. 97–99; Harrison, 1:161–63.

39. Woodford to the Reverend John Bagge, 2 Dec. 1723, Woodford to Welch, 31 July 1725; Woodford to Mason, 2 May 1723; Woodford to Bagge, 10 May 1723; Woodford to Welch, 30 Nov. 1725, Woodford Letter Book.

40. Jones, *Present State of Virginia*, p. 77.

41. Woodford to Mason, 25 Nov. 1723, Woodford Letter Book.

42. Fairfax D.B. D-1, fol. 184.

43. *Maryland Gazette* (Annapolis), 9 Dec. 1756; Gen. John Mason to Gen. Henry Dearborn, 26 Apr. 1821, GHL.

44. Brock, *Official Records of Robert Dinwiddie,* 1:xxiii.

45. Wright, *Letters of Robert Carter,* p. 50.

46. Prince William D.B. B, fols. 457–58.

47. *Exec. Jour. Council,* 3:543–44; King George County Court Order Book, 1:226–27.

48. King George County Deed Book 1-A, p. 165; Inventory and appraisement of the Estate of John Dinwiddie, Gent., Deasd., Inventory Book 1, p. 94, King George County Circuit Court, King George, Va.

49. George Harrison Sanford King, "Copies of Extant Wills from Counties Whose Records Have Been Destroyed," pp. 51–59.

50. John Mercer's Ledger, 1725, fols. 66, 98, 27, Bucks County Historical Society, Doylestown, Pa.

51. Ibid., fol. 10. John Mercer represented William Eilbeck in a series of legal actions in 1731–32.

52. Joseph Aderton and Peter How to William Eilbeck, 23 Sept. 1725. Dawson family papers, privately owned, microcopy in Mason Papers, LC.

53. C.O. 5 / 1442 / 14 and 26, PRO.

54. Araby was purchased in 1935 by Admiral and Mrs. Frank Jack Fletcher. Charles County Deeds, bk. O, no. 2, fol. 75; Charles County Debt Books, 1753, fol. 20, MdHR. Annapolis.

55. Mercer's Ledger, 1725, fols. 10, 20, 93, and 114. Edmund Bagge Account Book, fol. 55.

56. Mercer's Ledger, 1725, fol. 91.

57. Lois Mulkearn, ed., *George Mercer Papers,* pp. 204–5; letter from Trinity College Library, Dublin, 9 June 1971, P.C.C. Mason File.

58. Charles County Accounts, bk. 18, fol. 37, MdHR.

59. Charles County Inventories, bk. 21, fols. 90–91, MdHR.

60. Prince William County Will Book C, 1734–44, pp. 49–50, VSL.

61. Ibid., pp. 112–13.

62. George Harrison Sanford King, "John Mercer," p. 101.

63. Prince William County Will Book C, 1734–44, pp. 275–90, 374.

64. William Meade, *Old Churches, Ministers, and Families of Virginia,* 1:258; Richard Hewitt to the Bishop of London, Warwick County, 29 July 1725, Correspondence of the Bishop of London, 1679–1771, Church Commissioners for England, Fulham Palace Papers 14.

65. Prince William County Will Book C, 1734–44, fols. 275–90.

66. Susanne Hening Neale, "Charles Bridges, Painter and Humanitarian" (M.A. Thesis, College of William and Mary, 1969).

67. Prince William County Will Book C, 1734–44, p. 40.

68. Watkins, p. 24.

69. *Exec. Jour. Council,* 4:328.

70. Mercer's Ledger, 1730.

71. Mulkearn, *George Mercer Papers,* pp. 200–201.

72. Meade, 2:197–201; Brent, p. 101.

73. Hayden, pp. 151–54, 696–99.

74. Meade, 2:207–15.

75. Hester D. Richardson, *Side-Lights on Maryland History* (Baltimore, 1913), 2:118.

76. Hayden, p. 697.

77. Harrison, 2:395.

78. Advertisements in *Md. Gaz.* (Annapolis) 1729–70 and *Virginia Gazette* (Williamsburg) 1737–69.

79. Letter of Richard Dell, city archivist of the Corporation, Glasgow City Archives Office, 22 Jan. 1973, P.C.C. Mason File.

80. Account of William Hunt, Bank of England, London, 1733–42, P.C.C. Mason File.

81. Charles County Patent Book E-1, no. 2, fol. 754 and bk. G.B., fol. 194, Charles County Debt Books, 1753, fol. 69, MdHR.

82. Mercer Land Book, fols. 233–37.

83. Prince William County Will Book C, 1734–44, pp. 49–50, 275–90, 367–73.

84. C.O. 5 / 1322, fol. 383, PRO.

85. Rufus Jones, *The Quakers in the American Colonies* (New York, 1966) , p. 296.

86. Harrison, 1:239–49; Prince William D.B. D, fols. 9–16, 16–20.

87. Mercer Land Book, fol. 187.

88. Fairfax D.B. D-1, fols. 266–69.

89. Ibid., fols. 408–14, 422–424. Transcript of Bible records from the Rev. Melvin Lee Steadman, Virginia Beach, Va.

90. Ann Thomson Mason to John Thomson (draft) , c. 1743, Mason Papers, W&M.

91. Ann Thomson Mason to Haswell and Hunt (draft) , c. 1743, ibid.

92. The will of the Honorable Sir William Thomson was proved at London with two codicils on 21 Jan. 1742 / 43. John Thomson was one of the two executors.

93. Will of Ann Thomson Mason, Stafford D.B. O (Wills) , fols. 433–39.

94. *Md. Gaz.* (Annapolis) 23 Dec. 1762.

95. Inventory, Stafford D.B. O (Wills) , fols. 433–56.

Chapter IV   George Mason IV, Country Gentleman

1. Rowland, *Mason*, 1:57, 70, 104–5.

2. Fairfax D.B. A-1, fols. 382–83, B-1, fols. 331–33, 358–62, T-1, fols. 234–39; Prince William D.B. B, fols. 457–58, P, fol. 299; Fairfax Minute Book, 1749–56, fols. 18 and 182, VSL.

3. Will of Ann Thomson Mason, Stafford County Deed Book O (Wills) , fols. 433–39.

4. Will of French Mason, Fairfax County Will Book A-1, fols. 456–57, VSL.

5. George Mason to George Washington, 6 May 1758, Washington Papers, LC. French Mason was killed by his slaves in 1769 (*WMQ*, 2d ser., 13[1933]:59) .

6. King, "Copies of Extant Wills," pp. 59, 63–64.

7. Hayden, p. 534.

8. Will of George Mason IV, Fairfax County Will Book F, no. 1.

9. Meade, 2:200; King, "John Mercer," p. 107.

10. Vestry Records of Truro Parish, LC.

11. Mercer's ledger, fol. 108.

12. Hayden, p. 164.

13. Gosforth Parish Register, Cumberland, England. Daniel Hay, librarian, Whitehaven Public Library, established the identity of William Eilbeck through very extensive researches in West Cumberland.

14. Prince Georges County Wills, bk. 20, fol. 156, MdHR.

15. Durham Church Records, MdHR.

16. Louise Joyner Hienton, "Prince George's County, Md., Piscataway or St. Johns Parish (now called King Georges Parish) , Index to Register 1689–1878," typescript (Hyattsville, Md., 1961) , p. ii. M.H.S.

17. Will of John Edgar, 10 Nov. 1736, proved 22 Nov. 1736, Prince Georges County Wills, bk. 21, fol. 133.

18. Charles County Inventories, bk. 90, fols. 60–66; bk. 58, fols. 202–9.

19. "Economic Behavior in a Planting Society: The Eighteenth Century Chesapeake," pp. 471–73.

20. Mulkearn, *Mercer Papers*, pp. 4, 6, 170.

21. "Virginia Gazette Extracts," pp. 74–75.

22. Marquis François Jean de Chastellux, *Travels in North America in the Years 1780, 1781, and 1783* (London, 1787) .

23. King, "John Mercer," p. 109.

24. Rowland, *Mason*, 1:67.

25. Matriculation Records of the College of William and Mary.

26. Student's Ledger, The Library, Middle Temple, London, photocopy, P.C.C. Mason File.

27. Middleton, pp. 130–31.

28. Royle's *Va. Gaz.* (Williamsburg) 29 Aug. 1751.

29. Mason Family Bible, GHL.

30. "Field Notes upon a Survey of Dogue's Neck, 1754," LC, photocopy GHL.

31. Beirne and Scarff, pp. 11, 1, 4.

32. Mason Family Bible, GHL.

33. Watkins, p. 50.

34. George Mason to Alexander Henderson, 18 July 1763, GHL.

35. Melvin Lee Steadman, Jr., *Falls Church by Fence and Fireside* (Falls Church, Va., 1964), p. 22.

36. Truro Parish Records, LC.

37. Robert A. Rutland, ed., *The Papers of George Mason, 1725–1792*, 1:37.

38. Beirne and Scarff, pp. 37, 143.

39. Beverley, p. 290.

40. [Durand of Dauphiné], *A Frenchman in Virginia, Being the Memoirs of a Huguenot Refugee, 1686*, trans. "A Virginian" [Fairfax Harrison] (Richmond, 1923).

41. Rowland, *Mason*, 1:99–100.

42. King, "Extant Wills," p. 60.

43. Mason-Steadman Papers, P.C.C. Mason File; Rowland, *Mason*, 1:67.

44. King, "John Mercer," pp. 103, 155.

45. Will of Sarah Edgar Eilbeck, Charles County, Md., Will Book AF no. 7, fol. 583. MdHR.

46. Rutland, *Mason Papers*, 1:480–81; John Lee (1709–1789) was the son of Hancock and Sarah (Allerton) Lee.

47. John Fitzpatrick, ed., *Diaries of George Washington, 1784–1799*, 1:145–47, 199–200, 210.

48. Brooke Hindle, *The Pursuit of Science in Revolutionary America, 1735–1789* (Chapel Hill, N.C., 1956), pp. 197–98.

49. George Mason, "Subscription for Maurice Pound," Miscl. Collection, Historical Society of Pennsylvania, Philadelphia.

50. George Washington Account Books, ledger A, fol. 100, Research Library, Mount Vernon, Va.

51. George William Fairfax to Thomas Fairfax, n.d. (c. 1716), Fairfax of Cameron Papers, Gay's House, Holyport, Berkshire, England.

52. Purdie and Dixon's *Va. Gaz.* (Williamsburg) 2 Sept. 1773; Rind's *Va. Gaz.* (Williamsburg) 27 May 1773; Bolling to Pleasants, 29 Nov. 1774, Brock Collection, box 12, Henry E. Huntington Library, San Marʾ.no, Calif.; Pleasants Letter Book, 1, fol. 33, and passim, Friends Historical Library, Haverford College, Haverford, Pa.

53. Robert Bolling, "The Vintage of Parnassus, or little Poems intended to attract a stronger public attention to vine planting in Virginia," 1772, Brock Collection, box 64; Purdie and Dixon's *Va. Gaz.* (Williamsburg) 18 Mar. 1773.

54. Purdie and Dixon's *Va. Gaz.* (Williamsburg) 25 Feb. 1773, 11 Mar. 1773; Rind's *Va. Gaz.* (Williamsburg) 16 Sept. 1773.

55. Rind's *Va. Gaz.* (Williamsburg) 28 July 1774; Julian P. Boyd et al., eds., *The Papers of Thomas Jefferson*, 1:156–59.

56. Dixon and Hunter's *Va. Gaz.* (Williamsburg) 9 Sept. 1775; Philip Mazzei to John Page, 11 Jan. 1777, 24 May 1778, Ms. Div., New York Public Library, New York, N.Y.; Rind's *Va. Gaz.* (Williamsburg) 27 May 1773.

57. Rutland, *Mason Papers*, 1:130–31.

58. Fitzpatrick, *Washington Diaries*, 1:135; Purdie and Dixon's *Va. Gaz.* (Williams-

burg) 22 Jan. 1767; Paul Haworth, *George Washington, the Farmer* (Indianapolis, 1915) , pp. 94–97; *Md. Gaz.* (Annapolis) 8 July 1773.

59. Jennifer and Hooe Account Book, fols. 102, 106, NYPL. The deed from George Mason to George Mason, Jr., for the Lexington plantation described the land as in the son's possession for the previous two years, i.e., 1774–76 (Fairfax D.B. M-1, fols. 236–39) . Only by careful study of documents can one be certain which George Mason, Jr., is being referred to.

60. Rowland, *Mason,* 1:101.

61. William Fitzhugh to George Mason, 12 July 1768, Rutland, *Mason Papers,* 1:92.

62. Rowland, *Mason,* 1:100–101.

63. Mason Family Bible, GHL.

64. Martha Sprigg Poole, "Tudor Hall and Those Who Lived There," pp. 257–77.

65. *Jour. H.B.,* 8:80, 123–24.

66. *Jour. H.B.,* 8:7–8.

67. Joseph Albert Ernst, "Genesis of the Currency Act of 1764," pp. 1–27.

68. *Jour. H.B.,* 8:5, 12, 21, 24, 50.

69. Rowland, *Mason,* 1:73–75.

70. *Jour. H.B.,* 8:80, 123–24.

71. *Md. Gaz.* (Annapolis) 17 July 1760, 20 Aug. 1761.

72. Fitzpatrick, *Washington Diaries,* 2:143; Elswyth Thane, *Potomac Squire* (New York, 1963) , p. 65.

73. *Md. Gaz.* (Annapolis) , 27 Sept. 1764, 1 May 1766; Provincial Court Judgments 1761–62, bk. DD no. 2, fol. 94, MdHR.

74. Rowland, "Maryland Delegates"; Poole, "Tudor Hall."

75. John M. Jordon to Robert Carter, 27 Apr. 1762, Carter Papers, Duke University Library, Durham, N.C.; Purdie and Dixon's *Va. Gaz.* (Williamsburg) 28 Mar. 1766, 28 Dec. 1769; *Archives of Maryland,* 14:132–33, 31:545; Rowland, "Maryland Delegates."

76. Barnes and Ridgate advertised slaves from Africa *Md. Gaz.* (Annapolis) 23 Aug. 1770. Osgood Hanbury was represented by Barnes and Ridgate (ibid., 25 July 1771) . Osgood Hanbury was a Quaker.

77. *Md. Gaz.* (Annapolis) 1 July 1762, 29 July 1762.

78. Ibid., 19 Feb. 1761, 29 Oct. 1761, 21 June 1764. On 9 Aug. 1764 Thomson Mason drew a bill of exchange from "Maryland" on James Gildart of Liverpool in favor of Alexander McFarlane (C. E. French Collection, Massachusetts Historical Society, Boston) .

79. Mason-Steadman Papers, P.C.C. Mason File.

80. Rind's *Va. Gaz.* (Williamsburg) 22 Sept. 1768.

81. Cockburn Papers, fol. 10, LC.

82. Miscellaneous Petition 266A, VSL.

83. *Jour. H.B.,* 10:163, 10:115–16, 10:126–29.

84. Charles J. Stille, *Life and Times of John Dickinson* (Philadelphia, 1891) , pp. 21–34.

85. Rind's *Va. Gaz.* (Williamsburg) 9 Nov. 1769.

86. Purdie and Dixon's *Va. Gaz.* (Williamsburg) 24 May 1770.

87. Rind's *Va. Gaz.* (Williamsburg) 16 June 1774.

88. Harrison Williams, *Legends of Loudoun* (Richmond, 1938) , pp. 76–77, 102–3.

89. Rind's *Va. Gaz.* (Williamsburg) 31 Oct. 1771.

90. Purdie and Dixon's *Va. Gaz.* (Williamsburg) 22 Sept. 1773; Pinkney's *Va. Gaz.* (Williamsburg) 16 Feb. 1775.

91. Rutland, *Mason Papers,* 1:99.

92. Hayden, pp. 622, 623.

93. Fitzpatrick, *Washington Diaries,* 1:373.

94. Jack P. Greene, ed., The Diary of Colonel Landon Carter, 1752–1787, 2:807.

95. Rowland, *Mason,* 1:97.

96. Mason Family Bible, GHL.

97. Rowland, *Mason*, 1:163.

98. Rutland, *Mason Papers*, 1:433.

Chapter V   George Mason IV, Internal Improvements

1. Purdie and Dixon's *Va. Gaz.* (Williamsburg) 23 Apr. 1772; *Jour. H.B.*, 11:252, 292, 297, 310.

2. *Scots Magazine*, 1767.

3. John Semple, "Proposals," George Washington Papers, Minnesota Historical Society, Saint Paul.

4. *Jour. H.B.*, 10:214, 334; Richard Henry Lee to William Lee, 17 Dec. 1769, Lee Papers, VHS.

5. *Jour. H.B.*, 11:252, 292, 297, 310; Purdie and Dixon's *Va. Gaz.* (Williamsburg) 23 Apr. 1772.

6. George Armroyd, *A Connected View of the Whole Internal Navigation of the United States* (Philadelphia, 1830), p. 209; Thomas Johnson to George Washington, 10 May 1772, Washington Papers, LC.

7. *Md. Gaz.* (Annapolis), 3 Nov. 1774; Rind's *Va. Gaz.* (Williambsurg) 28 Nov. 1774; *Md. Gaz.* (Annapolis), 12 Jan. 1775; Dixon's *Va. Gaz.* (Williamsburg) 7 Jan. 1775.

8. George Mason to George Washington, 9 Mar. 1775, Washington Papers, LC; *Jour. H.B.*, 12:181; Pinkney's *Va. Gaz.* (Williamsburg) 26 Oct. 1775; Hening, 11:510.

9. Thomas Johnson to George Washington, 25 Feb. 1775, Washington Papers, LC; ibid., 24 Jan. 1775.

10. George Mason to George Washington, 17 Feb. 1775, Washington Papers, LC.

11. Ibid., 9 Mar. 1775; *Jour. H.B.*, 12:181; Pinkney's *Va. Gaz.* (Williamsburg) 26 Oct. 1775.

12. Hening, 11:510; Alexander Henderson to George Washington, 11 Jan. 1785, Washington Papers, LC.

13. Alfred P. James, *The Ohio Company*, pp. 128–29, 177–83.

14. Harrison, 2:618.

15. *Exec. Jour. Council*, 5:195.

16. James, p. 10; Kenneth P. Bailey, *The Ohio Company of Virginia and the Westward Movement* (Glendale, Calif., 1939), p. 297.

17. Mulkearn, *Mercer Papers*, p. 2.

18. Ibid., pp. 3, 464, 20n; James, p. 15.

19. James, pp. 24–25, 29; Mulkearn, *Mercer Papers*, p. 173.

20. *Exec. Jour. Council*, 5:295; Bailey, p. 67.

21. Mulkearn, *Mercer Papers*, p. 4; William A. Hunter, *Forts on the Pennsylvania Frontier, 1773–1758* pp. 39–42.

22. Thomas Lee to Governor Hamilton, 22 Nov. 1744, Lee Papers, University of Virginia Library, Charlottesville.

23. Lawrence Henry Gipson, *Lewis Evans* (Philadelphia, 1939), pp. 33–38.

24. Mulkearn, *Mercer Papers*, pp. 142, 171; N.N., bk. H, fols. 507–11, bk. P, fol. 185; James, p. 104.

25. George Washington to Lawrence Washington, 27 May 1750, National Park Service, Morristown National Historical Park, Morristown, N.J.; James, pp. 36 ff. 113; Bailey, pp. 320–27.

26. Mulkearn, *Mercer Papers*, p. 171.

27. N.N., bk. H, fols. 507–11; James, p. 104; N.N., bk. P, fol. 185.

28. Mulkearn, *Mercer Papers*, p. 7.

29. James, pp. 205–19.

30. Mulkearn, *Mercer Papers,* pp. 142–43.

31. Ibid., pp. 54–55, 66, 134.

32. James, pp. 55–76.

33. Rutland, *Mason Papers,* 1:28–31; Mulkearn, *Mercer Papers,* pp. 147–48.

34. Mulkearn, *Mercer Papers,* pp. 149–50, 172.

35. Ibid., pp. 174–75.

36. Hunter, pp. 44–60.

37. Ibid., pp. 128–67.

38. James, p. 111.

39. Ibid., pp. 115–18; Mulkearn, *Mercer Papers,* p. 359 (fac. 29) .

40. *Archives of Maryland,* 25:141–42, 619–20.

41. *Md. Gaz.* (Annapolis) , 28 July 1757.

42. *Md. Gaz.* (Annapolis) , 18 Jan. 1759, 10 Apr. 1760, 16 Aug. 1770, 19 Aug. 1762, 12 July 1764, 21 Aug. 1766. The firm was known as Stewart and Campbell after Duncan Campbell became a partner.

43. James, pp. 118–20, 125.

44. Ibid., pp. 236–39.

45. James, pp. 182–83, 291–93.

46. Mulkearn, *Mercer Papers,* pp. 181, 452; *Md. Gaz.* (Annapolis) , 17 Feb., 16 June 1763.

47. Ibid., pp. 29, 359.

48. *Md. Gaz.* (Annapolis) 14, 21, 28 July 1763.

49. Francis Parkman, *The Conspiracy of Pontiac* (New York, 1966) , pp. 290–319; James, pp. 128–29.

50. Henry S. Commager, ed., *Documents of American History* (New York, 1963) , pp. 47–50.

51. James, pp. 128–29.

52. Thomas P. Abernethy, *Western Lands,* pp. 25–29, 40–47.

53. *Md. Gaz.* (Annapolis) 12 Mar., 30 Apr. 1772; James, pp. 155, 265–66.

54. Rutland, *Mason Papers,* pp. 217–19.

55. James, p. 339; George Mason to John Francis Mercer, 1 May 1788, P.C.C. Mason File.

56. Brock, 2:96; John C. Fitzpatrick, *Writings of George Washington,* 2:467–71; Mulkearn, *Mercer Papers,* pp. 611–12.

57. Bailey, p. 274; James, p. 153.

58. George Mason, "Memorial of the Ohio Company," 20 Nov. 1778, Miscellaneous Petitions, 266 A. VSL.

59. James Scott, his certificate for the Importation of fifty-nine persons, Prince William County Court, June 5, 1773, Brock Collection, BR Box 78.

60. "1773, December 6th John Graham's Certificate of Rights for Importation of 85 persons and Assignment to Geo. Mason," Brock Collection, BR Box 78.

61. Bruce, *Economic History,* 1:512–26.

62. Fairfax County Minute Book, 1772–74, fols. 231, 238, VSL.

63. St. George L. Sioussat, "The Breakdown of the Royal Management of Lands in the Southern Provinces, 1773–1775," pp. 67–98; see also Boyd et al., *Jefferson Papers,* 1:115n.

64. C. Herbert Laub, "British Regulation of Crown Lands in the West," pp. 52–55.

65. Rutland, *Mason Papers,* 1:182.

66. George E. Lewis, *The Indiana Company* (Glendale, Calif., 1941) , pp. 127–42; Morris, *Encylcopedia of American History,* pp. 81–82.

67. Abernethy, pp. 101–12; *Exec. Jour. Council,* 6:562.

68. "March 11, 1774, Mr. Cumberland Willson's Certificate of Rights for Importation of 40 persons + Assignment to Geo: Mason," "March 11, 1774 Alexander Campbell's Certificate of Rights for Importation of 41 persons + Assignment to Geo: Mason," Brock Collection, BR Box 78.

69. *Exec. Jour. Council,* 6:562.

70. "May 1774. Thomas Smith Certificate and Affidavit of the Importation of 137 persons from Great Britain and Assignment thereof to William Harrison his Assignment to G. Mason," Brock Collection, BR Box 78.

71. "Petition of George Mason for Warrants for Lands in Fincastle County (June 1774)," Boyd et al., *Jefferson Papers,* 1:112–15; Rowland, *Mason,* 1:415–18; Rutland, *Mason Papers,* 1:193–96.

72. *Exec. Jour. Council,* 6:578.

73. Brock Collection, BR Box 78.

74. Samuel M. Wilson, *The Ohio Company of Virginia, 1748–1798* (Lexington, Ky., 1926), pp. 29–39; James, pp. 150–63; Bailey, pp. 274–75; Abernethy, p. 128.

75. Rutland, *Mason Papers,* 1:263–64.

76. Abernethy, pp. 133, 224.

77. Rutland, *Mason Papers,* 1:399–408, 424; James, p. 166.

78. George Mason, "Memorial of the Ohio Company."

79. Petition of the Reverend James Scott, 21 May 1778, Prince William County Legislative Petitions, VSL.

80. Boyd et al., *Jefferson Papers,* 2:249–52.

81. Hening, 10:35–50.

82. Hening, 10:50–65.

83. Abernethy, p. 224.

84. Hening, 10:50–65.

85. George Mason to Richard Henry Lee, 19 June 1779, Lee Papers, UVa.

86. Lewis, pp. 215–22.

87. Mason to Lee, 19 June 1779, Lee Papers, UVa. Rowland, *Mason,* 1:333–36.

88. Hugh O. Potter, *In the Beginning,* pp. 6–17.

89. George Mason to John Harvie, 10 Dec. 1785, Brock Collection, BR Box 78.

90. George Mason to George Muter, 28 Sept. 1785, Mason Papers, LC.

91. Fairfax D.B. 10–1, fols. 191–98. The same deed is filed in Daviess County Deeds, bk. A, fols. 210–18, Daviess County Courthouse, Owensboro, Ky.

Chapter VI   George Mason IV, Plantation Economy

1. Hening, 6:214; Harrison, 2:670–75.

2. *Archives of Maryland,* 22:345.

3. The Dumfries board in 1761 was composed of John Baylis, William Carr, John Champe, James Douglas, Thomas Lawson, Henry Lee, Richard Henry Lee, Allan Macrae, the Reverend John Moncure, Henry Peyton, the Reverend James Scott, John Tayloe, Foushee Tebbs, and Presley Thornton (Harrison, 2:663). Besides the clergymen, Tayloe, Thornton, and Lawson were partners in the Neabsco ironworks; Tayloe and Thornton were partners in the Occoquan ironworks; and Carr, Douglass, and Macrae were Scottish merchants. In addition, all the members of the group were large-scale landowners. Tayloe, Thornton, Scott, and Richard Lee were members of the Ohio Company; Thornton and Richard Henry Lee belonged to the Mississippi Company. Of such were the town boards of trustees.

4. Minute Book of Alexandria Trustees, Alexandria City Hall Archives, Alexandria, Va.; Hening, 10:172.

5. Fairfax D.B. C-1, fols. 296–97.

6. Ibid., bk. E-1, fols. 102–9. Richard Arell was licensed by Fairfax County Court in 1768 to keep an ordinary at Alexandria. The license was renewed in 1769 and thereafter until 1773 (Fairfax County Court Order Books, 1768–70, fols. 53, 243, 128, and 303, 1772–74, fols. 141 and 291). There are many references to Richard Arell's tavern in the diaries

of George Washington. The most interesting is the entry for July 5, 1774, when the Fairfax Resolves, written by George Mason, were adopted, and Washington and the others repaired to Arell's for supper (Fitzpatrick, *Washington Diaries*, 1:284, 301, 2:34, 41, 43, 61, 75, 79, 80, 139, 156, 169.

7. Fairfax D.B. D-1 fols. 313–14; bk. E-1, fols. 210–17.

8. *Md. Gaz.* (Annapolis) 3 Apr. 1760. Carlyle and Dalton were business partners; Ramsay, Hunter, Muir, and Adams were also merchants. Gerard Alexander was married to a daughter of Dr. Gustavus Brown, and, like Fairfax and Mason, was primarily a landowner. George Johnson, attorney-at-law, had married a daughter of Dennis McCarty of Pohick, and William Ramsay had married her sister. George Johnston was the target of some satirical verses in the *Md. Gaz.* (Annapolis) 26 Feb. and 9 Dec. 1756.

9. *Archives of Maryland*, 44:595; *Md. Gaz.* (Annapolis) 5 Apr., 24 May, 12 July 1753.

10. *Archives of Maryland*, 44:44–45. George Gordon was a Scot from Banffshire who settled in Saint Marys County, Md.

11. Mulkearn, *Mercer Papers*, pp. 146–622; James, pp. 36–37.

12. Hening, 6:396; Harrison, 2:430–31.

13. William Lux to James Russell, 20 July 1763, William Lux Letter Book, New York Historical Society, New York, N.Y.; Harry Piper to John Dixon and Isaac Littledale, Harry Piper Letter Book, UVa.

14. James Lawson to Alexander Hamilton, 31 Jan. 1764.

15. Nicholas Cresswell, *The Journal of Nicholas Cresswell 1774–1777* (New York, 1924), pp. 18, 27.

16. Craven, *Soil Exhaustion*, p. 72; Harrison, 2:416–17.

17. Alexander Hamilton to Neil Jamieson, 24 Jan. 1774, Jamieson Papers, LC.

18. *Md. Gaz.* (Annapolis) 21 Dec. 1752. The records of the Commissioners for the Sale of Confiscated British Property in the Maryland Land Office, Annapolis, provide a useful index to this type of economic penetration, MdHR.

19. Evans, "Planter Indebtedness," pp. 511–33; Ernst, "Genesis of the Currency Act," pp. 22–74.

20. William Allason to James Dunlop, 12 Sept. 1762, William Allason Letter Book, VSL.

21. Henry Hamilton, *An Economic History of Scotland in the Eighteenth Century* (Oxford, 1963), pp. 308 ff.

22. Lawrence H. Gipson, *The Coming of the Revolution* (New York, 1945) pp. 40–54; ibid., "Virginia Planter Debts before the American Revolution," pp. 259–77.

23. *Md. Gaz.* (Annapolis) 6 Dec. 1770; Charles Albro Barker, *The Background of the Revolution in Maryland* (New Haven, 1940), pp. 345–58; David C. Skaggs, Jr., "Maryland's Impulse toward Social Revolution: 1750–1776," pp. 779–80.

24. *Md. Gaz.* (Annapolis) 21 Feb. and 7 Mar. 1771.

25. Glassford Papers, Vol. 28, fol. 1, LC; Richard McMaster and David C. Skaggs, eds., "Letter Books of Alexander Hamilton," p. 311.

26. Purdie and Dixon's *Va. Gaz.* (Williamsburg) 14 June 1770; James Pagan, *Sketch of the History of Glasgow* (Glasgow, 1847), p. 80; Andrew MacGeorge, *Old Glasgow* (Glasgow, 1880), pp. 157, 237; *Dictionary of National Biography*, s.v. "Glassford, John."

27. *Md. Gaz.* (Annapolis) 14 Oct. 1773; Purdie and Dixon's *Va. Gaz.* (Williamsburg) 4 June 1767; Rind's *Va. Gaz.* (Williamsburg) 5 Nov. 1772 and 4 Nov. 1773.

28. Richard Henry Lee to William Lee, 4 July 1773, Lee Papers, UVa.

29. Frederick County Deeds, bk. N, fol. 587, MdHR.

30. *Md. Gaz.* (Annapolis) 20 May 1773.

31. Purdie and Dixon's *Va. Gaz.* (Williamsburg) 22 Aug. 1771 and 28 Oct., 1773; Rind's *Va. Gaz.* (Williamsburg) 22 July 1773.

32. Fairfax D.B. K-1, fols. 429–33; *Md. Gaz.* (Annapolis) 3 Nov. 1774; Martin Cockburn Account Book, fols. 32–33, LC.

33. Frederick Nichols to George Mason and Martin Cockburn, 26 May 1773; Edward Smith to Mason and Cockburn, 28 July 1773, P.C.C. Mason File; Fairfax County Court Order Book, 1772–74, fols. 265–76, VSL; VHS Ms.2Un3a22.

34. Saint Marys County Wills, bk. JJ-1, fol. 39, MdHR.

35. *Md. Gaz.* (Annapolis) 23 Aug. 1770.

36. Mulkearn, *Mercer Papers,* pp. 212–13.

37. George Mason, "Scheme for Replevying Goods under Distress for Rent," 23 Dec. 1765, Washington Papers, LC.

38. Mason to Washington and George William Fairfax, 23 Dec. 1765, Washington Papers, LC.

39. Francis Fauquier, "Answers to inquiries sent to me by the Right Honorable the Lords Commissioners for Trade and Plantation Affairs," 30 Jan. 1763 (ms. copy), Sparks Transcripts, Houghton Library, Harvard University, Cambridge, Mass.

40. Rowland, *Mason,* 2:160–61; Fauquier, "Answers"; *Jour. H.B.,* 10:39, 52, 64.

41. *Jour. H.B.,* 10:101, 118, 125, 129; Hening, 8:237; *Jour. H.B.,* 10:142, 155, 248–49, 263, 289, 302.

42. C.O. 5 / 1132 Aa75 and C.O. 5 / 1332 Aa76, PRO, copy of text only in Sparks Transcripts, HL; R. Jackson to Board of Trade, 18 July 1770, ibid.

43. Rind's *Va. Gaz.* (Williamsburg) 16 Nov. 1769, 29 Mar. 1770; Harry Piper to John Dixon and Isaac Littledale, 16 Dec. 1770, Piper Letter Book.

44. Text in Benjamin Rush, *An Address to the Inhabitants of the British Settlements in America* (Philadelphia, 1773), Appendix; John Pownall to the Clerk of the Council in Waiting, 9 July 1772, C.O. 5 / 133, PRO.

45. *Jour. H.B.,* 12:85, 91.

46. Rowland, *Mason,* 1:391; *Jour. H.B.,* 11:xxviii.

47. Purdie and Dixon's *Va. Gaz.* (Williamsburg) 2 July 1771.

48. Rind's *Va. Gaz.* (Williamsburg) 4 Aug. and 11 Aug. 1774; Hening, 9:302.

49. Marraro, Howard R., ed., *Philip Mazzei, Virginia's Agent in Europe* (New York, 1935).

50. Rutland, *Mason Papers,* 3:1086.

CHAPTER VII   George Mason IV, Civic and Parish Interests

1. Charles S. Sydnor, *Gentleman Freeholders,* pp. 91–93.

2. Truro Vestry Book, fol. 28.

3. *Exec. Jour. Council,* 5:231; Fairfax M.B., 1749–56, fol. 17.

4. George Mason to Patrick Henry, 6 May 1783, Pierpont Morgan Library, New York, N.Y.

5. Hugh F. Rankin, *Criminal Trial Proceedings in the General Court of Colonial Virginia* (Charlottesville, Va., 1966) pp. 7–19, and passim.

6. Fairfax M.B., 1749–56, fol. 225; 1755–63, fol. 636.

7. Ibid., 1756–63, fol. 899; 1768–70, fol. 252.

8. Petitions to move the courthouse from Alexandria or retain it in the more central location in the back country were received at several sessions of the county court, ibid., 1749–56, fol. 183; 1756–63, fol. 331.

9. Bruce, *Institutional History,* 1:79–93.

10. Truro Vestry Book, fol. 33; Captain Jeremiah Bronaugh died 11 Nov. 1749. His tombstone in Pohick Churchyard is clearly legible.

11. Ibid., fols. 34–35, 37–38, 41–49; Beirne and Scarff, p. 30.

12. Truro Vestry Book, fol. 44; Hening, 8:43.

13. Truro Vestry Book, fols. 53–57.

14. Ibid., fol. 68.

15. Ibid., fol. 71.

16. Fairfax D.B. L-1, fols. 179–82; Harry Piper to John Dixon and Isaac Littledale, 2 Aug. 1770, Piper Letter Book; Truro Vestry Book, fol. 80.

17. Truro Vestry Book, fol. 42; fols. 47–49, 87–88.

18. Ibid., fols. 67, 70. On 8 Feb. 1768 Daniel McCarty and William Payne, wardens of Truro Parish, agreed to deliver 16,738 pounds of tobacco to Henry Riddell, chief factor for Glassford and Henderson, upon his paying to the late churchwardens £429 4s. 5d. or the equivalent of 18 shillings per hundredweight (Fairfax Parish Vestry Book, fol. 15, Christ Church, Alexandria, Va.) .

19. Truro Vestry Book, fol. 61; Rowland, *Mason,* 1:114.

20. Wesley M. Gewehr, *The Great Awakening in Virginia,* pp. 99, 107 ff.; Howard M. Wilson, *Tinkling Springs: A Study of the Church and Her People, 1732–1952* (Fisherville, Va., 1954) , pp. 21–25.

21. Fairfax M.B., 1772–74, fols. 264–75.

22. Robert B. Semple, *History of the Rise and Progress of the Baptists in Virginia* (Richmond, 1810) , p. 308; James B. Taylor, *Virginia Baptist Ministers* (Richmond, 1860) , p. 219.

23. Purdie and Dixon's *Va. Gaz.* (Williamsburg) 15 Aug. 1771 and 20 Feb. 1772.

24. General Assembly Religious Petitions, VSL.

25. Rutland, *Mason Papers,* 1:278.

26. Hening, 9:164.

27. Truro Vestry Book, fols. 87–88.

28. Fairfax County Petitions, 21 Nov. 1783, Legislative Petitions, VSL.

29. Hening, 11:532.

30. Rowland, *Mason,* 2:87; *Virginia Journal and the Alexandria Advertiser* 14 Apr. 1785.

31. George Mason to Robert Carter, 5 Oct. 1785, Rutland, *Mason Papers,* 2:832.

32. Fairfax Petition filed as 14 Nov. 1785, General Assembly Religious Petitions, VSL. *Virginia Journal and the Alexandria Advertiser* 17 Nov. 1785.

33. Hening, 12:84 ff.

CHAPTER VIII   George Mason IV, the American Revolution

1. George Mason to George William Fairfax and George Washington, 23 Dec. 1765, Washington Papers, LC.

2. Letter to the Committee of Merchants in London in June 1766, Mason Papers, LC; Purdie and Dixon's *Va. Gaz.* (Williamsburg) 20 May 1767.

3. Francis Norton Mason, ed., *John Norton and Sons, Merchants of London and Virginia—Being the Papers from their Counting House for the Years 1750–1795* (Richmond, 1937) , p. 8–9; Rowland, *Mason,* 1:125–27.

4. Purdie and Dixon's *Va. Gaz.* (Williamsburg) 18 July 1766; Rind's *Va. Gaz.* (Williamsburg) 18 July 1766; Purdie and Dixon's *Va. Gaz.* (Williamsburg) 28 May 1767; Rind's *Va. Gaz.* (Williamsburg) 23 July 1767.

5. *Jour. H.B.,* 10:172; Arthur M. Schlesinger, *The Colonial Merchants and the American Revolution* (New York, 1966) , pp. 134–38; John R. Alden, *The South in the Revolution, 1763–1789* (Baton Rouge, La., 1957) , pp. 99–108.

6. Mason to Washington, 5 Apr. 1769, Washington Papers, LC.

7. Rutland, *Mason Papers,* 1:100.

8. Draft of Non-importation Agreement, Washington Papers, LC; Rutland, *Mason Papers,* 1:94–95.

9. *Jour. H.B.,* 10:189.

10. Draft of Non-importation Agreement; Rutland, *Mason Papers,* 1:105.

11. Rutland, *Mason Papers,* 1:103.

12. Purdie and Dixon's *Va. Gaz.* (Williamsburg) 18 May 1769.

13. Rutland, *Mason Papers,* 1:127; Mason to a kinsman, 6 Dec. 1770, Mason Papers, LC.

14. Mason to Richard Henry Lee, 6 June 1770, Rutland, *Mason Papers,* 1:116–119.

15. Rind's *Va. Gaz.* (Williamsburg) 7 Nov. 1771.

16. Ibid., 26 May 1774; Benjamin W. Labaree, *The Boston Tea Party* (New York, 1964), pp. 218–19.

17. George Mason to Martin Cockburn, 26 May 1774, Rowland, *Mason,* 1:168–69; James C. Ballagh, ed., *Letters of Richard Henry Lee* (New York, 1911), 1:150.

18. Rind's *Va. Gaz.* (Williamsburg) 26 May 1774.

19. Arthur Lee to Francis Lightfoot Lee, 2 Apr. 1774, Arthur Lee Papers, HL.

20. McMaster and Skaggs, "Letter Books of Alexander Hamilton, p. 162.

21. Rind's *Va. Gaz.* (Williamsburg) 9 June 1774.

22. Purdie and Dixon's *Va. Gaz.* (Williamsburg) 2 June 1774.

23. Rind's *Va. Gaz.* (Williamsburg) 21 July 1774.

24. Ibid., 9 June 1774.

25. Purdie and Dixon's *Va. Gaz.* (Williamsburg) 30 June 1774; Harry Piper to John Dixon and Isaac Littledale, 9 June 1774, Piper Letter Book; William Reynolds to George Norton, 3 June 1774, William Reynolds Letter Book, LC.

26. Rutland, *Mason Papers,* 1:201–9.

27. William Reynolds to John Norton, 6 Aug. 1774, Reynolds Letter Book, 1: fol. 56.

28. Rind's *Va. Gaz.* (Williamsburg) 25 Aug. 1774.

29. Greene, *Diary of Landon Carter,* 2:848.

30. Thomson Mason to John Dickinson, 17 June 1775, Logan Papers, Historical Society of Pennsylvania.

31. Rowland, *Mason,* 1:181–82, 418, 427; Rind's *Va. Gaz.* (Williamsburg) 25 Aug. 1774.

32. Rowland, *Mason,* 1:179.

33. Rutland, *Mason Papers,* 1:213; Fitzpatrick, *Washington Diaries,* 2:193.

34. Rutland, *Mason Papers,* 1:210–11.

35. Pinkney's *Va. Gaz.* (Williamsburg) 27 Oct. 1774, 2 Feb. 1775; Rowland, *Mason,* 1:181–82; George Mason to Martin Cockburn, 5 Aug. 1775, Mason Papers, LC.

36. Rowland, Mason 1:430–33.

37. John Dalton, William Ramsay, et al. to George Mason and Charles Broadwater, 9 Dec. 1775, VSL.

38. George Mason to Martin Cockburn, 24 July 1775, VHS; George Mason to George Washington, 14 Oct. 1775, Washington Papers, LC.

39. Rutland, *Mason Papers,* 1:242–43.

40. George Mason to Martin Cockburn, 22 Aug. 1775, Rutland, *Mason Papers,* 1:250.

41. George Mason to Maryland Council of Safety, 31 Jan. 1776, Rutland, *Mason Papers,* 1:262.

42. William Bell Clark, ed., *Naval Documents of the American Revolution,* 3:1068, 1179–80.

43. Benjamin Harrison to Edmund Pendleton, 13 Feb. 1776; John Page to Thomas Jefferson, 26 Apr. 1776, Boyd et al., *Jefferson Papers,* 1:288.

44. Adam Stephen to Thomas Jefferson, 29 July 1776, Boyd, et al., *Jefferson Papers,* 1:480–82.

45. *Md. Gaz.* (Annapolis) 5 Nov. 1776; Petition of Thomas Collis, 30 May 1777, Legislative Petitions, VSL; Cockburn Day Book, fol. 36, LC.

46. Rowland, *Mason,* 1:213; Richard Graham to Leven Powell, 20 Feb. 1777, Leven Powell Papers, W&M.

47. Rutland, *Mason Papers,* 1:316.

48. Clark, *Naval Documents,* 1:617–19.

49. *Jour. H.B.,* 12:233–37.

50. George Mason to George Washington, 2 Apr. 1776, Washington Papers, LC.

51. Rowland, "Merchants and Mills," pp. 245–46; Jenifer and Hooe Account Book, fol. 106.

52. Clark, *Naval Documents,* 2:1268; 3:754–55; J. Franklin James, "St. Eustatius in the American Revolution," pp. 683–708.

53. Curtis P. Nettels, *The Emergence of a National Economy, 1775–1815* (New York, 1962), pp. 14–15; George Mason to Richard Henry Lee, 18 May 1776, Lee Family Papers, VHS; George Mason to Patrick Henry, 22 Aug. 1777, VSL.

54. George Mason to William Aylett, 19 Apr. 1777, VSL.

55. *Md. Gaz.* (Annapolis) 6 Feb. 1777, 12 and 26 June 1777; Robert A. East, *Business Enterprise in the American Revolutionary Era* (New York, 1938), p. 106, and passim.

56. George Mason to William Bingham, 10 Mar. 1780, Gratz Collection, Historical Society of Pennsylvania.

57. George Mason to Richard Harrison, 24 Oct. 1778, GHL, 9 Nov. 1778, Rutland, *Mason Papers*, 1:442–43.

58. George Mason to George Washington, 8 Mar. 1779, Washington Papers, LC.

59. George Washington to Benjamin Franklin, 27 Mar. 1779, Benjamin Franklin Papers, American Philosophical Society, Philadelphia, Pa.

60. Rutland, *Mason Papers*, 2:490.

61. George Mason to Thomas Jefferson, 16 July 1779, Brock Collection. George Mason to George Mason, Jr., 3 June 1781, Mason Papers, LC. Dixon's *Va. Gaz.* (Williamsburg) 17 July, 24 July, 21 Aug. 1779; Clarkson and Davis' *Va. Gaz.* (Williamsburg) 19 Aug. 1780.

62. George Mason to James Madison, 2 Aug. 1780, Madison Papers, LC; William T. Hutchinson and William M. E. Rachal, eds., *The Papers of James Madison* (Chicago, 1962–), 2:53n.

63. Rutland, *Mason Papers*, 2:691.

64. William Lee to William Hicks, 29 Aug. 1776, Lee Letter Book, Stratford Hall, Stratford, Va.

65. Neil Jamieson to Sir Henry Clinton, 11 Dec. 1780, Clinton Papers, William L. Clements Library, Ann Arbor, Michigan.

66. Joshua Johnson to George Mason, Jr., 20 Feb. 1781, Wallace, Johnson, and Muir Letter Book, 1, fol. 8; Joshua Johnson to John Muir, 20 Feb. 1781, ibid., 1, fol. 14; Johnson to Wallace, Johnson and Muir, 20 Mar. 1781, ibid., 1, fol. 33. NYPL.

67. Joshua Johnson to George Mason, Jr., 20 Apr. 1782; Joshua Johnson to Thomas Ridout, 8 May 1782; ibid., bk. 1, fols. 411 and 426; Johnson to George Mason, 25 Oct. 1782, ibid., 1, fol. 624.

68. Joshua Johnson to Wallace, Johnson, and Muir, 25 July 1781, ibid., 1, fol. 129.

69. Pinkney's *Va. Gaz.* (Williamsburg) 22 Mar., 31 Mar., 23 Apr. 1775; George Mason to Patrick Henry, 6 Apr. 1777, Henry Papers, LC.

70. George Mason to Richard Henry Lee, Rutland, *Mason Papers*, 2:522–24; Thomas Jefferson to Benjamin Harrison, 30 Oct. 1779, Boyd, et al., *Jefferson Papers*, 3:125–30; Kathleen Bruce, *Virginia Iron Manufacture in the Slave Era* (New York, 1930), pp. 44–56. Randolph W. Church, "John Ballendine," pp. 39–46.

71. Boyd et al., *Jefferson Papers*, 3:49–50, and 70 ff.; Palmer et al., *Calendar of Virginia State Papers*, 1:352–55; George Mason to George Mason, Jr., 3 June 1781 (copy), Mason Papers, LC.

72. Prince William County Petition, 10 Dec. 1781, Legislative Petitions, VSL; Dr. Robert Honyman Journal, fols. 523–25, LC.

73. John Parke Custis to George Washington, 26 Oct. 1777, George Bolling Lee Papers, VHS.

74. Hening, 10:169–71, 279–286; Lancaster County Petition, 20 Oct. 1779, Legislative Petitions, VSL.

75. George Mason to Richard Henry Lee, 18 May 1776, Lee Family Papers, VHS; Edmund Randolph, *History of Virginia*, ed. Arthur H. Shaffer (Charlottesville, 1970), p. 254; George Washington to John Parke Custis, 14 Nov. 1777, George Bolling Lee Papers, VHS; Fitzpatrick, *Writings of Washington*, 10:60.

76. Draft in George Mason's handwriting, Mason Papers, LC, facsimile in Rowland, *Mason*, 1:240; Purdie's *Va. Gaz.* (Williamsburg) 17 May and 14 June 1776.

77. Purdie's *Va. Gaz.* (Williamsburg) 5 July 1776.

78. George Mason to Richard Henry Lee, 4 June 1779, Rutland, *Mason Papers,* 2:506–8.

79. George Mason to James Mercer, ibid., 2:617–18, letter of Stevens Thomson Mason, 16 Feb. 1837, quoting an excerpt from an original letter of George Mason to William Fitzhugh, now in the possession of Mrs. Alfred Whittell, Jr., a descendant of Thomson Mason of Hollin Hall.

80. Rowland, *Mason,* 1:348–50.

81. Brent, pp. 101–2.

82. Rowland, *Mason,* 1:348–49; George Mason Graham Stafford, *General George Mason Graham of Tyrone and His People* (New Orleans, La., 1947) , p. 58.

83. Cresswell, pp. 142, 144, and passim.

84. Thomson Mason to Daniel of St. Thomas Jenifer, 22 Sept. 1773, P.C.C. Mason File.

85. Alexander Purdie, ed., *Journal of the House of Delegates, October 1777* (Williamsburg, 1778) .

86. Rutland, *Mason Papers,* 2:655, 676, 677.

87. Ibid., pp. 689–94.

88. George Mason V to William Temple Franklin, W. T. Franklin Papers, vol. 3, fol. 100.

89. Ibid., vol. 4, fol. 128.

90. Rutland, *Mason Papers,* 2:773.

91. E. C. Branchi, trans., "Memoirs of Philip Mazzei," p. 5.

92. W. T. Franklin Papers, vol. 5, fols. 45, 50.

93. George Mason to Arthur Lee, 25 Mar. 1783, Rutland, *Mason Papers,* 2:765–67.

94. Will of Thomson Mason, Stafford D.B. S, fols. 308–22.

95. "The Wallace Family," pp. 177–182.

96. Will of Thomson Mason.

97. Will of George Mason IV, Fairfax County Will Book F, No. 1.

98. "An Act Concerning Awards," Dumfries District Court Records at Large, May 1798–99, VSL.

99. Deposition of George Mason Graham, pp. 64–67, photocopy GHL.

CHAPTER IX   George Mason IV, the Sage of Gunston Hall

1. Rowland, *Mason,* 2:63–66; John T. Faris, *Historical Shrines of America* (New York, 1918) , p. 282.

2. U.S., Bureau of the Census, *Heads of Families at the First Census of the United States, Virginia, Records of the State Enumerations: 1782–1785.* (Washington, D.C., 1908) , pp. 18, 85.

3. James Mercer to John F. Mercer, 23 Sept. 1783, Mercer Papers, VHS.

4. *Heads of Families at the First Census,* p. 18.

5. Richard Graham to Leven Powell, 22 Feb. 1777, Leven Powell Papers, W&M.

6. Rutland, *Mason Papers,* 2:759.

7. Curtis P. Nettels, p. 50.

8. Craven, *Soil Exhaustion,* p. 82; G. Melvin Herndon, *William Tatham and the Cultivation of Tobacco* (Coral Gables, Fla., 1969) , pp. 301–5.

9. David Pagan to William Murray, 8 Aug. 1775, Brock Collection; Alexander Hamilton to George Mason, 14 June 1784, MacMaster and Skaggs, "Post-Revolutionary Letters," pp. 53–54.

10. George Mason to Patrick Henry, 6 May 1783, Pierpont Morgan Library. On the opposition in Virginia to the payment of British debts, see James Mercer to John F. Mercer, 5 Apr. 1783, Mercer Papers.

11. Hening, 9:377–80; H. J. Eckenrode, *The Revolution in Virginia* (Hamden, Conn., 1964), p. 188; A.O. 13 / 133 fol. 379, Whitehaven Public Library, Whitehaven, Cumberland, PRO.

12. George Mason to Patrick Henry, 6 May 1783, Pierpont Morgan Library; Richard B. Morris, *The Peacemakers* (New York, 1965), pp. 366–67.

13. Hayes's *Va. Gaz.* (Richmond) 7 June 1783.

14. Ibid., 14 June 1783. Similar views are expressed in Thomson Mason to John F. Mercer, 22 June 1783, Mercer Papers, Rutland, *Mason Papers*, 2:780; Rowland, *Mason*, 2:54.

15. Alexander Hamilton to James Brown and Co., 25 Jan. 1784, MacMaster and Skaggs, "Post-Revolutionary Letters," pp. 26–29.

16. Alexander Henderson to Robert Ferguson, 7 Oct. 1784, Miscl. Manuscripts, Alexander Henderson, New York Historical Society.

17. Nettels, p. 50; Frederick L. Nussbaum, "American Tobacco and French Politics, 1783–1798," pp. 501–3.

18. Thomas Rutland to John F. Mercer, 28 July 1788, Thomas Rutland Letter Book, 2, fol. 76, MHS; Louis F. Magazin, "The Economic Depression in Maryland and Virginia 1785–1787" (Ph.D. diss., Georgetown University, 1967).

19. Rutland to Mason, 8 Sept. 1784, Rutland Letter Book, 2 fol. 34. Rutland had married a niece of Charles Wallace of the Annapolis firm of Wallace, Johnson, and Muir.

20. Rutland to Mason, 1 May 1786; Rutland to Thomas Stone, 6 June 1786, ibid., 1, fols. 231 and 245; George Mason to William Carr, 3 Mar. 1786, P.C.C. Mason File, Rutland to Stephen West, 10 July 1786, Rutland Letter Book, 1, fol. 239.

21. Rutland to Mason, 27 Aug. 1786, ibid., 1, fol. 255; 12 June 1787, ibid., 2, fol. 37; 17 Mar. 1788, ibid., 1, fol. 58.

22. In addition to his Maryland stores, Rutland maintained stores at Dumfries and Alexandria between 1784 and 1788 (Rutland to John Love, 22 Mar. 1788, Rutland to Mason, 22 Mar. 1788, ibid., 2, fols. 59–60; George Mason to John F. Mercer, 1 May 1788, P.C.C. Mason File.

23. Thomas Rutland to John F. Mercer, 4 July 1788, Rutland Letter Book, 2, fol. 75; Mason to John F. Mercer, 12 May 1792, Gratz Collection, Historical Society of Pennsylvania, Mason to John F. Mercer, 26 Nov. 1788, Rutland, *Mason Papers*, 3:1132–34.

24. Mason to John Mercer, 31 Oct. 1789, Dreer Collection, Historical Society of Pennsylvania.

25. Prince William County Petitions, Legislative Petitions, VSL, filed as 21 May and 14 Oct. 1779, 21 Nov. 1786, 19 Mar. 1787; ibid., filed as 5 and 6 Dec. 1786.

26. George Mason, "A Private Citizen Begs Leave Humbly to Submit the Following Queries to the Consideration of the General Assembly now Sitting," MS. copy made in 1842 from original owned by Thomson F. Mason of Alexandria, Rutland, *Mason Papers*, 2:859–63.

27. Fairfax County Petitions, Legislative Petitions filed as 27 May 1782, VSL.

28. Jacques P. Brissol de Warville, *New Travels in the United States of America, 1788*, ed. Durand Echeverria (Cambridge, Mass., 1964), pp. 341–42.

29. Rutland, *Mason Papers*, 2:775.

30. John C. Robert, *The Tobacco Kingdom* (1938; repr. ed. Gloucester, Mass., 1965), p. 162; Lewis C. Gray, *History of Agriculture in the Southern United States to 1860* (Washington, D.C., 1922), 2:1030.

31. Fitzpatrick, *Washington Diaries*, 2:349–53; "The Mount Vernon Compact," Rutland, *Mason Papers*, 2:812–16.

32. Fitzpatrick, *Washington Diaries*, 2:373–75; George Washington to George Mason, 3 Oct. 1785, Rutland, *Mason Papers*, 2:831–32.

33. Fitzpatrick, 2:423.

34. George Mason to George Washington, 9 Nov. 1785, Rowland, *Mason*, 2:90–91; Fitzpatrick, *Washington Diaries*, 2:454–55.

35. George Mason to William Fitzhugh, 26 Feb. 1786, Rutland, *Mason Papers*, 2:454–55.
36. Ibid., 2:843, 846–50.
37. Rowland, *Mason*, 2:94, 96; George Mason to John Fitzgerald, 28 Nov. 1786, Rutland, *Mason Papers*, 2:858.
38. Edmund Randolph to George Mason, 6 Dec. 1786, Rutland, *Mason Papers*, 2:864.
39. John T. Goolrick, *Historic Fredericksburg* (Richmond, 1922), p. 72; Fairfax County Tax Lists, 1787, VSL; George Mason to Edmund Randolph, 12 Apr. 1787, Rutland, *Mason Papers*, 3:874.
40. Fitzpatrick, 3:196; Rowland, *Mason*, 2:96.
41. Rutland, *Mason Papers*, 3:875–81.
42. Ibid., pp. 876–79.
43. Ibid., p. 881.
44. Ibid., pp. 884, 1045.
45. Ibid., pp. 994–95.
46. Ibid., p. 1037.
47. Ibid., pp. 1037, 1039–40.
48. Ibid., pp. 1047, 1072, 1120.
49. Boyd et al., *Jefferson Papers*, 16:7.
50. Ibid., pp. 493–94; Kenneth Russell Bowling, "Politics in the First Congress, 1788–1791" (Ph.D. diss., Univ. of Wisc., 1968), pp. 183, 325.
51. Bowling, pp. 325–26.
52. Ibid., p. 195.
53. Boyd et al., *Jefferson Papers*, 17:466.
54. Bowling, p. 196; Rutland, *Mason Papers*, 3:1226–27.
55. Rutland, *Mason Papers*, 3:1146–47; 1161–62.
56. Rowland, *Mason*, 2:363–65.
57. Ibid., p. 365.

CHAPTER X   George Mason IV, Siblings and Progeny

1. Rutland, *Mason Papers*, 2:761, 3:1235–36.
2. Will of William Eilbeck, Charles County Wills, bk. AD, no. 5, fols. 316–18; Will of Sarah (Edgar) Eilbeck, ibid., bk. AF, no. 7, fols. 582–85; Rutland, *Mason Papers*, 1:434; VHS, Mss. 6:1, M. 382:2; Clara S. McCarty, *McCartys of Virginia with Emphasis on the First Four Generations in the Colony* (Richmond, 1972), pp. 102–3.
3. *Biographical Directory of the American Congress, 1774–1961* (Washington, D.C., 1961), pp. 1283–84; *National Genealogical Society Quarterly* 28, no. 3 (1940):71; *Biographical Directory*, pp. 1283–84.
4. Emily Virginia Mason to Catherine Mason Rowland, 25 Mar. 1846, Burton Historical Collection, Detroit Public Library, Detroit, Mich., photocopy GHL.
5. Richmond City Marriage Bonds, 69-2557, VSL, photocopy GHL; *Biographical Directory*, pp. 1283–84.
6. *Biographical Directory*, p. 1510; McCarty, pp. 102–3.
7. McCarty, pp. 115–121; Hayden, p. 85.
8. "Bronaugh Family," pp. 235, 237.
9. King, "John Mercer," p. 156.
10. P.C.C. Mason File.
11. Watkins, pp. 64, 96; P.C.C. Mason File.
12. King, *Register of Overwharton Parish*, p. 179; John Mason," Recollections," Mason Papers, LC.
13. Mason Family Bible, GHL; Rowland, *Mason*, 2:307; Rutland, *Mason Papers*, 3:1266; P.C.C. Mason File.

14. Martha von Briesen, ed., *The Letters of Elijah Fletcher* (Charlottesville, Va., 1965) , pp. 15–19; Prince William County Will Book K, fol. 492.

15. Dorothy Vandegrift Lee, *Virginia Ghosts* (Richmond, 1930) , pp. 9–10; Mutual Assurance Society, Declaration for Assurance no. 2045, VSL.

16. Stafford, p. 206; P.C.C. Mason File.

17. Rutland, *Mason Papers*, 2:891.

18. Mason Family Bible; Rutland, *Mason Papers*, 3:1227, 1253.

19. Rutland, *Mason Papers*, 2:620–22; Alexandria City Will Book B, 1804–7, pp. 237–38, Alexandria, Va., VSL.

20. Fairfax County Will Book G, fol. 258.

21. David Bailie Warden, *A Chorological-and-Statistical Description of the District of Columbia* (Paris, 1816) , p. 39, and passim.

22. Fairfax County Court Inventories, photocopy, P.C.C. Mason File.

23. Rowland, *Mason*, 1:103; Deposition of George Graham in the City of Washington at the Land Offices, photocopy GHL.

24. Will of William Eilbeck, Charles County Wills, bk. AD, no. 5, fols. 316–18.

25. Personal correspondence of Robert Barnes, Baltimore, GHL; Charles C. Sellers, *Portraits and Miniatures by Charles Willson Peale* (Philadelphia, 1952) , 1:112.

26. P.C.C. Mason File; *Pennsylvania Gazette* (Philadelphia) , 1811.

27. Hayward File, MHS; P.C.C. Mason File.

28. Stella Pickett Hardy, *Colonial Southern Families of the Southern States of America* (Baltimore, 1958) , p. 493.

29. *Baltimore Sun*, 4 Oct. 1906; Charles County Wills, bk. HB no. 14, fols. 50–51.

30. Garnett. "James Mercer," pp. 216–17.

31. Rutland, *Mason Papers*, 3:1269.

32. Will of George Mason IV.

33. Harrison, 2:578; Samuel Shepherd, *The Statutes at Large of Virginia, 1792–1807* (Richmond, 1835–36) , 1: 430; 2: 119; 3: 169.

34. Stafford, p. 97.

35. Grace Nadine Mason Saunders. "The Genealogy and Short History of My Ancestors and Their Descendants the Gunston Branch of Masons," mimeographed (Estill, S.C.) , p. 30; Gerard Mason's Estate Accounts, Prince William County Will Book P, pp. 476–481.

36. Mason Family Bible, GHL.

37. John Mason, "Autobiography," Mason Papers, LC.

38. Rutland, *Mason Papers*, 3:1005.

39. Ibid., p. 881

40. Archives Departmentales de la Gironde, Bordeaux, 2 E Series; Richard K. MacMaster, ed., "The Tobacco Trade with France," pp. 26–53.

41. MacMaster, ed., "Maryland Students in Flanders," pp. 185–92.

42. Merrill Jensen, *The New Nation* (New York, 1958) , pp. 203–4.

43. MacMaster, "Tobacco Trade with France," pp. 26–38.

44. Rutland, *Mason Papers*, 3:1044.

45. George Mason to John Mason, 31 July 1789, Mason Family Papers, LC, and, 14 May 1789, Mason Papers, W&M.

46. Joseph Fenwick to Ignatius Fenwick, 11 Oct. 1788, MacMaster, "Tobacco Trade with France," pp. 39–42.

47. George Mason to John Mason, 12 June 1788, Mason Family Papers, LC.

48. George Mason to John Mason, 14 May 1789, Mason Papers, W&M.

49. George Mason to John Mason, 20 May 1790, Mason Papers, LC.

50. Rutland, *Mason Papers*, 3:1142.

51. Ibid., pp. 1157–61.

52. *The Writings of Thomas Jefferson*, Publication of the Thomas Jefferson Memorial Association of the United States (Washington, D.C., 1903) , 7:409.

53. Rutland, *Mason Papers*, 3:1150–53.

54. Memorandum from George Mason to Joshua Johnson, Dawson Papers; Scharf, *History of Maryland*, 2:504.

55. Records of the Chamberlain of London, Chamberlain's Court, Guildhall, London; John P. Fallon, *The Marks of the London Goldsmiths and Silversmiths* (London, 1972), p. 108.

56. Fenwick Mason & Co. to Thomas Jefferson, 16 May 1793, Coolidge Collection, Massachusetts Historical Society, Boston.

57. Rutland, *Mason Papers*, 3:1147.

58. Ibid., pp. 1193–98.

59. Ibid., p. 1217.

60. Fenwick, Mason & Co. to Christopher Champlin, 1 Nov. 1790, Wetmore Collection, Massachusetts Historical Society.

61. John Mason, "Recollections," Mason Papers, LC.

62. Victor Marie du Pont, *Journey to France and Spain 1801*, ed. Charles W. David (Ithaca, N.Y., 1961), p. 53.

63. *Diary of Mrs. William Thornton 1800*, Records of the Columbia Historical Society, vol. 10 (Washington, D.C., 1907), p. 176.

64. Mary E. Curry, *Theodore Roosevelt Island: A Broken Link to Early Washington, D.C. History*, Records of the Columbia Historical Society, vol. 48 (Washington, D.C., 1971–72), p. 20.

65. George Mason to John Mason, 6 Dec. 1791, Ruthland, *Mason Papers*, 3:1247.

66. George Mason to John Mason, 16 Apr. 1791, Mason Papers, W&M.

67. George Mason to John Mason, 9 Dec. 1791, Mason Family Papers. LC.

68. Rutland, *Mason Papers*, 3:1265; MacMaster, "Tobacco Trade with France," pp. 51–52; Joseph Fenwick to Citoyens Administrateurs de la Department de la Gironde, 10 March 1796, with enclosures, Archives Departmentales, Bordeaux, France, Series 3L, No. 240.

69. John Mason to George Washington, 22 Apr. 1793; Tobias Lear to John Mason, 6 May 1793, Washington Papers, LC.

70. Samuel Davis to Mason, Fenwick & Co., 26 Sept. 1793. Jesse Dewees to John Mason, 6 and 10 July 1795, microcopy in Mason Papers, LC.

71. George McCandless to Mason, Fenwick & Co., 25 Feb. 1794; Archibald Campbell to John Mason, 20 Mar. 1794; Governeur and Kemble to Fenwick, Mason & Co. 12 July, 1794, 23 July 1794; Nathaniel Fellowes to Mason, Fenwick & Co., 10 Aug. 1794; Jesse Dewees to John Mason, 10 July 1795, microcopies in Mason Papers, LC.

72. Jonathan Sterns to John Mason, 18 Dec. 1795, 22 May, 1796; John Mason to Samuel Smith, 4 Apr. 1803; Joseph Fenwick to John Mason, 25 Aug. 1803, microcopies in Mason Papers, LC.

73. John Joseph Walsh, *Early Banks and Banking in the District of Columbia* (Washington, D.C., 1940), pp. 59–77.

74. Commissioners for Confiscated British Property, Sale Book, 1792–1795, fols. 6–7, MdHR; Shepherd's *Statutes at Large*, 2:177.

75. Ann Hollingsworth Wharton, *Social Life in the Early Republic* (Philadelphia, 1902), p. 87.

76. Mollie Somerville, "General John Mason," pp. 3–11.

77. Warden, *Chorological and Statistical Description of the District of Columbia*.

78. Cora Bacon-Foster, *Early Chapters in the Development of the Potomac Route to the West* (Washington, D.C. 1912), p. 123.

79. Thomas Mendenhall to John Mason, 21 Mar. 1801, Historical Society of Delaware, Wilmington.

80. John Mason to Thomas Jefferson, 13 May 1805; Thomas Jefferson to John Mason, 17 Dec. 1805, Coolidge Collection.

81. "Stories of General John Mason" as recorded by his favorite daughter Anna Maria (Mason) Lee, transcription P.C.C. Mason File.

82. Ibid.

83. *The Agricultural Museum*, 1 (1811) 12, 350, 368.

84. Burton Collection, Detroit Public Library.

85. The *Globe,* Washington, D.C., 23 Mar. 1849.

Chapter XI Notes on Other Masons

1. Carolyn Thomas Foreman, "General Richard Barnes Mason," p. 14.

2. Ibid., pp. 32, 36.

3. Hugh O. Potter, *In the Beginning,* pp. 18–19.

4. Foreman, "General Mason," p. 33.

5. William T. Sherman, *Memoirs of General William T. Sherman by Himself* (New York, 1875) , p. 64.

6. Stafford, p. 150.

7. Mason to Linell, 29 Apr. 1865, Burton Collection.

8. Thomas Hurray-Houghton, *Memorials to the Family of Hurray* (Liverpool, 1926) , p. 101.

9. *Wolverhampton Chronicle,* 19 Apr. 1865, William Salt Library, Brewood, Stafford, England; P.C.C. Mason File.

10. *Encyclopedia of the New West* (1881) , pp. 454–55; *Galveston Daily News,* 4 Feb. 1896.

11. P.C.C. Mason File.

12. "Stories of General John Mason" as recorded by his favorite daughter Anna Maria (Mason) Lee, P.C.C. Mason File.

13. Gunston Hall School Records (1892–1942) , GHL.

14. Rowland, *Mason,* 1:109–10.

Bibliography and Abbreviations

Bibliography and Abbreviations

Books

Abernethy, Thomas Perkins. *Western Lands and The American Revolution*. New York, 1937.

Bailey, Kenneth P. *The Ohio Company of Virginia and the Westward Movement 1748–1792: A Chapter in the History of the Colonial Frontier*. Glendale, Calif. 1939.

Beirne, Rosamond Randall, and John Henry Scarff. *William Buckland 1734–1744: Architect of Virginia and Maryland*. Baltimore, 1958.

Beverley, Robert. *The History and Present State of Virginia*. Edited by Louis B. Wright. Chapel Hill, N.C., 1947.

Bowling, Kenneth Russell. "Politics In The First Congress 1789–1791." Ph.D. dissertation, University of Wisconsin, 1968.

Boyd, Julian P., et al., eds. *The Papers of Thomas Jefferson*. Princeton, 1950–.

Brent, Chester Horton. *The Descendants of Col. Giles Brent, Capt. George Brent, and Robert Brent, Gent., Immigrants to Maryland and Virginia*. Rutland, Vt., 1946.

Brock, R. A., ed. *The Official Records of Robert Dinwiddie: Lieutenant-Governor of the Colony of Virginia 1751–1758*. Richmond, 1883.

Bruce, Philip Alexander. *Institutional History of Virginia in the Seventeenth Century: An Inquiry into the Religious, Moral, Educational, Legal, Military, and Political Condition of the People Based upon Original and Contemporaneous Records*. 2 vols. 1910. Reprint. Gloucester, Mass., 1964.

Clark, William Bell, ed. *Naval Documents of the American Revolution*. 3 vols. Washington, D.C., 1968.

Craven, Avery O. *Soil Exhaustion as a Factor in the Agricultural History of Virginia and Maryland 1606–1860*. Gloucester, Mass., 1965.

Davis, Richard Beale, ed. *William Fitzhugh and His Chesapeake World 1676–1701: The Fitzhugh Letters and Other Documents*. Chapel Hill, N.C., 1963.

Fitzpatrick, John, ed. *Diaries of George Washington 1748–1799*. 4 vols. Boston, 1925.

——. *Writings of George Washington*. 39 vols. Washington, D.C., 1931–44.

Gewehr, Wesley M. *The Great Awakening in Virginia, 1740–1790*. Durham, N.C., 1930.

Greene, Jack P., ed., *The Diary of Colonel Landon Carter of Sabine Hall, 1752–1778.* 2 vols. Charlottesville, Va., 1965.

Harrison, Fairfax. *Landmarks of Old Prince William: A Study of Origins in Northern Virginia.* 2 vols. Richmond, 1924.

Hayden, the Rev. Horace Edwin. *Virginia Genealogies.* 1891. Reprint. Washington, D.C., 1931.

Hening, William Waller., ed. *The Statutes at Large, Being a Collection of All the Laws of Virginia. . . .* 13 vols. 1819–23. Facsimile reprint. Charlottesville, Va., 1969.

Hunter, William A. *Forts on the Pennsylvania Frontier, 1753–1758.* Harrisburg, Pa., 1960.

James, Alfred P. *The Ohio Company: Its Inner History.* Pittsburg, 1959.

Jones, the Rev. Hugh. *The Present State of Virginia from Whence Is Inferred a Short View of Maryland and North Carolina.* Edited by Richard L. Morton. Chapel Hill, N.C., 1956.

Kennedy, John P., and Henry R. McIlwaine, eds. *Journals of the House of Burgesses of Virginia* [1619–1776]. 13 vols. Richmond, 1905–15. *Jour. H.B.*

King, George Harrison Sanford, comp. *The Register of Overwharton Parish, Stafford County, Virginia, 1723–1758, and Sundry Historical and Genealogical Notes.* Fredericksburg, Va., 1961.

McIlwaine, Henry R., ed. *Legislative Journals of the Council of Colonial Virginia.* Richmond, 1918–19. *Leg. Jour. Council.*

——. *Minutes of the Council and General Court of Colonial Virginia, 1622–1632 and 1570–1676.* Richmond, 1934. *Minutes of Council.*

——, and Wilmer L. Hall., eds. *Executive Journals of the Council of Colonial Virginia.* Richmond, 1925–45. *Exec. Jour. Council.*

Maryland Historical Society. *Archives of Maryland.* Edited by William H. Browne et al. 59 vols. Baltimore, 1883–.

Meade, William. *Old Churches, Ministers, and Families of Virginia.* 2 vols. Philadelphia, 1889.

Middleton, Arthur Pierce. *Tobacco Coast: A Maritime History of Chesapeake Bay in the Colonial Era.* Edited by George C. Mason. Newport News, Va., 1953.

Mulkearn, Lois, comp. and ed., *George Mercer Papers: Relating to the Ohio Company of Virginia.* Pittsburgh, 1954.

Palmer, William P., et al., eds. *Calendar of Virginia State Papers and Other Manuscripts. . . .* 11 vols. Richmond, 1875–93.

Potter, Hugh O. *In the Beginning: Historical Facts about the Earliest Days of Present Owensboro and Daviess County, Kentucky.* Owensboro, Ky., 1968.

Rowland, Kate Mason. *The Life of George Mason 1725–1792: Including His Speeches, Public Papers, and Correspondence, with an Introduction by General Fitzhugh Lee.* 2 vols. 1892. Reprint. New York, 1964.

Rutland, Robert A., ed. *The Papers of George Mason 1725–1792.* 3 vols. Chapel Hill, N.C., 1970.

Scharf, John T. *History of Maryland from the Earliest Period to the Present Day.* 3 vols. 1879. Reprint. Hatboro, Vt., 1967.

———. *History of Western Maryland, Being a History of Frederick, Montgomery, Carroll, Washington, Alleghany, and Garrett Counties.* 2 vols. Philadelphia, 1882.

Sydnor, Charles S. *Gentlemen Freeholders: Political Practices in Washington's Virginia.* Chapel Hill, N.C., 1952.

Watkins, C. Malcolm. *The Cultural History of Marlborough, Virginia, an Archeological and Historical Investigation of the Port Town for Stafford County and the Plantation of John Mercer, Including Data Supplied by Frank M. Setzler and Oscar H. Darter.* Smithsonian Institution Bulletin no. 253. Washington, D.C., 1968.

Periodicals

Andrews, Francis Baugh. "Notes on Pershore Abbey at the Time of the Suppression." *Laudate* 8 (1930) :232–43.

Billings, Warren M. "The Causes of Bacon's Rebellion: Some Suggestions." *Virginia Magazine of History and Biography* 78 (1970) :409–35.

Branchi, E. C., trans. "Memoirs of Philip Mazzei." *William and Mary Quarterly,* 2d. ser. 10 (1930) :5.

"Bronaugh Family." *William and Mary Quarterly,* 1st ser. (1908) :235–37.

Church, Randolph W. "John Ballendine, Unsuccessful Entrepreneur of the Eighteenth Century." *Virginia Calvacade* 8 (1959) :39–46.

"Colonial Attorney-Generals." *William and Mary Quarterly,* 1st ser. 10 (1901) :140–41.

Craven, Wesley Frank. "Indian Policy in Early Virginia." *William and Mary Quarterly,* 3d ser. 1 (1944) :77–79.

"Deposition of George Graham." *Louisiana Genealogical Register* 1, no. 2 (1945) :64–67.

East, Robert A. "The Business Entrepreneur in a Changing Colonial Economy 1763–1795." *Journal of Economic History* 6 (1946) :1–27.

"Economic Behavior in a Planting Society: The Eighteenth Century Chesapeake." *Journal of Southern History* 33 (1967) :471–73.

Ernst, Joseph Albert. "Genesis of the Currency Act of 1764: Virginia Paper Money and the Protection of British Investments." *William and Mary Quarterly,* 3d ser. 22 (1965) :33–74.

Evans, Emory G. "Planter Indebtedness and the Coming of the Revolution in Virginia." *William and Mary Quarterly,* 3d ser. 19 (1962) :511–33.

"The Fitzhugh Family." *Virginia Magazine of History and Biography* 7 (1900) :317–19.

Foreman, Carolyn Thomas. "General Richard Barnes Mason." *Chronicles of Oklahoma* 19 (1941) :14–36.

Fowke, Gerard. "Colonel Gerard Fowke of Virginia and Maryland from 1651." *Maryland Historical Magazine* 16 (1921) :5.

Garnett, James Mercer. "James Mercer, Born February 26, 1736; Died October 31, 1793; Judge of the General Court of Virginia; 1779–89, and of the Court of Appeals of Five Judges, 1789–93." *William and Mary Quarterly*, 1st ser. 17 (1908) :85–99.

Gipson, Lawrence H. "Virginia Planter Debts before the American Revolution." *Virginia Magazine of History and Biography* 69 (1961) :259–77.

James, J. Franklin. "St. Eustatius in the American Revolution." *American Historical Review* 8 (1903) :683–708.

Kammer, Michael G. "The Causes of the Maryland Revolution of 1689." *Maryland Historical Magazine* 55 (1960) :293–333.

King, George Harrison Sanford. "Copies of Extant Wills from Counties Whose Records Have Been Destroyed: Will of Major John Dinwiddie of King George County, Virginia." *Virginia Genealogist* 3 (1959) :51–59.

——. "Notes from the Journal of John Mercer, Esquire (1704/5–1768) of Marlborough, Stafford County, Virginia." *Virginia Genealogist* 4 (1960) :99–109.

Laub, C. Herbert. "British Regulations of Crown Lands in the West: The Last Phase, 1773–1775." *William and Mary Quarterly*, 2d ser. 10 (1930) :52–55.

MacMaster, Richard K., ed. "Maryland Students in Flanders: Letters of the Reverend John Ceslas Fenwick, O.P., 1784–1789." *Records of the American Catholic Historical Society* 74 (1963) :185–92.

——. "The Tobacco Trade with France: Letters of Joseph Fenwick, U.S. Consul at Bordeaux 1787–1795." *Maryland Historical Magazine* 60 (1965) :26–55.

——, and David C. Skaggs, eds. "The Letterbooks of Alexander Hamilton." *Maryland Historical Magazine* 61 (1966) :162.

——. "Post-Revolutionary Letters of Alexander Hamilton, Piscataway Merchant, Part I, January–June 1784." *Maryland Historical Magazine* 63 (1968) :26.

Nussbaum, Frederick L. "American Tobacco and French Politics 1783–1798." *Political Science Quarterly* 40 (1925) :501–3.

Poole, Martha Sprigg. "Tudor Hall and Those Who Lived There." *Maryland Historical Magazine* 46 (1951) :257–77.

Rowland, Kate Mason. "Maryland Delegates to the Albany Congress." *Dixie* 2 (1899) :274–99.

——. "Merchants and Mills: From the Letter Book of Robert Carter of Nominy, Westmoreland County." *William and Mary Quarterly*, 1st ser. 11 (1903) :245–46.

Sheridan, Richard B. "The British Credit Crisis of 1772 and the American Colonies." *Journal of Economic History* 20 (1960) :161–86.

Sioussat, St. George Leakin. "The Breakdown of the Royal Management of Lands in the Southern Provinces, 1773–1775." *Agricultural History* 3 (1929) :67–98.

Skaggs, David C., Jr. "Maryland's Impulse towards Social Revolution: 1750–1776." *Journal of American History* 54 (1968) :771–86.

Somerville, Mollie. "General John Mason of Analostan Island." *Ironworker* 26 (1962) :3–11.

Steiner, Bruce E. "The Catholic Brents of Colonial Virginia." *Virginia Magazine of History and Biography* 70 (1962) :387–409.

——. "The Royal Province of Maryland in 1692." *Maryland Historical Magazine* 15 (1920) :123–68.

"Virginia Gazette Extracts." *William and Mary Quarterly,* 1st ser. 12 (1903) :74–75.

Wagner, Anthony, and F. S. Andrus. "The Origin of the Family of Taliaferro." *Virginia Magazine of History and Biography* 77 (1969) :22–25.

"The Wallace Family." *William and Mary Quarterly,* 1st ser. 13 (1905) :177–82.

Manuscripts

Annapolis, Md. Maryland Hall of Records.   MdHR
    Charles County Accounts, Deeds, Debt Books, Inventories, Wills
    Commissioners for Confiscated British Property, Sale Book 1792–95
    Frederick County Deeds
    Patent Books
    Prince Georges County Deeds, Will Books 20, 21
    Provincial Court Judgements 1761–62
Baltimore, Md. Maryland Historical Society.   MHS
    Ignatius Fenwick Papers
    Alexander Hamilton Papers
    Hayward File
    Thomas Rutland Letter Books
Boston, Mass. Massachusetts Historical Society.
    Bancroft Papers
    Coolidge Collection
    Pickering Papers
    Wetmore Collection
Cambridge, Mass. Houghton Library, Harvard University.   HL
    Arthur Lee Papers
    Sparks Transcripts
Charlottesville, Va. University of Virginia Library.   UVa
    Lee Papers
    Harry Piper Letter Book
Detroit, Mich. Detroit Public Library.
    Burton Historical Collection
Doylestown, Pa. Bucks County Historical Society.
    John Mercer's Ledgers 1725–37, 1744–49.

Durham, No. Carolina. Duke University Library.
  Robert Carter Papers
Haverford, Pa. Friends Historical Library, Haverford College.
  Robert Pleasants Letter Book
Lexington, Ky. Margaret I. King Library, University of Kentucky.   UK
  William Woodford Letter Books 1723–37
London, England.
  Principal Probate Registry, Somerset House
  Public Record Office.   PRO
Lorton, Va. Gunston Hall Library.   GHL
  Pamela C. Copeland Mason Family Research File.   P.C.C. Mason File
New York, N.Y. New York Historical Society.
  William Lux Letter Book, 1763–69
  Alexander Henderson Papers
——. New York Public Library. Manuscript Division.   NYPL
  Bancroft Collection
  Emmet Collection
  Jenifer and Hooe Account Books
  Wallace, Johnson, and Muir Letter Book
Philadelphia, Pa. American Philosophical Society.
  Benjamin Franklin Papers
  William Temple Franklin Papers
——. Historical Society of Pennsylvania.
  Dreer Collection
  Gratz Collection
  Logan Collection
  "Subscription for Maurice Pound, Fairfax County, October 1759," Mis-
    cellaneous Collection, 5-C.
Richmond, Va. Virginia Historical Society.   VHS
  Lee Family Papers, 1638–1876
  George Bolling Lee Papers
  Mercer Papers
——. Virginia State Library.   VSL
  William Allason Letter Book
  General Assembly Religious Petitions
  Legislative Petitions
  "Memorial of the Ohio Co." 20 Nov. 1778, Miscellaneous Petitions, 266A
  John Mercer Land Book, microcopy
  County Records, microcopies
    Fairfax County Deed Books.   Fairfax D.B.
    Fairfax County Minute Books 1749–56.   Fairfax M.B.
    Fairfax County Petitions
    Fairfax County Land Cause Book no. 1, 1812–32
    Fairfax County Will Books A-1, F-1, and O
    Northern Neck Proprietary of the Grants, books 2, 5, H, and P.
      N.N.

Northumberland County Court Order Book no. 2

Northumberland County Patent Book no. 4, 1655–62

Prince William County Deed Books A, B, C, and D.   Prince William D.B.

Prince William County Will Books C, K, and P.

Stafford County Court Order Book, 1664–1668, 1691–93.   Stafford O.B.

Stafford County Deed Books W-Z and L.

Stafford County Court Records, 1689–93.

Westmoreland County Court Order Book no. 1.   Westmoreland O.B.

Westmoreland County Patent Books nos. 3 and 5

San Marino, Calif. Henry E. Huntington Library.

Robert Carter Letter Book

Brock Collection

Washington, D.C. Library of Congress, Manuscript Division.   LC

Cockburn Papers

Glassford Papers

William Gooch Papers, Microcopy

Dr. Robert Honyman Journal

Henry Papers

Jamieson Papers

George Mason Papers, 1763–91

"Field Notes upon a Survey made of Dogues Neck February 1754"

William Reynolds Letter Book

Truro Parish Vestry Book

Washington Papers

Williamsburg, Va. Library of the College of William and Mary.   W&M

Leven Powell Papers

Mason Papers

Provisional List of Alumni of the College of William and Mary from 1693 to 1888

Index

Index

Virginia: boundary disputes, 122, 125, 210; British invasion, 203; British raids, 211; colonial problems, 19-20; colonial society, 11; Committee of Safety, 191, 192; constitution, 204-7; dominion status, 107n; English institutions, 6, 9; Great Seal, 208; laws of, 178; legal code, 206-7; local government, 6-7; public lands policy, 137-40, 142-46; revolutionary army, 190-91; *see also* House of Burgesses
Virginia Company of London, 137
Virginia Convention, 166, 188, 191, 201, 204, 229, 230
Viticulture, 101-4

Wagener, Peter, 153, 182
Wahangonche, 13
Waite, William, 88-89, 96, 97, 171; Gunston Hall and, 97
Waite, Mrs. William (Jane Dinwiddie), 88
Wallace, Johnson & Muir, 201, 213
Waller, Benjamin, 107, 120, 123, 142
Waller, William, 123
Walpole, Thomas, 134, 136, 139n
Walpole Company, 139n
Ward, Edward, 129
Warden, David Bailie, 258
Wardrop, James, 126
Warville, Jacques Brissot de, 224
Washington, Augustine, 93, 123
Washington, George, 188, 203, 230; Alexandria office, 154; Clifton affair and, 109; Constitutional Convention and, 227-28; Continental Congress and, 188; farm crops, 105; on federal city, 231, 232; French and Indian War and, 129-30; frontier expedition, 96; landholdings, 217; marriage, 100; George Mason IV and, 98, 101, 104, 121, 178, 188, 194, 198, 217, 225-26, 232, 251; George Mason V and, 238, 239; John Mason and, 253; military bounty lands, 136; Neutrality Proclamation, 256; nonimportation agreements and, 180-82; Potowmack Co. and, 258; slaves, 218; tax evasion, 227; viticulture and, 102
Washington, Mrs. George (Martha Dandridge Custis), 100
Washington, George Augustine, 226
Washington, John, 15
Washington, Lawrence, 90, 93, 123
Washington, Lund, 232

Washington, D.C., 230-32, 240, 258
Washington, 250
Watson, Josiah, 199
Waugh, John, 21, 24-28, 46
Waugh, Mrs. John (Elizabeth), 21
Waugh, Joseph, 47
Waywardens, English, 4
Welch, Reuben, 65
West, Hugh, 151, 170, 171
West, John, 46n, 182
West, Pearson, 46n
West, Stephen, 161, 222, 223, 250
West, Thomas, 74
West & Hobson, 222
West family, 46
West Indies trade, 193, 198
Western lands, 118, 122-49, 204
Westmoreland County, 10, 12, 14
Wharton, Samuel, 139n
Wheat trade, 105, 156, 221, 246, 249, 255
Wheatly, David, 29
Wheaton, Frank, 263
Wheaton, Mrs. Frank (Sarah Maria Cooper), 263
Wheaton, Mrs. Frank (Emma Twiggs Mason), 263
Whiting & Montague, 69
Wilks, Mr., 37
William and Mary, 23-25
Williams, Master, 75
Williams, Mrs. Devereaux, 263
Williams, Evans, 137
Williams, W., 73
Williamsburg, 51; Bruton Parish Church, 51; Governor's Palace, 51; society, 54
Willing, Charles, 214
Wilson, Cumberland, 140
Wilson, George, 148
Wilson, John, 70, 71
Wilson, William, 255
Wilson, Woodrow, 237
Window tax, 204
Wine industry, 101-4
Wishart, Sydney, 237
Wishart, Mrs. Sydney (Nancy Cooke), 237
Withers, John, 29, 42, 43
Woodbridge, 58, 244
Woodford, William, 58, 63, 65, 66
Woods, John, 255
Woodward, Mr., 111
Wren, James, 97
Wright, Charles, 252
Wright, Richard, 39